SQUARE ENIX

KINGDOM HEARTS

Adapted by
Shiro Amano

HAN

Kingdom Hearts II Volume 1
Adapted by Shiro Amano

Assistant Editors - Alethea & Athena Nibley
Associate Editor - Peter Ahlstrom
Retouch and Lettering - Star Print Brokers
Production Artist - Michael Paolilli
Graphic Designer - James Lee

Editor - Bryce P. Coleman
Digital Imaging Manager - Chris Buford
Pre-Production Supervisor - Erika Terriquez
Art Director - Anne Marie Horne
Production Manager - Elisabeth Brizzi
Managing Editor - Vy Nguyen
VP of Production - Ron Klamert
Editor-in-Chief - Rob Tokar
Publisher - Mike Kiley
President and C.O.O. - John Parker
C.E.O. and Chief Creative Officer - Stuart Levy

A  Manga

TOKYOPOP Inc.
5900 Wilshire Blvd. Suite 2000
Los Angeles, CA 90036

E-mail: info@TOKYOPOP.com
Come visit us online at www.TOKYOPOP.com

ISBN: 978-1-4278-0058-9

First TOKYOPOP printing: July 2007

10 9 8 7 6 5 4 3 2

Printed in the USA

KINGDOM HEARTS II

A scattered dream that's like a far-off memory. A far-off memory that's like a scattered dream. I want to line the pieces up, yours and mine.

Adapted by
Shiro Amano
Original Concept by
Tetsuya Nomura

Disney · SQUARE ENIX

KINGDOM HEARTS

キングダム ハーツ II

CONTENTS

KINGDOM HEARTS II

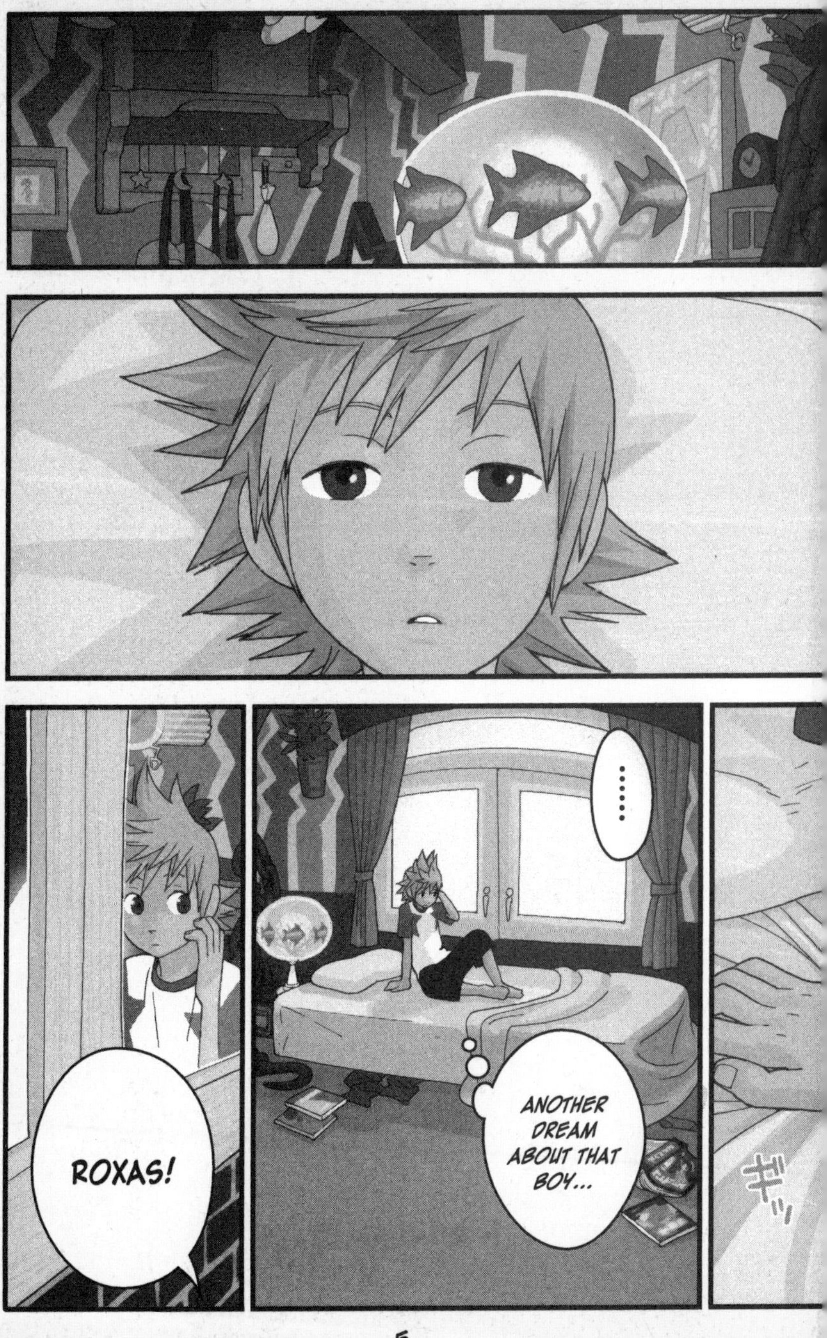
ギッ
......
ANOTHER DREAM ABOUT THAT BOY...
ROXAS!

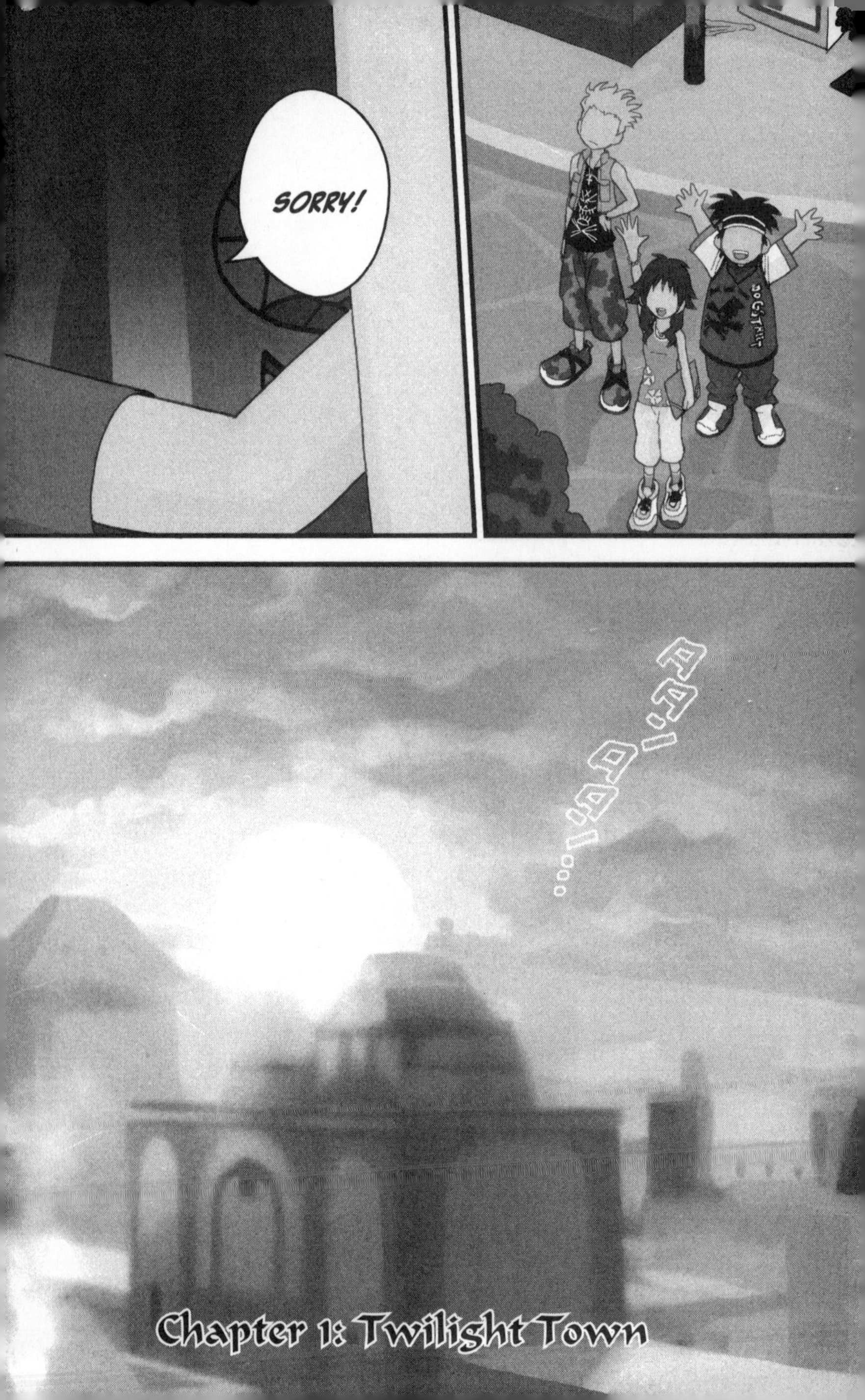
SORRY!
AA! AA!...
Chapter 1: Twilight Town

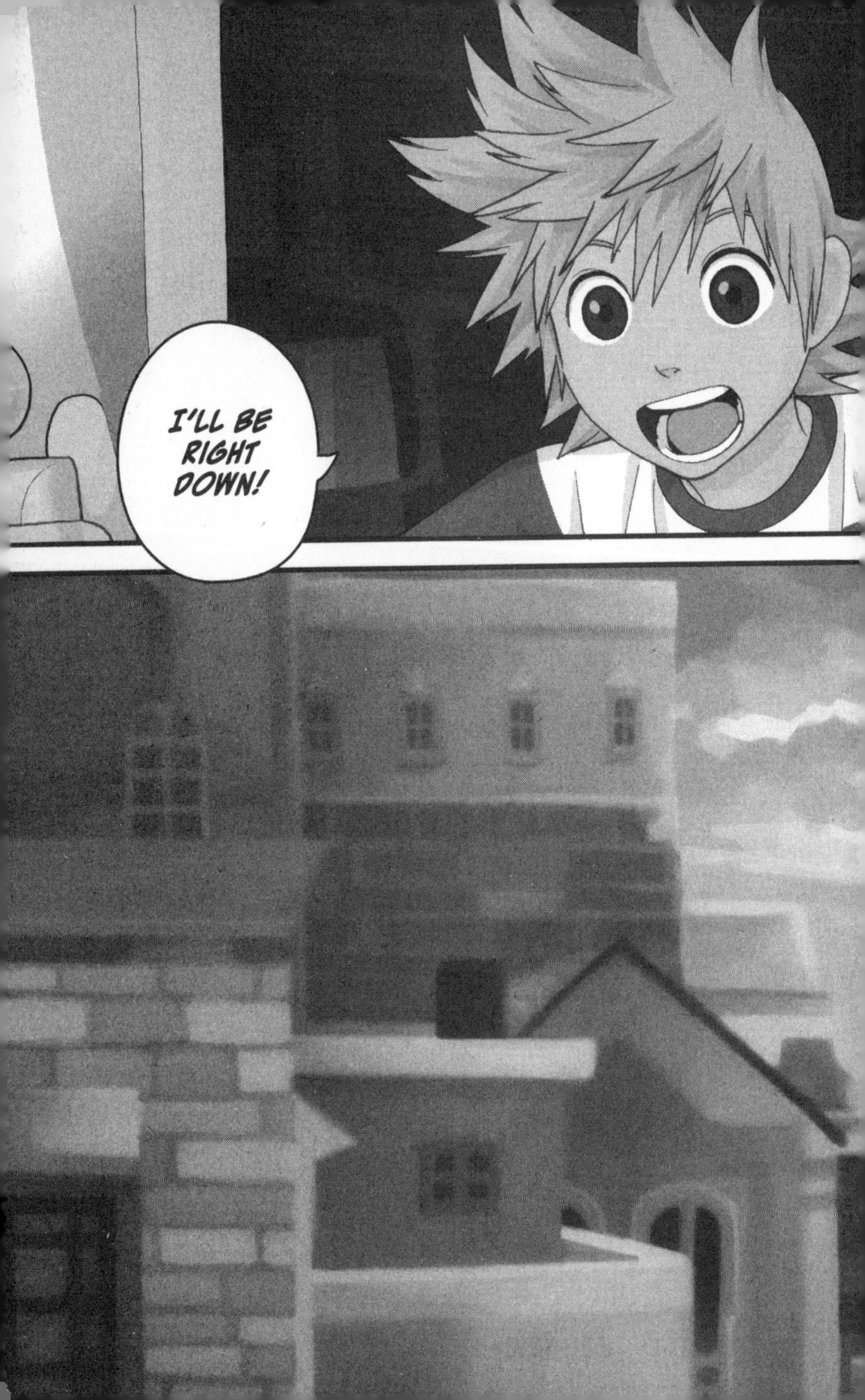
I'LL BE RIGHT DOWN!

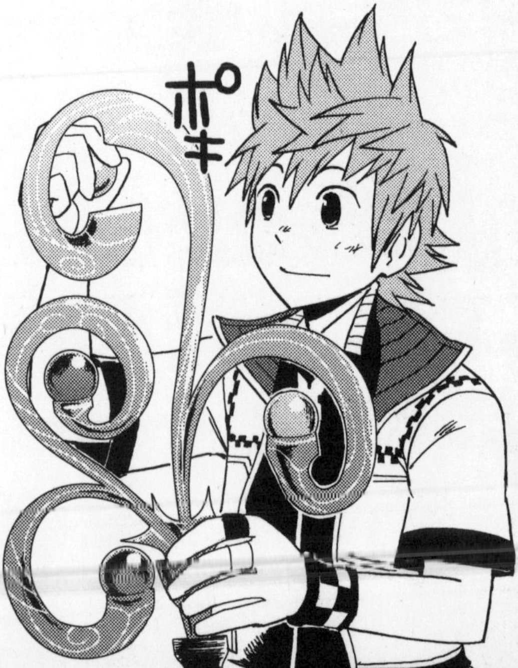
ポキ

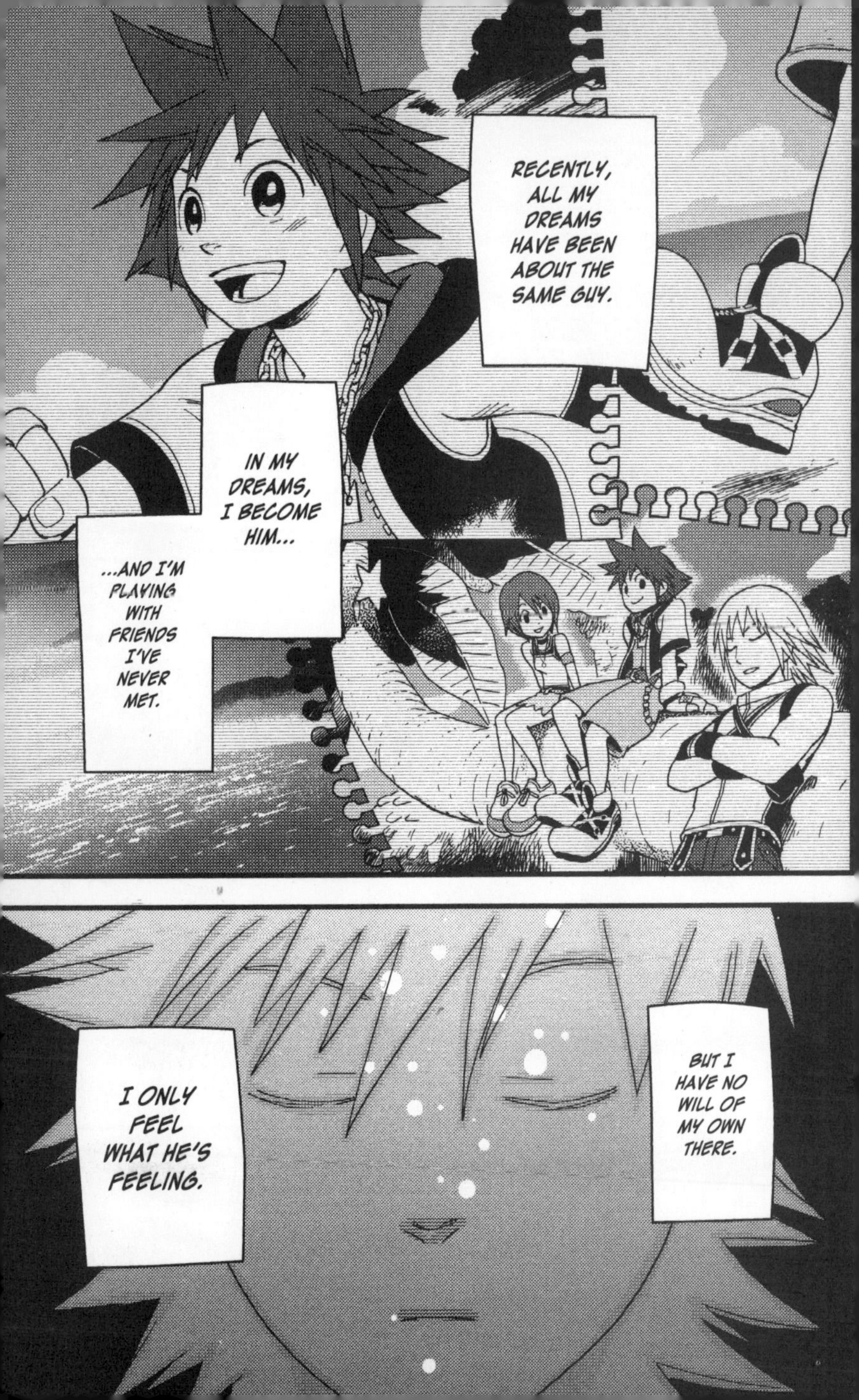
RECENTLY, ALL MY DREAMS HAVE BEEN ABOUT THE SAME GUY.
IN MY DREAMS, I BECOME HIM...
...AND I'M PLAYING WITH FRIENDS I'VE NEVER MET.
BUT I HAVE NO WILL OF MY OWN THERE.
I ONLY FEEL WHAT HE'S FEELING.

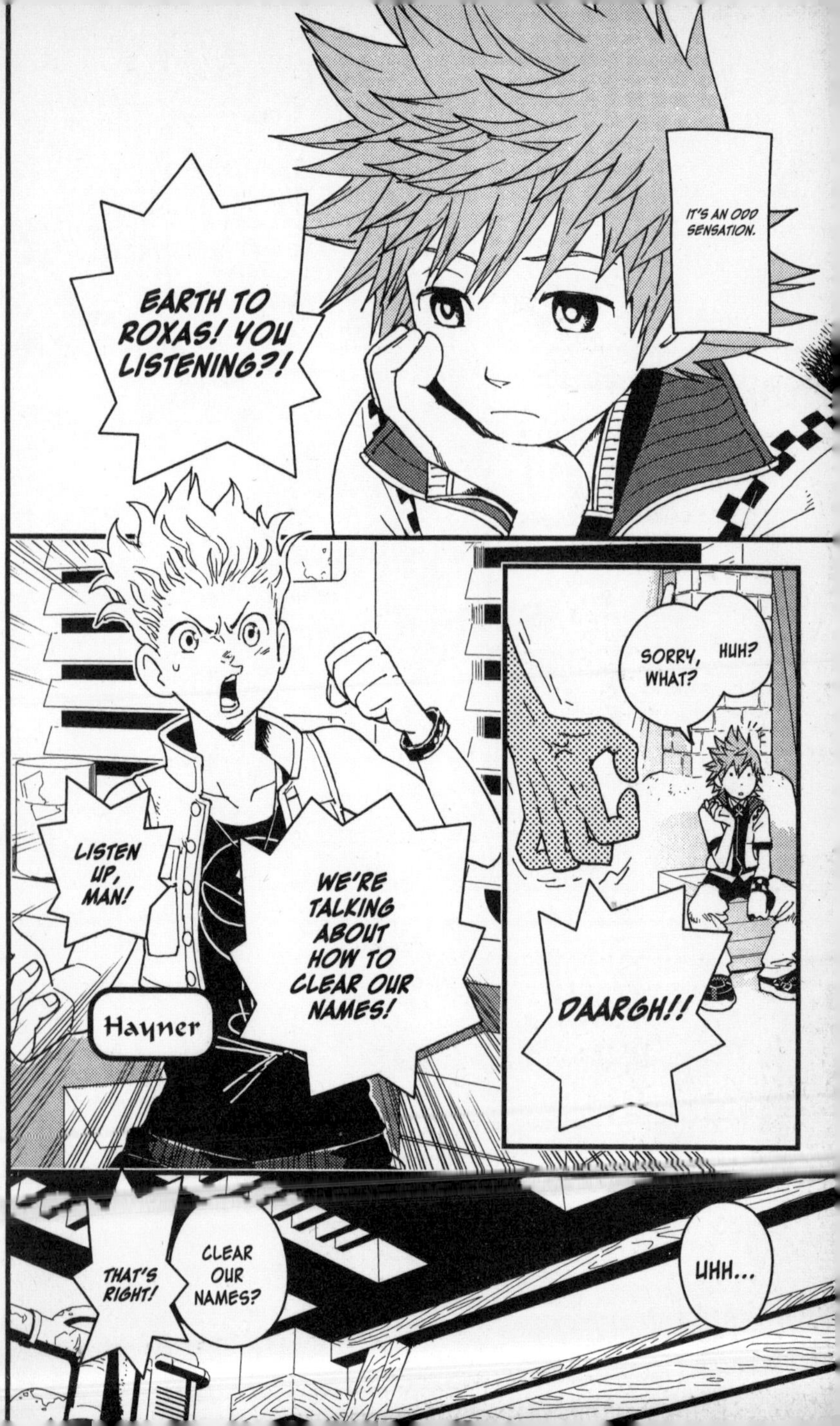
IT'S AN ODD SENSATION.
EARTH TO ROXAS! YOU LISTENING?!
HUH?
SORRY, WHAT?
DAARGH!!
LISTEN UP, MAN!
WE'RE TALKING ABOUT HOW TO CLEAR OUR NAMES!
Hayner
UHH...
CLEAR OUR NAMES?
THAT'S RIGHT!

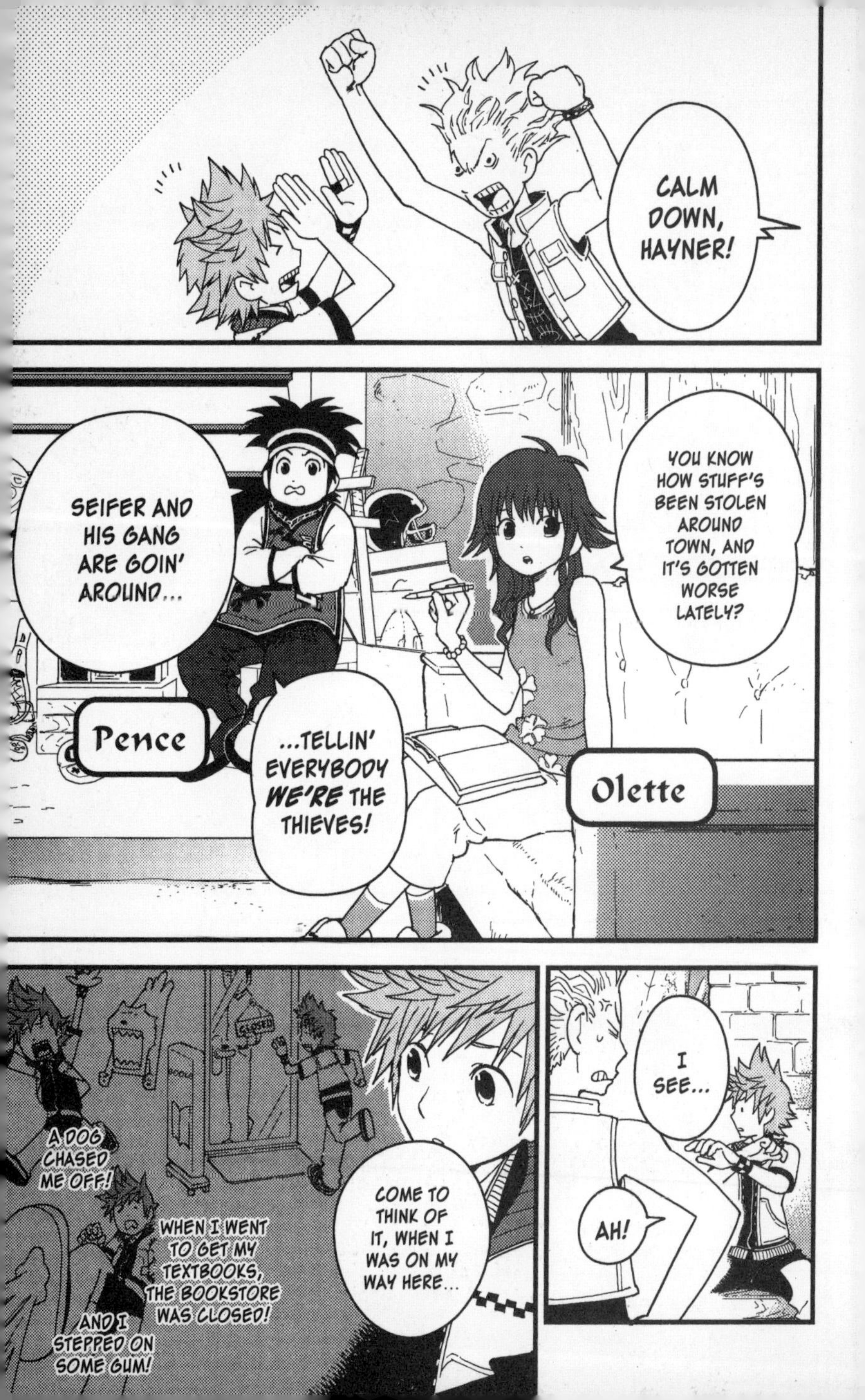
CALM DOWN, HAYNER!
YOU KNOW HOW STUFF'S BEEN STOLEN AROUND TOWN, AND IT'S GOTTEN WORSE LATELY?
Olette
SEIFER AND HIS GANG ARE GOIN' AROUND...
...TELLIN' EVERYBODY *WE'RE* THE THIEVES!
Pence
I SEE...
AH!
COME TO THINK OF IT, WHEN I WAS ON MY WAY HERE...
A DOG CHASED ME OFF!
WHEN I WENT TO GET MY TEXTBOOKS, THE BOOKSTORE WAS CLOSED!
AND I STEPPED ON SOME GUM!

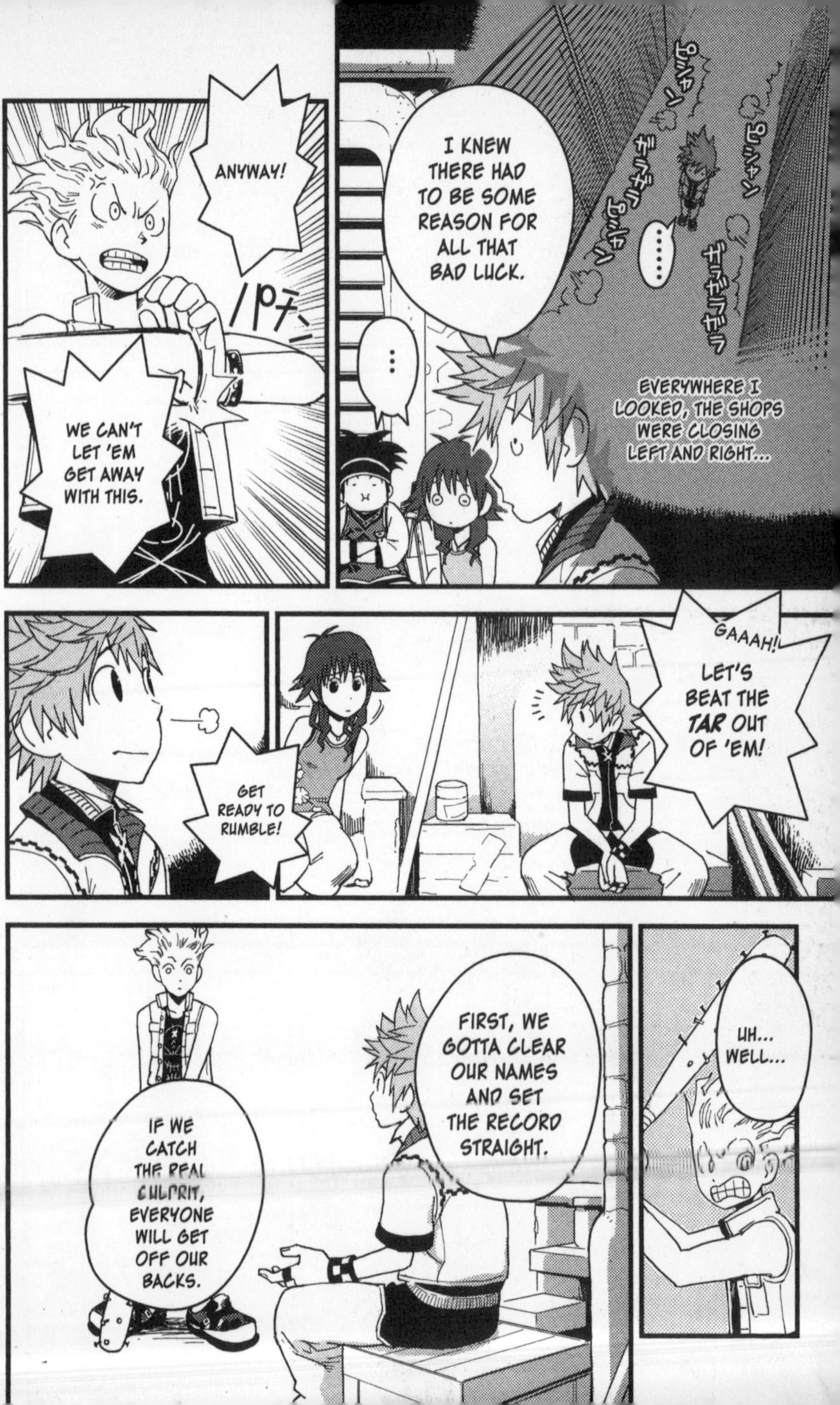
......
I KNEW THERE HAD TO BE SOME REASON FOR ALL THAT BAD LUCK.
EVERYWHERE I LOOKED, THE SHOPS WERE CLOSING LEFT AND RIGHT...
...
ANYWAY!
WE CAN'T LET 'EM GET AWAY WITH THIS.
GAAAH!
LET'S BEAT THE *TAR* OUT OF 'EM!
GET READY TO RUMBLE!
UH... WELL...
FIRST, WE GOTTA CLEAR OUR NAMES AND SET THE RECORD STRAIGHT.
IF WE CATCH THE REAL CULPRIT, EVERYONE WILL GET OFF OUR BACKS.

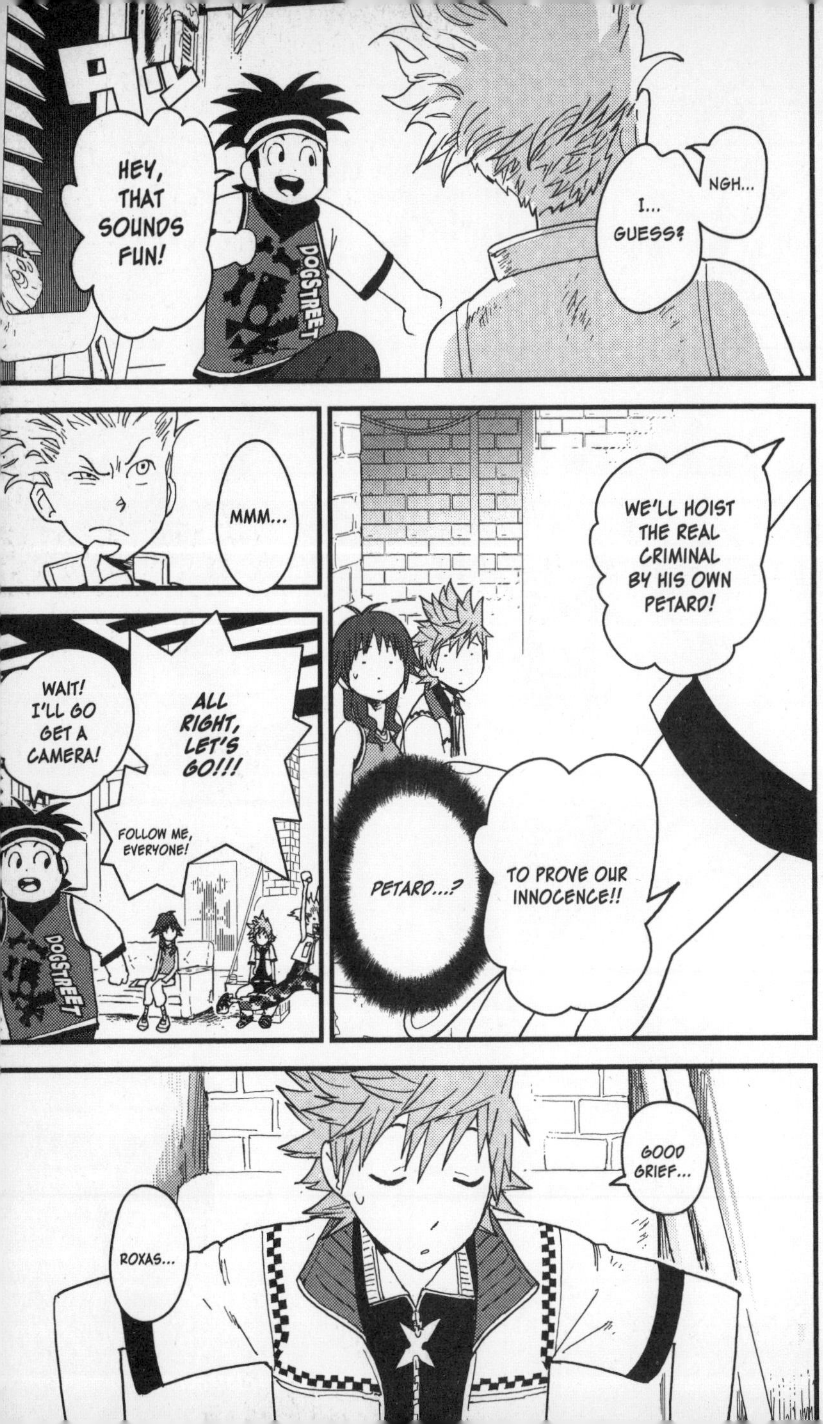
NGH...
I... GUESS?
HEY, THAT SOUNDS FUN!
DOGSTREET
WE'LL HOIST THE REAL CRIMINAL BY HIS OWN PETARD!
TO PROVE OUR INNOCENCE!!
PETARD...?
MMM...
ALL RIGHT, LET'S GO!!!
WAIT! I'LL GO GET A CAMERA!
FOLLOW ME, EVERYONE!
DOGSTREET
GOOD GRIEF...
ROXAS...

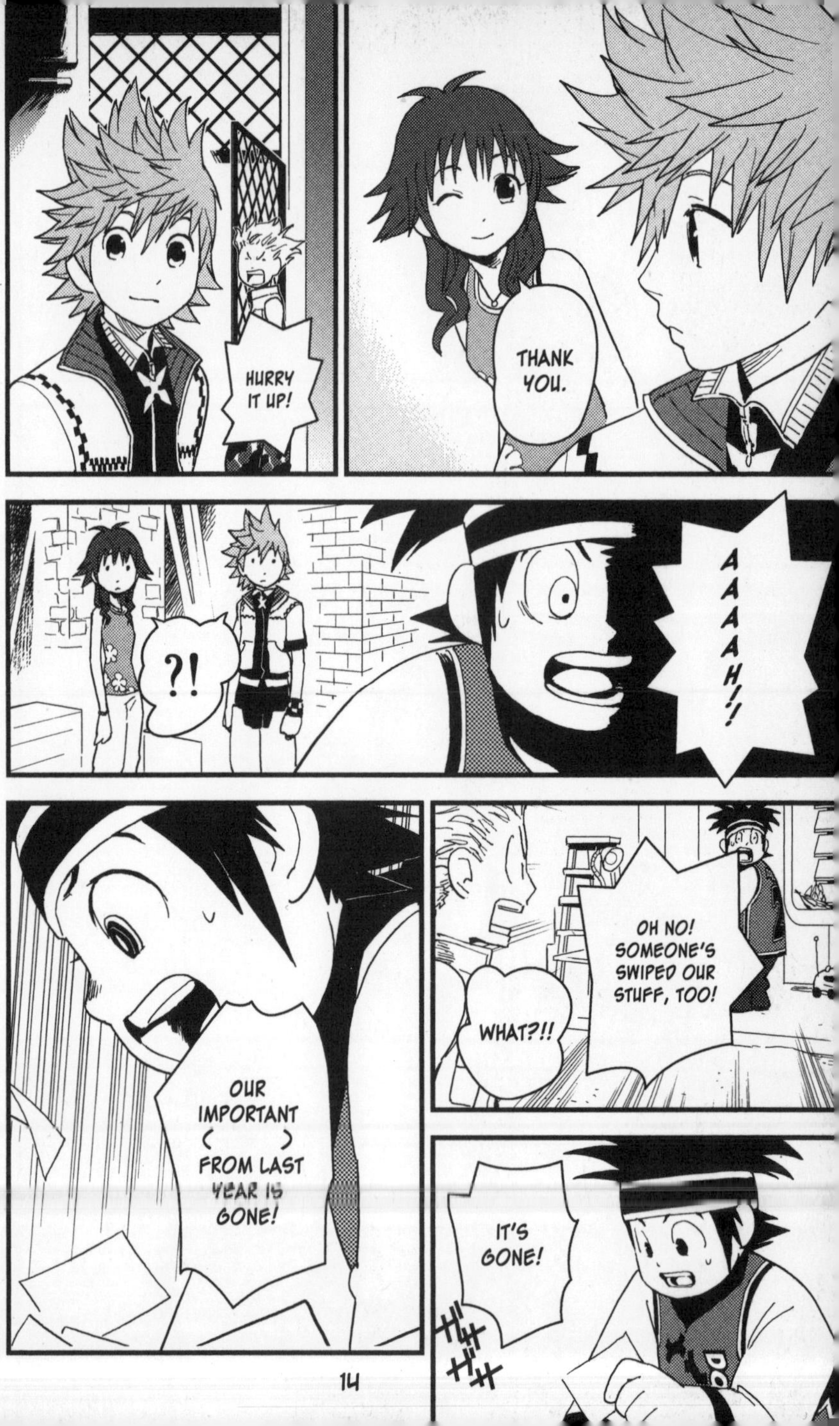
THANK YOU.
HURRY IT UP!
AAAAAH!!
?!
OH NO! SOMEONE'S SWIPED OUR STUFF, TOO!
WHAT?!!
IT'S GONE!
OUR IMPORTANT ( ) FROM LAST YEAR IS GONE!

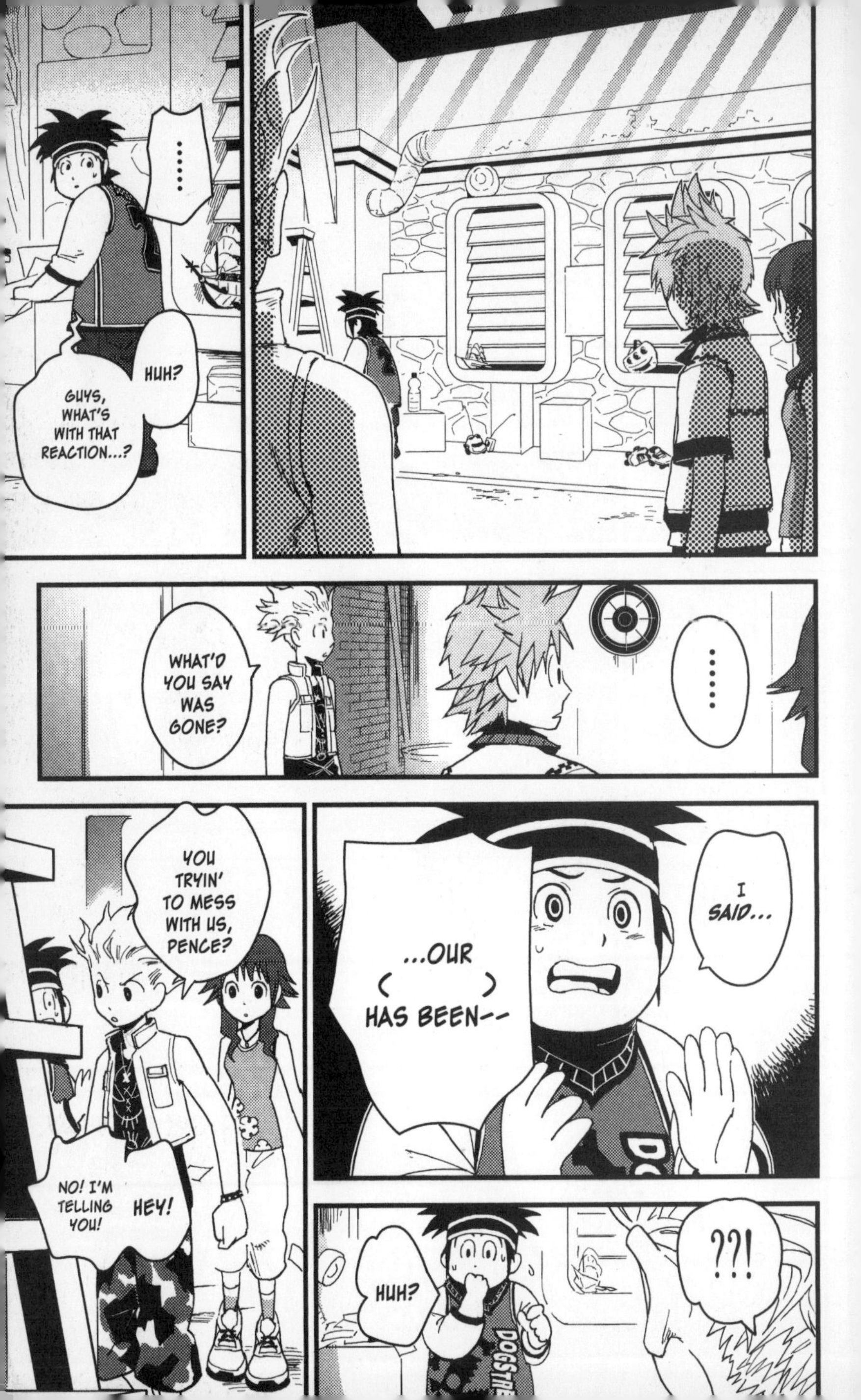
......
HUH?
GUYS, WHAT'S WITH THAT REACTION...?
......
WHAT'D YOU SAY WAS GONE?
I SAID...
...OUR ( ) HAS BEEN--
??!
HUH?
YOU TRYIN' TO MESS WITH US, PENCE?
HEY!
NO! I'M TELLING YOU!

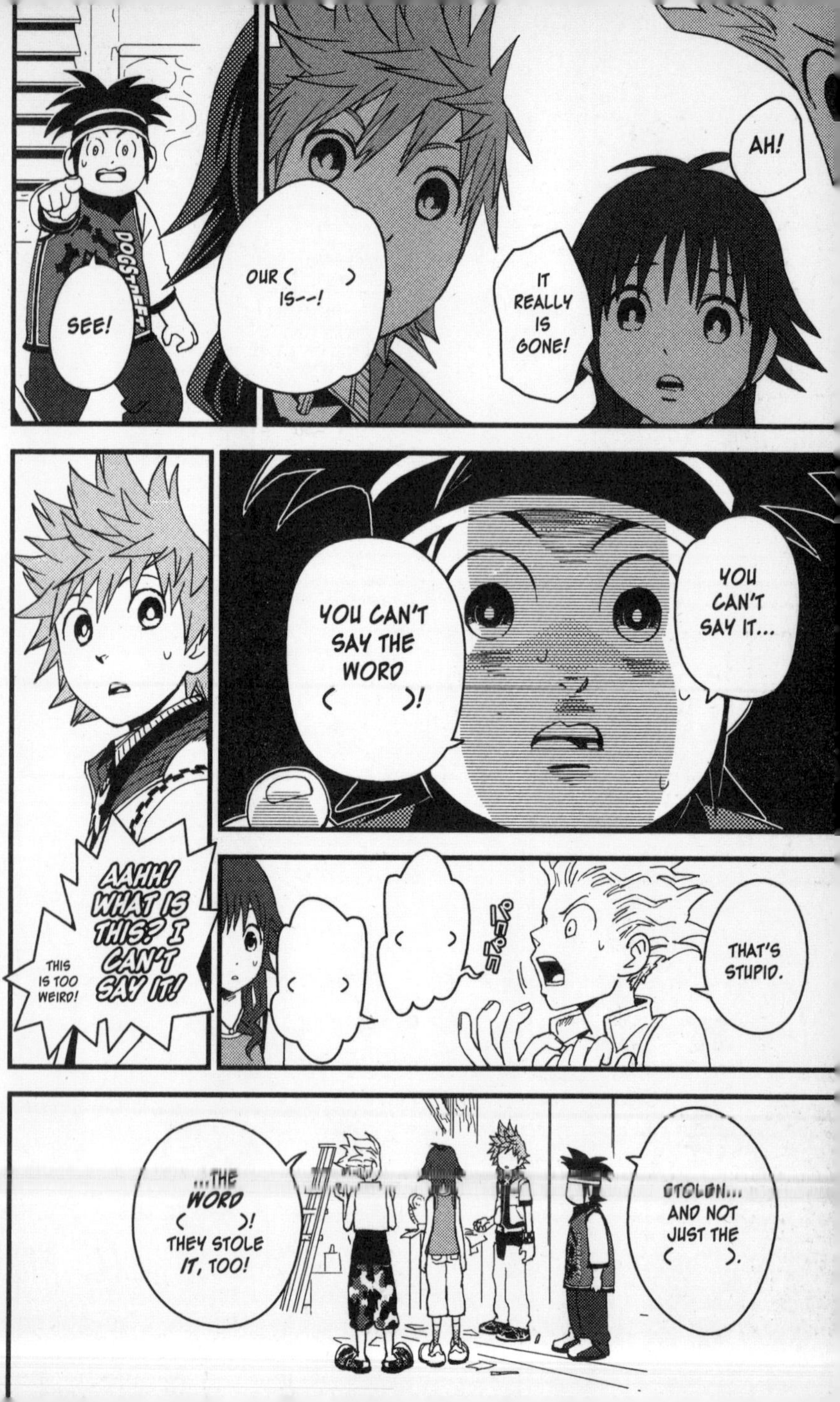
AH!
IT REALLY IS GONE!
OUR ( ) IS--!
SEE!
YOU CAN'T SAY IT...
YOU CAN'T SAY THE WORD ( )!
THAT'S STUPID.
( )
( )
AAHH! WHAT IS THIS? I CAN'T SAY IT!
THIS IS TOO WEIRD!
STOLEN... AND NOT JUST THE ( ).
...THE WORD ( )! THEY STOLE IT, TOO!

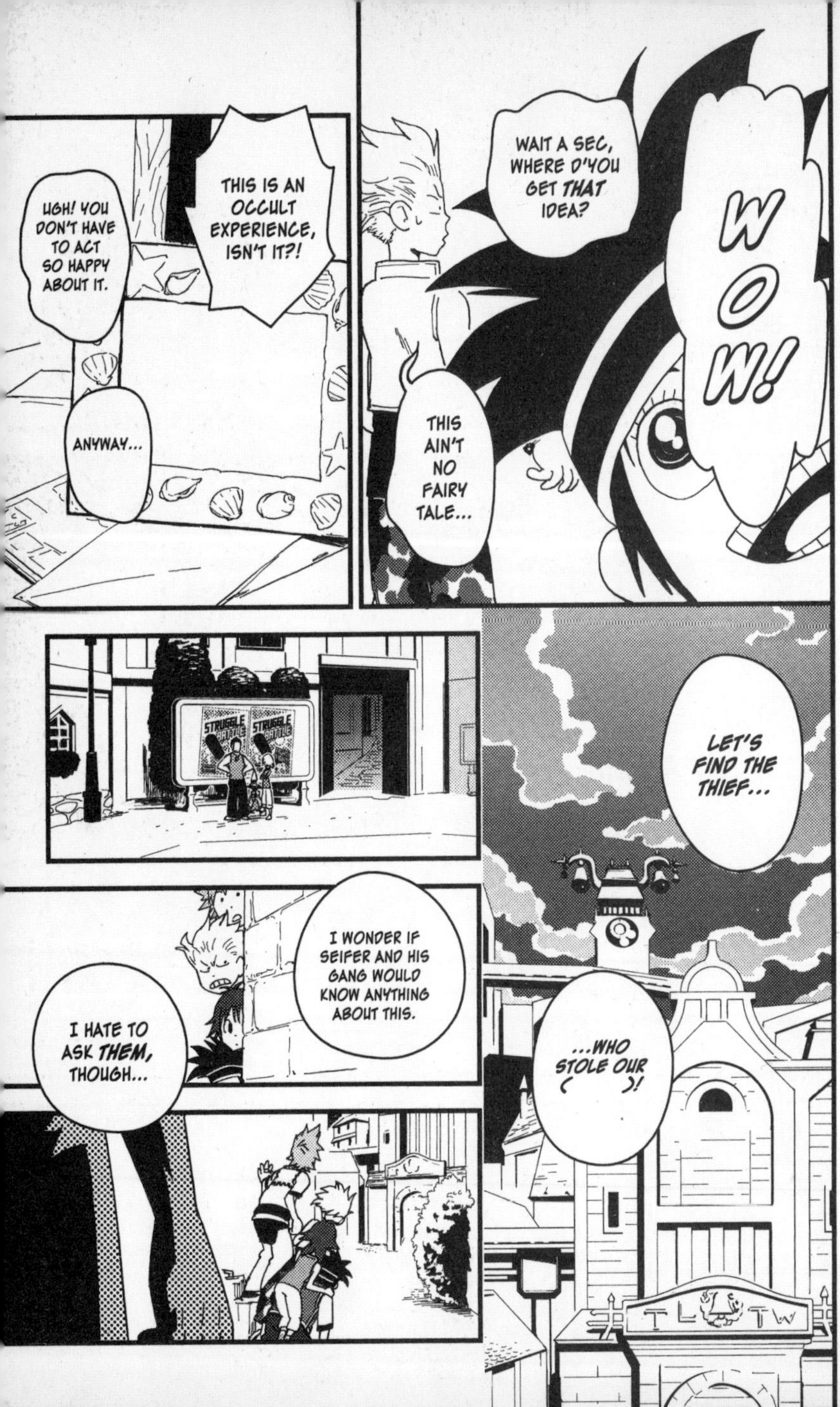
WOW!
WAIT A SEC, WHERE D'YOU GET THAT IDEA?
THIS AIN'T NO FAIRY TALE...
THIS IS AN OCCULT EXPERIENCE, ISN'T IT?!
UGH! YOU DON'T HAVE TO ACT SO HAPPY ABOUT IT.
ANYWAY...
LET'S FIND THE THIEF...
...WHO STOLE OUR ( )!
STRUGGLE BATTLE
STRUGGLE BATTLE
I WONDER IF SEIFER AND HIS GANG WOULD KNOW ANYTHING ABOUT THIS.
I HATE TO ASK THEM, THOUGH...

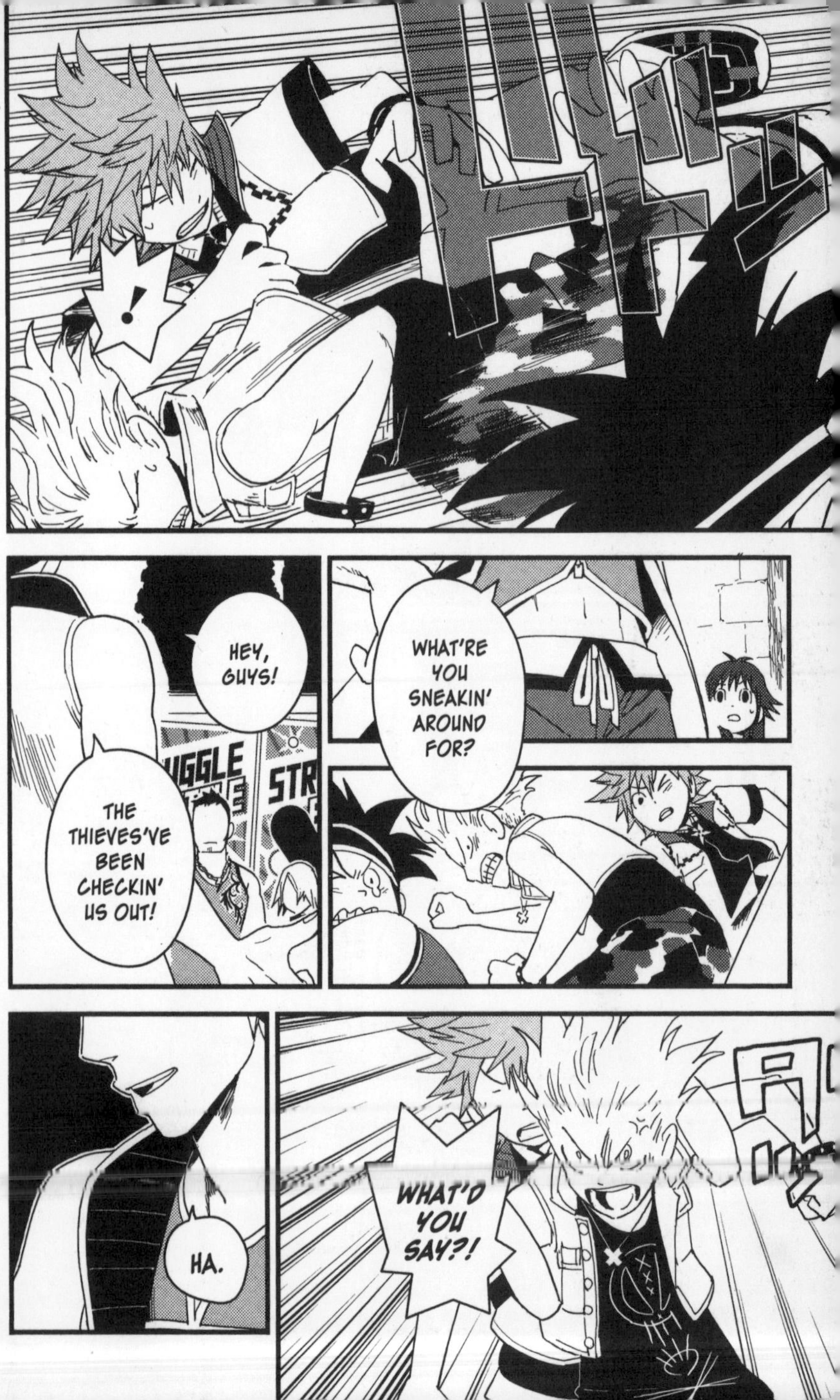
!
WHAT'RE YOU SNEAKIN' AROUND FOR?
HEY, GUYS!
THE THIEVES'VE BEEN CHECKIN' US OUT!
WHAT'D YOU SAY?!
HA.

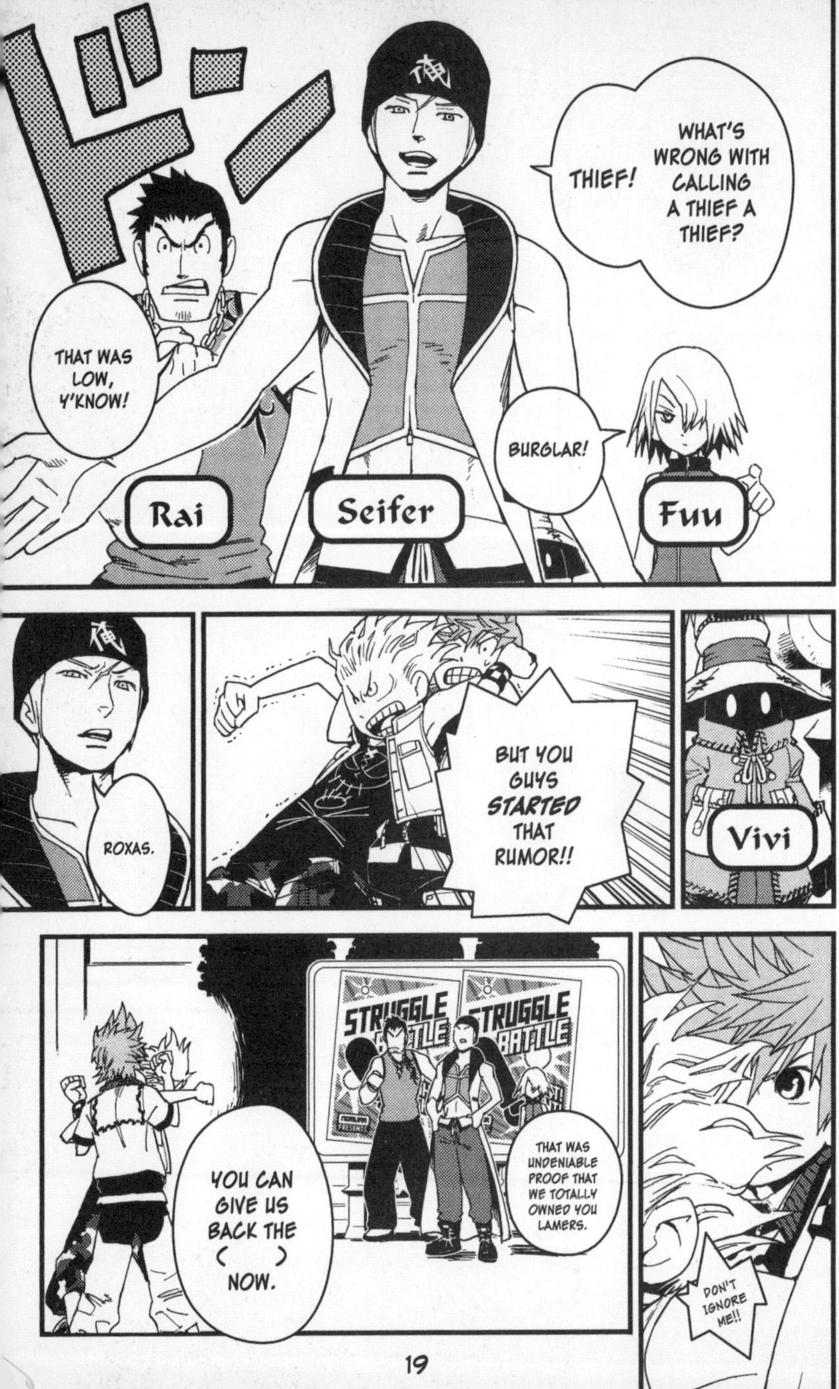
ドー
THIEF! WHAT'S WRONG WITH CALLING A THIEF A THIEF?
BURGLAR!
Fuu
Seifer
THAT WAS LOW, Y'KNOW!
Rai
Vivi
BUT YOU GUYS *STARTED* THAT RUMOR!!
ROXAS.
DON'T IGNORE ME!!
STRUGGLE BATTLE
STRUGGLE BATTLE
THAT WAS UNDENIABLE PROOF THAT WE TOTALLY OWNED YOU LAMERS.
YOU CAN GIVE US BACK THE ( ) NOW.

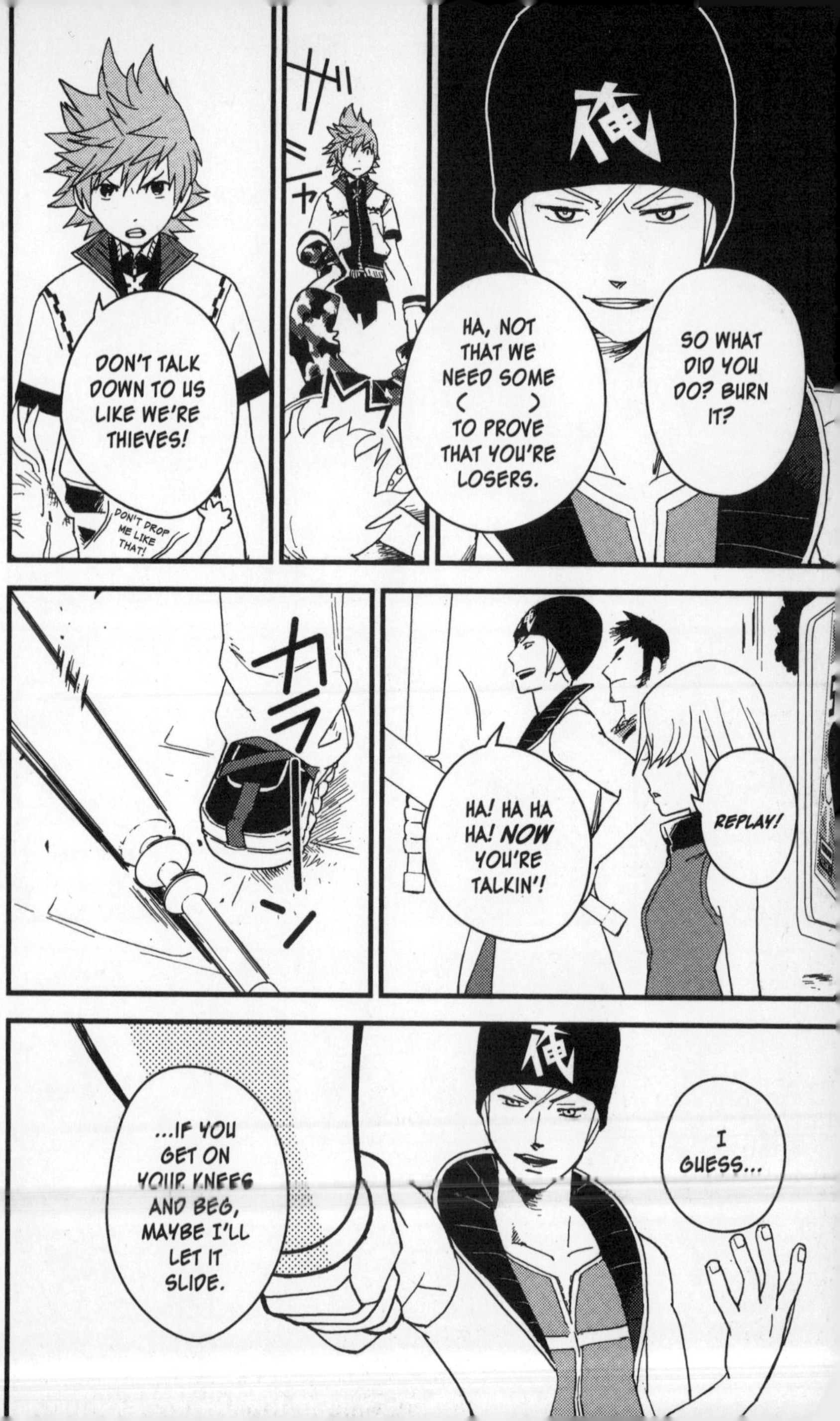
SO WHAT DID YOU DO? BURN IT?
HA, NOT THAT WE NEED SOME ( ) TO PROVE THAT YOU'RE LOSERS.
DON'T TALK DOWN TO US LIKE WE'RE THIEVES!
DON'T DROP ME LIKE THAT!
REPLAY!
HA! HA HA HA! *NOW* YOU'RE TALKIN'!
I GUESS...
...IF YOU GET ON YOUR KNEES AND BEG, MAYBE I'LL LET IT SLIDE.

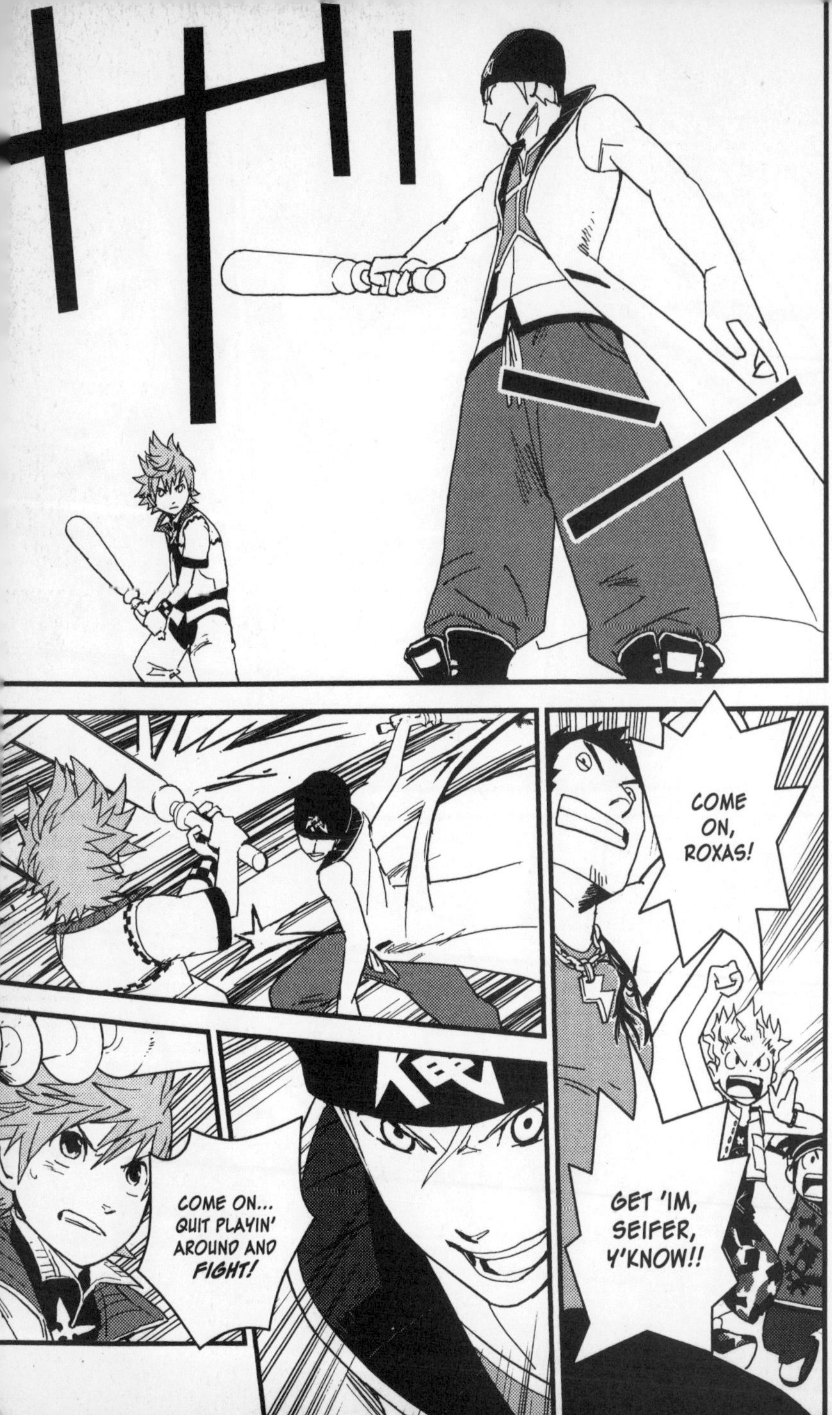
COME ON, ROXAS!
GET 'IM, SEIFER, Y'KNOW!!
COME ON... QUIT PLAYIN' AROUND AND *FIGHT!*

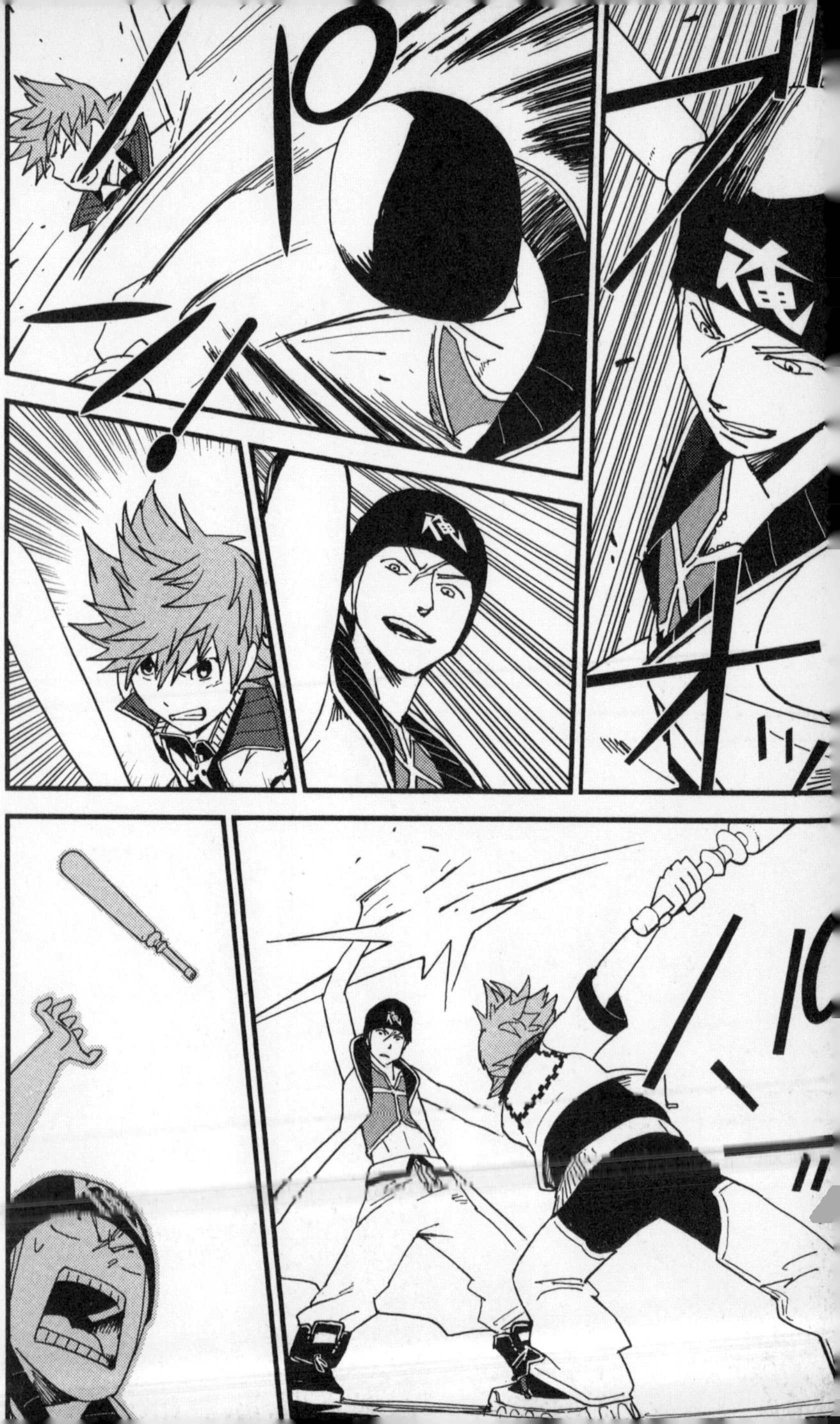

俺
ブオッ
パーン!!

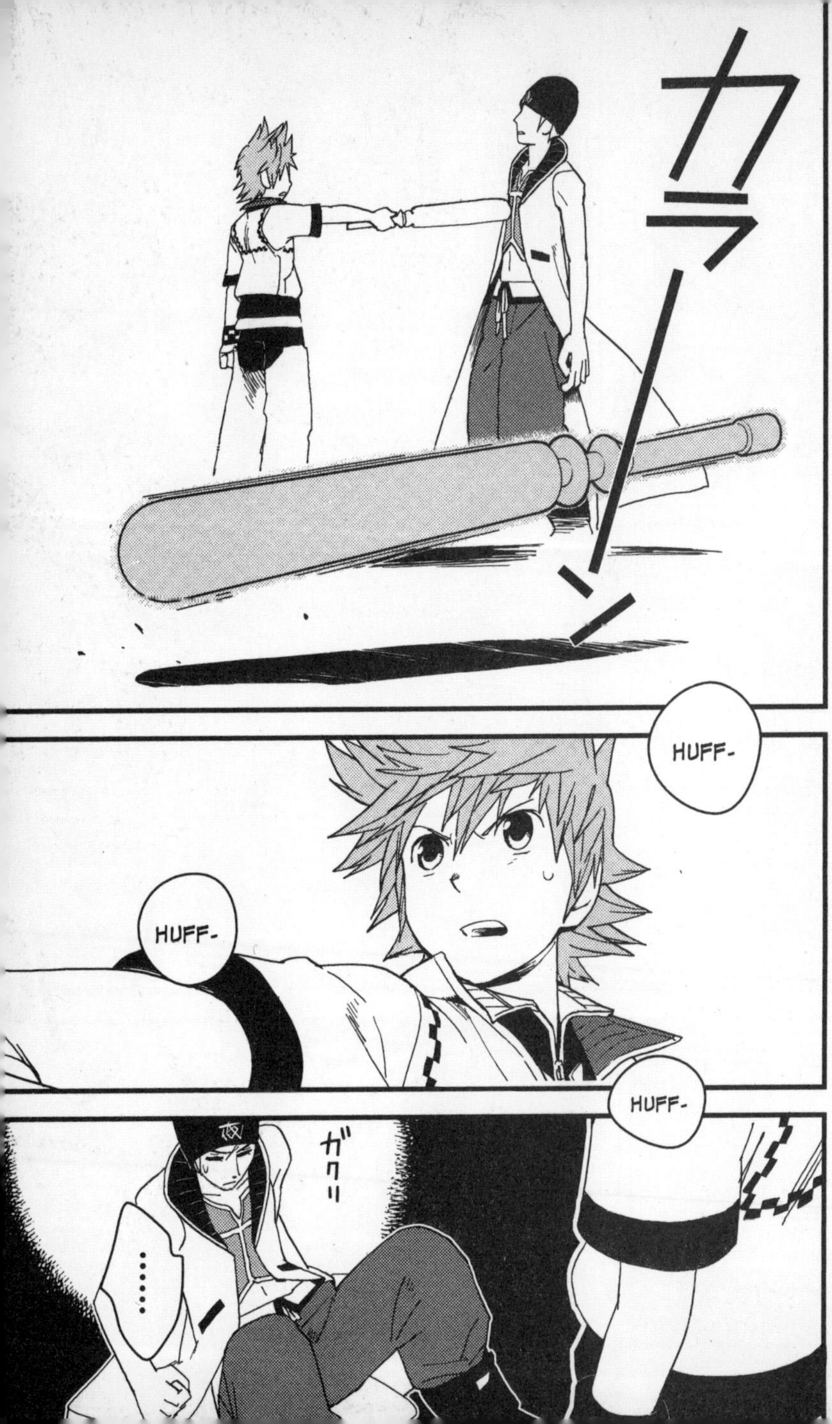
カラーン
HUFF-
HUFF-
HUFF-
ガクッ
......

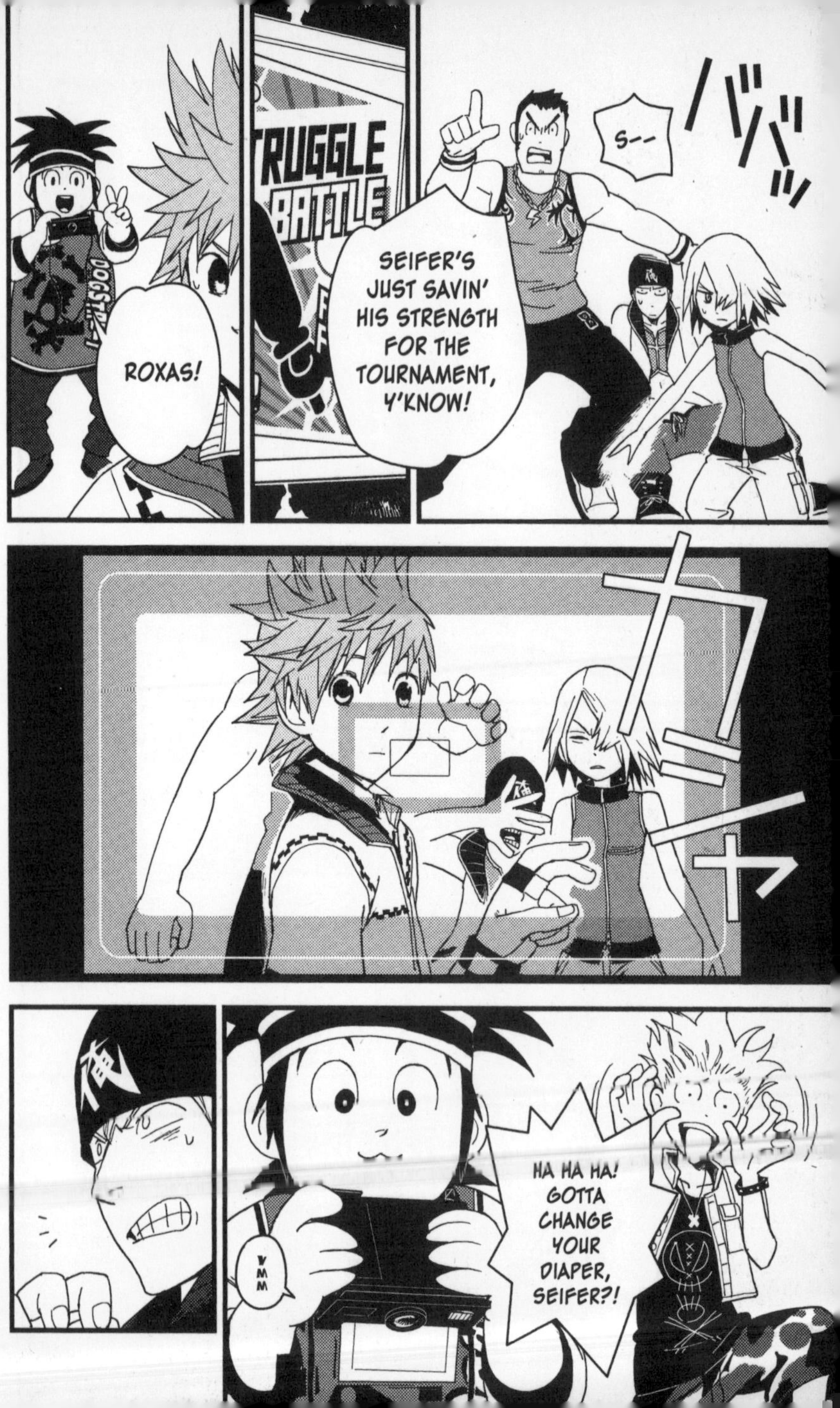
S--
TRUGGLE BATTLE
SEIFER'S JUST SAVIN' HIS STRENGTH FOR THE TOURNAMENT, Y'KNOW!
ROXAS!
HA HA HA! GOTTA CHANGE YOUR DIAPER, SEIFER?!
WMM

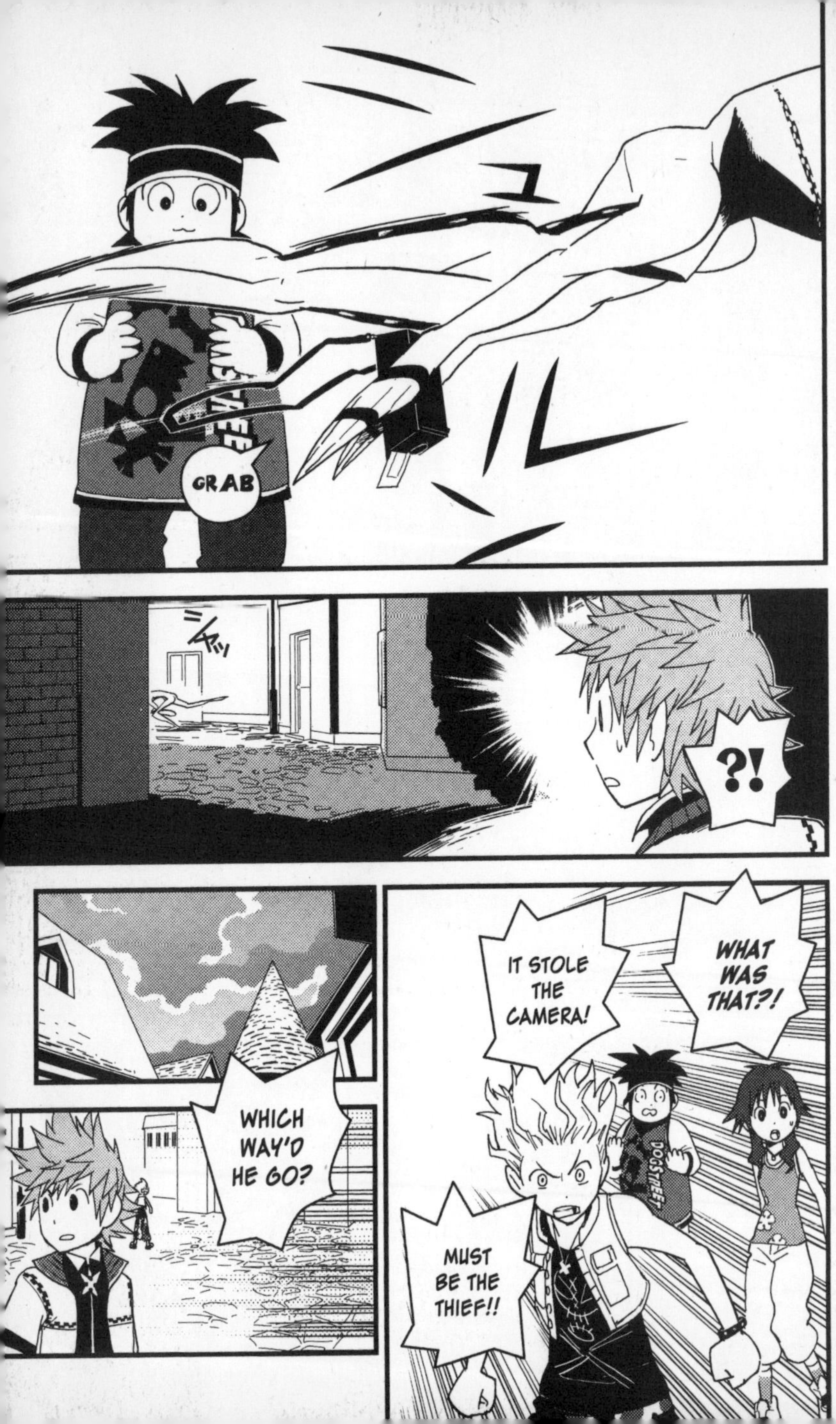
GRAB
?!
WHAT WAS THAT?!
IT STOLE THE CAMERA!
MUST BE THE THIEF!!
WHICH WAY'D HE GO?

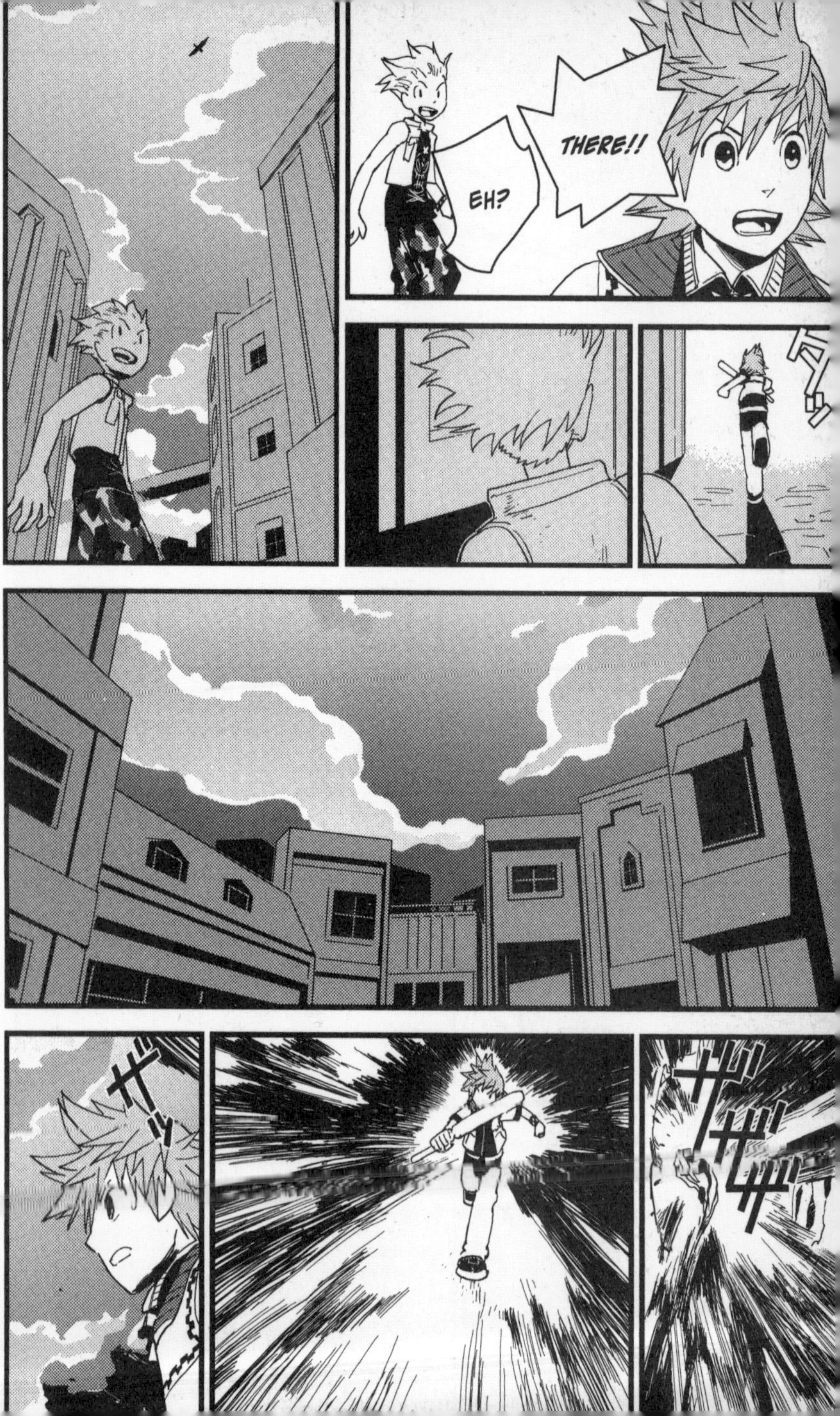
THERE!!
EH?

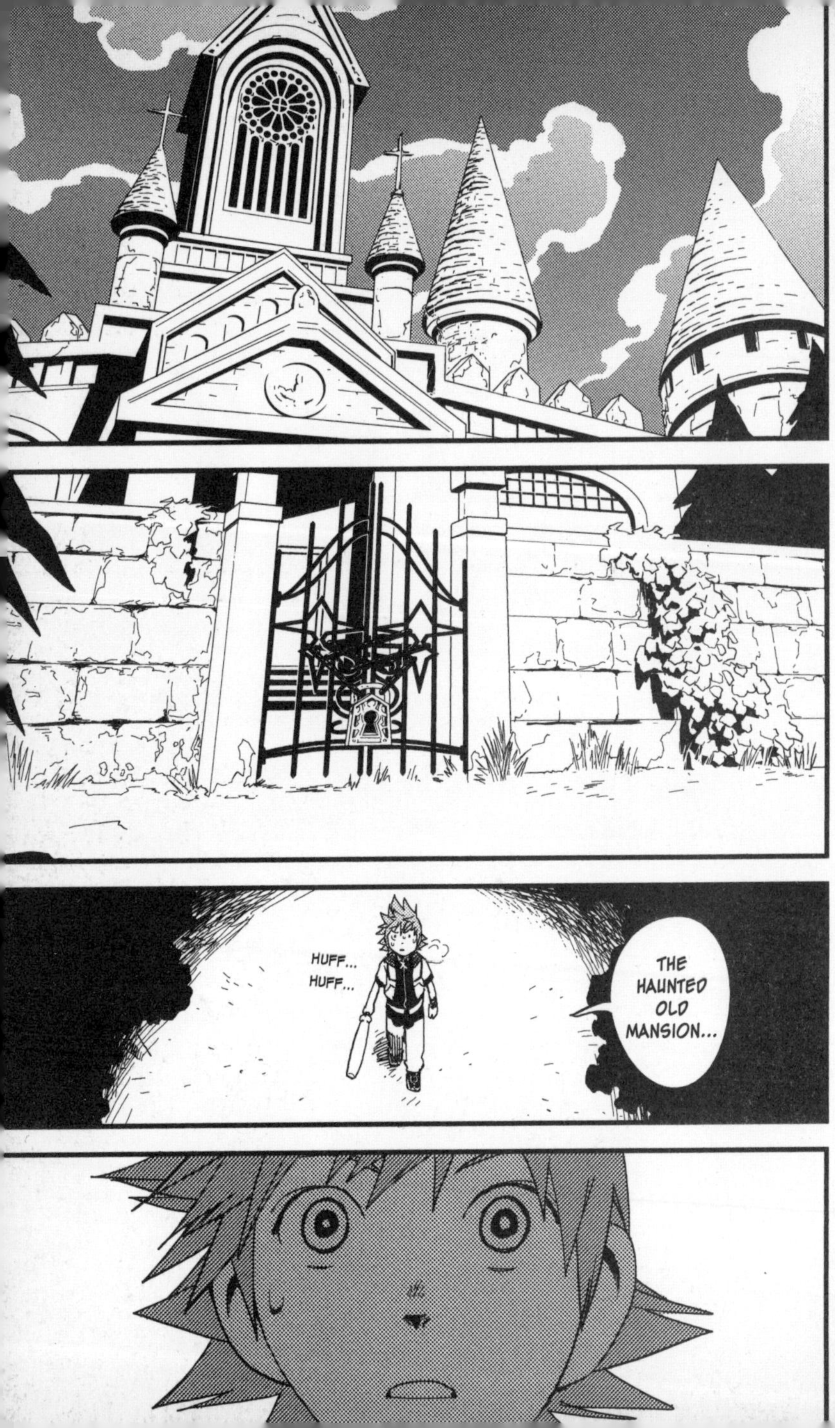
THE HAUNTED OLD MANSION...
HUFF... HUFF...

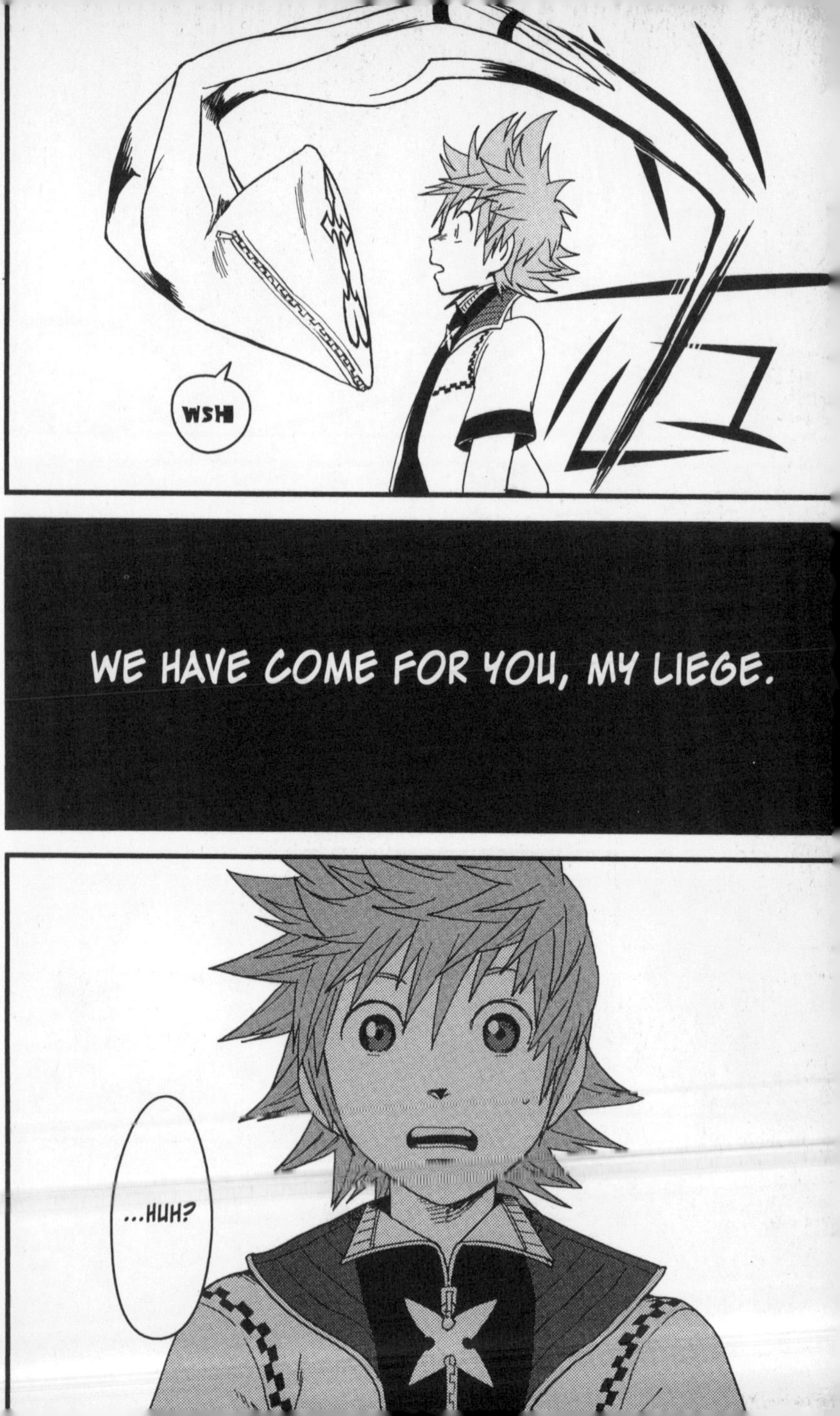
WSH
WE HAVE COME FOR YOU, MY LIEGE.
...HUH?

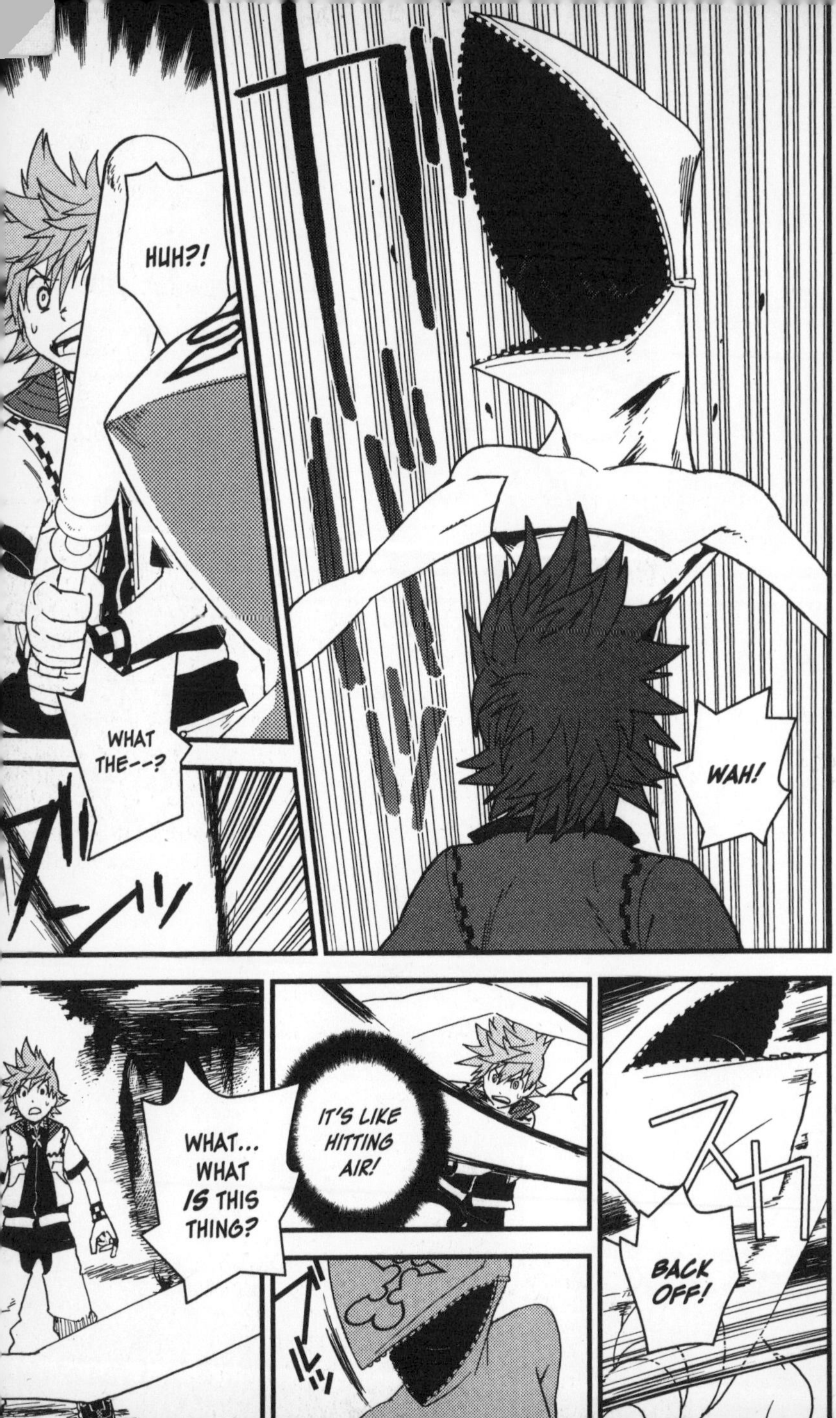
WAH!
HUH?!
WHAT THE--?
BACK OFF!
IT'S LIKE HITTING AIR!
WHAT... WHAT *IS* THIS THING?

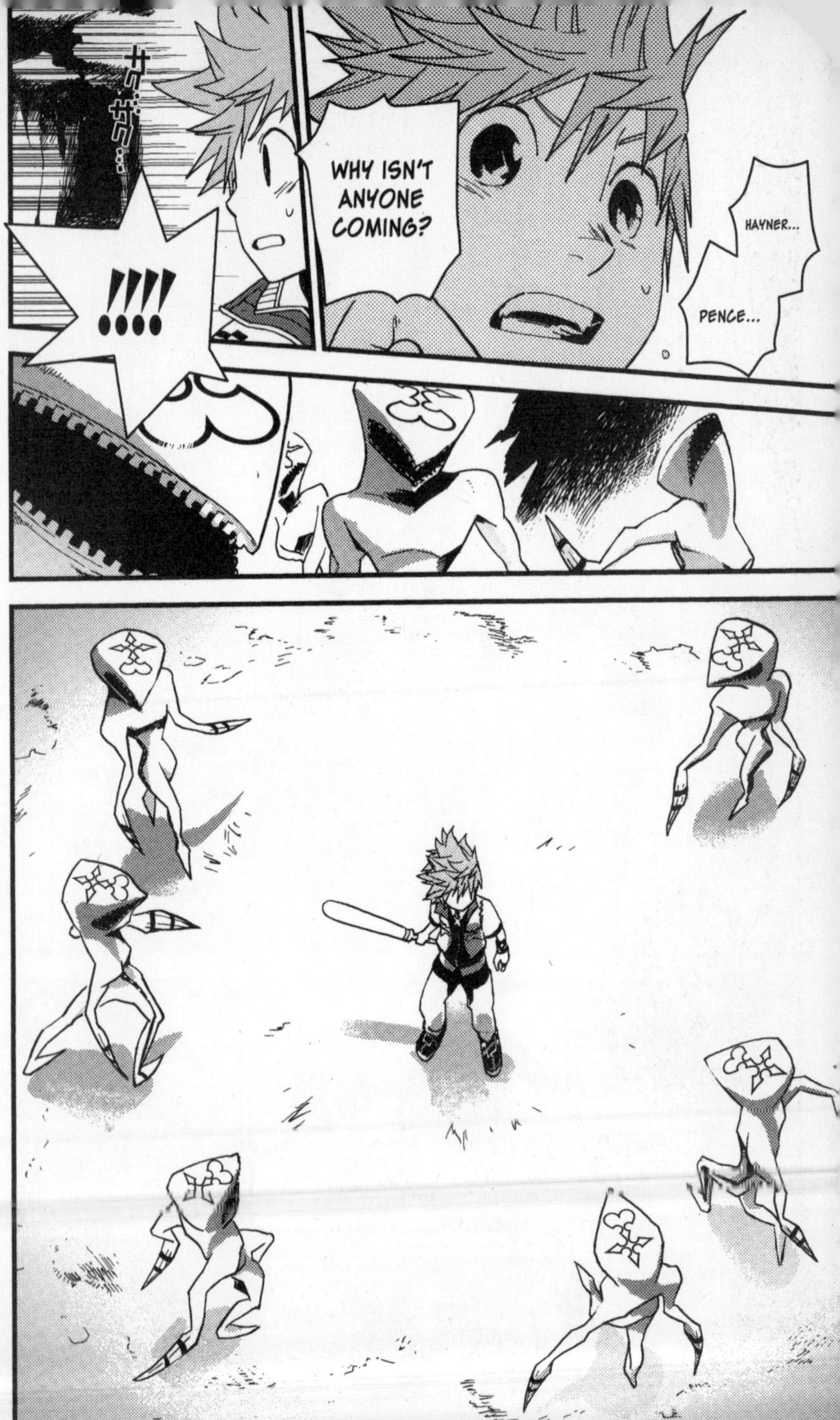
HAYNER...
PENCE...
WHY ISN'T ANYONE COMING?
サク…ザク…
!!!!

Chapter 2: Intruders

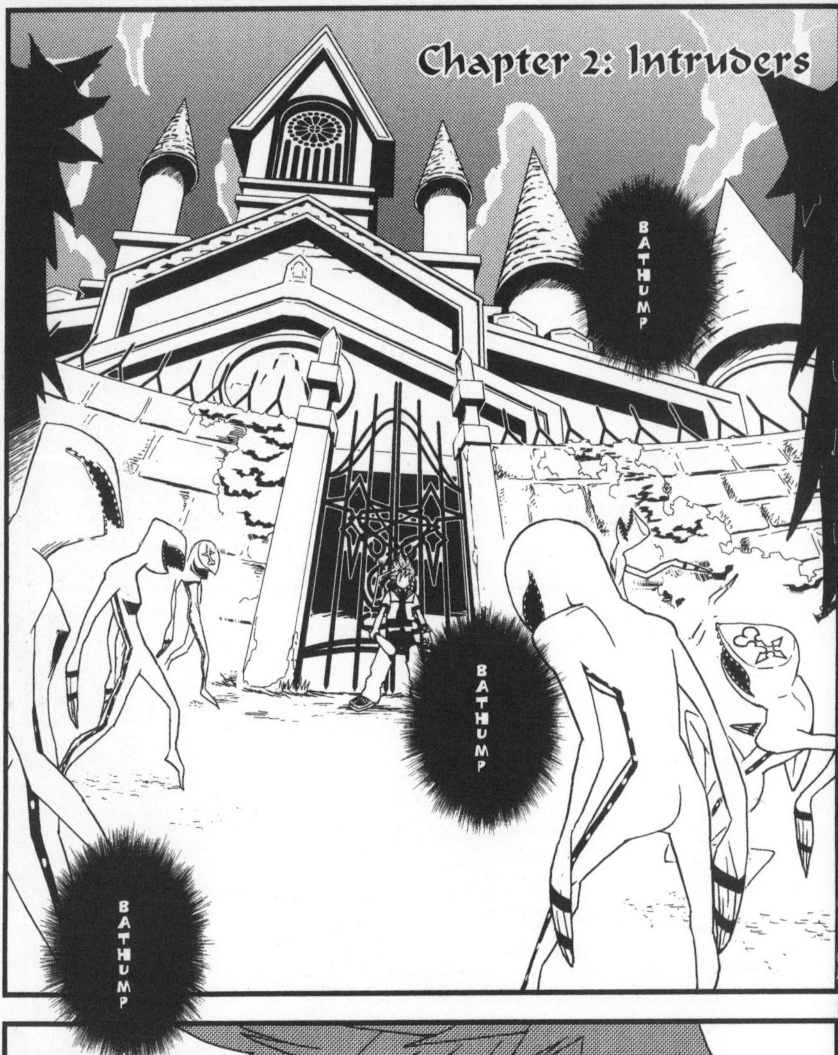
BATHUMP
BATHUMP
BATHUMP

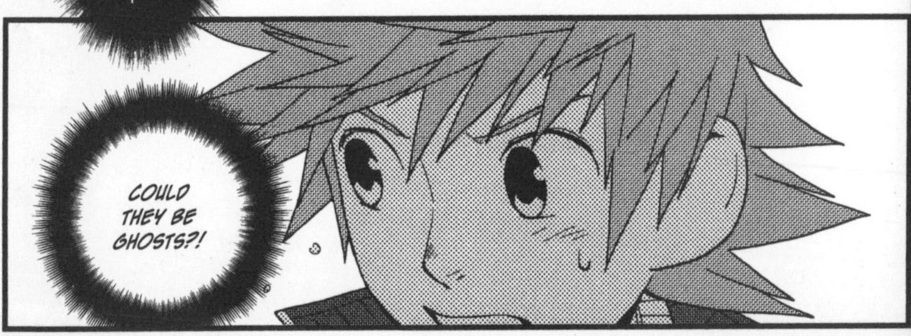
COULD THEY BE GHOSTS?!

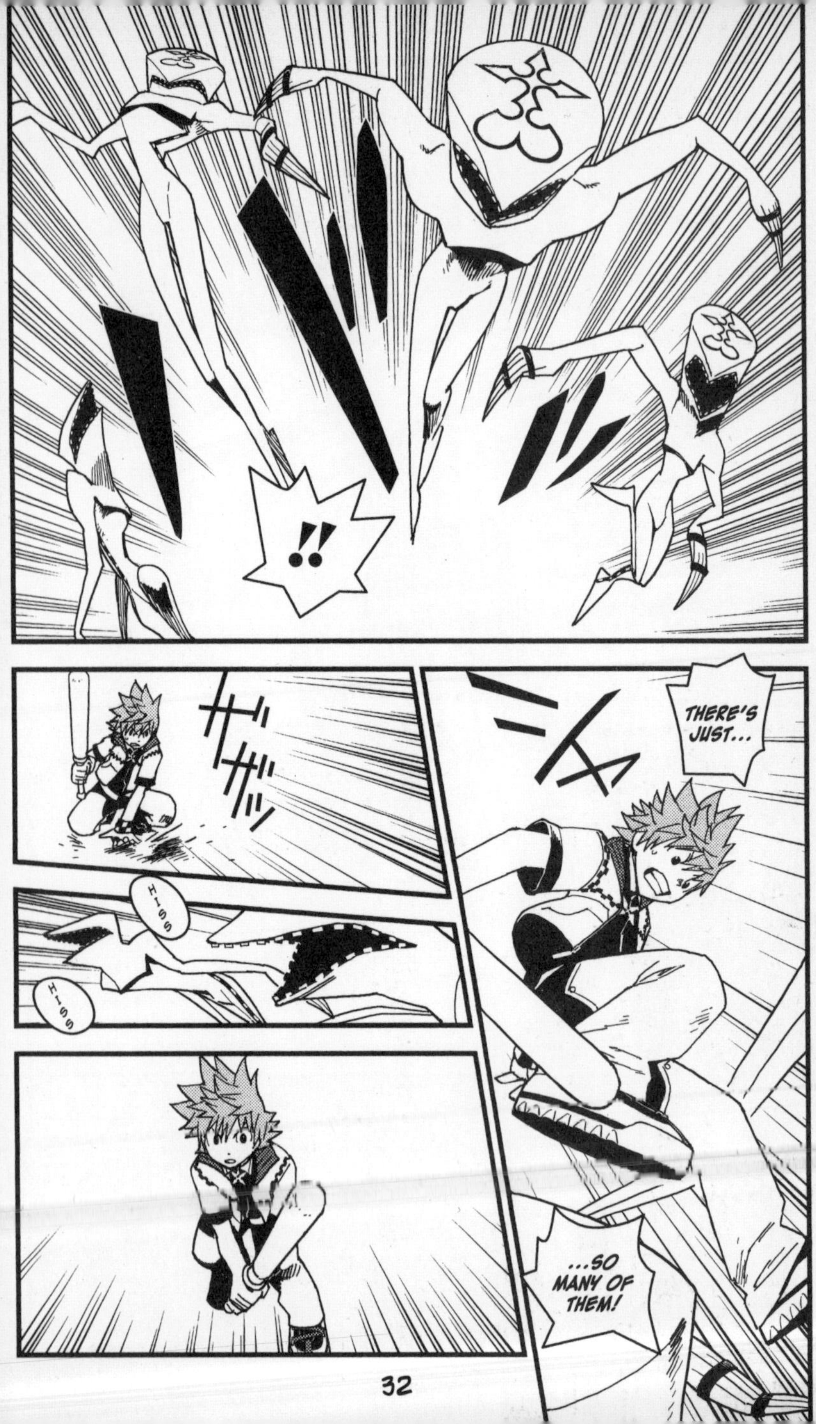
!!
THERE'S JUST...
...SO MANY OF THEM!
HISS
HISS

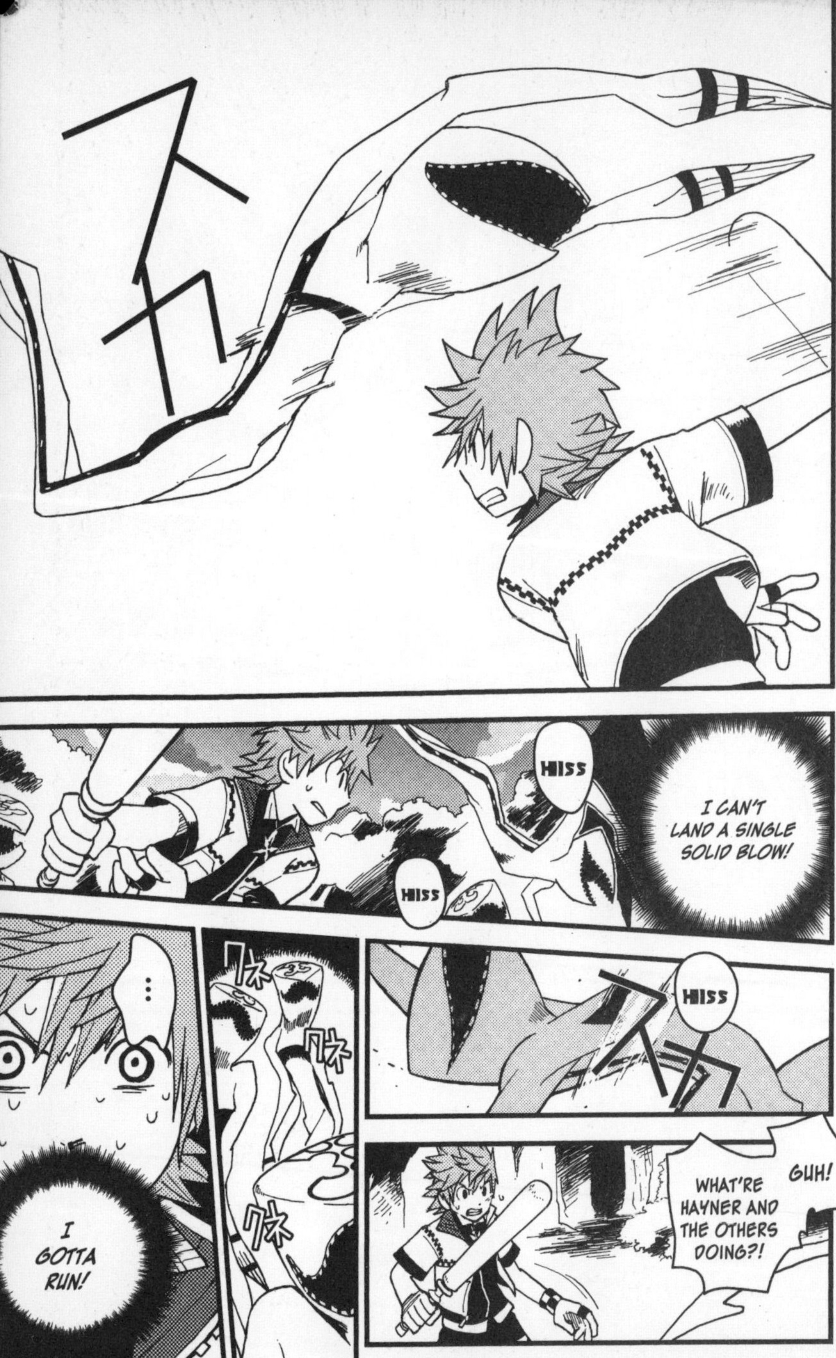
I CAN'T LAND A SINGLE SOLID BLOW!
HISS
HISS
HISS
GUH!
WHAT'RE HAYNER AND THE OTHERS DOING?!
...
I GOTTA RUN!

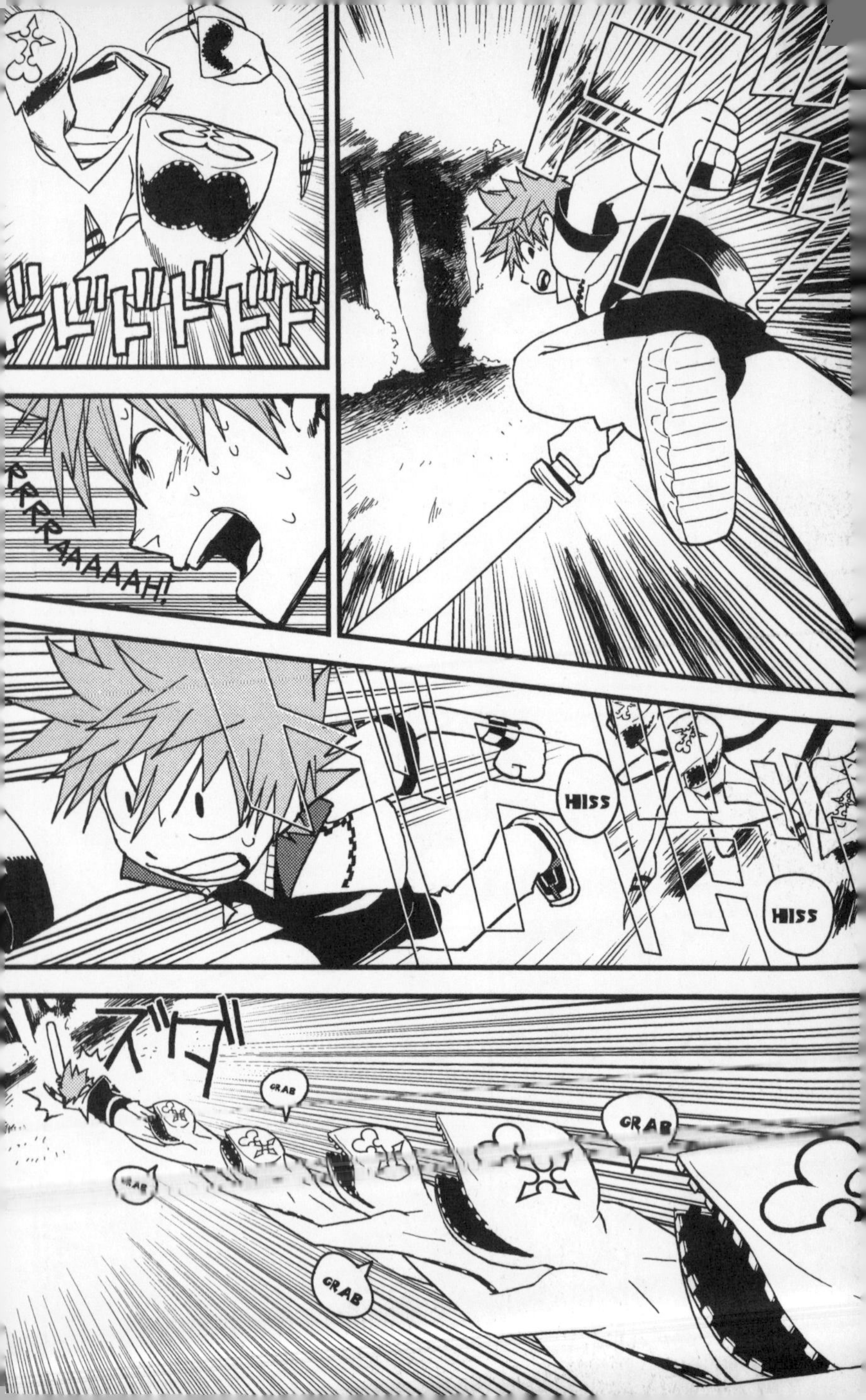
RRRRAAAAAAH!
HISS
HISS
GRAB
GRAB
GRAB
GRAB

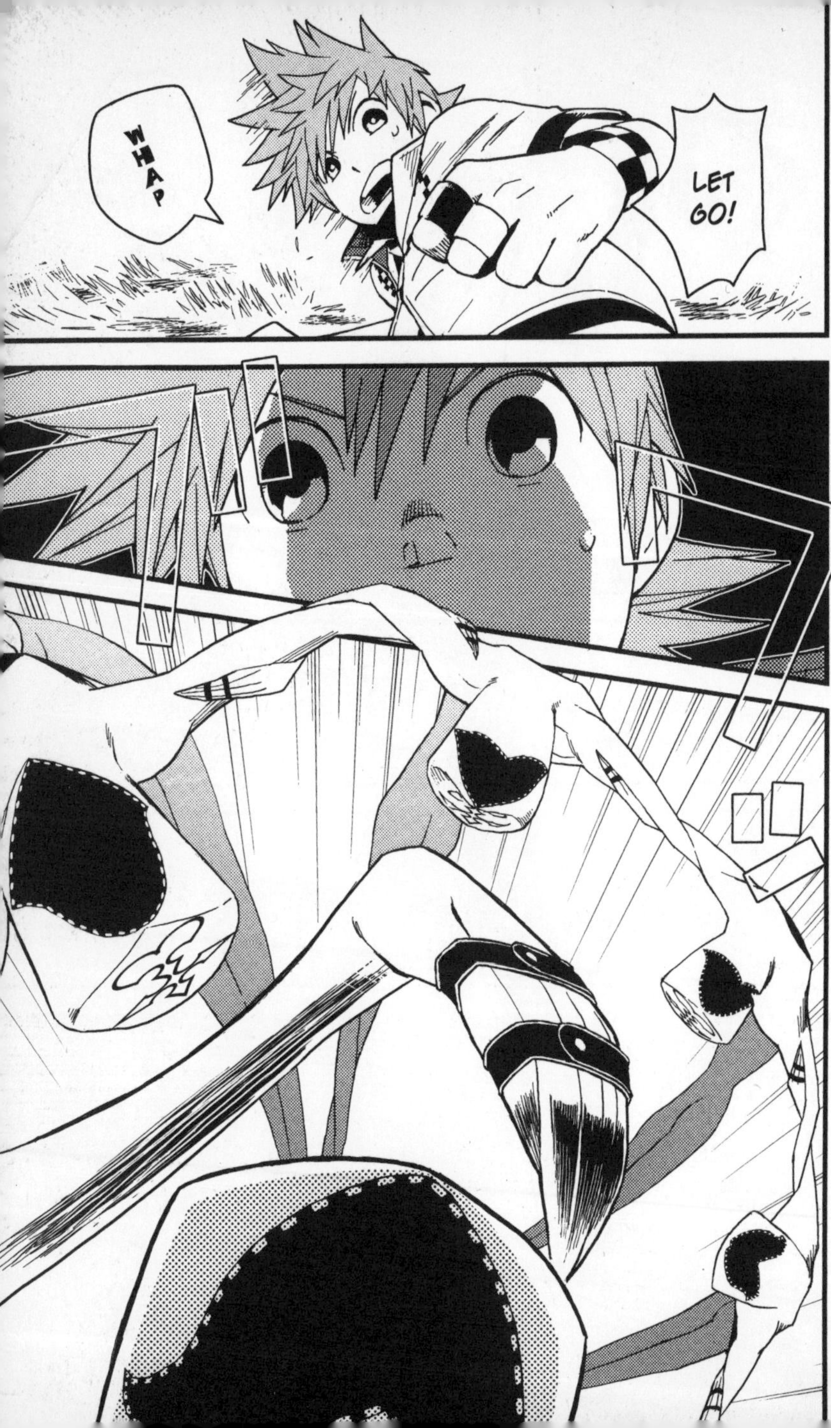
LET GO!
WHAP

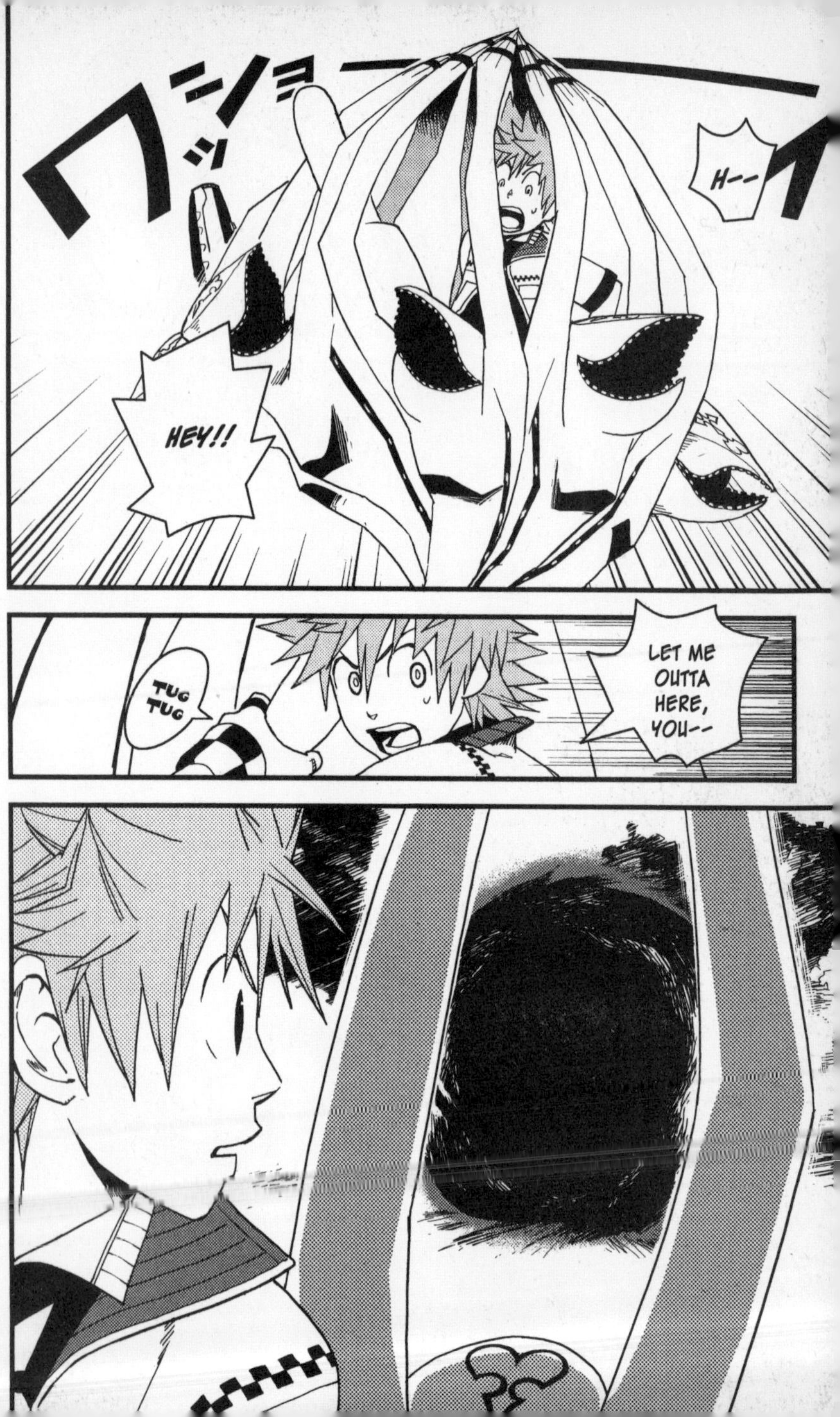
H--
ワッショーイ
HEY!!
LET ME OUTTA HERE, YOU--
TUG TUG

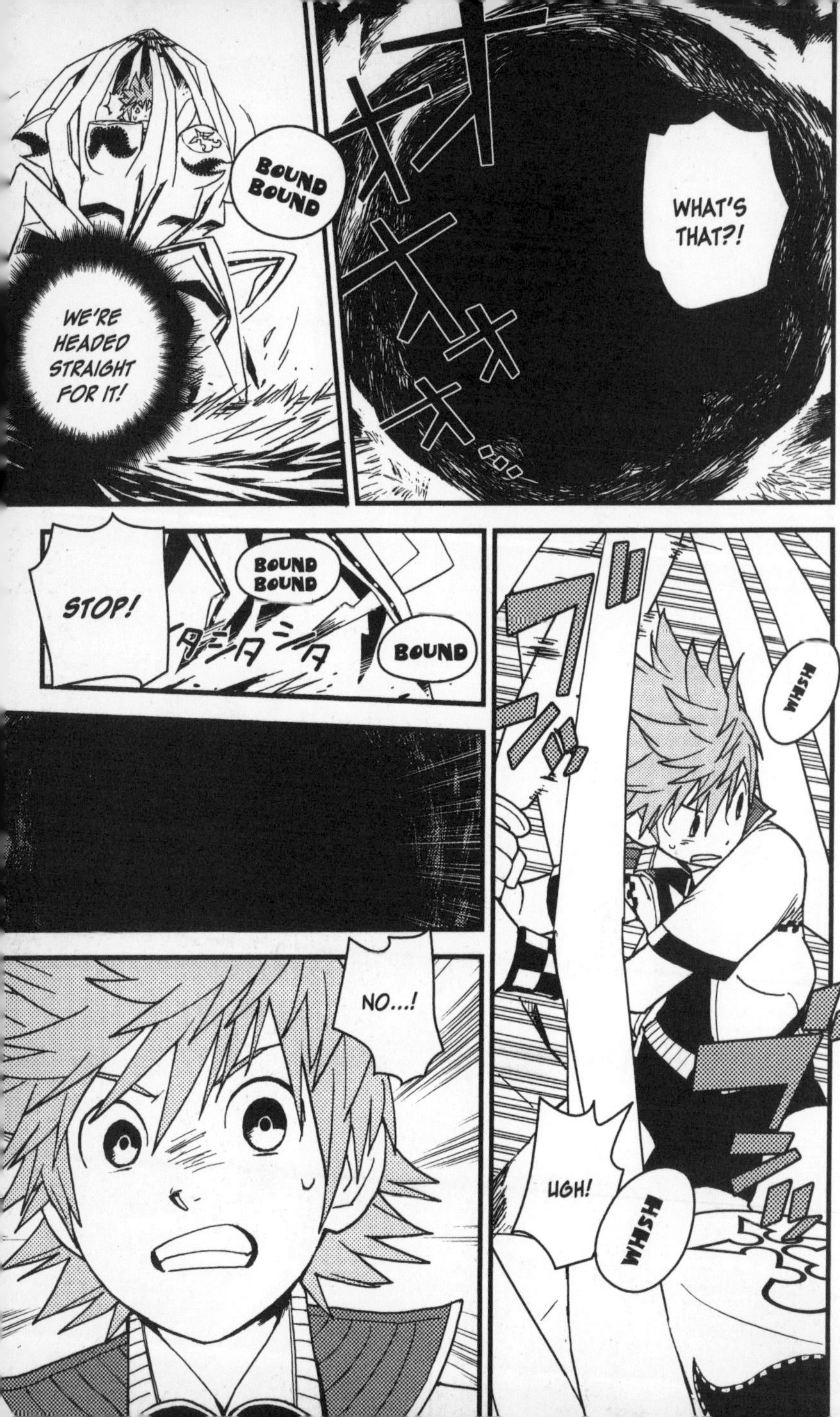
WHAT'S THAT?!
BOUND BOUND
WE'RE HEADED STRAIGHT FOR IT!
WHSH
UGH!
WHSH
STOP!
BOUND BOUND
BOUND
NO...!

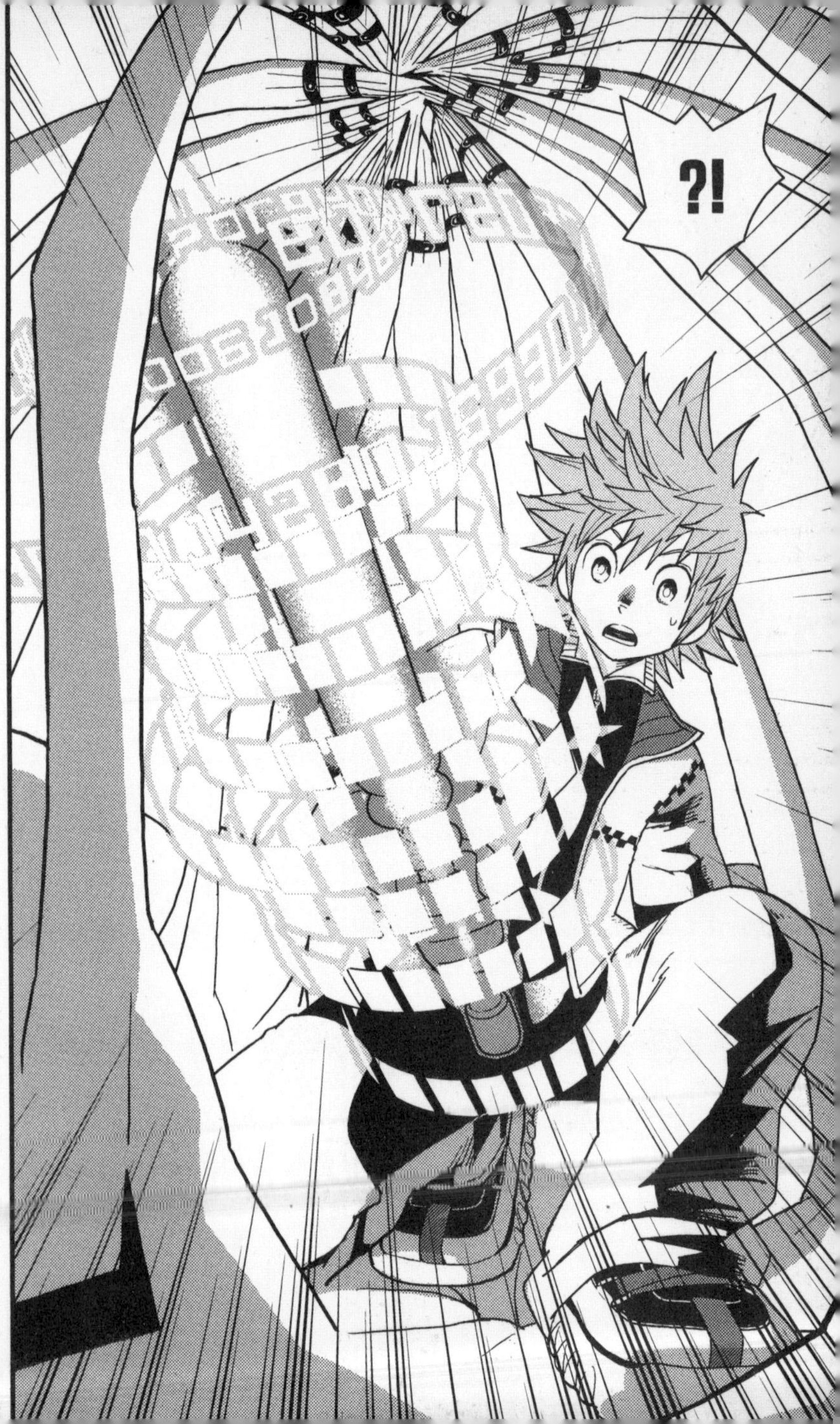
?!

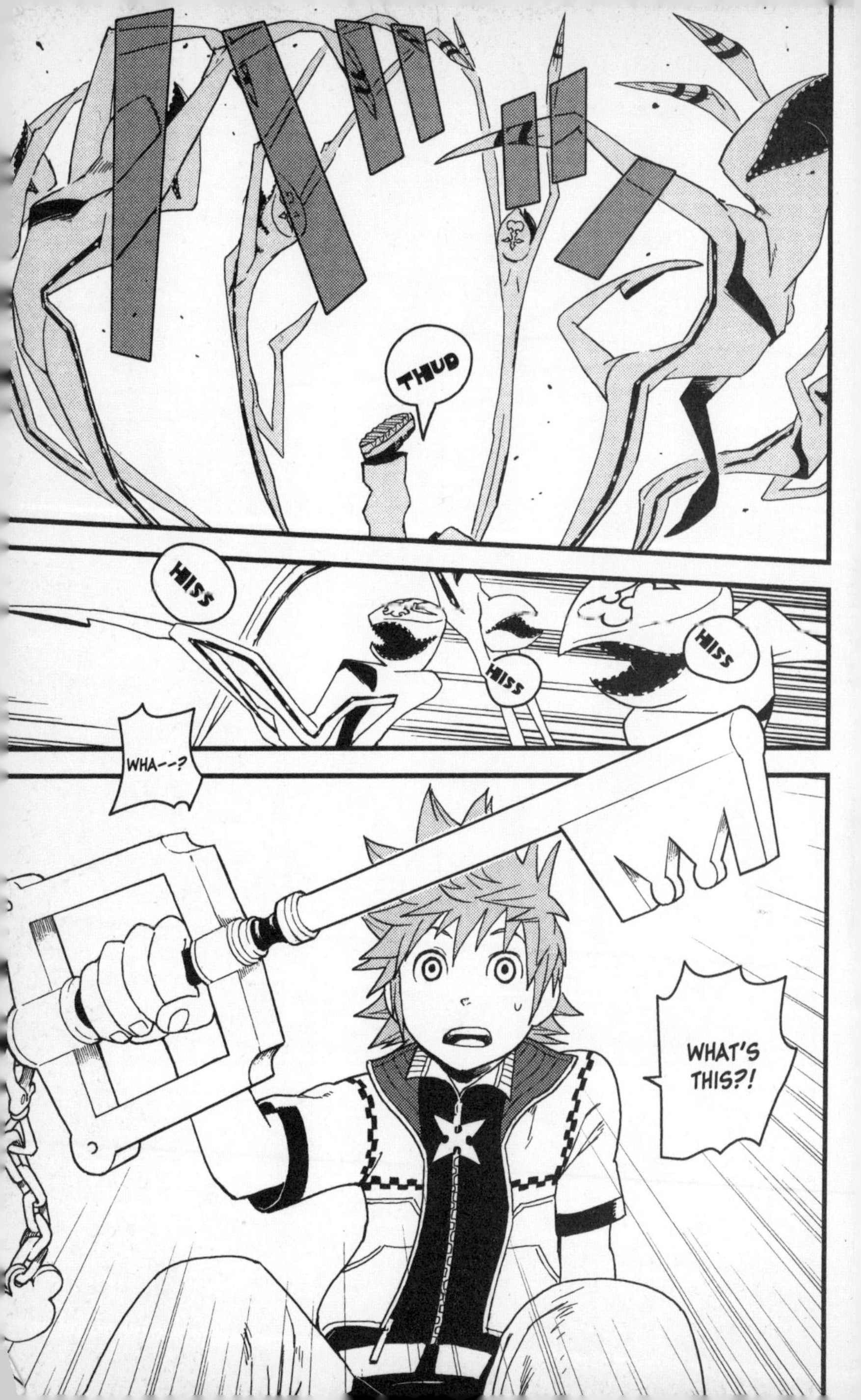
THUD
HISS
HISS
HISS
WHA--?
WHAT'S THIS?!

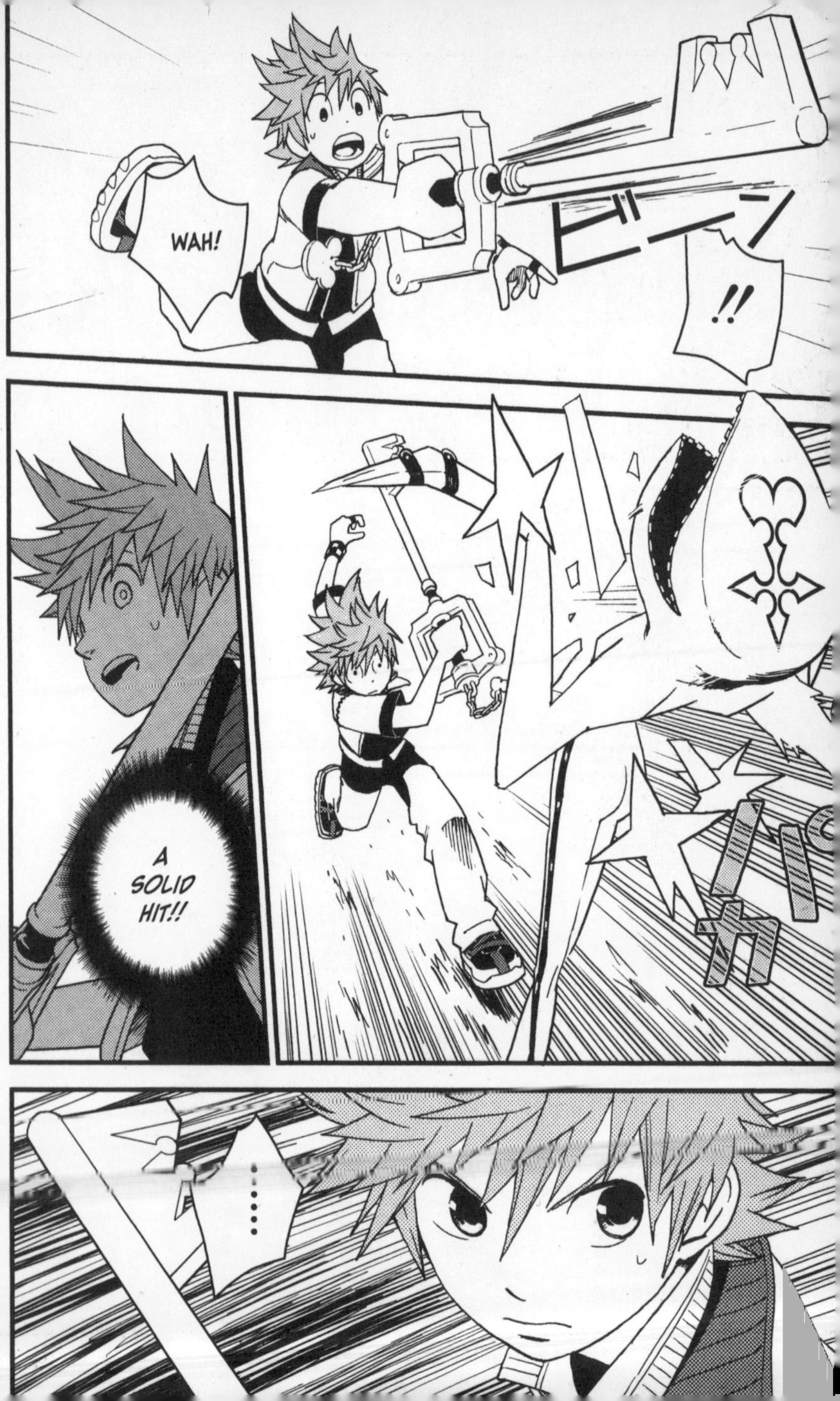
!!
WAH!
A SOLID HIT!!
......

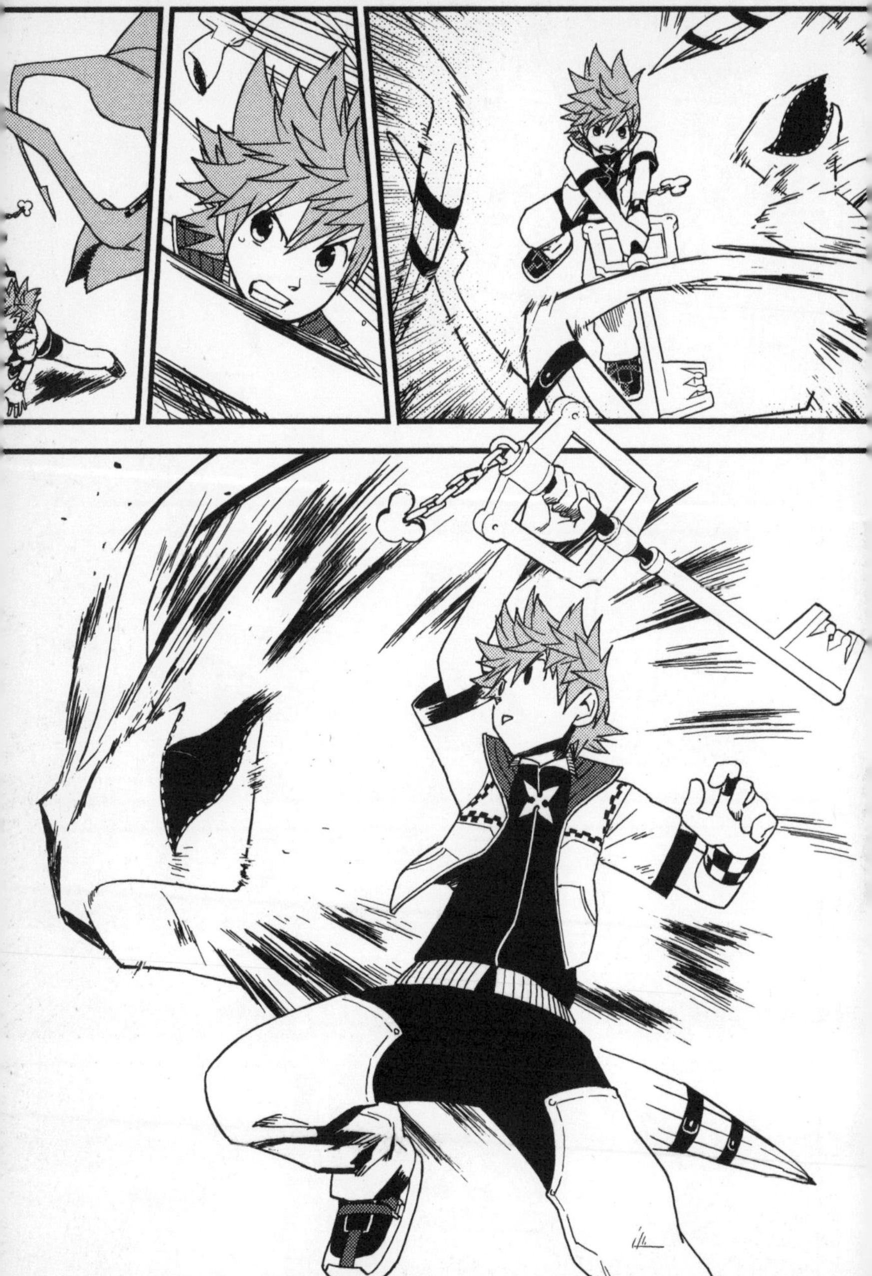

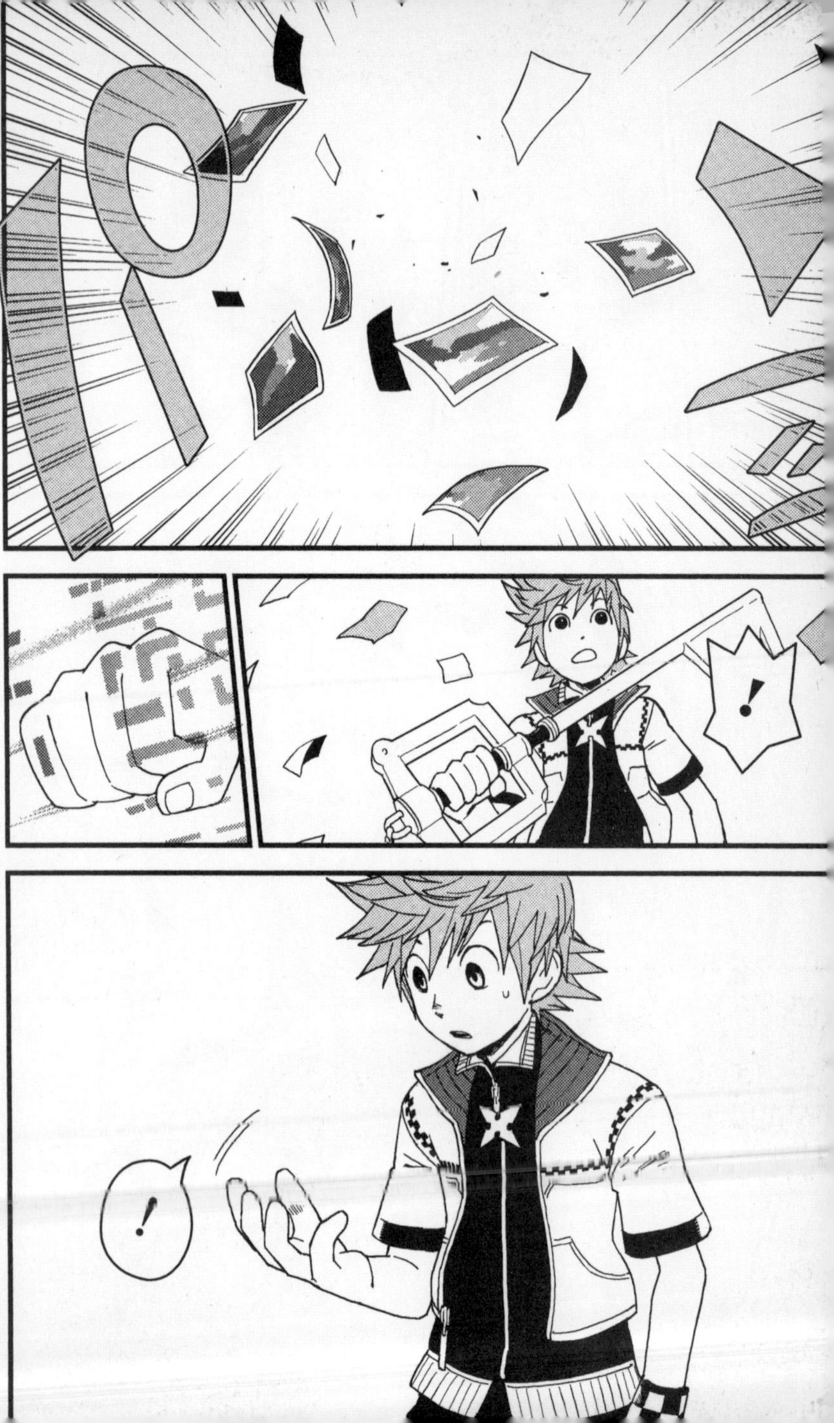
!
!

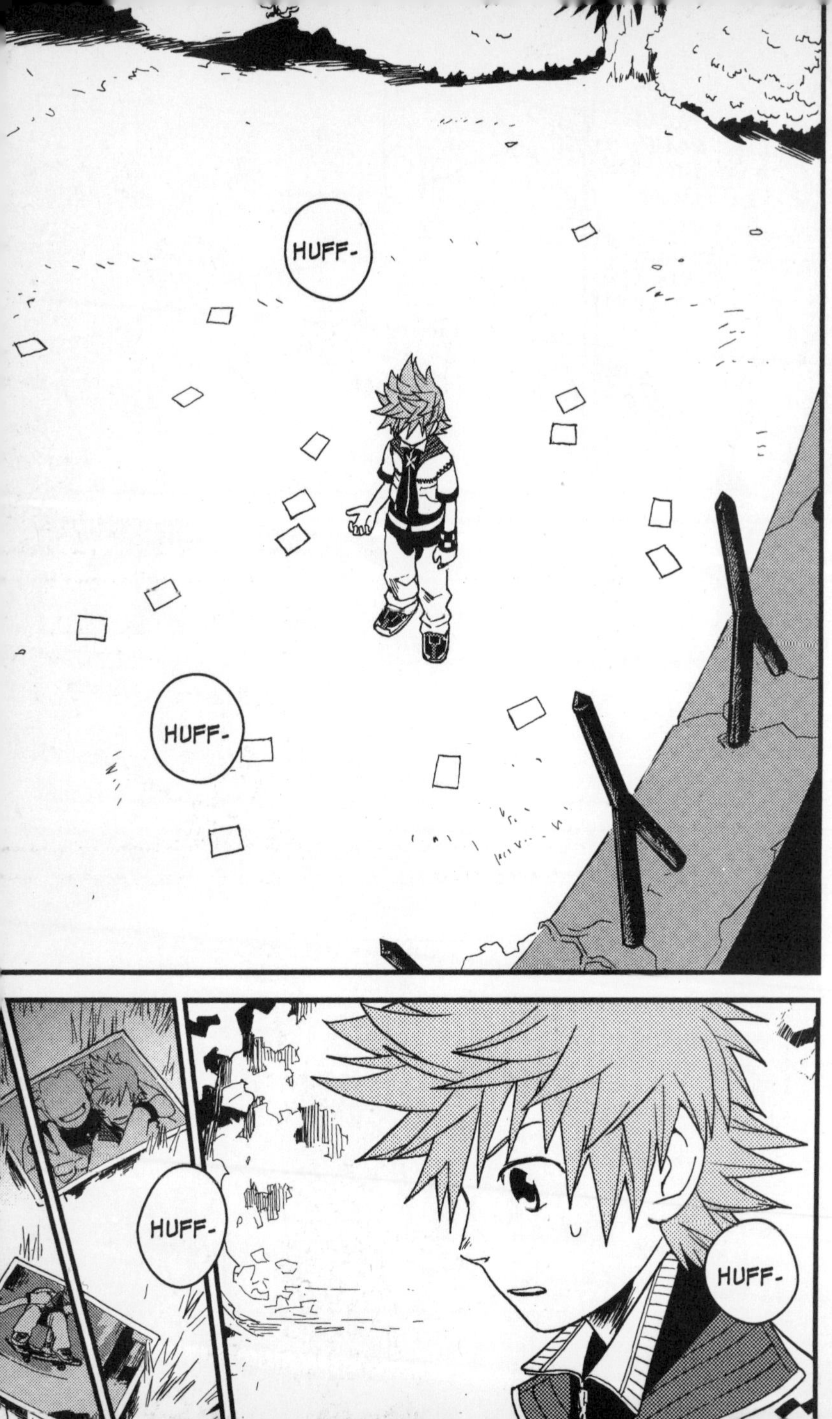
HUFF-
HUFF-
HUFF-
HUFF-

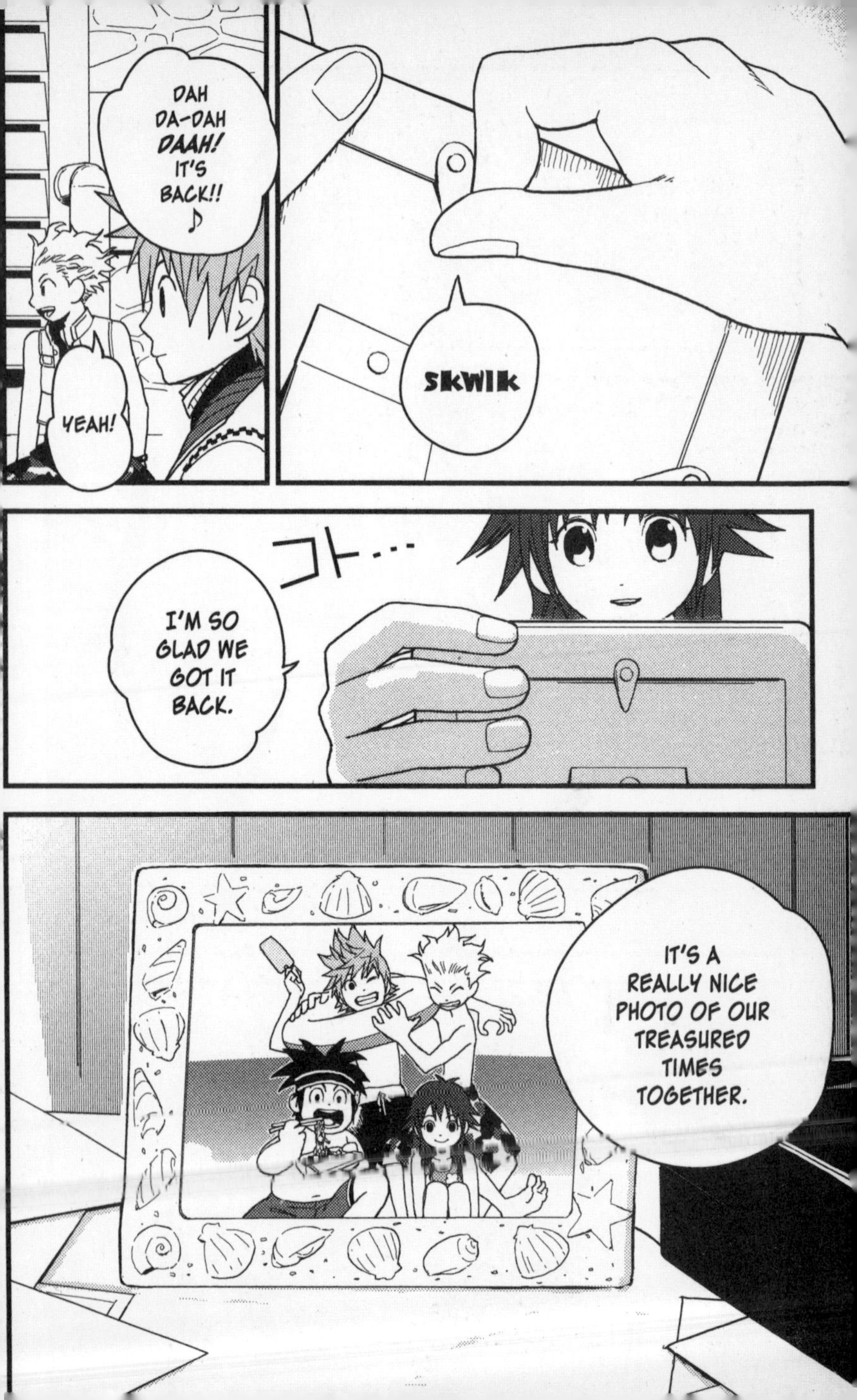
SKWIK
DAH DA-DAH DAAH! IT'S BACK!! ♪
YEAH!
コト...
I'M SO GLAD WE GOT IT BACK.
IT'S A REALLY NICE PHOTO OF OUR TREASURED TIMES TOGETHER.

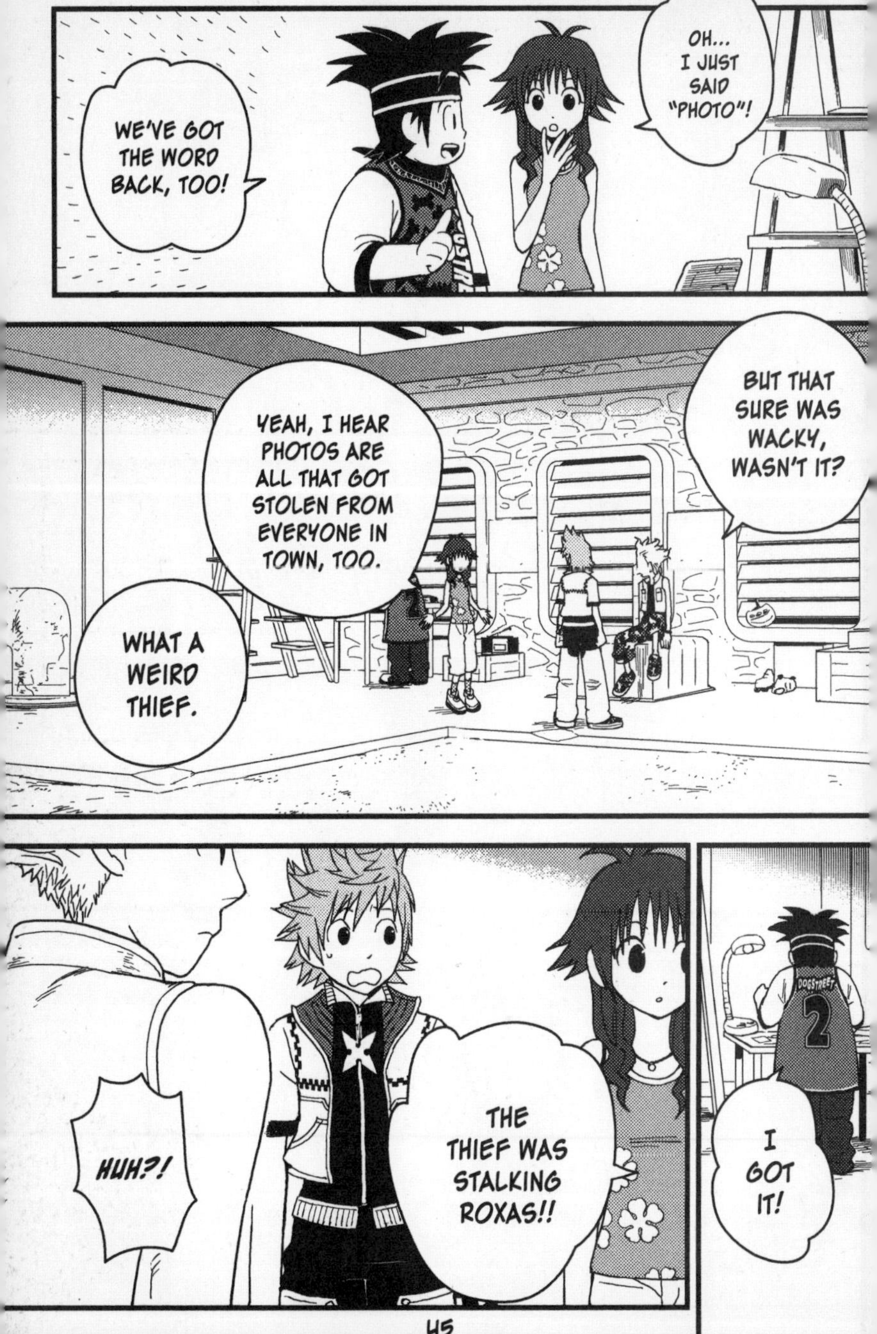
OH... I JUST SAID "PHOTO"!
WE'VE GOT THE WORD BACK, TOO!
BUT THAT SURE WAS WACKY, WASN'T IT?
YEAH, I HEAR PHOTOS ARE ALL THAT GOT STOLEN FROM EVERYONE IN TOWN, TOO.
WHAT A WEIRD THIEF.
DOGSTREET
I GOT IT!
THE THIEF WAS STALKING ROXAS!!
HUH?!

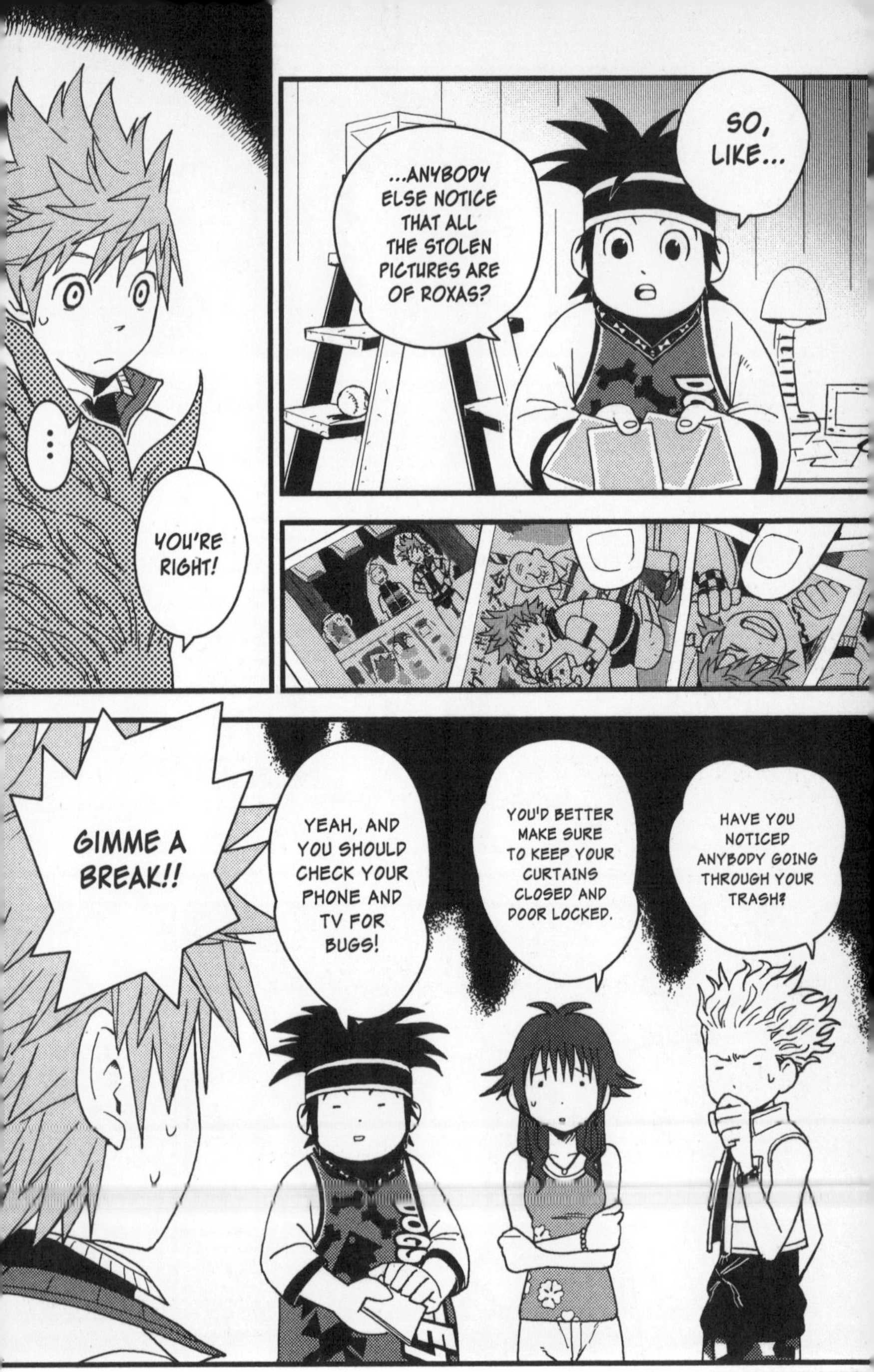
SO, LIKE...
...ANYBODY ELSE NOTICE THAT ALL THE STOLEN PICTURES ARE OF ROXAS?
...
YOU'RE RIGHT!
HAVE YOU NOTICED ANYBODY GOING THROUGH YOUR TRASH?
YOU'D BETTER MAKE SURE TO KEEP YOUR CURTAINS CLOSED AND DOOR LOCKED.
YEAH, AND YOU SHOULD CHECK YOUR PHONE AND TV FOR BUGS!
GIMME A BREAK!!

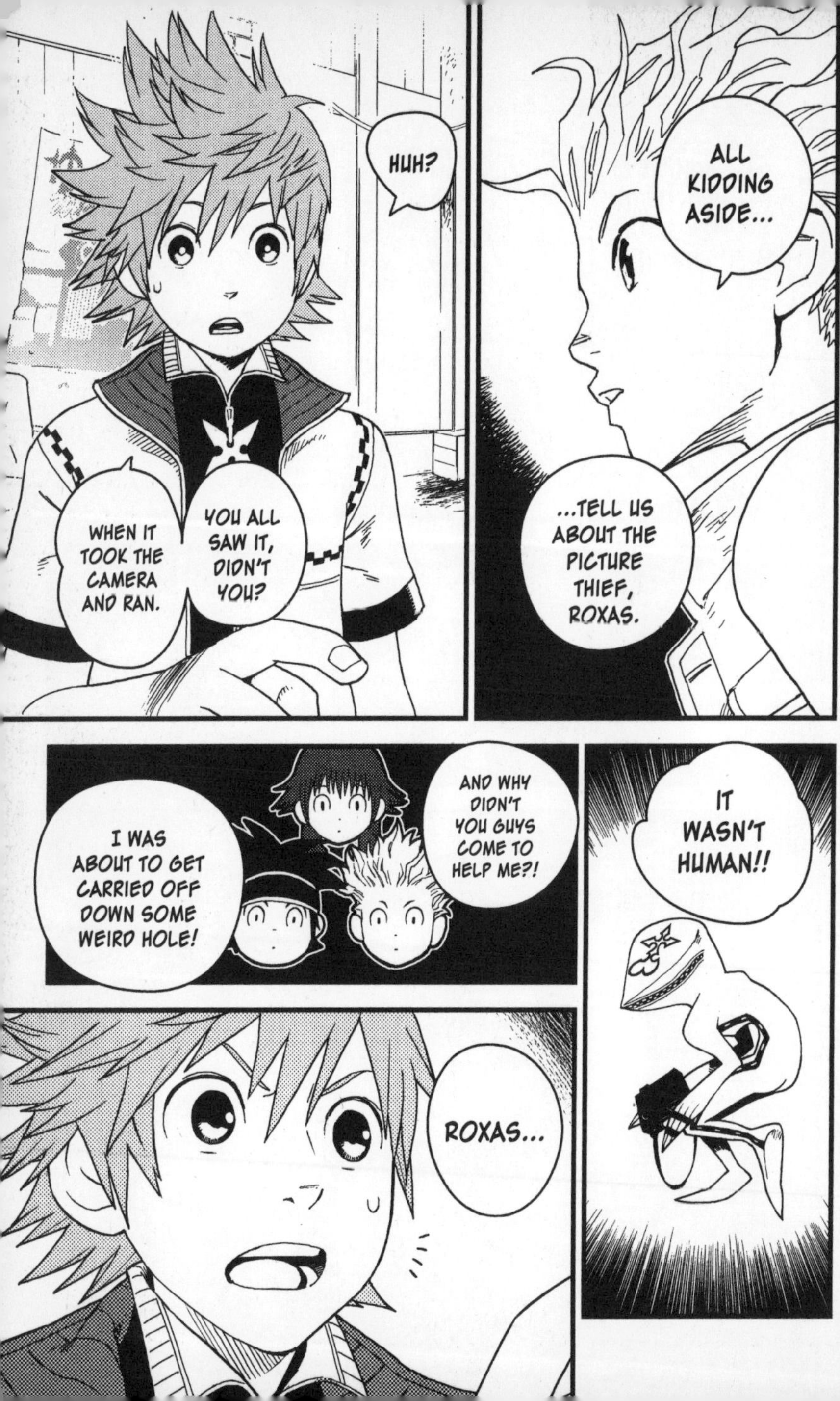

ALL KIDDING ASIDE...
...TELL US ABOUT THE PICTURE THIEF, ROXAS.
HUH?
YOU ALL SAW IT, DIDN'T YOU?
WHEN IT TOOK THE CAMERA AND RAN.
IT WASN'T HUMAN!!
AND WHY DIDN'T YOU GUYS COME TO HELP ME?!
I WAS ABOUT TO GET CARRIED OFF DOWN SOME WEIRD HOLE!
ROXAS...

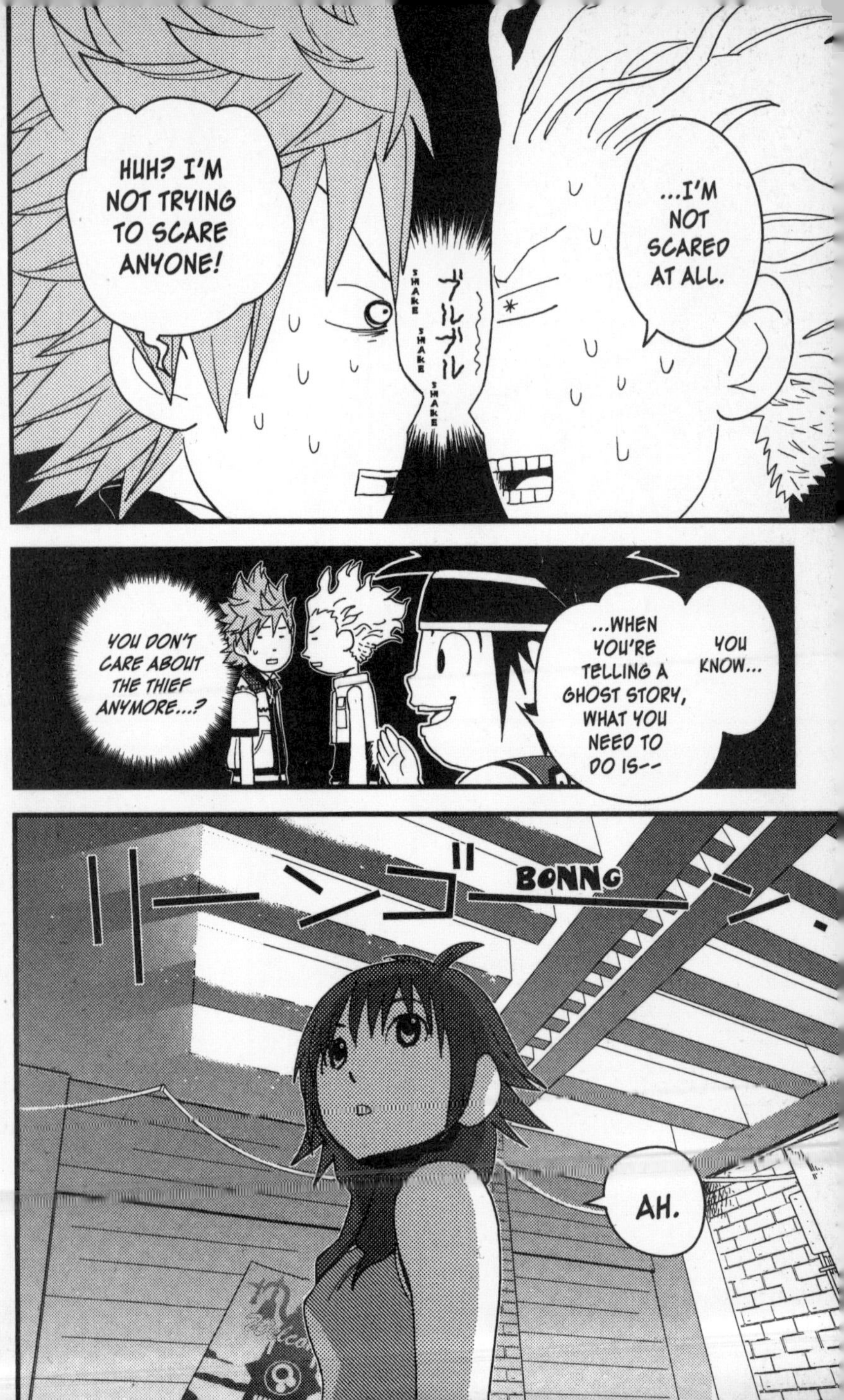
...I'M NOT SCARED AT ALL.
ブルブル
SHAKE SHAKE SHAKE
HUH? I'M NOT TRYING TO SCARE ANYONE!
YOU KNOW...
...WHEN YOU'RE TELLING A GHOST STORY, WHAT YOU NEED TO DO IS--
YOU DON'T CARE ABOUT THE THIEF ANYMORE...?
ゴーン
BONNG
AH.

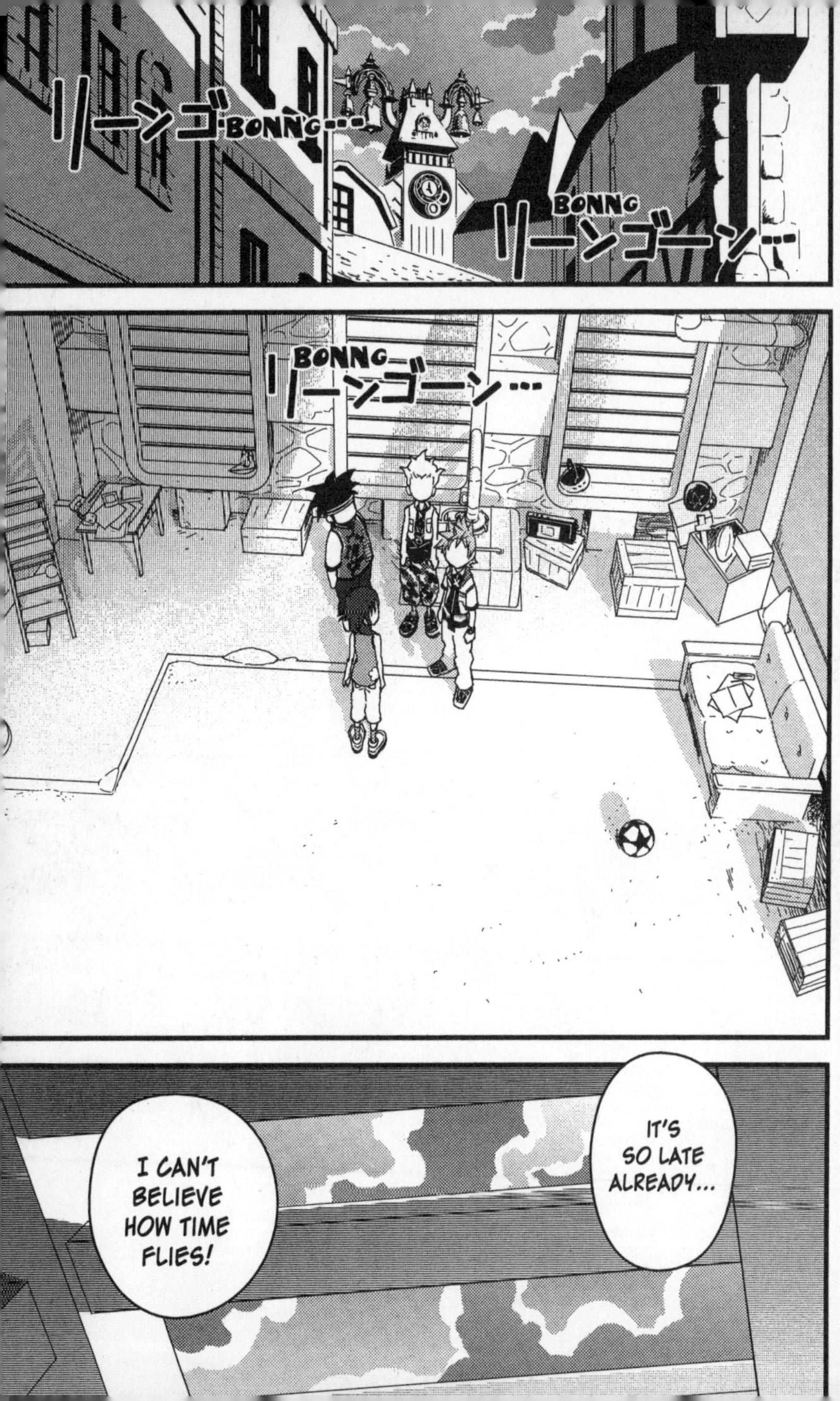
リーンゴ BONNG...
BONNG リーンゴーン
BONNG リーンゴーン...
IT'S SO LATE ALREADY...
I CAN'T BELIEVE HOW TIME FLIES!

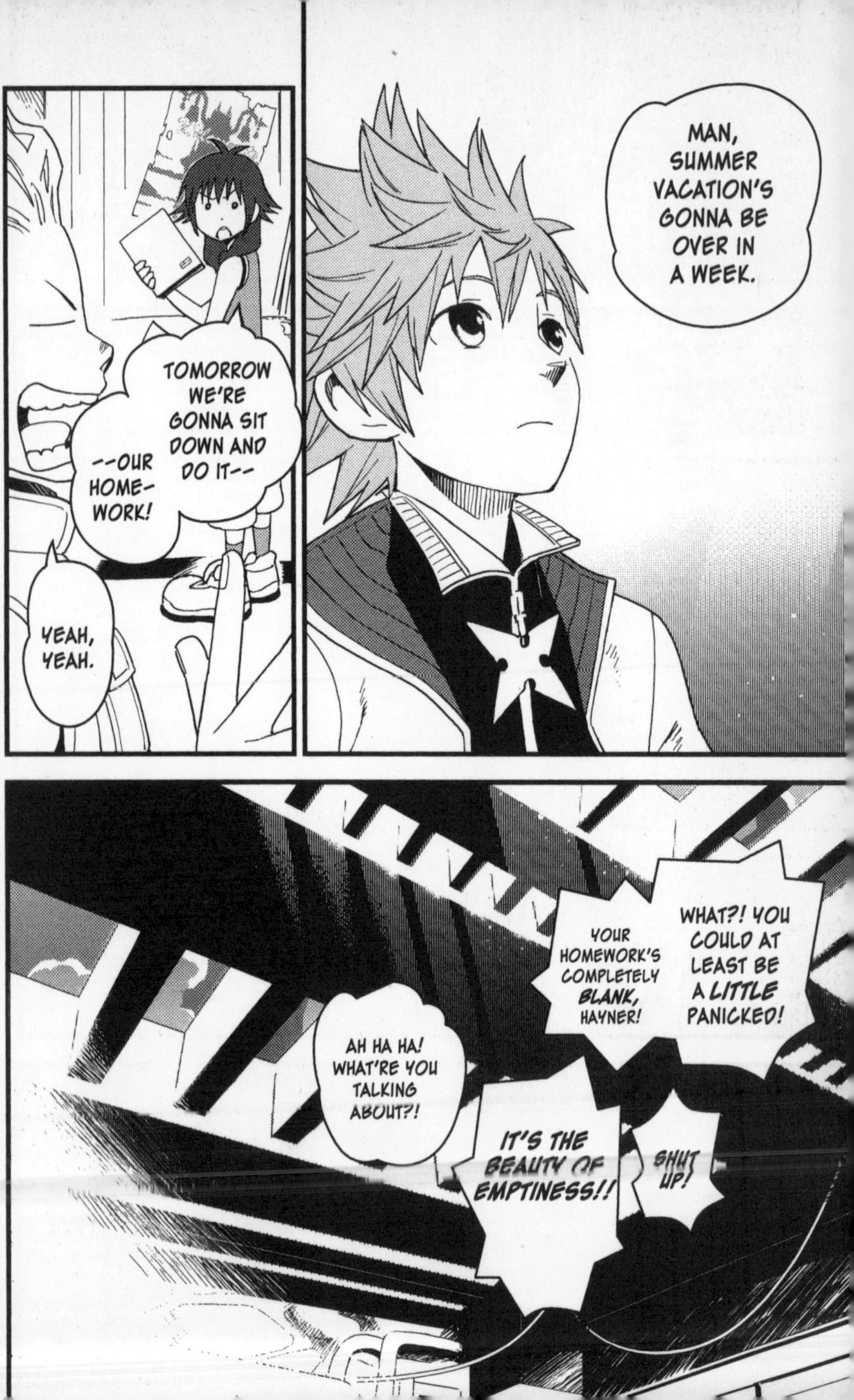
MAN, SUMMER VACATION'S GONNA BE OVER IN A WEEK.
TOMORROW WE'RE GONNA SIT DOWN AND DO IT--
--OUR HOMEWORK!
YEAH, YEAH.
WHAT?! YOU COULD AT LEAST BE A LITTLE PANICKED!
YOUR HOMEWORK'S COMPLETELY BLANK, HAYNER!
AH HA HA! WHAT'RE YOU TALKING ABOUT?!
IT'S THE BEAUTY OF EMPTINESS!!
SHUT UP!

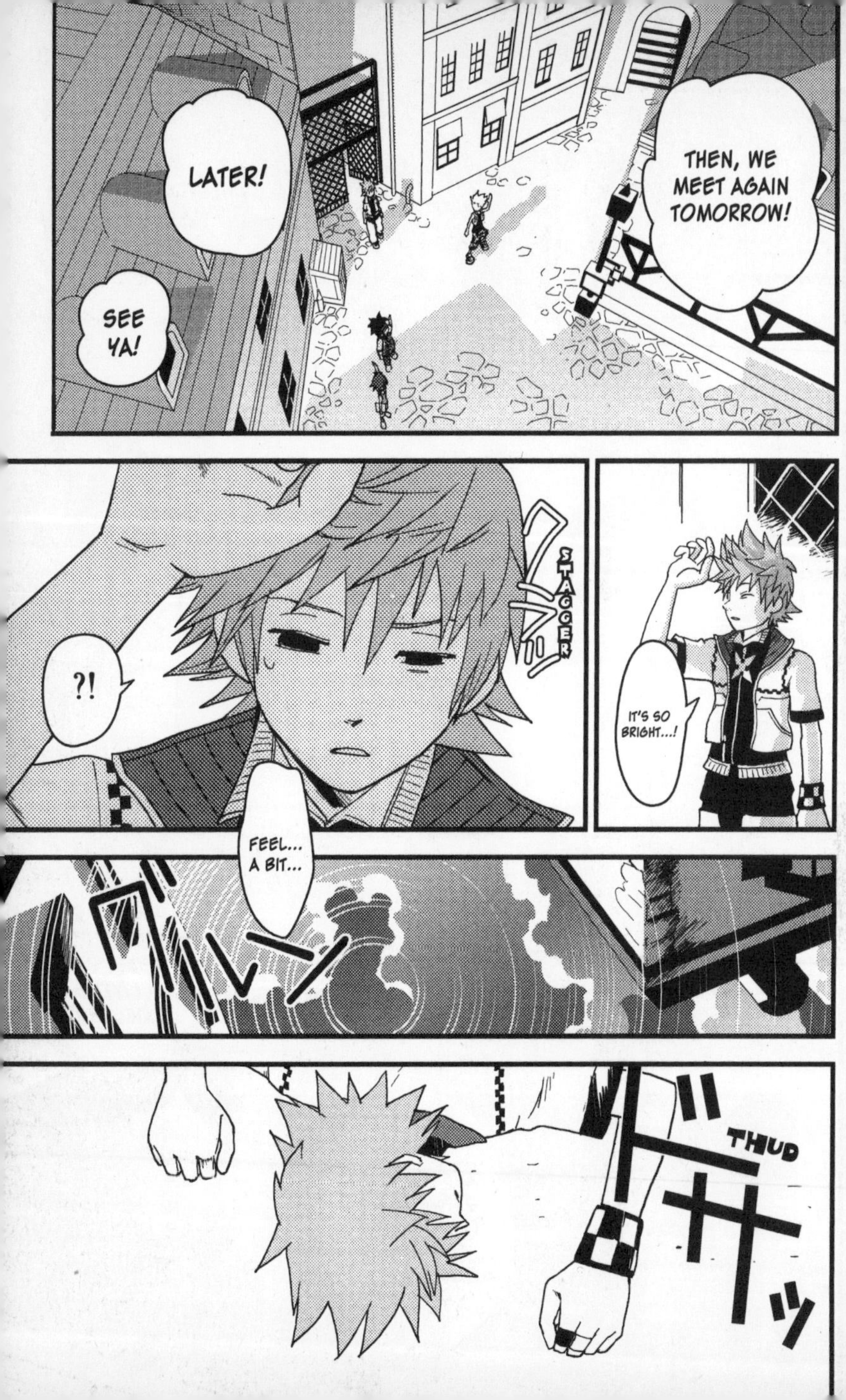
THEN, WE MEET AGAIN TOMORROW!
LATER!
SEE YA!
IT'S SO BRIGHT...!
STAGGER
?!
FEEL... A BIT...
THUD

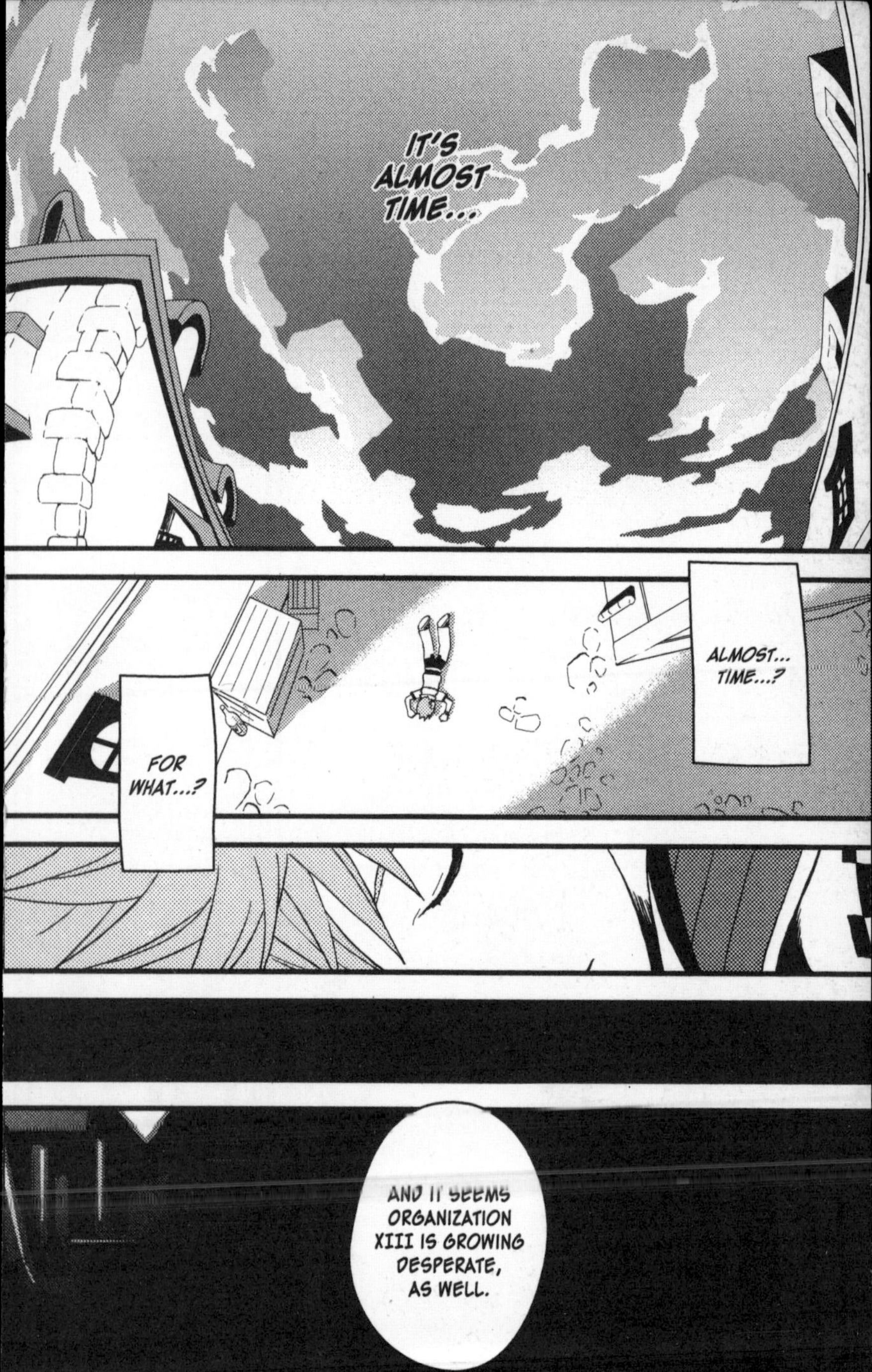
IT'S ALMOST TIME...
ALMOST... TIME...?
FOR WHAT...?
AND IT SEEMS ORGANIZATION XIII IS GROWING DESPERATE, AS WELL.

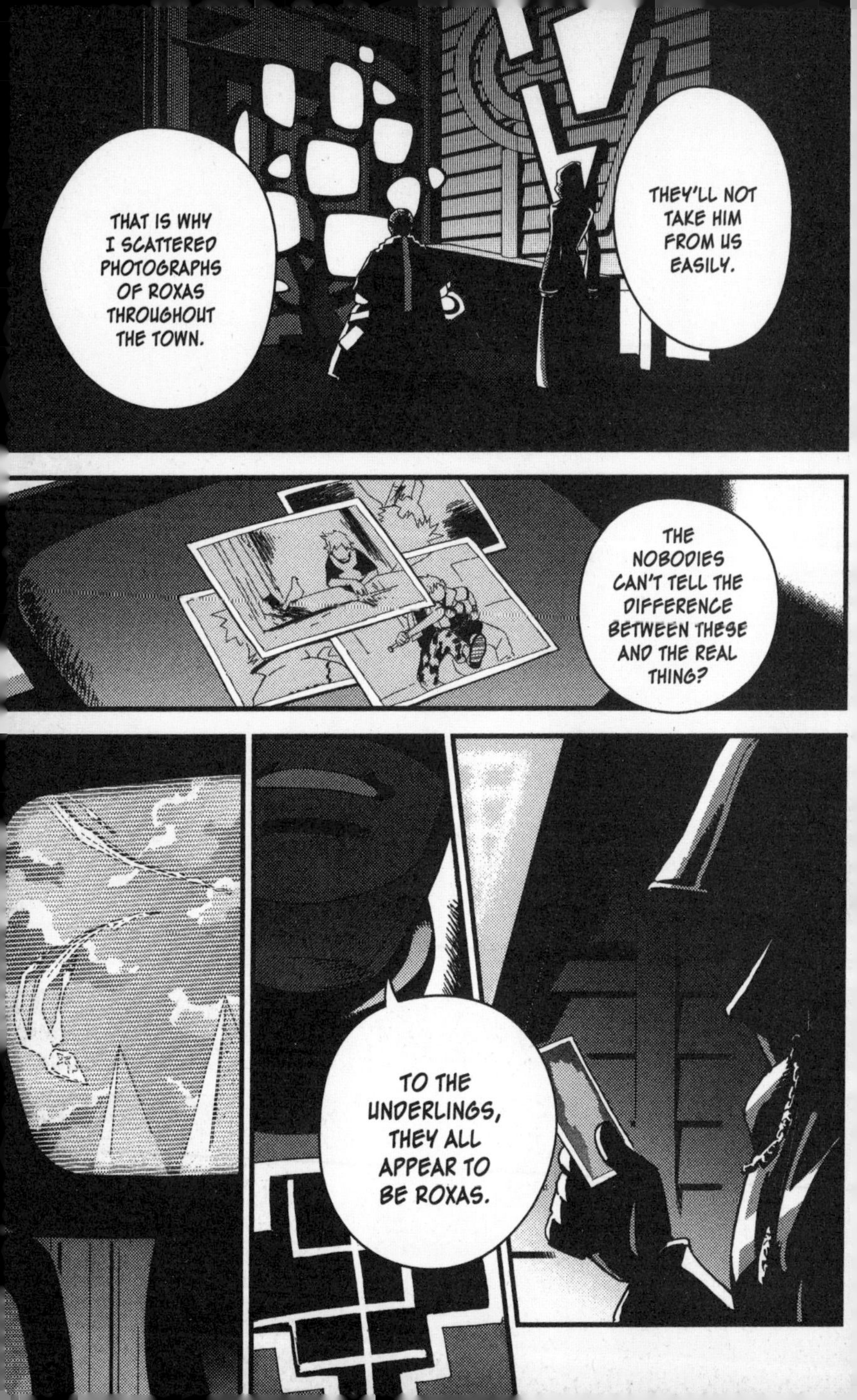
THEY'LL NOT TAKE HIM FROM US EASILY.
THAT IS WHY I SCATTERED PHOTOGRAPHS OF ROXAS THROUGHOUT THE TOWN.
THE NOBODIES CAN'T TELL THE DIFFERENCE BETWEEN THESE AND THE REAL THING?
TO THE UNDERLINGS, THEY ALL APPEAR TO BE ROXAS.

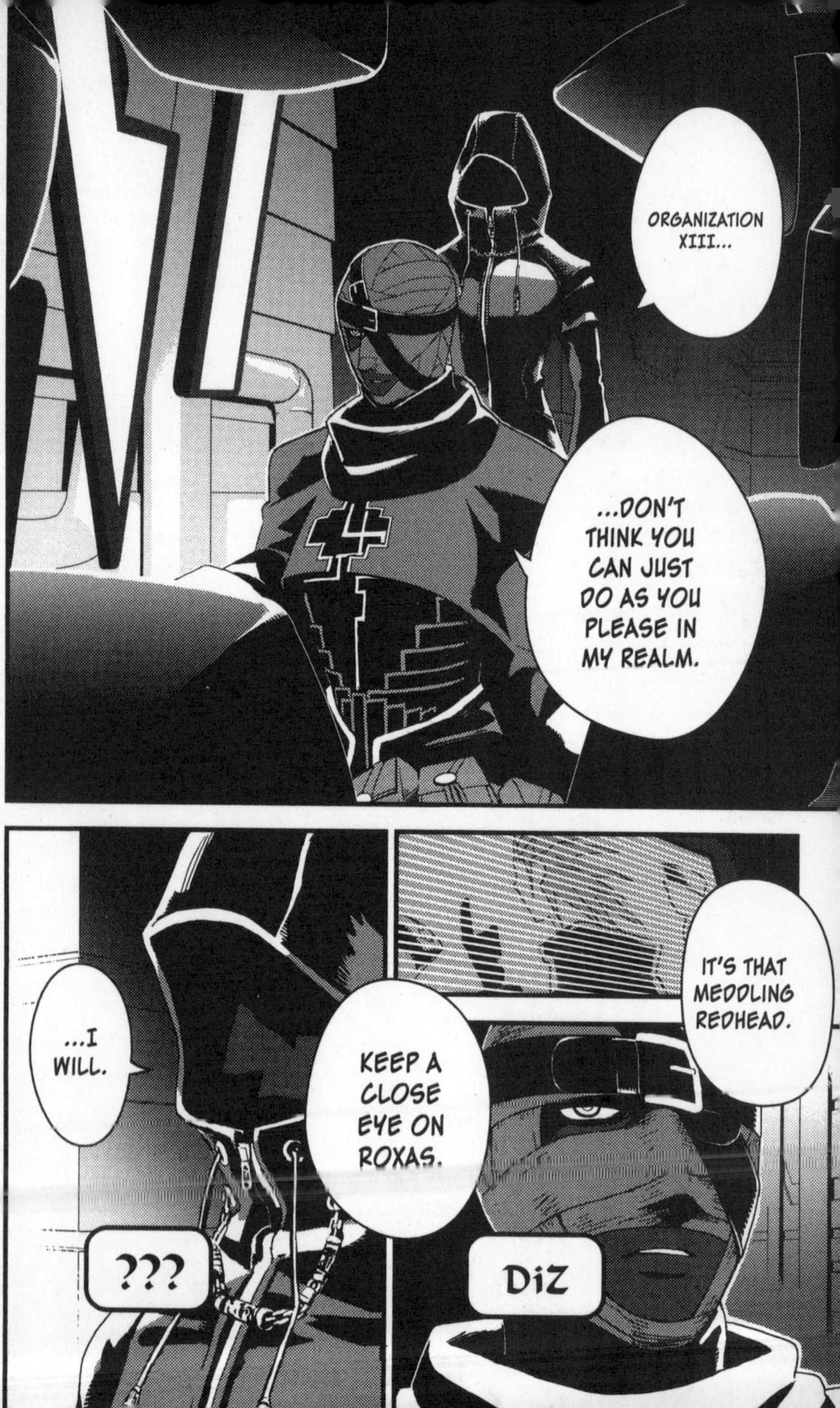
ORGANIZATION XIII...
...DON'T THINK YOU CAN JUST DO AS YOU PLEASE IN MY REALM.
IT'S THAT MEDDLING REDHEAD.
KEEP A CLOSE EYE ON ROXAS.
DiZ
...I WILL.
???

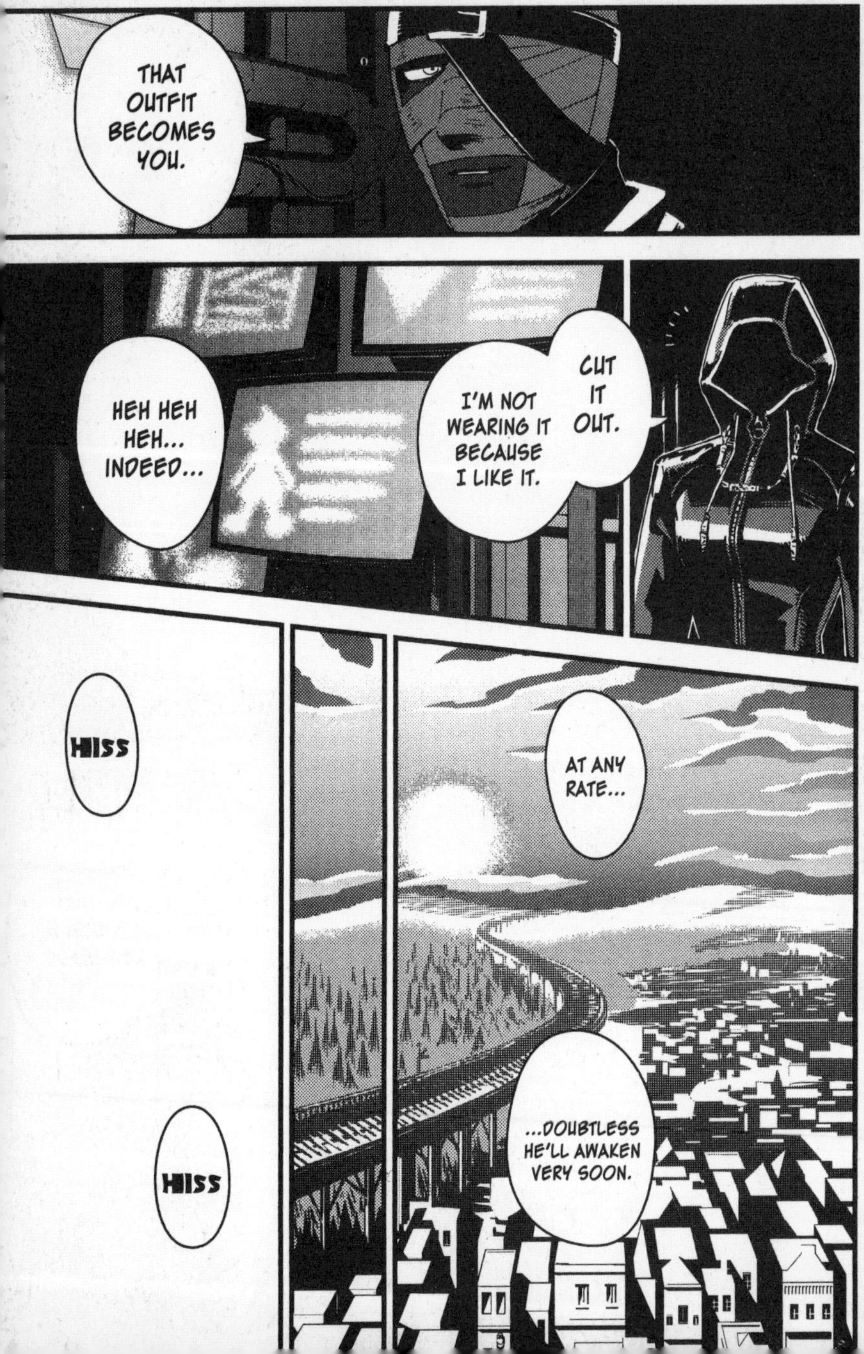
THAT OUTFIT BECOMES YOU.
CUT IT OUT.
I'M NOT WEARING IT BECAUSE I LIKE IT.
HEH HEH HEH... INDEED...
AT ANY RATE...
...DOUBTLESS HE'LL AWAKEN VERY SOON.
HISS
HISS

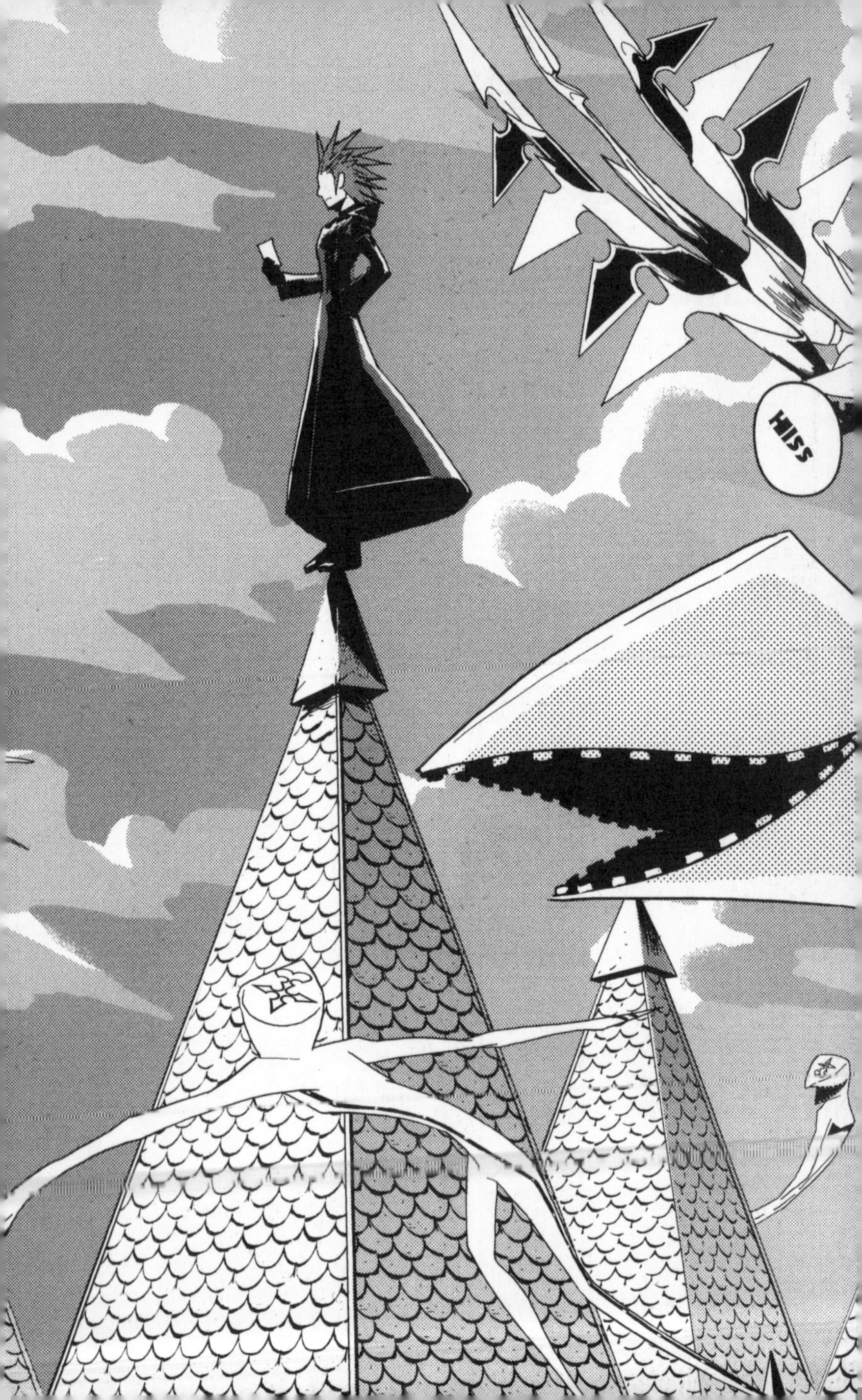
HISS

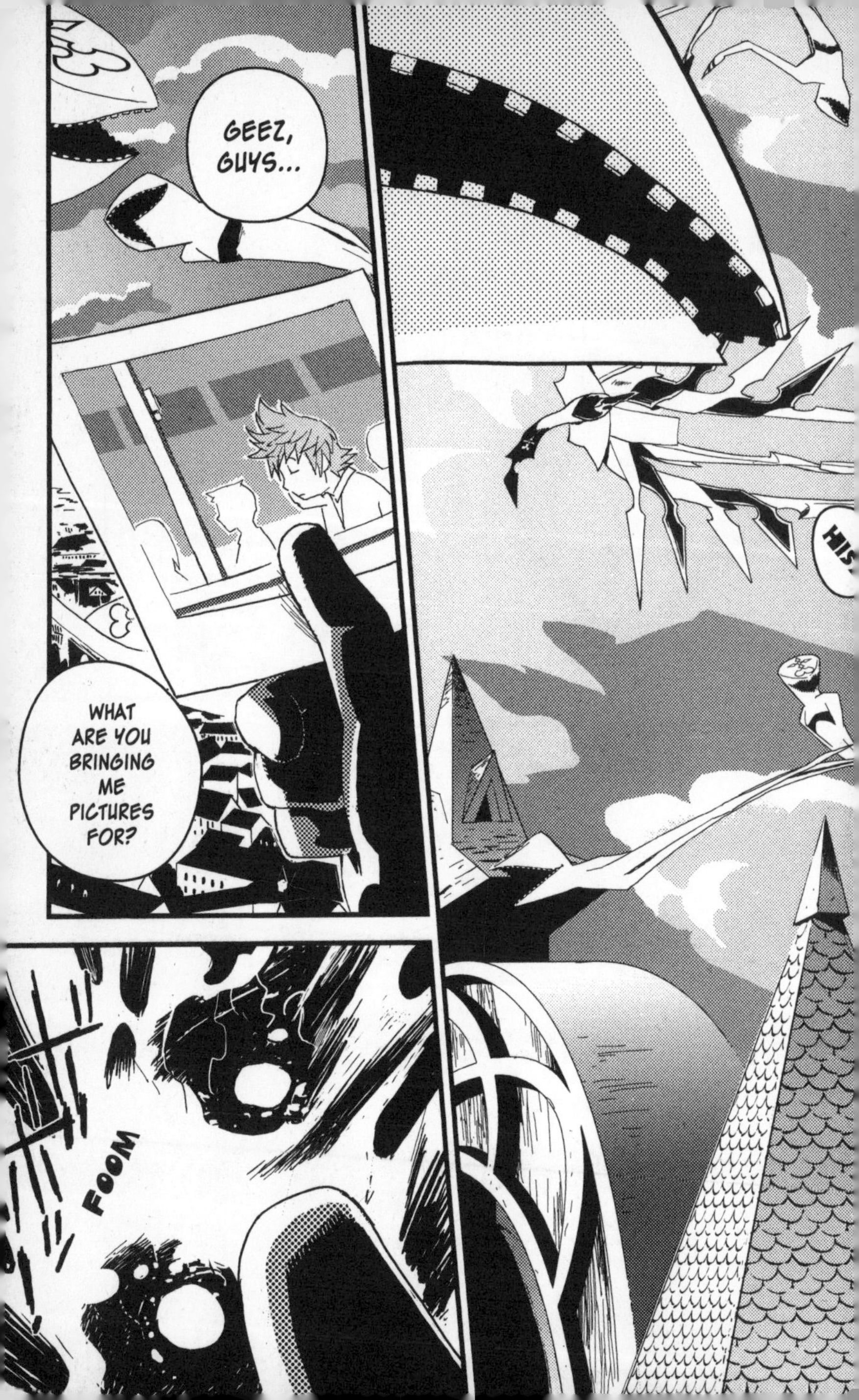
HIS
GEEZ, GUYS...
WHAT ARE YOU BRINGING ME PICTURES FOR?
FOOM

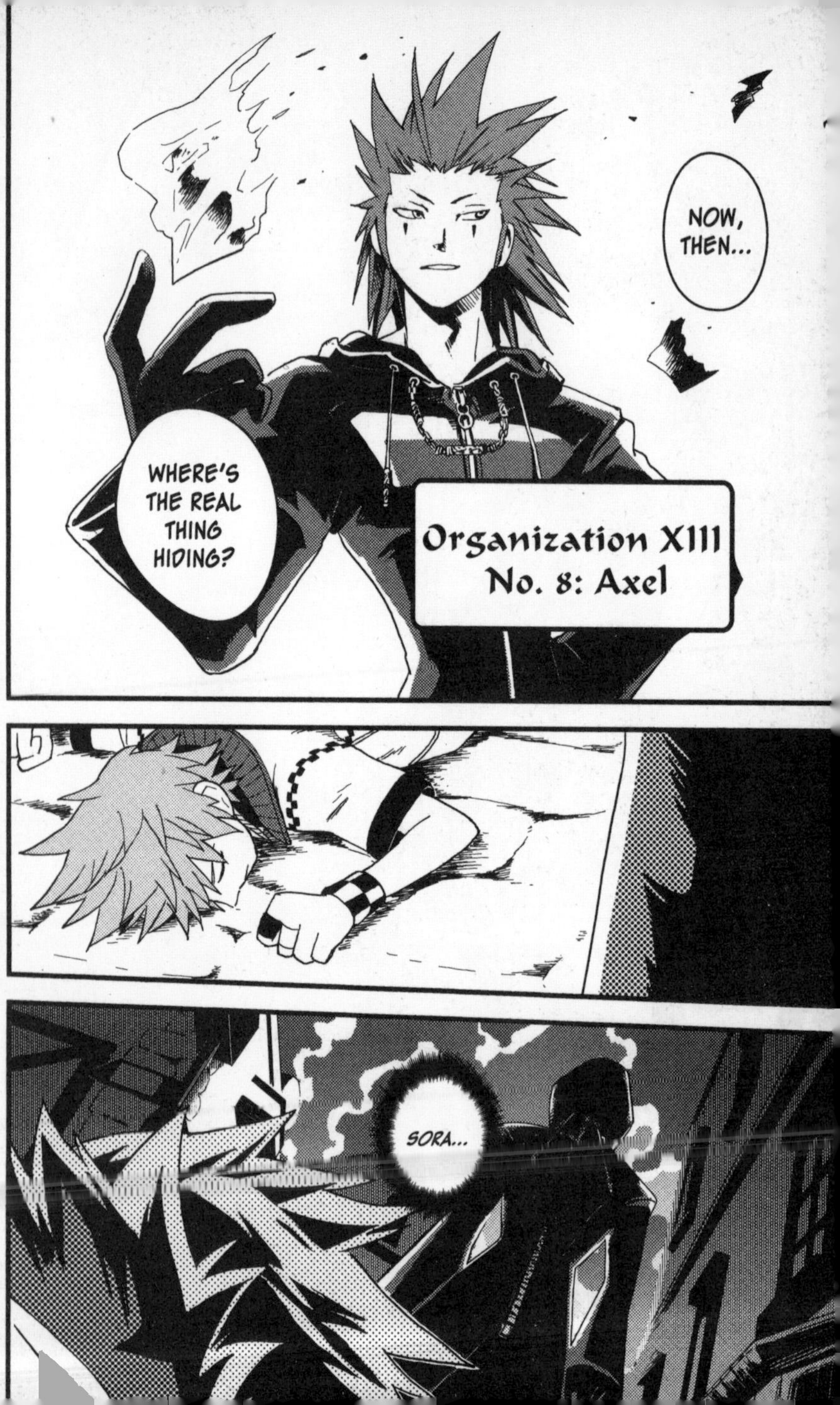
NOW, THEN...
WHERE'S THE REAL THING HIDING?
Organization XIII
No. 8: Axel
SORA...

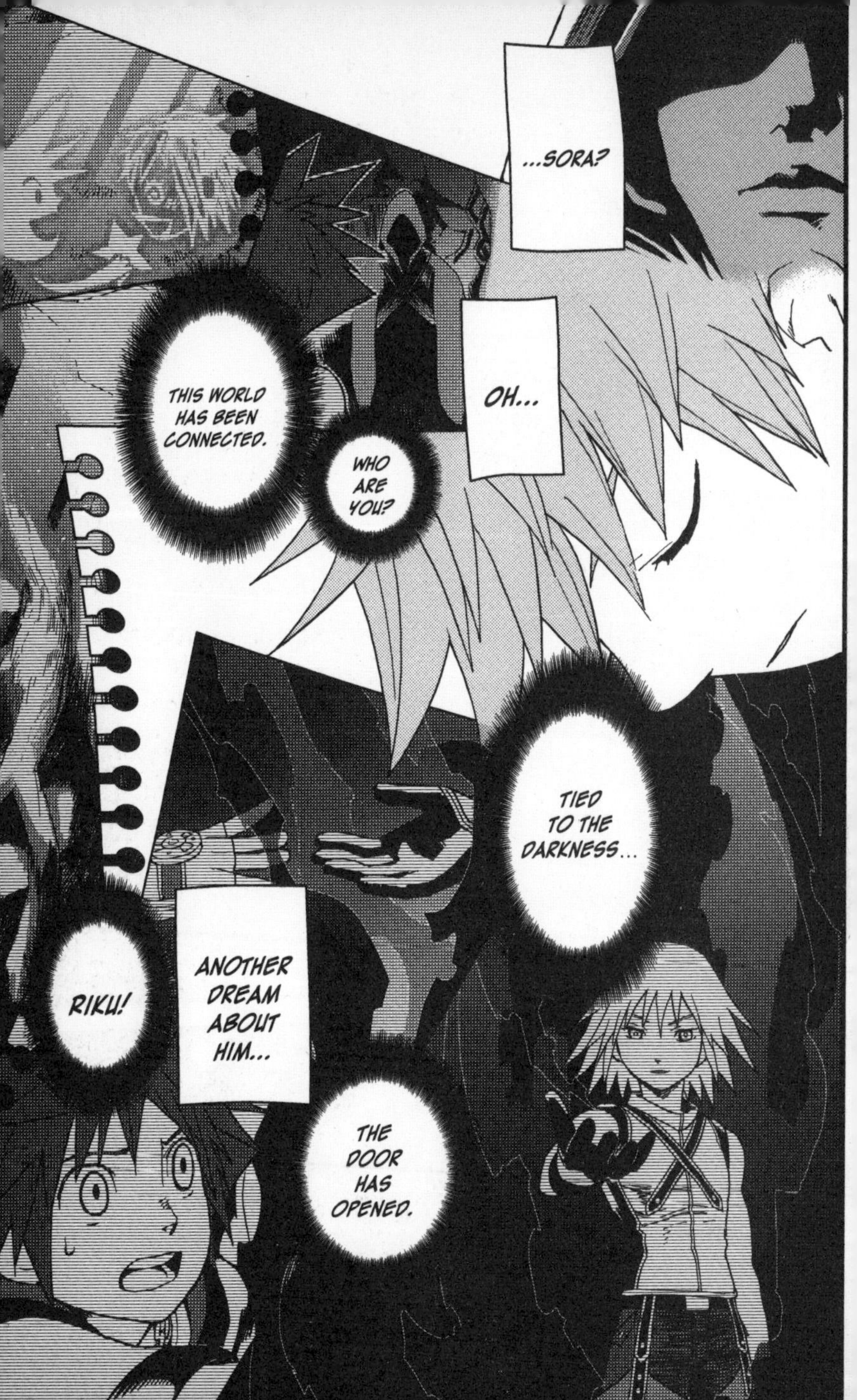
...SORA?
OH...
THIS WORLD HAS BEEN CONNECTED.
WHO ARE YOU?
TIED TO THE DARKNESS...
ANOTHER DREAM ABOUT HIM...
RIKU!
THE DOOR HAS OPENED.

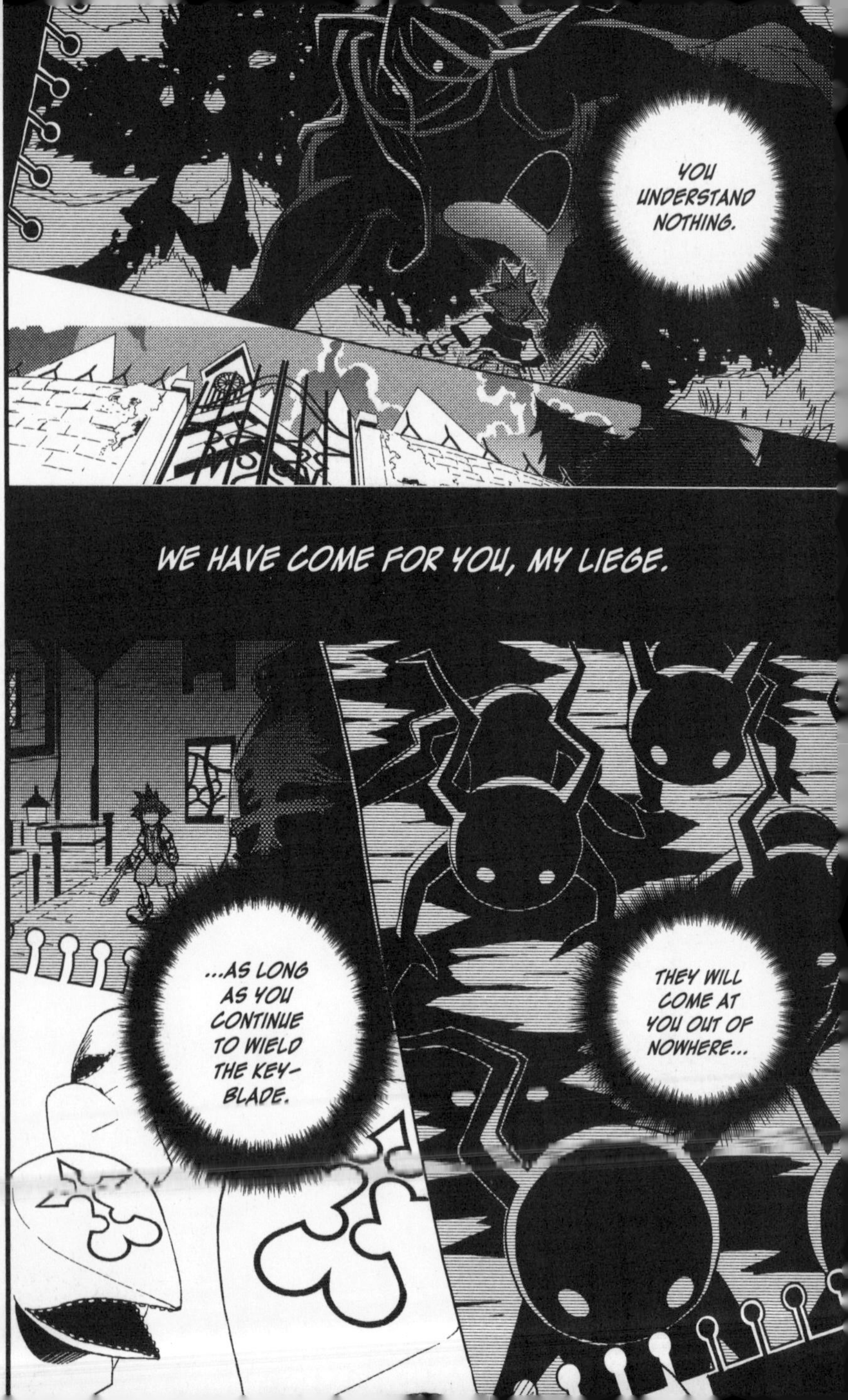
YOU UNDERSTAND NOTHING.
WE HAVE COME FOR YOU, MY LIEGE.
THEY WILL COME AT YOU OUT OF NOWHERE...
...AS LONG AS YOU CONTINUE TO WIELD THE KEY-BLADE.

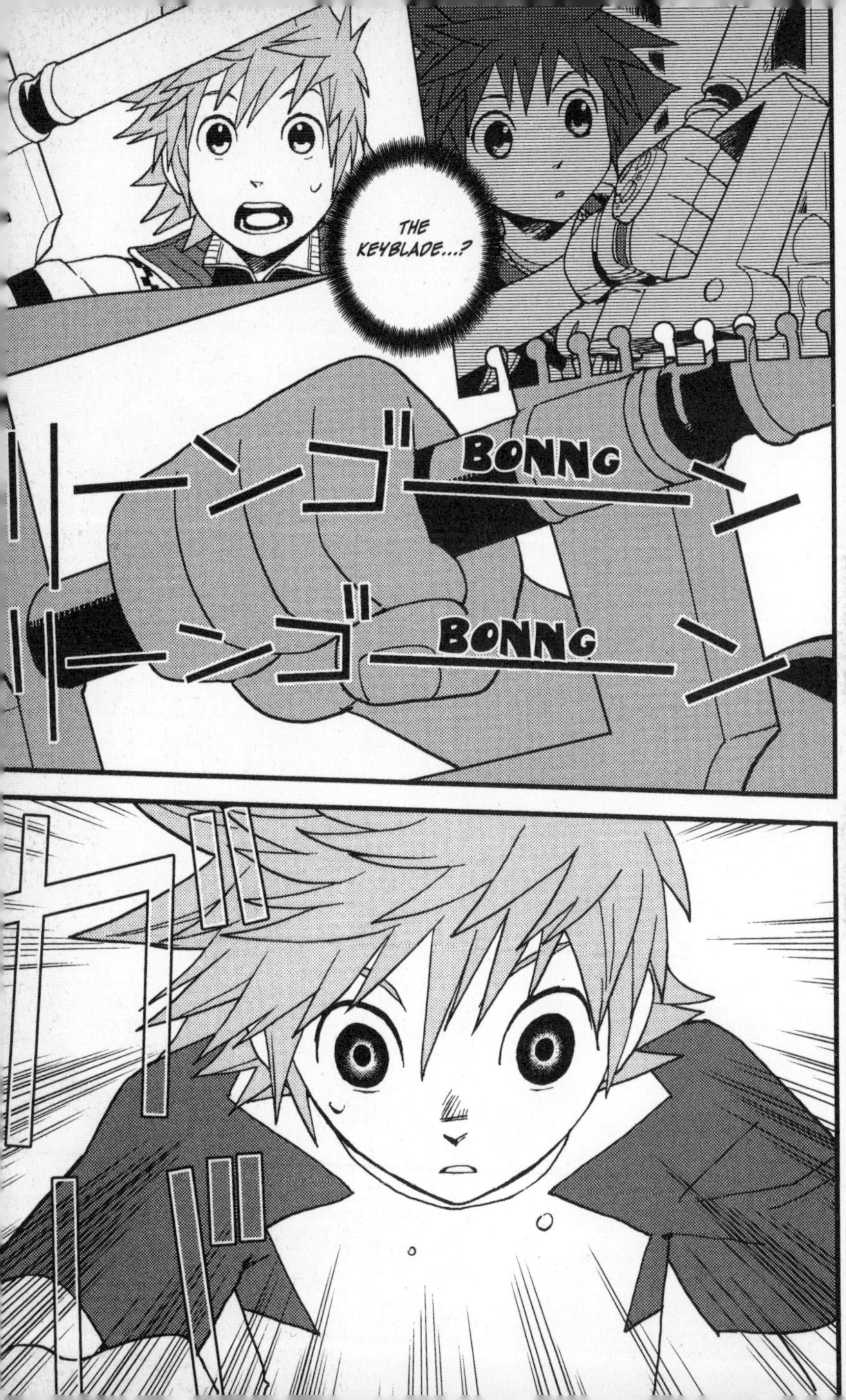
THE KEYBLADE...?
BONNG
BONNG

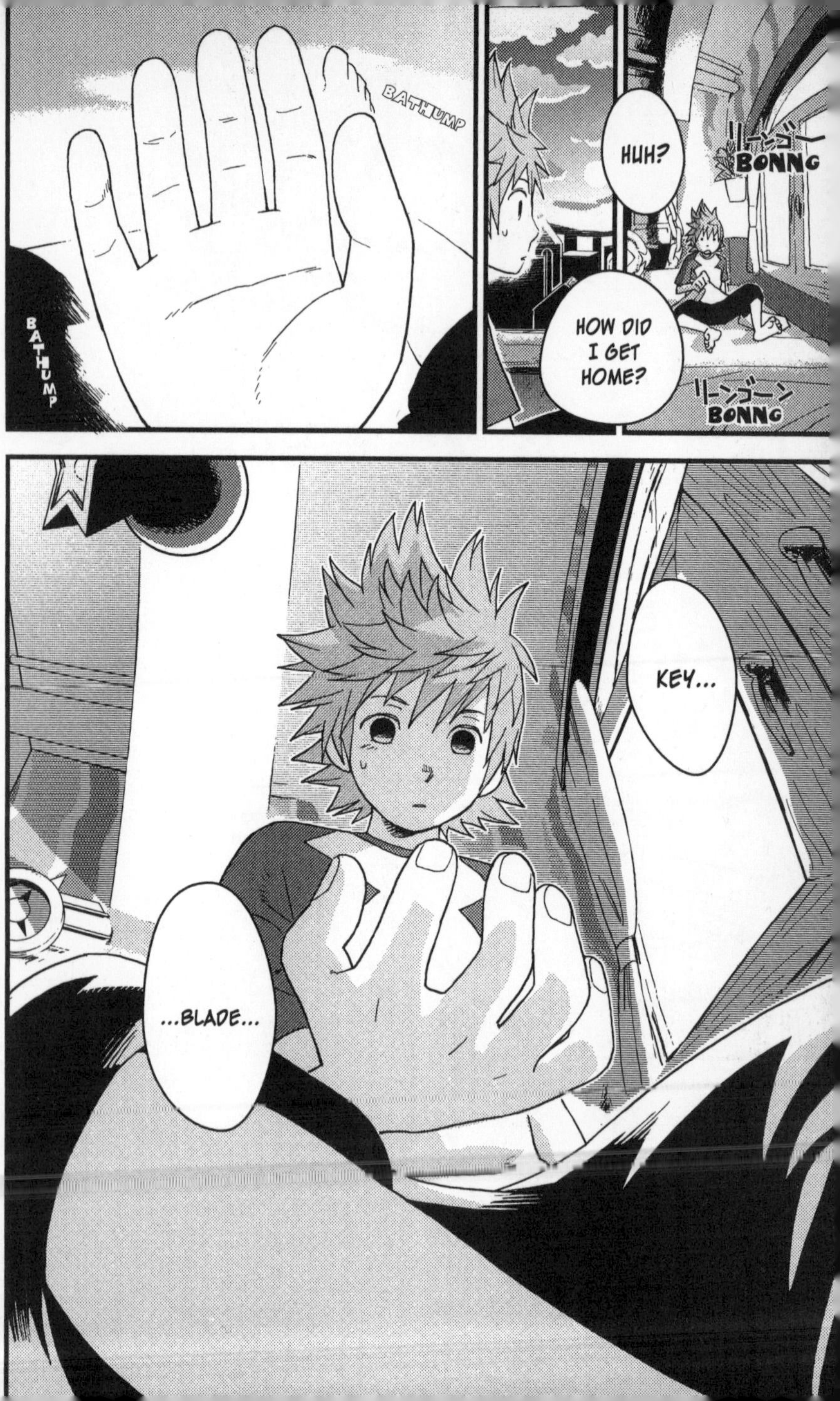
HUH?
BONNG
HOW DID I GET HOME?
リーンゴーン
BONNG
BATHUMP
BATHUMP
KEY...
...BLADE...

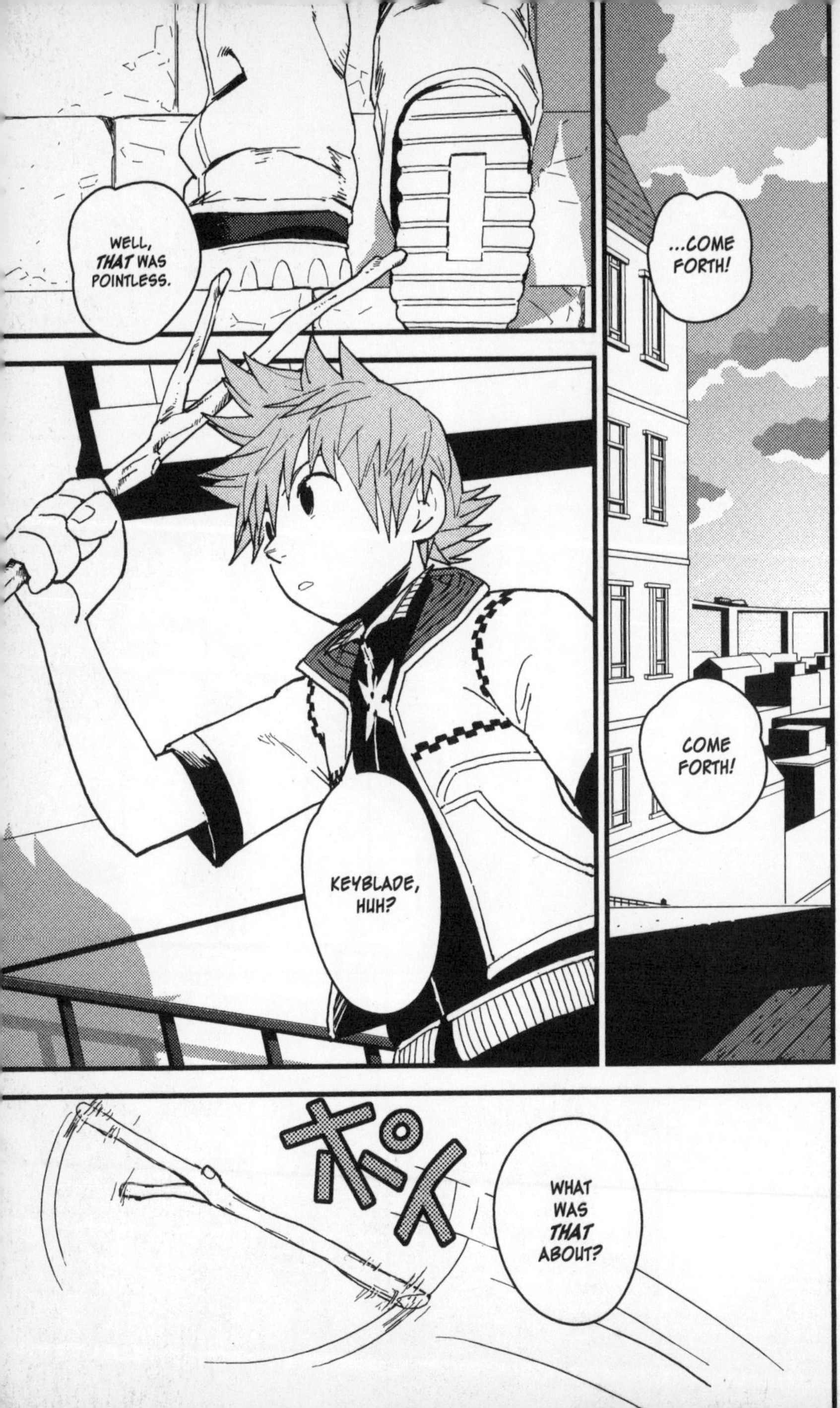
...COME FORTH!
COME FORTH!
WELL, *THAT* WAS POINTLESS.
KEYBLADE, HUH?
WHAT WAS *THAT* ABOUT?
ポイ

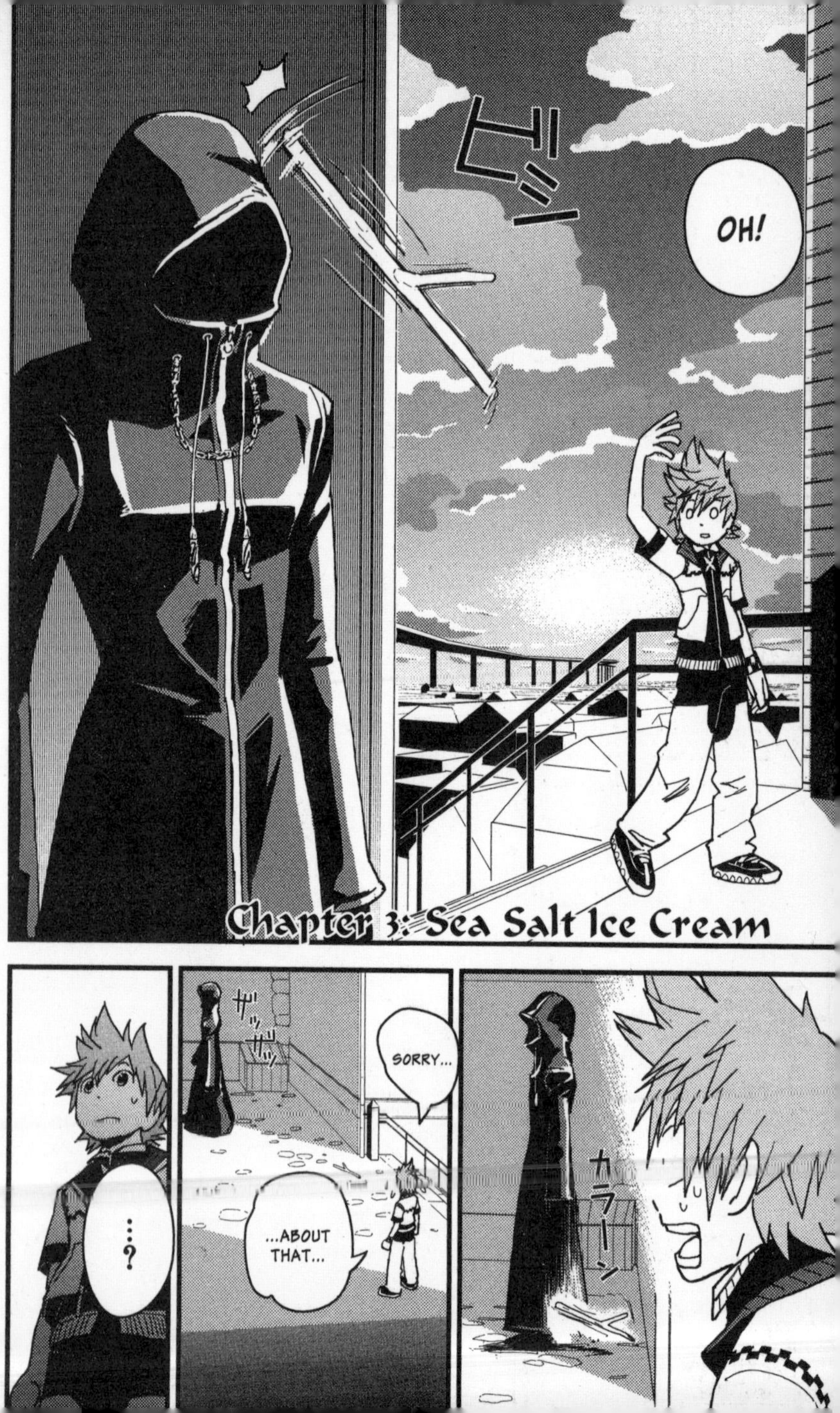
OH!
Chapter 3: Sea Salt Ice Cream
カラーン
ザッ ザッ
SORRY...
...ABOUT THAT...
...?

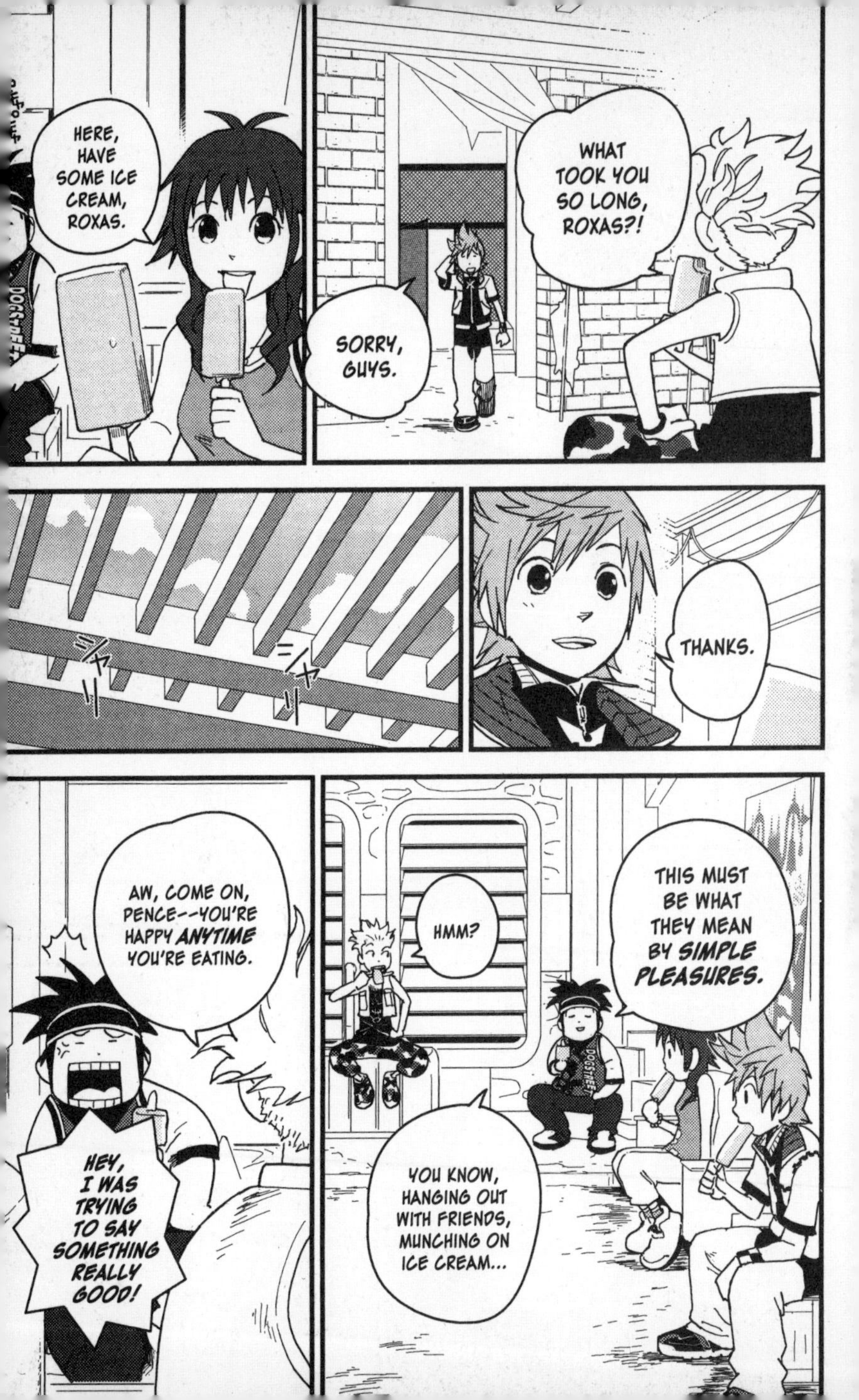
WHAT TOOK YOU SO LONG, ROXAS?!
SORRY, GUYS.
HERE, HAVE SOME ICE CREAM, ROXAS.
THANKS.
THIS MUST BE WHAT THEY MEAN BY *SIMPLE PLEASURES.*
HMM?
YOU KNOW, HANGING OUT WITH FRIENDS, MUNCHING ON ICE CREAM...
AW, COME ON, PENCE--YOU'RE HAPPY *ANYTIME* YOU'RE EATING.
HEY, I WAS TRYING TO SAY SOMETHING REALLY GOOD!

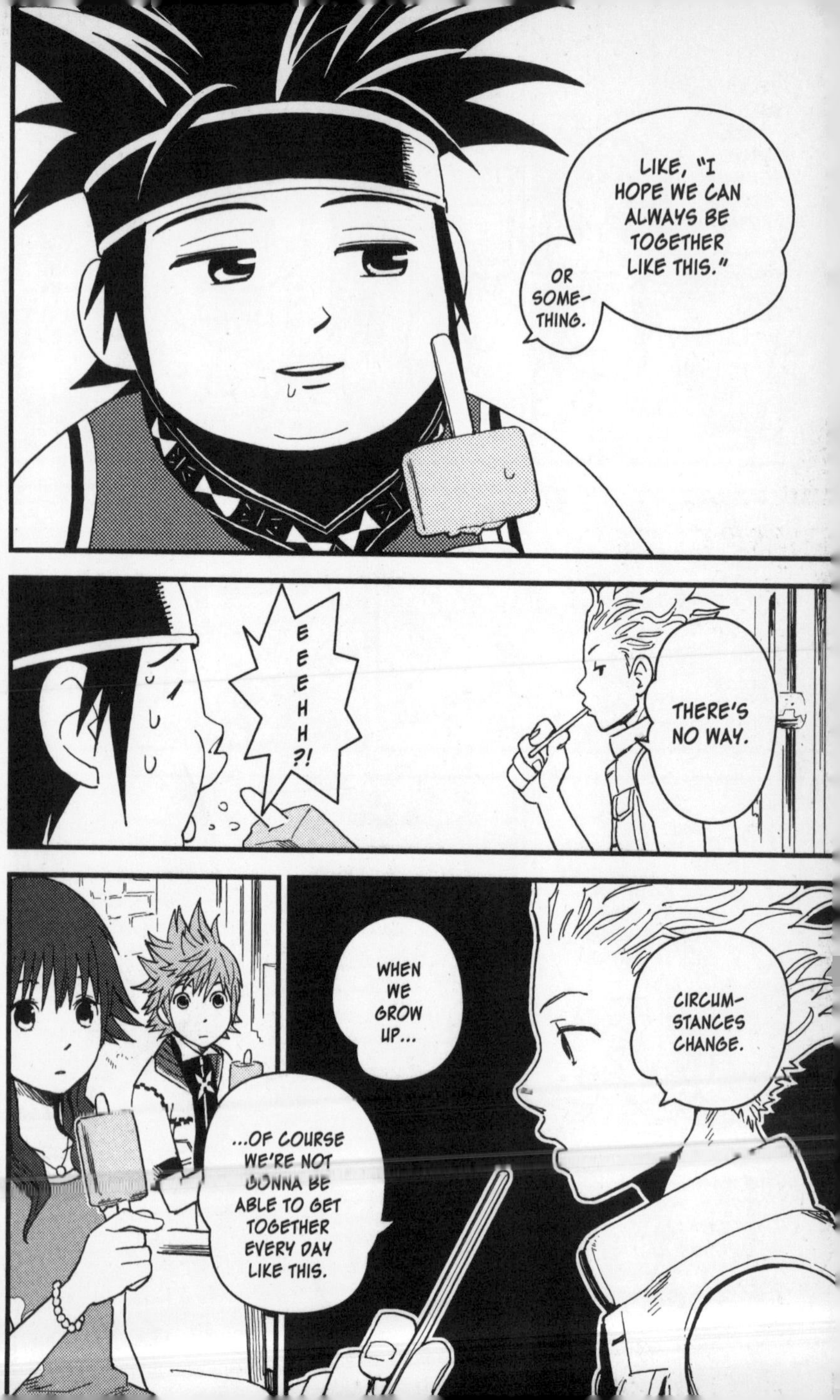
LIKE, "I HOPE WE CAN ALWAYS BE TOGETHER LIKE THIS."
OR SOMETHING.
THERE'S NO WAY.
EEEEHH?!
CIRCUM-STANCES CHANGE.
WHEN WE GROW UP...
...OF COURSE WE'RE NOT GONNA BE ABLE TO GET TOGETHER EVERY DAY LIKE THIS.

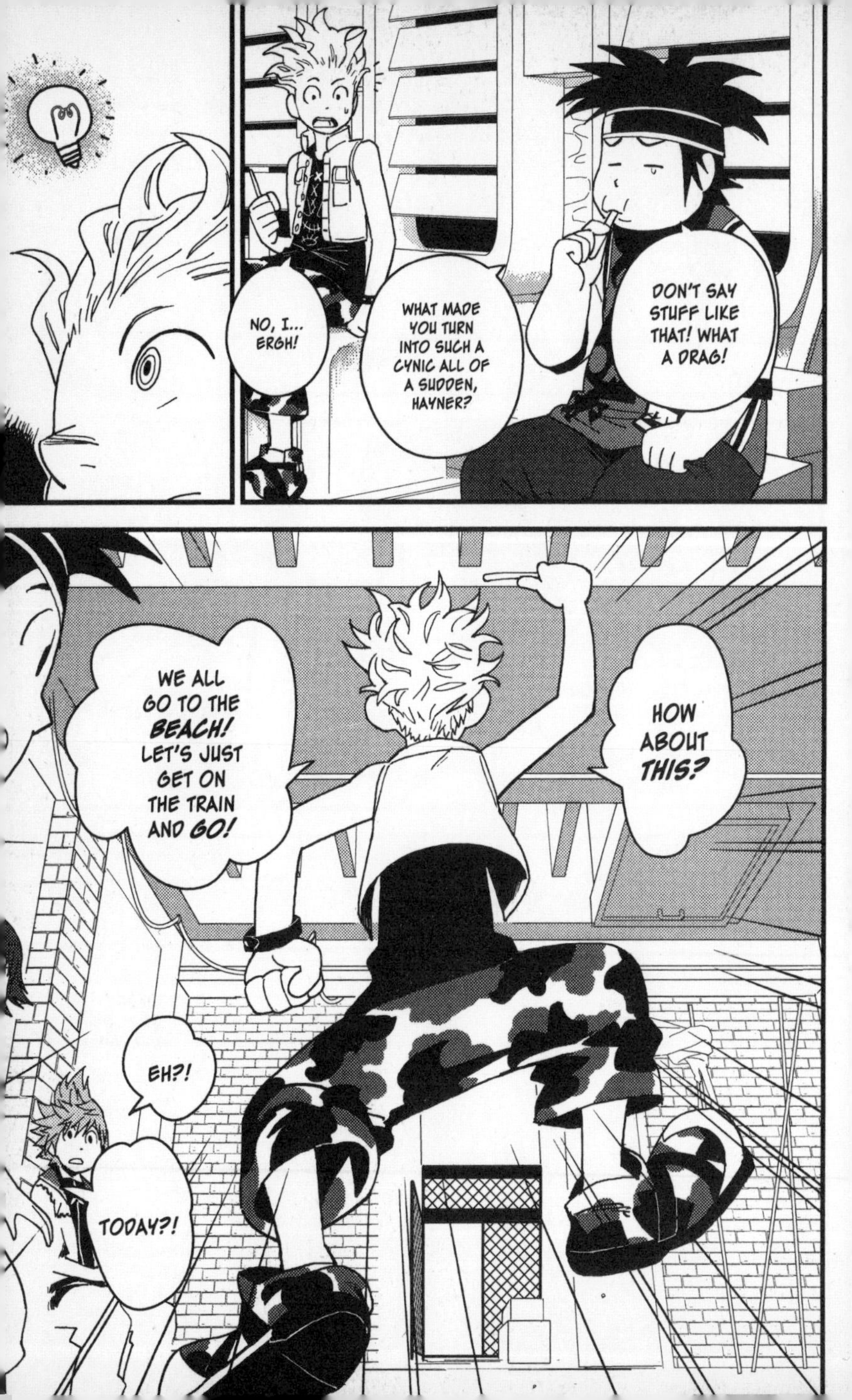
DON'T SAY STUFF LIKE THAT! WHAT A DRAG!
WHAT MADE YOU TURN INTO SUCH A CYNIC ALL OF A SUDDEN, HAYNER?
NO, I... ERGH!
HOW ABOUT THIS?
WE ALL GO TO THE BEACH! LET'S JUST GET ON THE TRAIN AND GO!
EH?!
TODAY?!

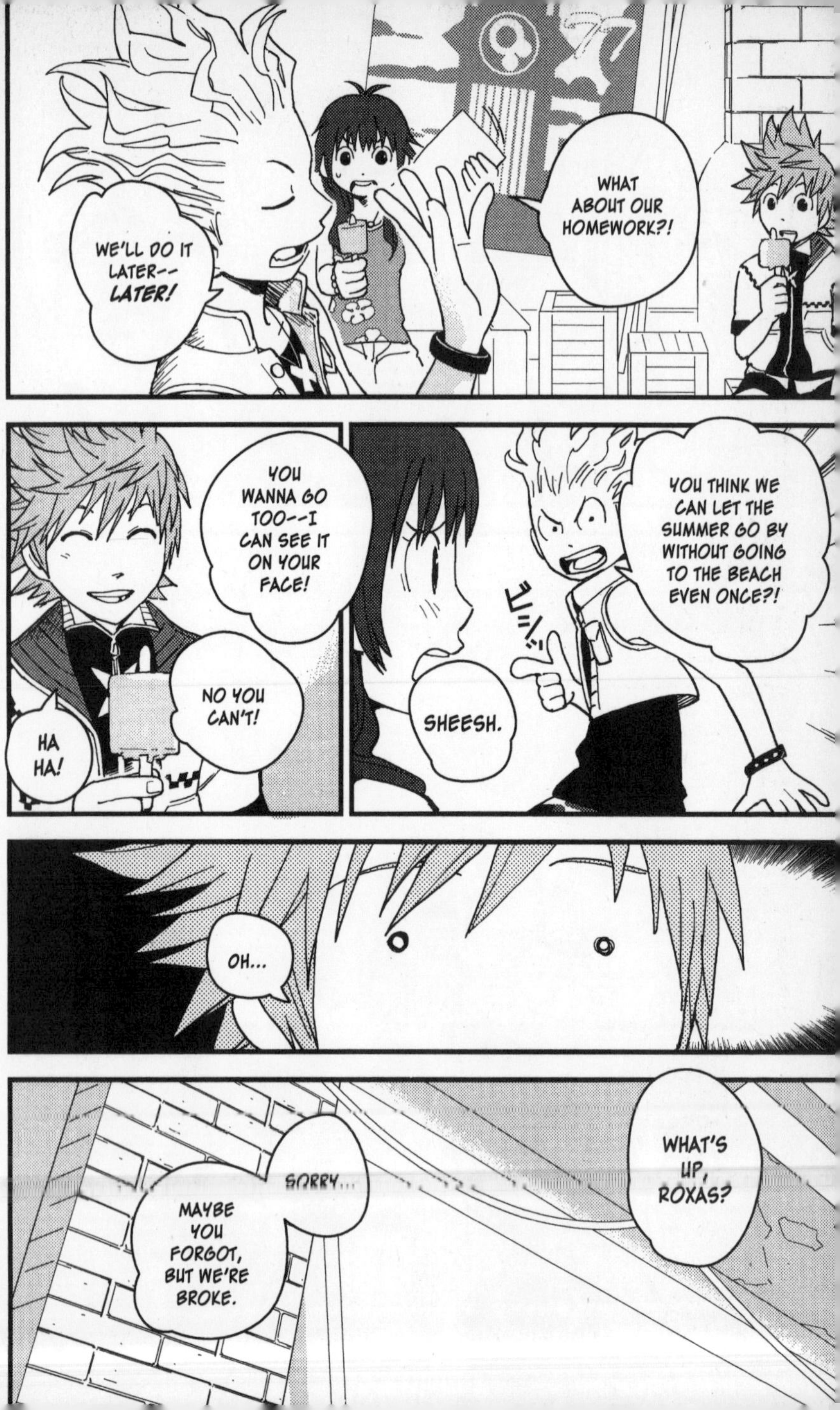
WHAT ABOUT OUR HOMEWORK?!
WE'LL DO IT LATER-- LATER!
YOU THINK WE CAN LET THE SUMMER GO BY WITHOUT GOING TO THE BEACH EVEN ONCE?!
SHEESH.
YOU WANNA GO TOO--I CAN SEE IT ON YOUR FACE!
NO YOU CAN'T!
HA HA!
OH...
WHAT'S UP, ROXAS?
SORRY...
MAYBE YOU FORGOT, BUT WE'RE BROKE.

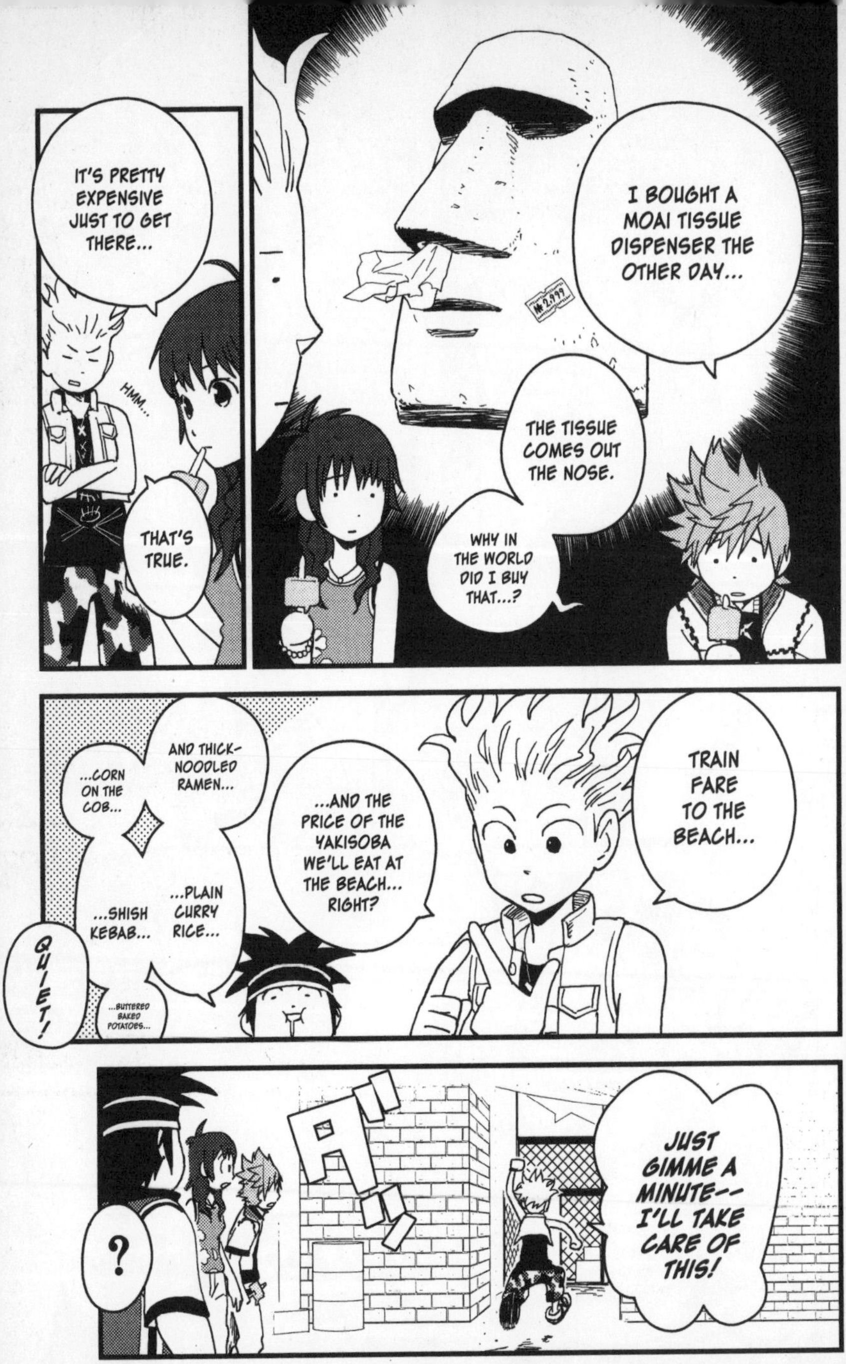
I BOUGHT A MOAI TISSUE DISPENSER THE OTHER DAY...
THE TISSUE COMES OUT THE NOSE.
WHY IN THE WORLD DID I BUY THAT...?
IT'S PRETTY EXPENSIVE JUST TO GET THERE...
HMM...
THAT'S TRUE.
TRAIN FARE TO THE BEACH...
...AND THE PRICE OF THE YAKISOBA WE'LL EAT AT THE BEACH... RIGHT?
AND THICK-NOODLED RAMEN...
...CORN ON THE COB...
...PLAIN CURRY RICE...
...SHISH KEBAB...
...BUTTERED BAKED POTATOES...
QUIET!
JUST GIMME A MINUTE--I'LL TAKE CARE OF THIS!
?

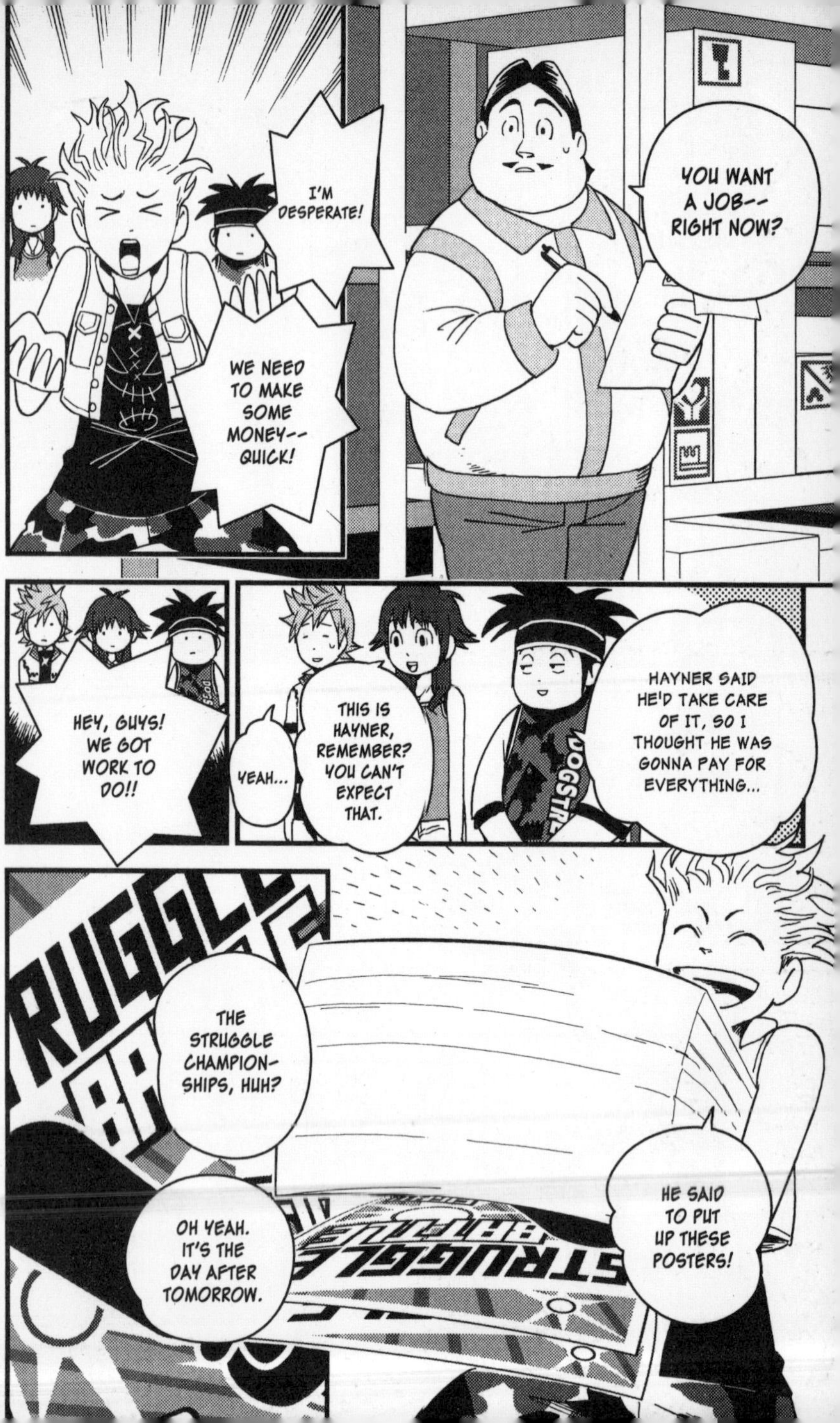
YOU WANT A JOB-- RIGHT NOW?
I'M DESPERATE!
WE NEED TO MAKE SOME MONEY-- QUICK!
HAYNER SAID HE'D TAKE CARE OF IT, SO I THOUGHT HE WAS GONNA PAY FOR EVERYTHING...
THIS IS HAYNER, REMEMBER? YOU CAN'T EXPECT THAT.
YEAH...
HEY, GUYS! WE GOT WORK TO DO!!
HE SAID TO PUT UP THESE POSTERS!
THE STRUGGLE CHAMPION-SHIPS, HUH?
OH YEAH. IT'S THE DAY AFTER TOMORROW.

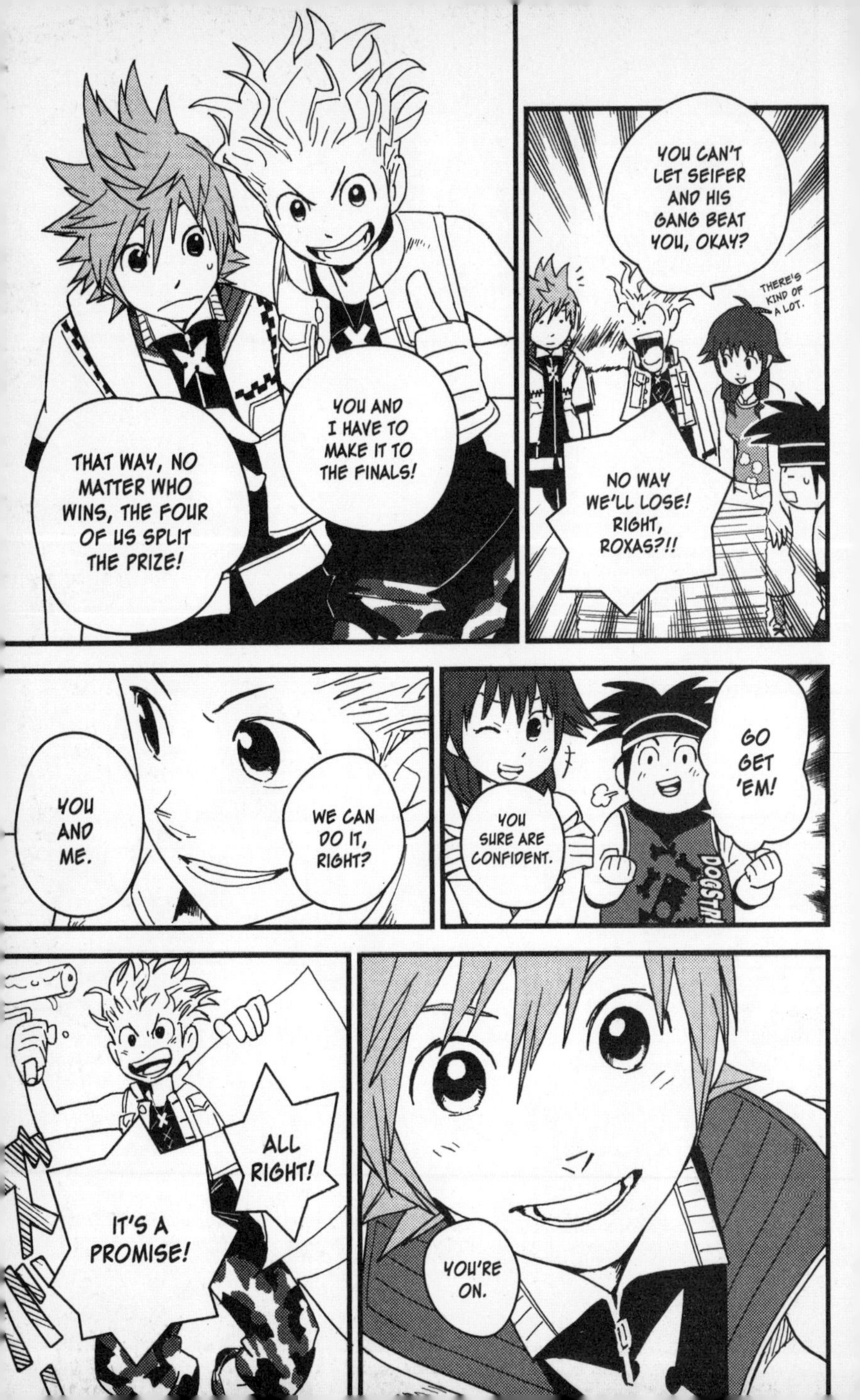
YOU CAN'T LET SEIFER AND HIS GANG BEAT YOU, OKAY?
THERE'S KIND OF A LOT.
NO WAY WE'LL LOSE! RIGHT, ROXAS?!!
YOU AND I HAVE TO MAKE IT TO THE FINALS!
THAT WAY, NO MATTER WHO WINS, THE FOUR OF US SPLIT THE PRIZE!
GO GET 'EM!
YOU SURE ARE CONFIDENT.
WE CAN DO IT, RIGHT?
YOU AND ME.
YOU'RE ON.
ALL RIGHT!
IT'S A PROMISE!

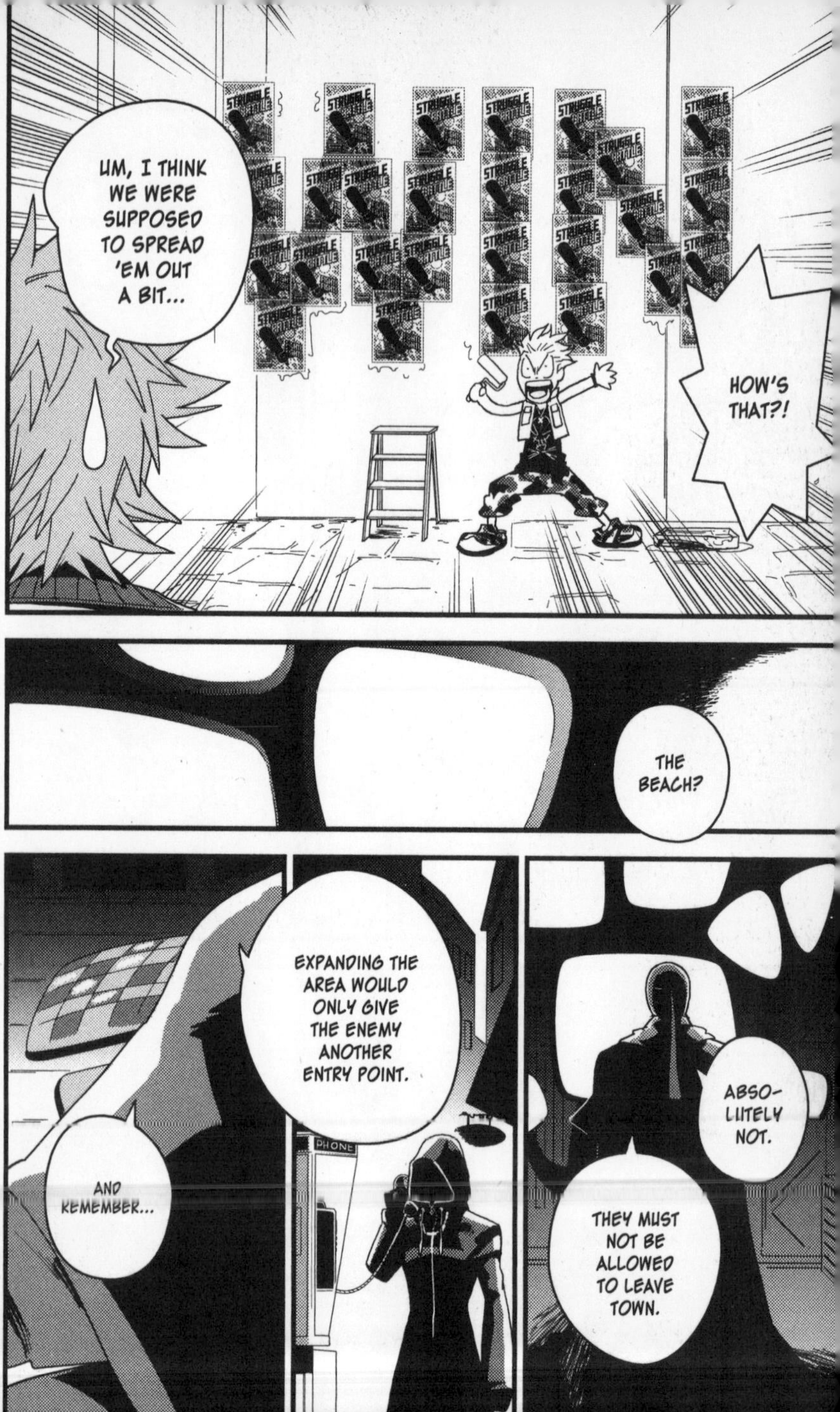
HOW'S THAT?!
UM, I THINK WE WERE SUPPOSED TO SPREAD 'EM OUT A BIT...
THE BEACH?
ABSO-LUTELY NOT.
THEY MUST NOT BE ALLOWED TO LEAVE TOWN.
EXPANDING THE AREA WOULD ONLY GIVE THE ENEMY ANOTHER ENTRY POINT.
PHONE
AND REMEMBER...

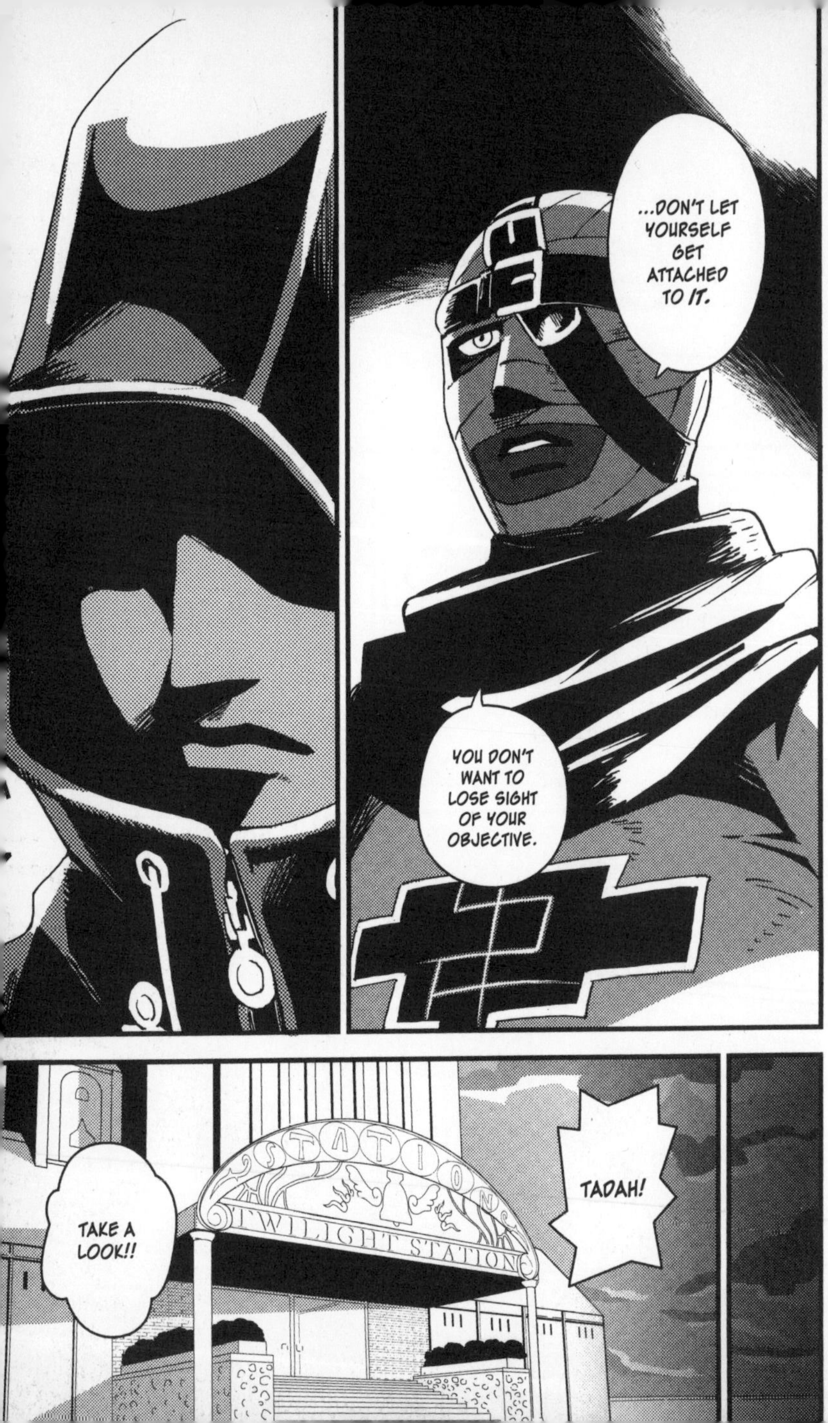
...DON'T LET YOURSELF GET ATTACHED TO *IT*.
YOU DON'T WANT TO LOSE SIGHT OF YOUR OBJECTIVE.
TADAH!
STATION
TWILIGHT STATION
TAKE A LOOK!!

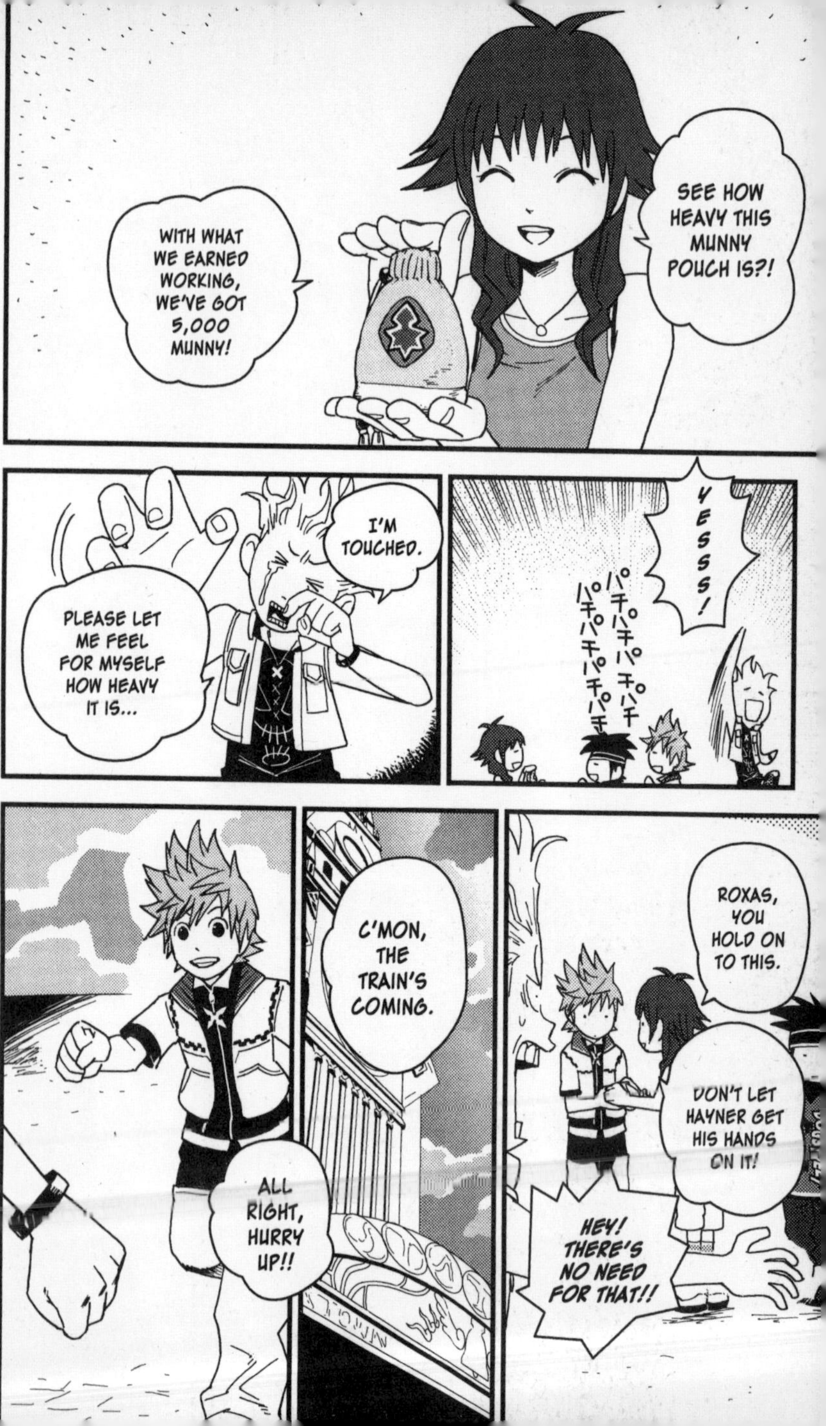
SEE HOW HEAVY THIS MUNNY POUCH IS?!
WITH WHAT WE EARNED WORKING, WE'VE GOT 5,000 MUNNY!
YESSS!
パチパチパチパチ
I'M TOUCHED.
PLEASE LET ME FEEL FOR MYSELF HOW HEAVY IT IS...
ROXAS, YOU HOLD ON TO THIS.
DON'T LET HAYNER GET HIS HANDS ON IT!
HEY! THERE'S NO NEED FOR THAT!!
C'MON, THE TRAIN'S COMING.
ALL RIGHT, HURRY UP!!

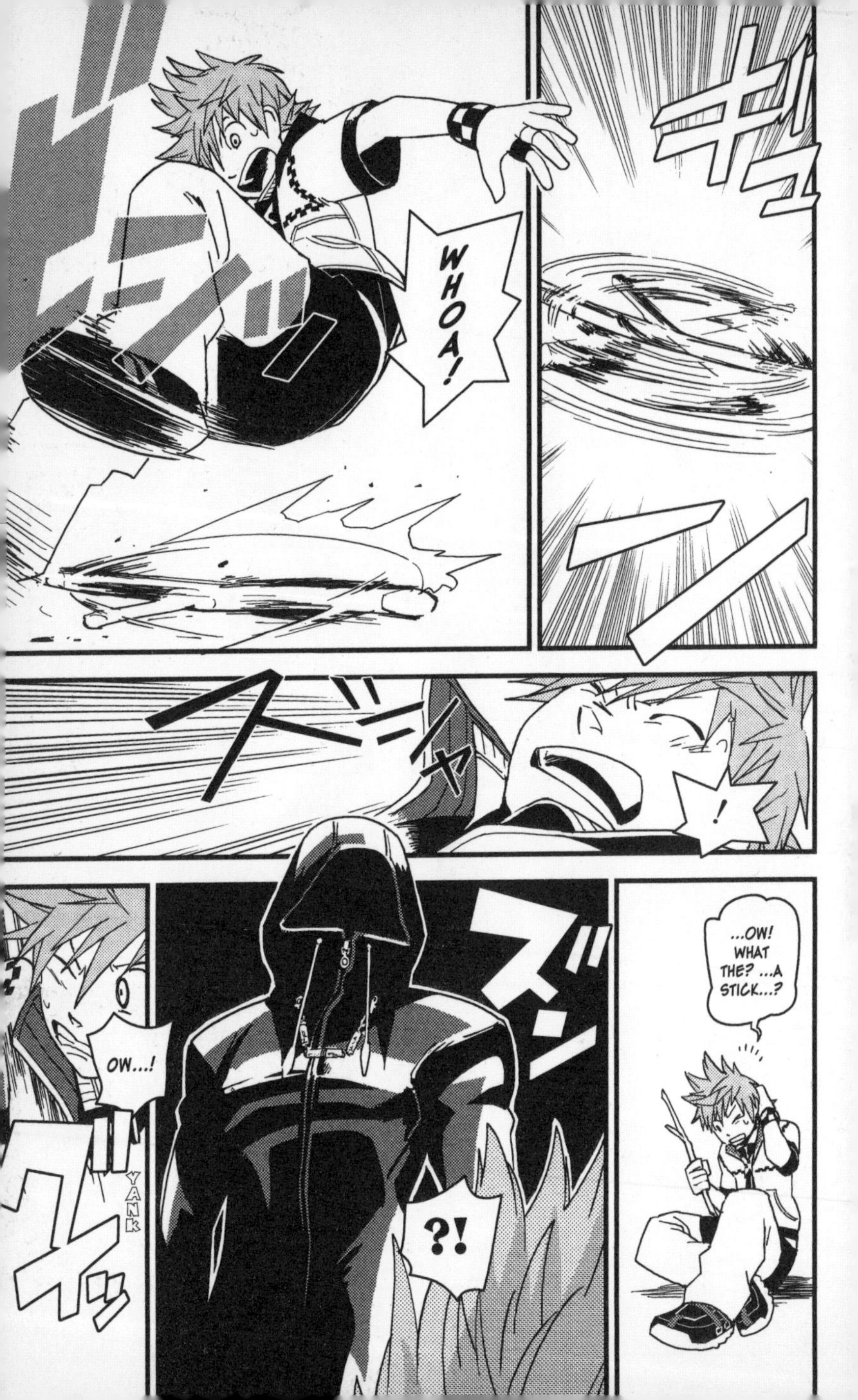
WHOA!
!
...OW! WHAT THE? ...A STICK...?
?!
OW...!
YANK

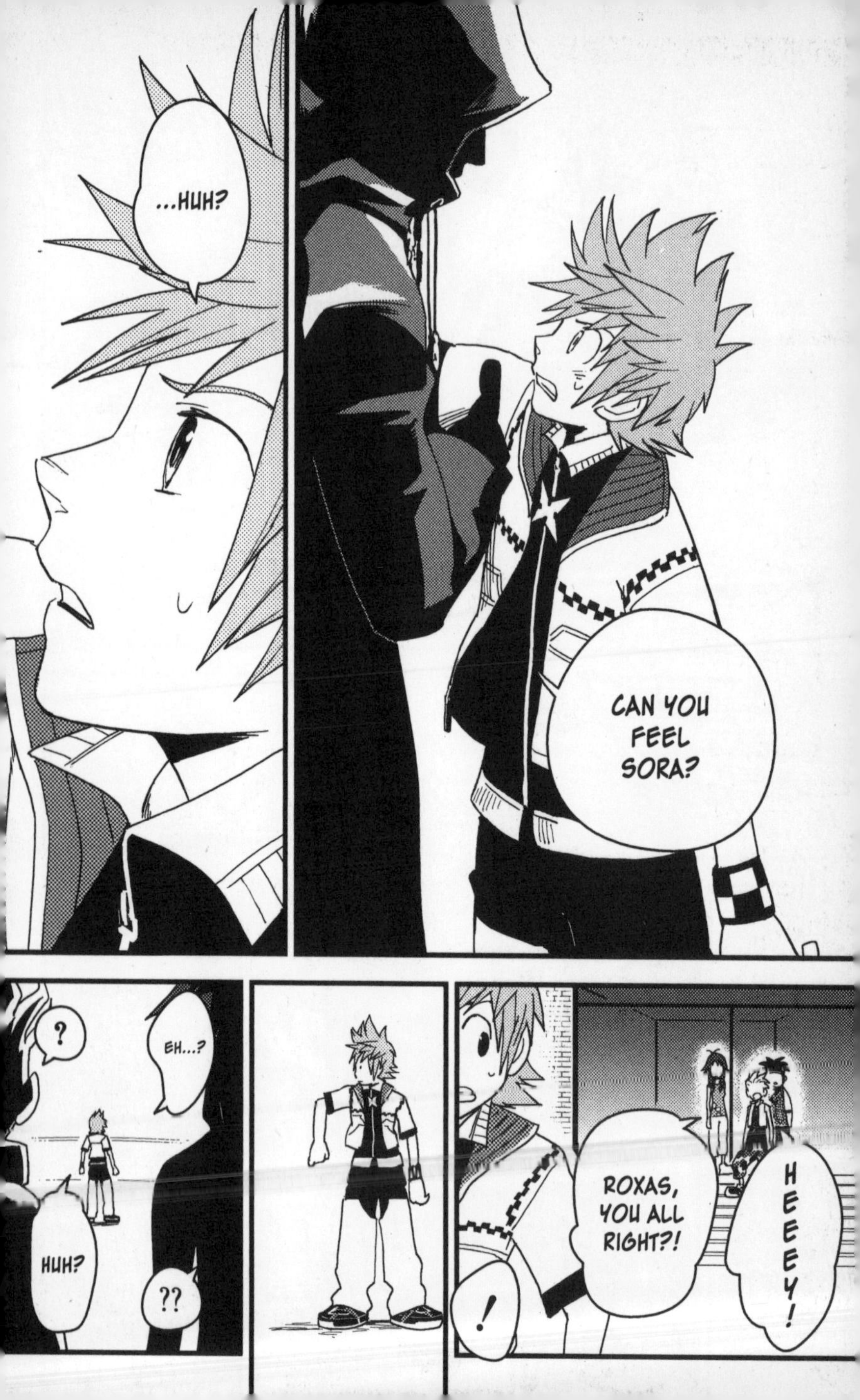
CAN YOU FEEL SORA?
...HUH?
HEEEY!
ROXAS, YOU ALL RIGHT?!
!
EH...?
?
??
HUH?

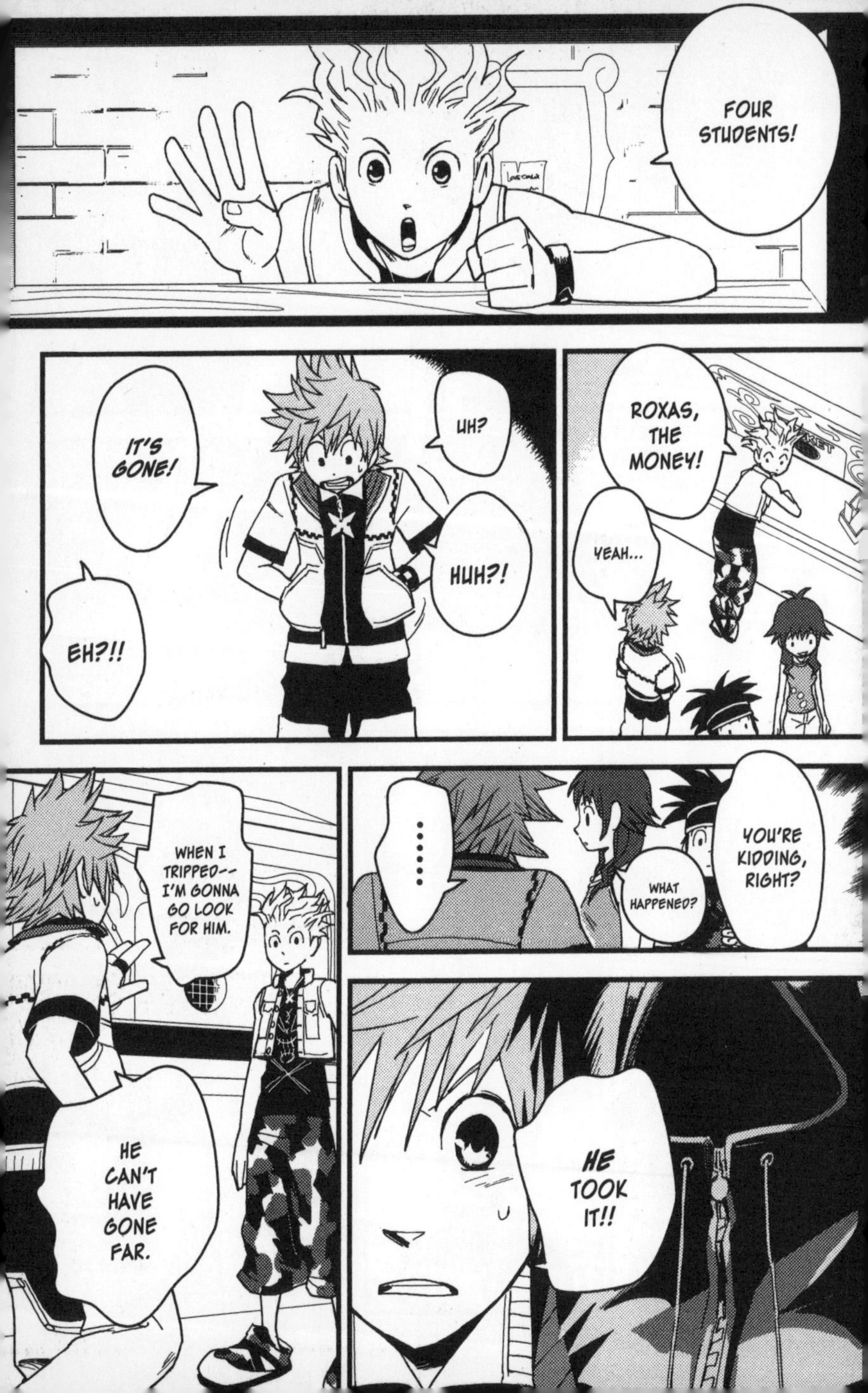
FOUR STUDENTS!
ROXAS, THE MONEY!
YEAH...
UH?
IT'S GONE!
HUH?!
EH?!!
YOU'RE KIDDING, RIGHT?
WHAT HAPPENED?
......
HE TOOK IT!!
WHEN I TRIPPED-- I'M GONNA GO LOOK FOR HIM.
HE CAN'T HAVE GONE FAR.

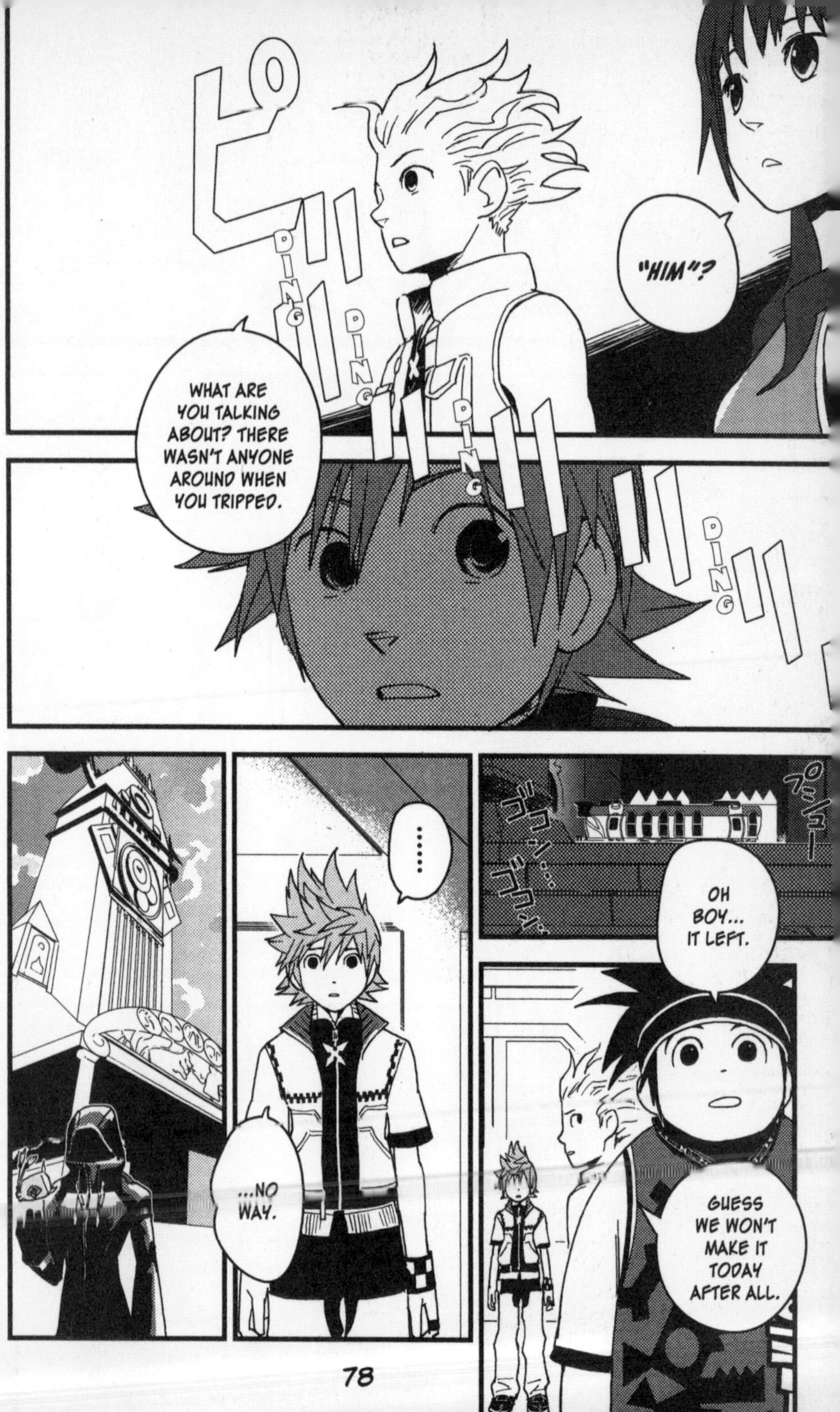
"HIM"?
DING DING DING DING DING
WHAT ARE YOU TALKING ABOUT? THERE WASN'T ANYONE AROUND WHEN YOU TRIPPED.
OH BOY... IT LEFT.
GUESS WE WON'T MAKE IT TODAY AFTER ALL.
......
...NO WAY.

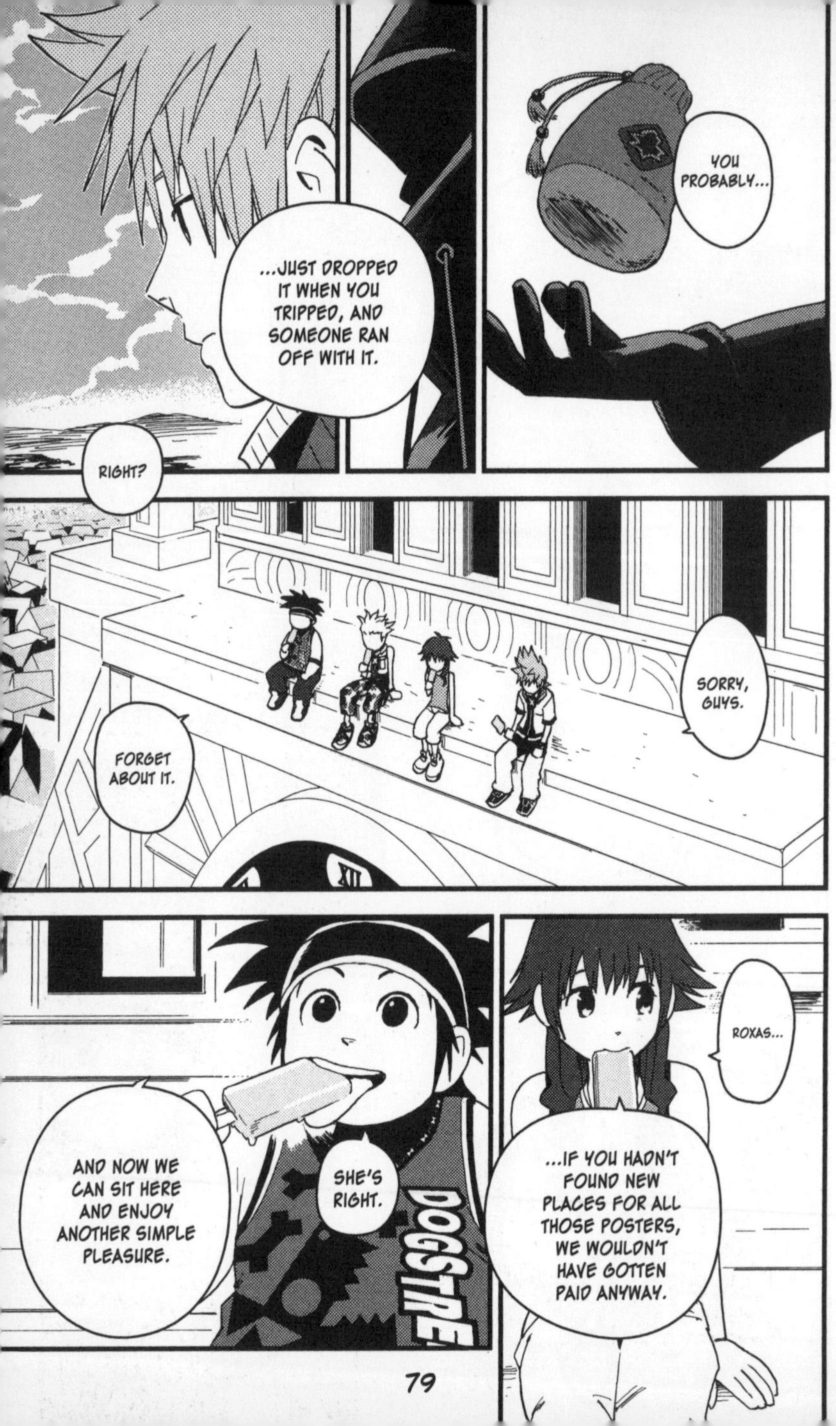
YOU PROBABLY...
...JUST DROPPED IT WHEN YOU TRIPPED, AND SOMEONE RAN OFF WITH IT.
RIGHT?
SORRY, GUYS.
FORGET ABOUT IT.
ROXAS...
...IF YOU HADN'T FOUND NEW PLACES FOR ALL THOSE POSTERS, WE WOULDN'T HAVE GOTTEN PAID ANYWAY.
SHE'S RIGHT.
AND NOW WE CAN SIT HERE AND ENJOY ANOTHER SIMPLE PLEASURE.
DOGSTRE

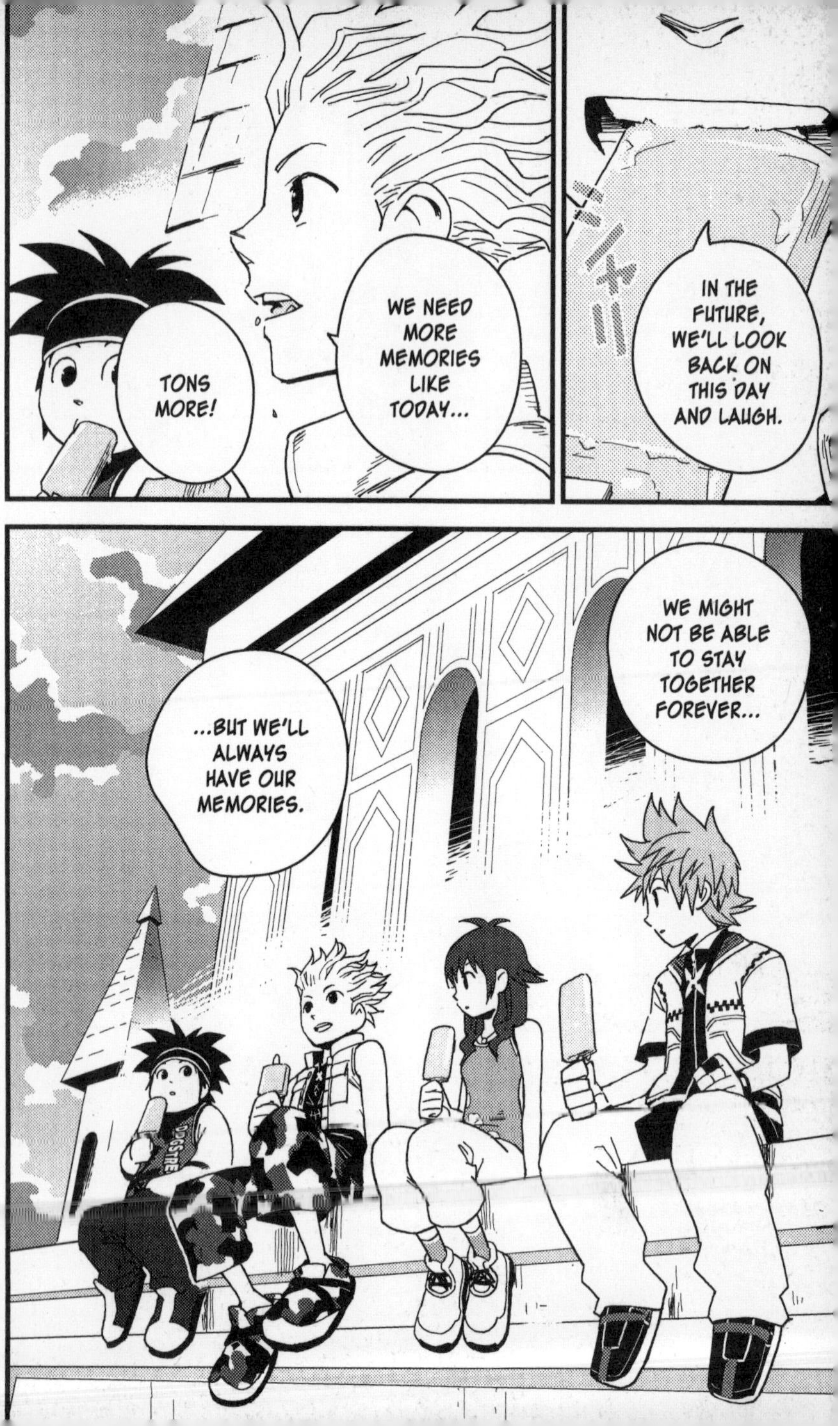
IN THE FUTURE, WE'LL LOOK BACK ON THIS DAY AND LAUGH.
WE NEED MORE MEMORIES LIKE TODAY...
TONS MORE!
WE MIGHT NOT BE ABLE TO STAY TOGETHER FOREVER...
...BUT WE'LL ALWAYS HAVE OUR MEMORIES.

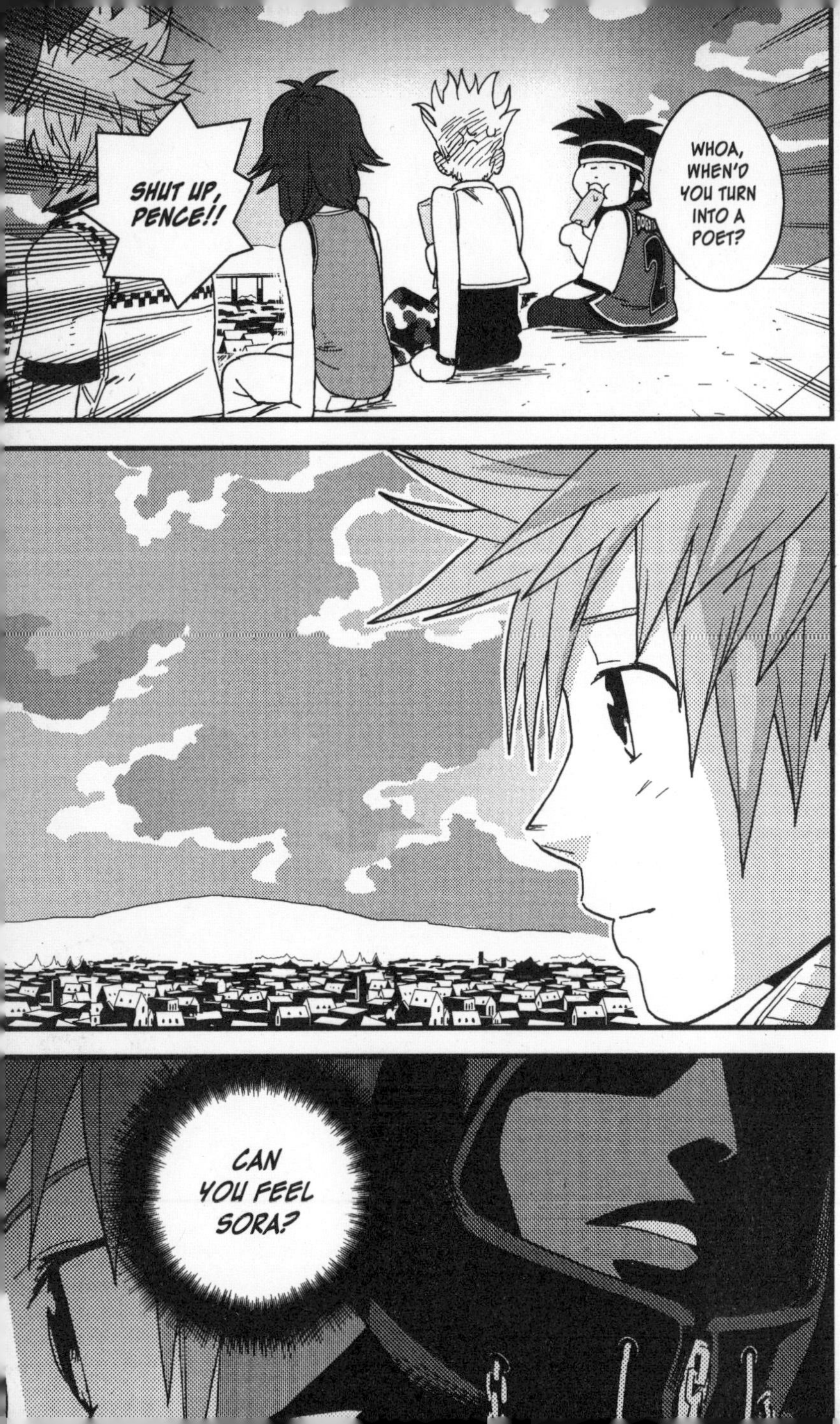
WHOA, WHEN'D YOU TURN INTO A POET?
SHUT UP, PENCE!!
CAN YOU FEEL SORA?

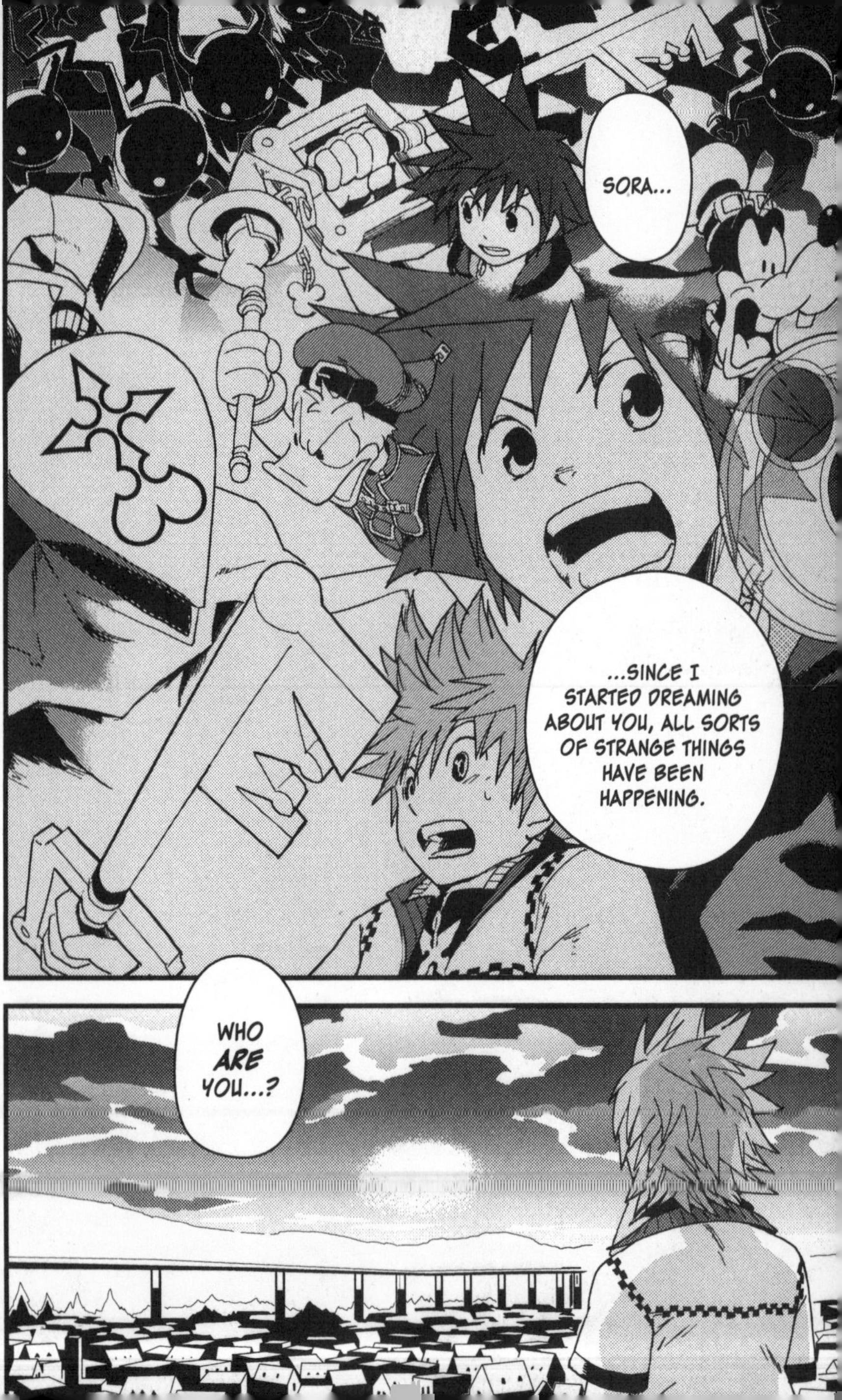
SORA...
...SINCE I STARTED DREAMING ABOUT YOU, ALL SORTS OF STRANGE THINGS HAVE BEEN HAPPENING.
WHO ARE YOU...?

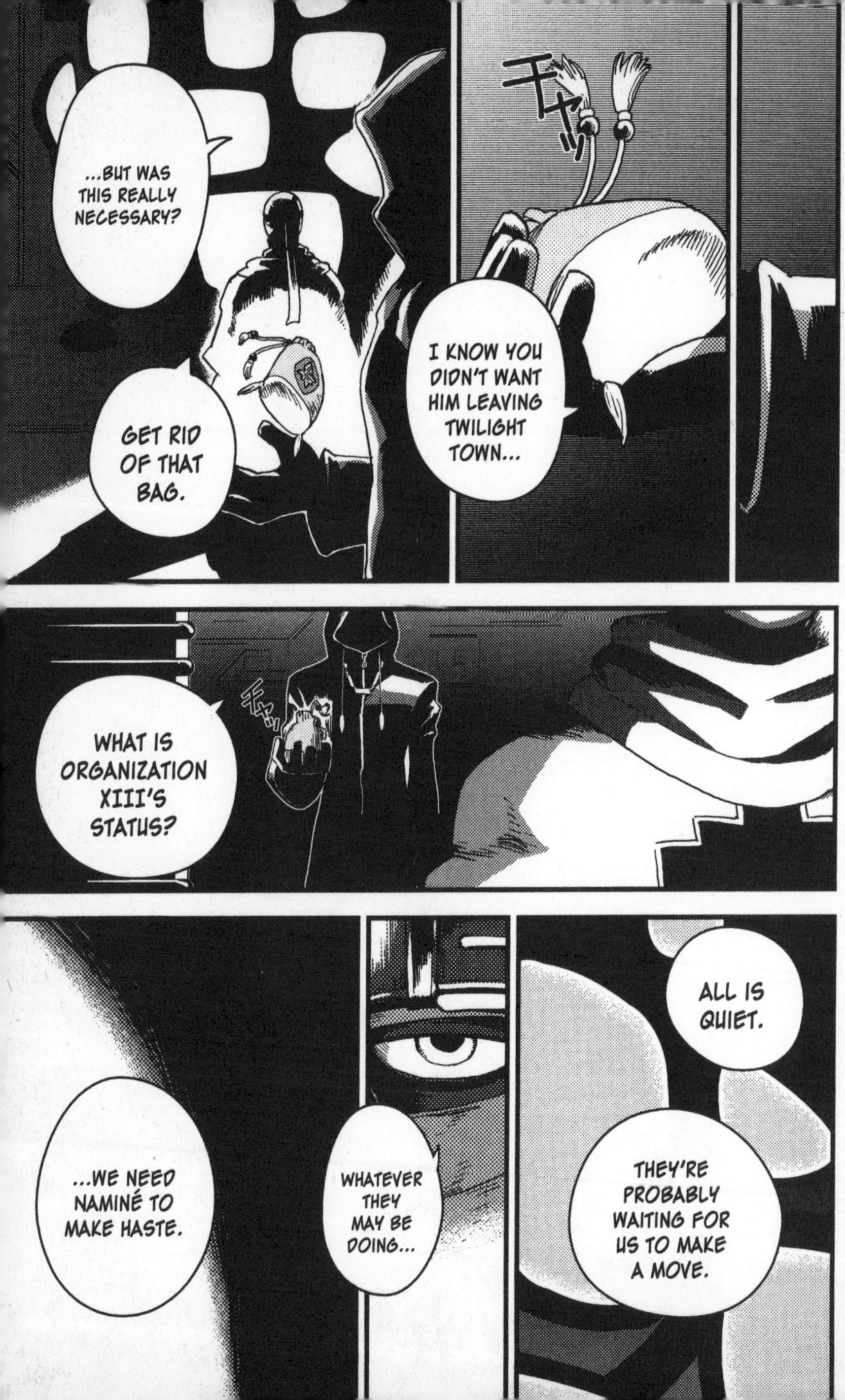
I KNOW YOU DIDN'T WANT HIM LEAVING TWILIGHT TOWN...
...BUT WAS THIS REALLY NECESSARY?
GET RID OF THAT BAG.
WHAT IS ORGANIZATION XIII'S STATUS?
ALL IS QUIET.
THEY'RE PROBABLY WAITING FOR US TO MAKE A MOVE.
WHATEVER THEY MAY BE DOING...
...WE NEED NAMINÉ TO MAKE HASTE.

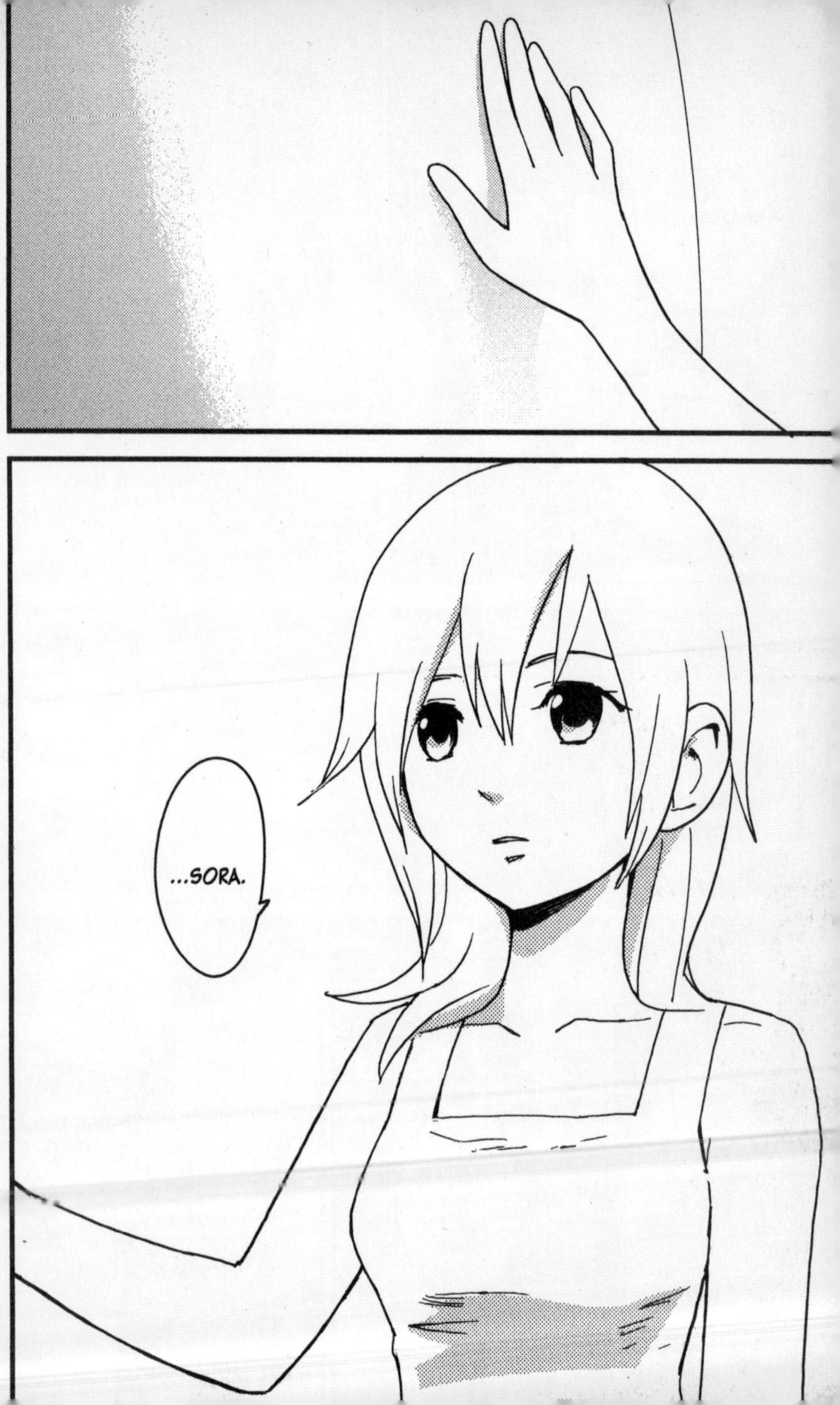
...SORA.

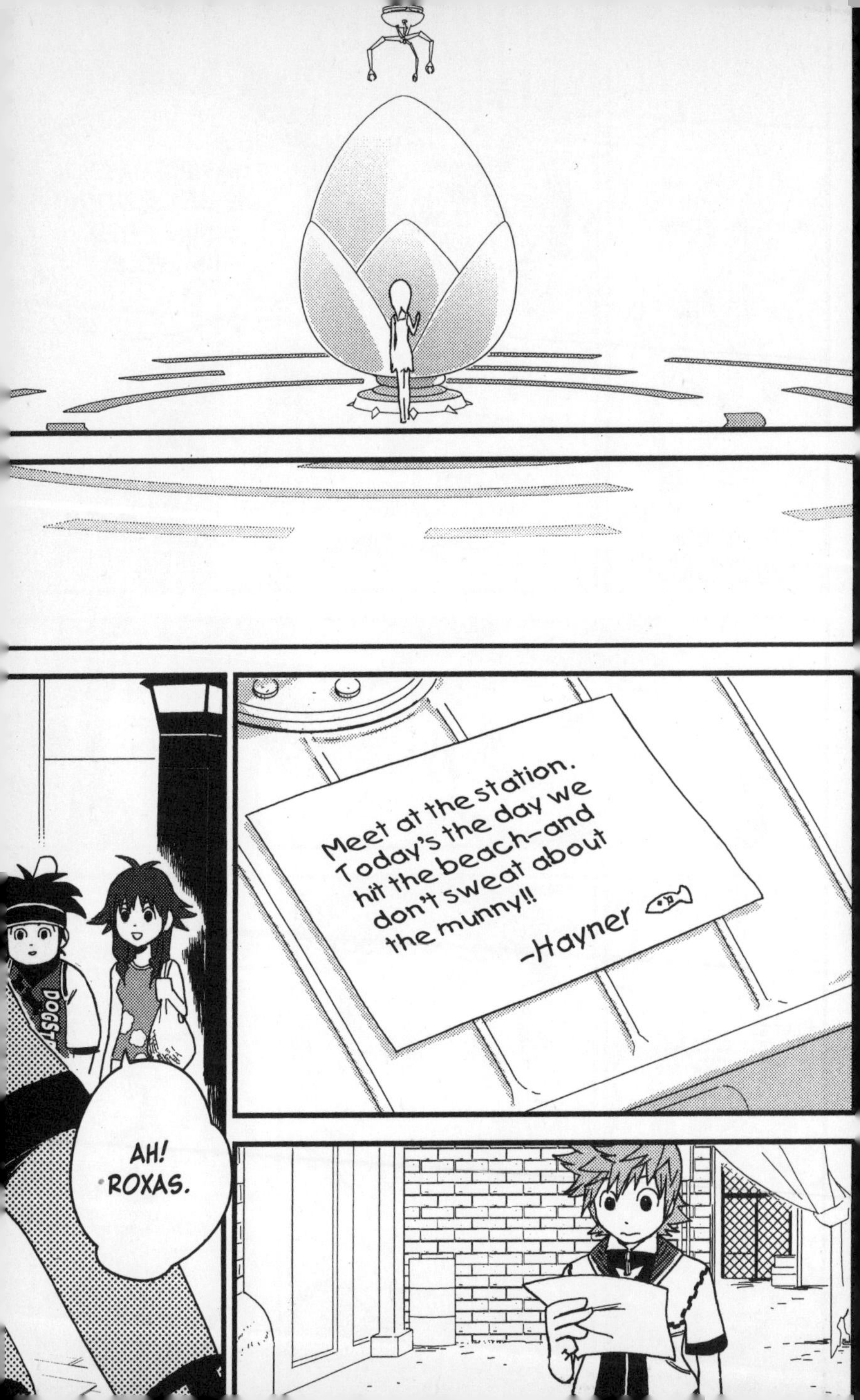
Meet at the station. Today's the day we hit the beach—and don't sweat about the munny!!
-Hayner
AH! ROXAS.

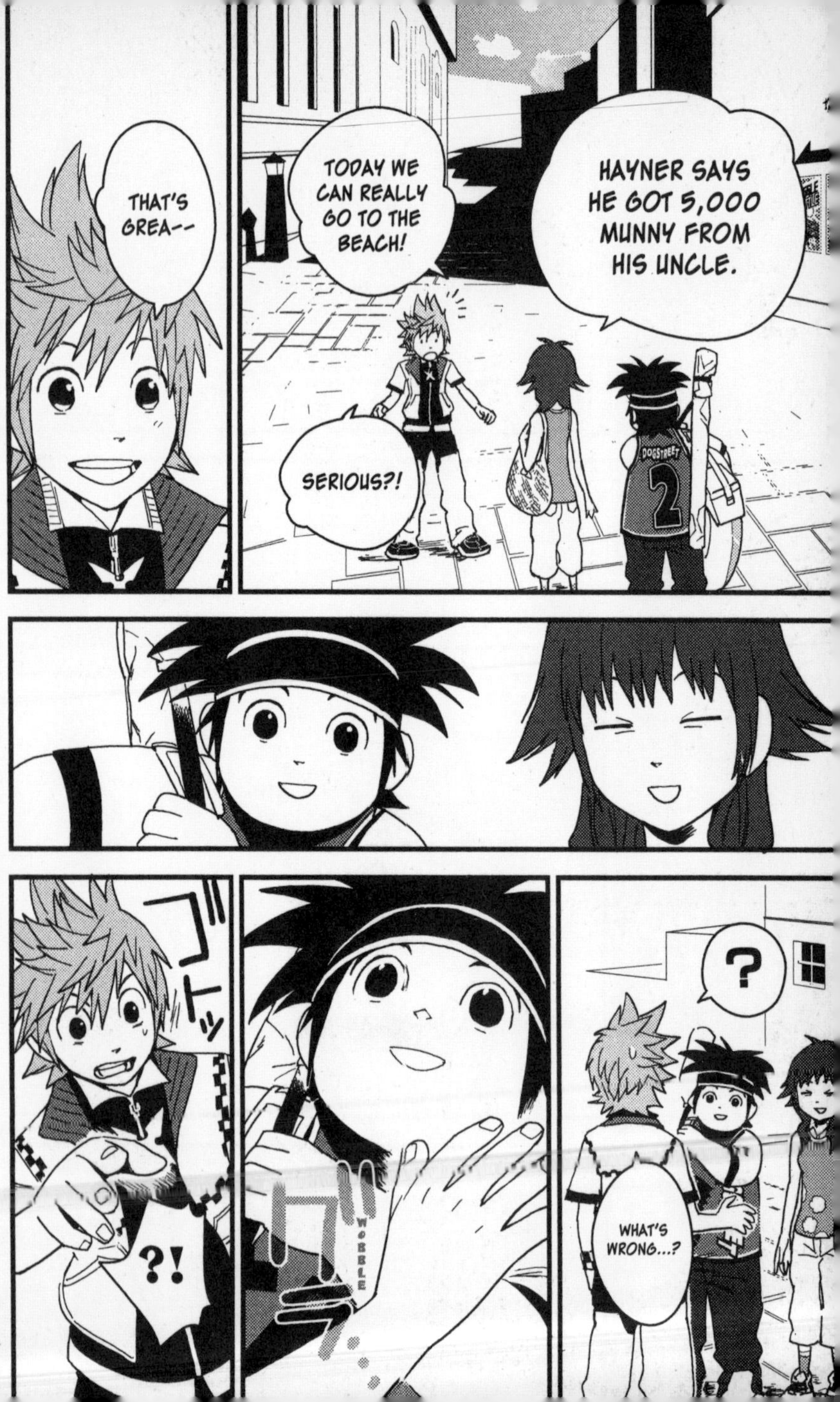
HAYNER SAYS HE GOT 5,000 MUNNY FROM HIS UNCLE.
TODAY WE CAN REALLY GO TO THE BEACH!
SERIOUS?!
THAT'S GREA--
?
WHAT'S WRONG...?
WOBBLE
ゴトッ
?!

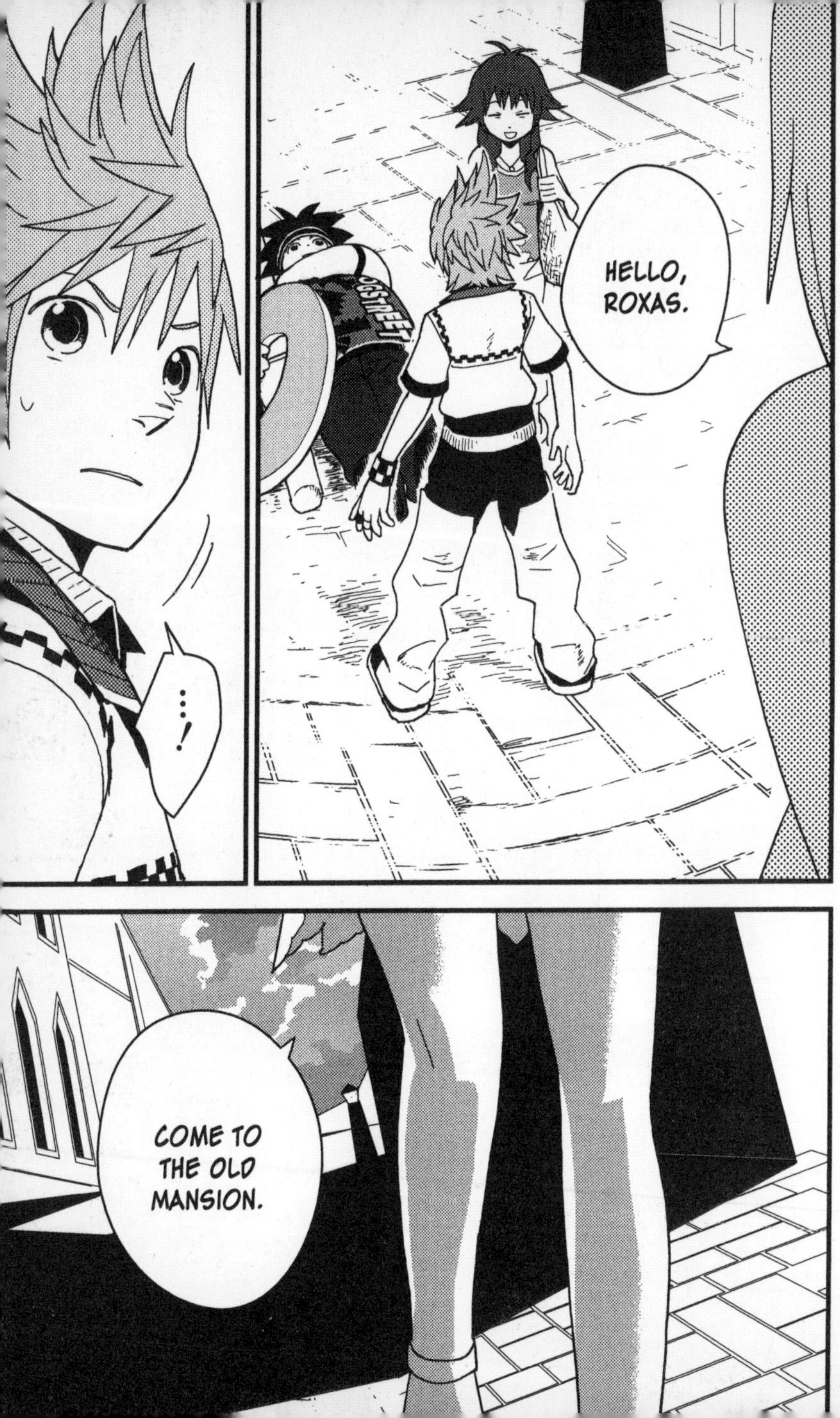
HELLO, ROXAS.
...!
COME TO THE OLD MANSION.

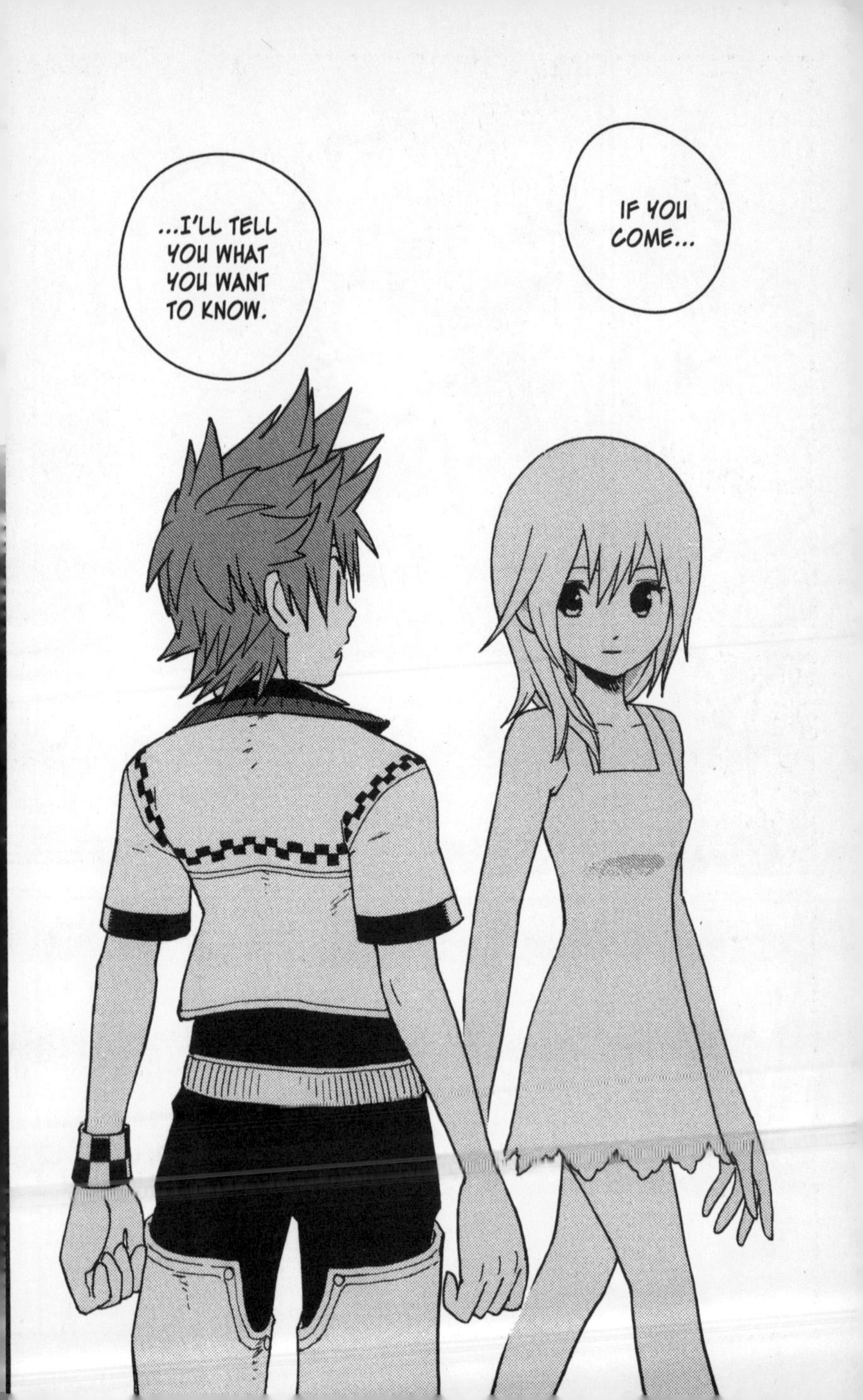
IF YOU COME...
...I'LL TELL YOU WHAT YOU WANT TO KNOW.

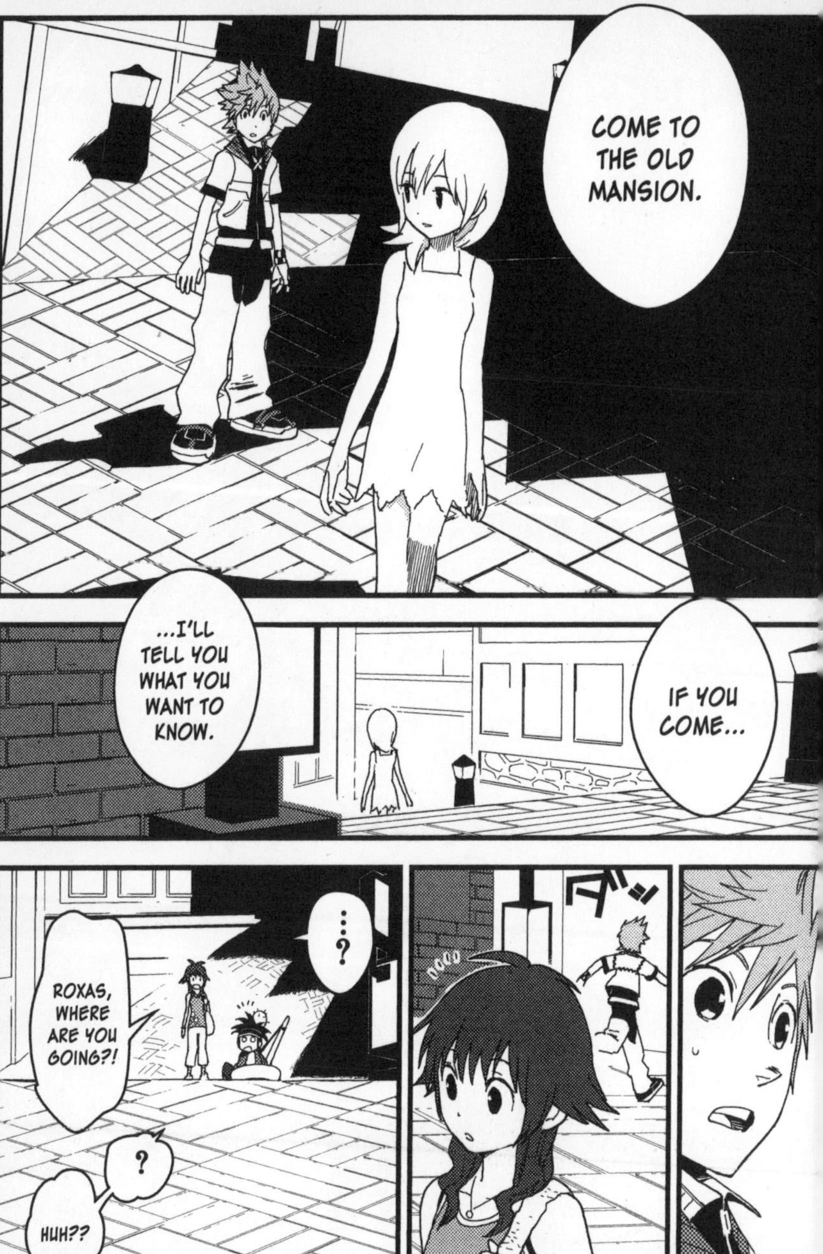
COME TO THE OLD MANSION.
IF YOU COME...
...I'LL TELL YOU WHAT YOU WANT TO KNOW.
...?
ROXAS, WHERE ARE YOU GOING?!
?
HUH??

Chapter 4: The Distant Sound of Waves

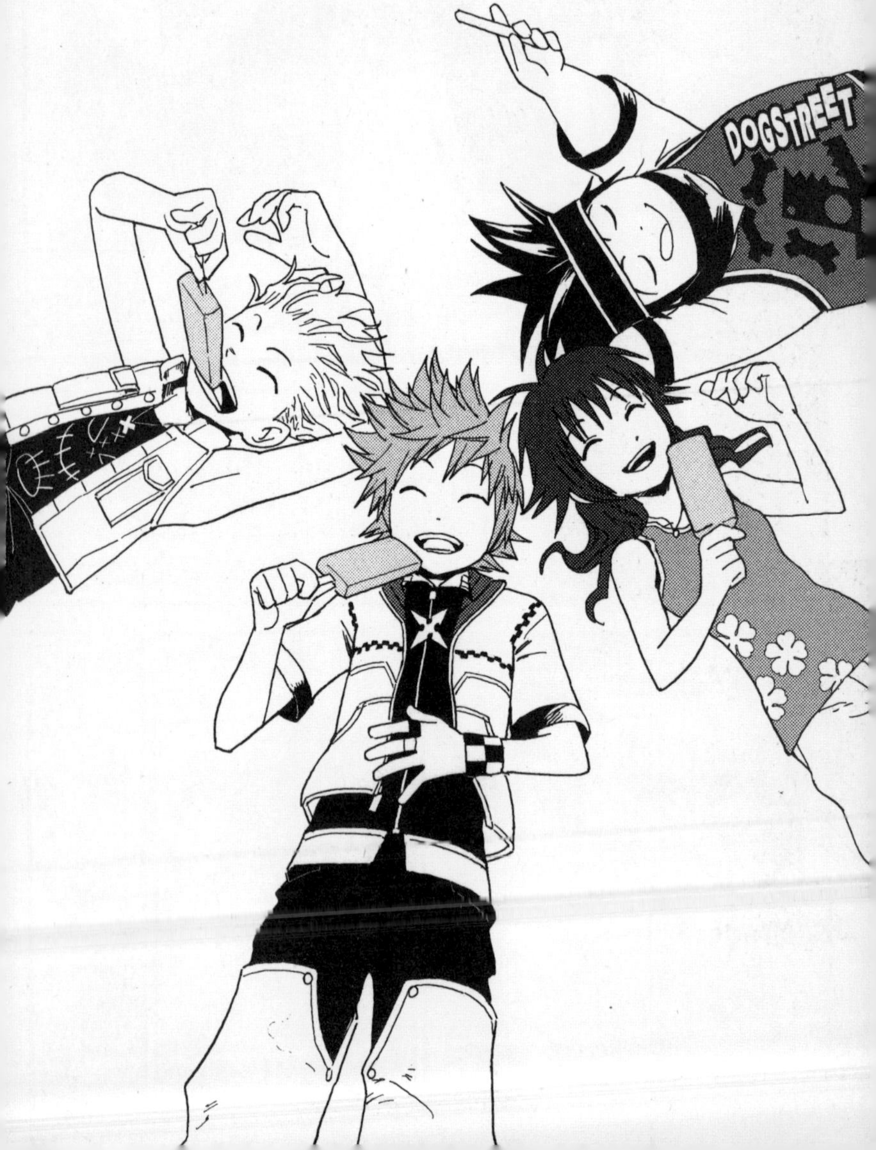
DOGSTREET

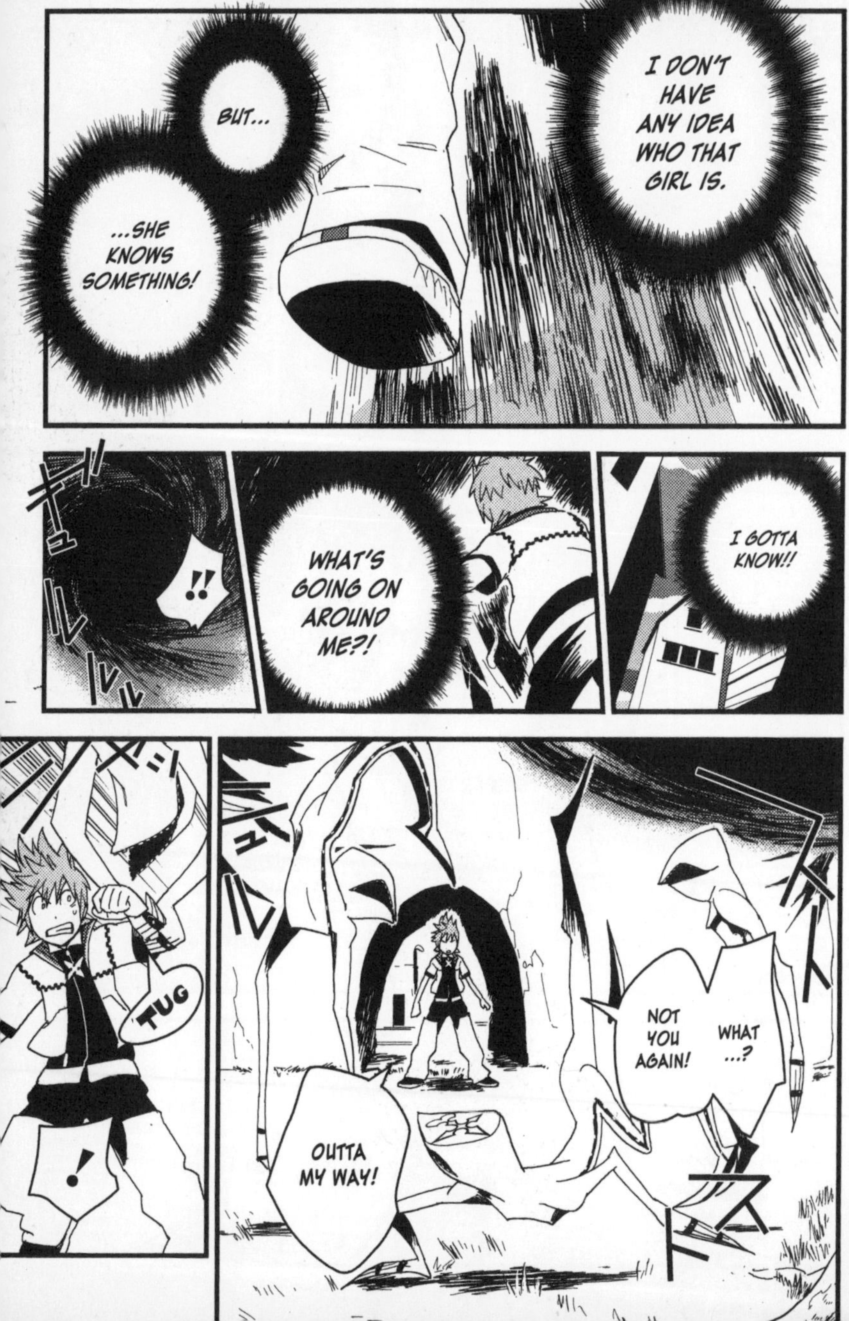

I DON'T HAVE ANY IDEA WHO THAT GIRL IS.
BUT...
...SHE KNOWS SOMETHING!
I GOTTA KNOW!!
WHAT'S GOING ON AROUND ME?!
!!
WHAT ...?
NOT YOU AGAIN!
OUTTA MY WAY!
TUG
!

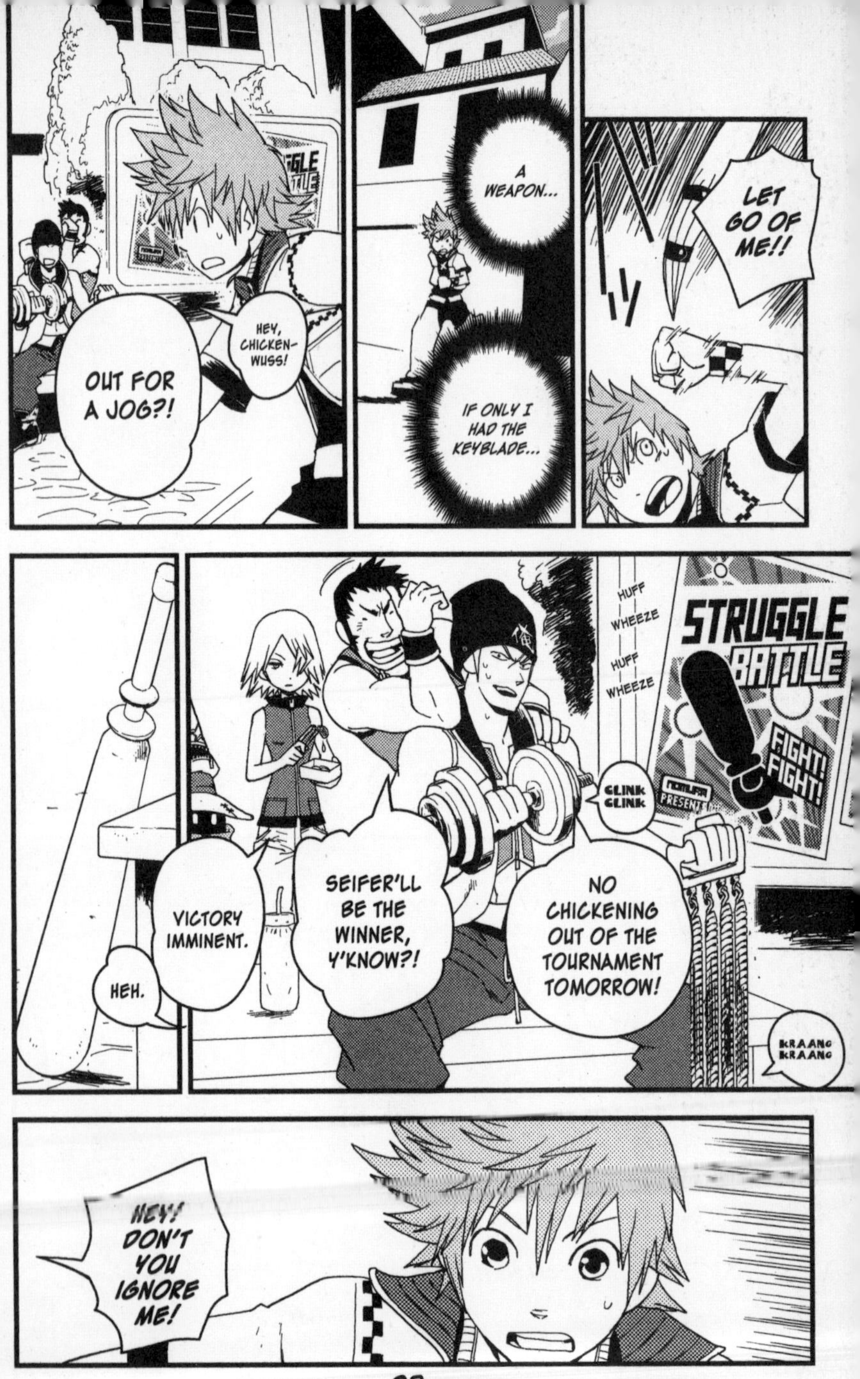
LET GO OF ME!!
A WEAPON...
IF ONLY I HAD THE KEYBLADE...
HEY, CHICKEN-WUSS!
OUT FOR A JOG?!
KRAANG KRAANG
STRUGGLE BATTLE
FIGHT! FIGHT!
HUFF WHEEZE
HUFF WHEEZE
CLINK CLINK
NO CHICKENING OUT OF THE TOURNAMENT TOMORROW!
SEIFER'LL BE THE WINNER, Y'KNOW?!
VICTORY IMMINENT.
HEH.
HEY! DON'T YOU IGNORE ME!

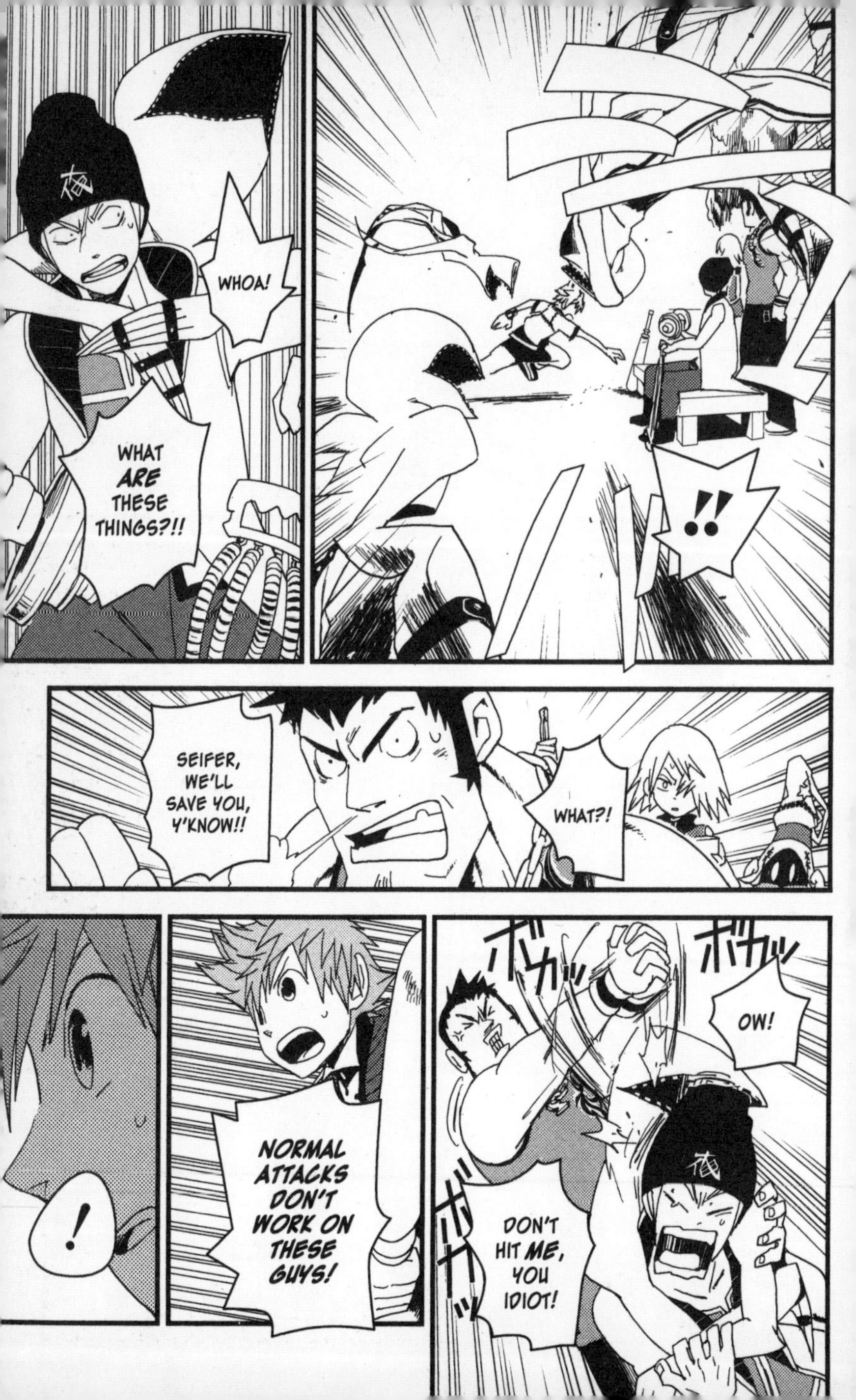
!!
WHOA!
WHAT ARE THESE THINGS?!!
WHAT?!
SEIFER, WE'LL SAVE YOU, Y'KNOW!!
ボカッ
OW!
ボカッ
DON'T HIT ME, YOU IDIOT!
ボカッ
NORMAL ATTACKS DON'T WORK ON THESE GUYS!
!

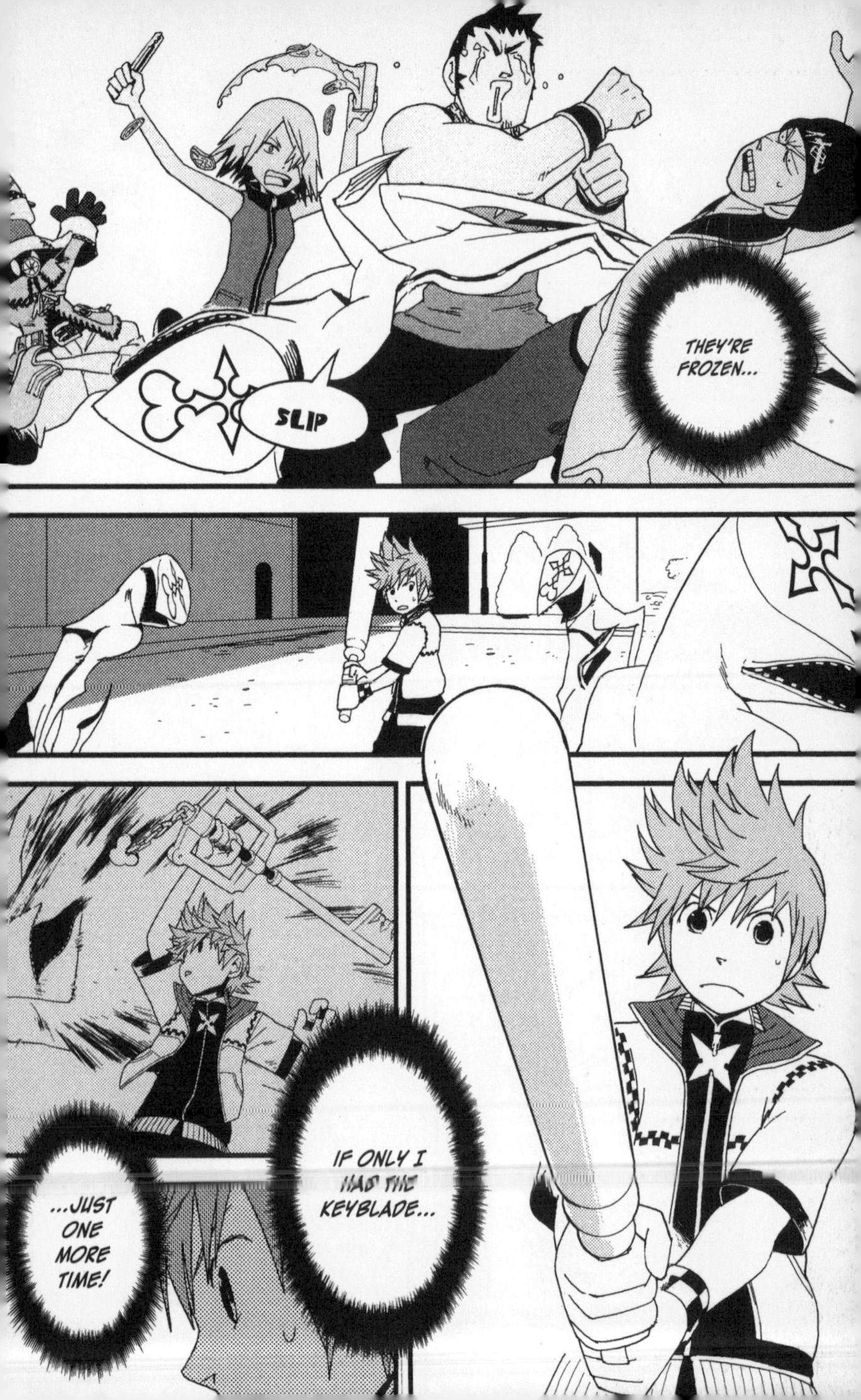
THEY'RE FROZEN...
SLIP
IF ONLY I HAD THE KEYBLADE...
...JUST ONE MORE TIME!

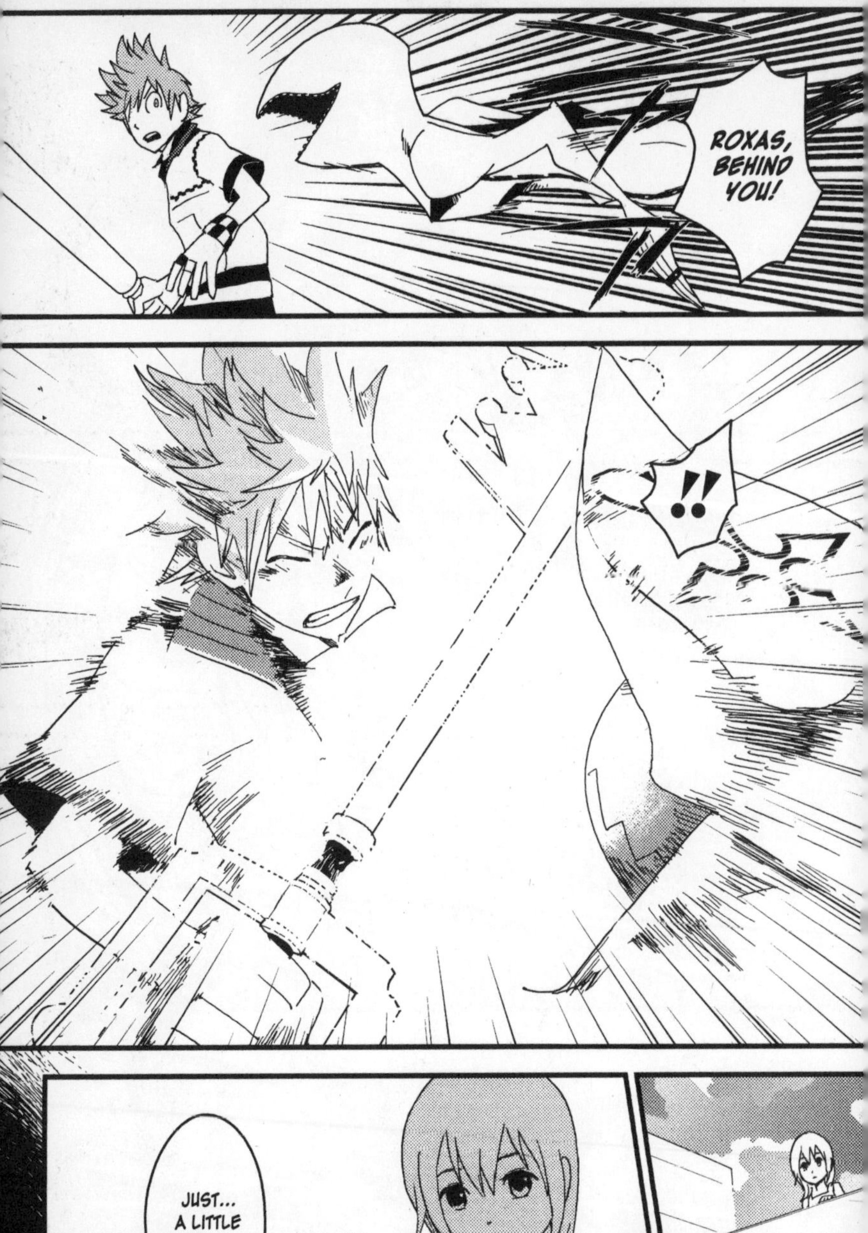
ROXAS, BEHIND YOU!
!!
JUST... A LITTLE LONGER...

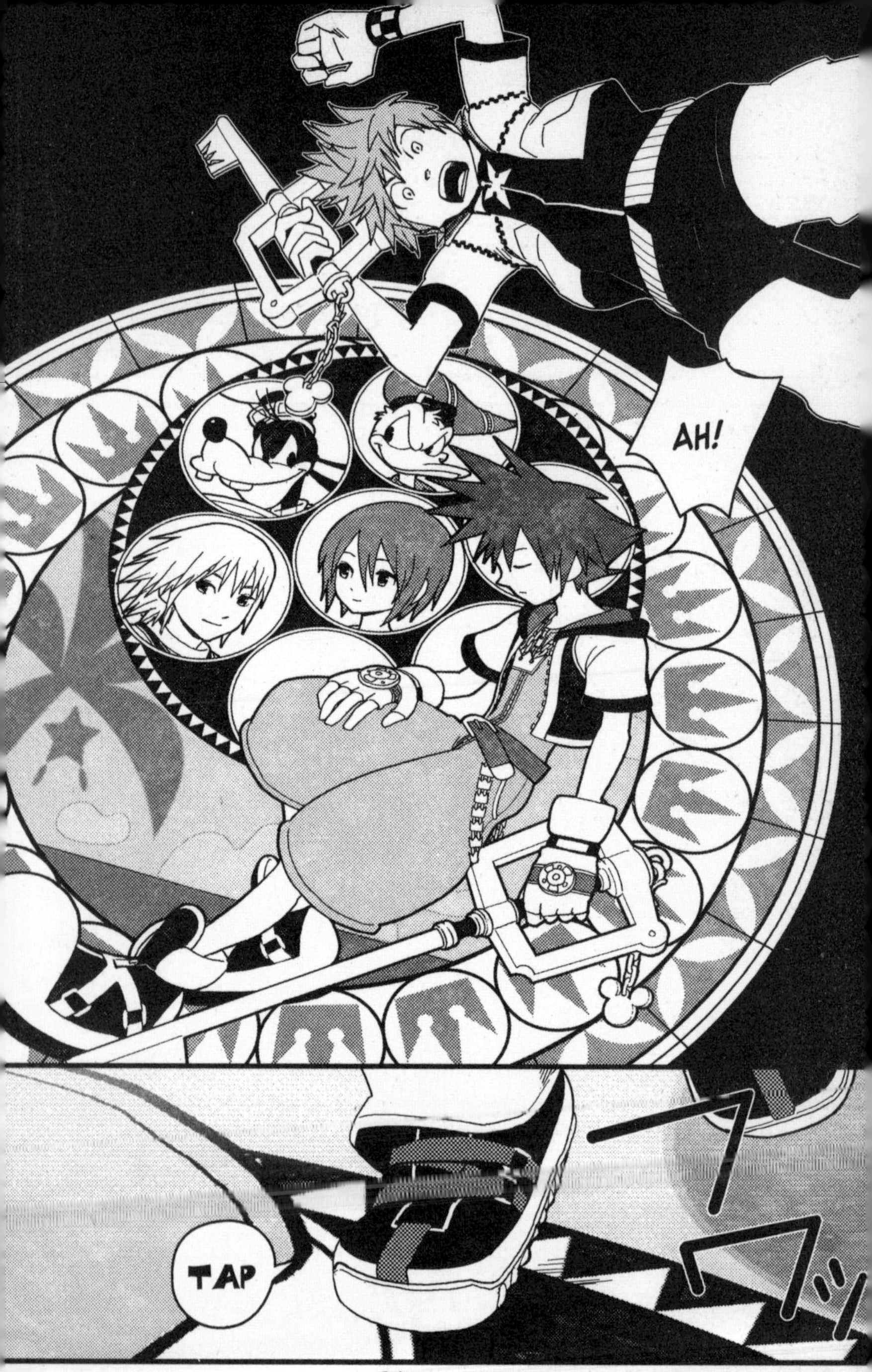
AH!
TAP

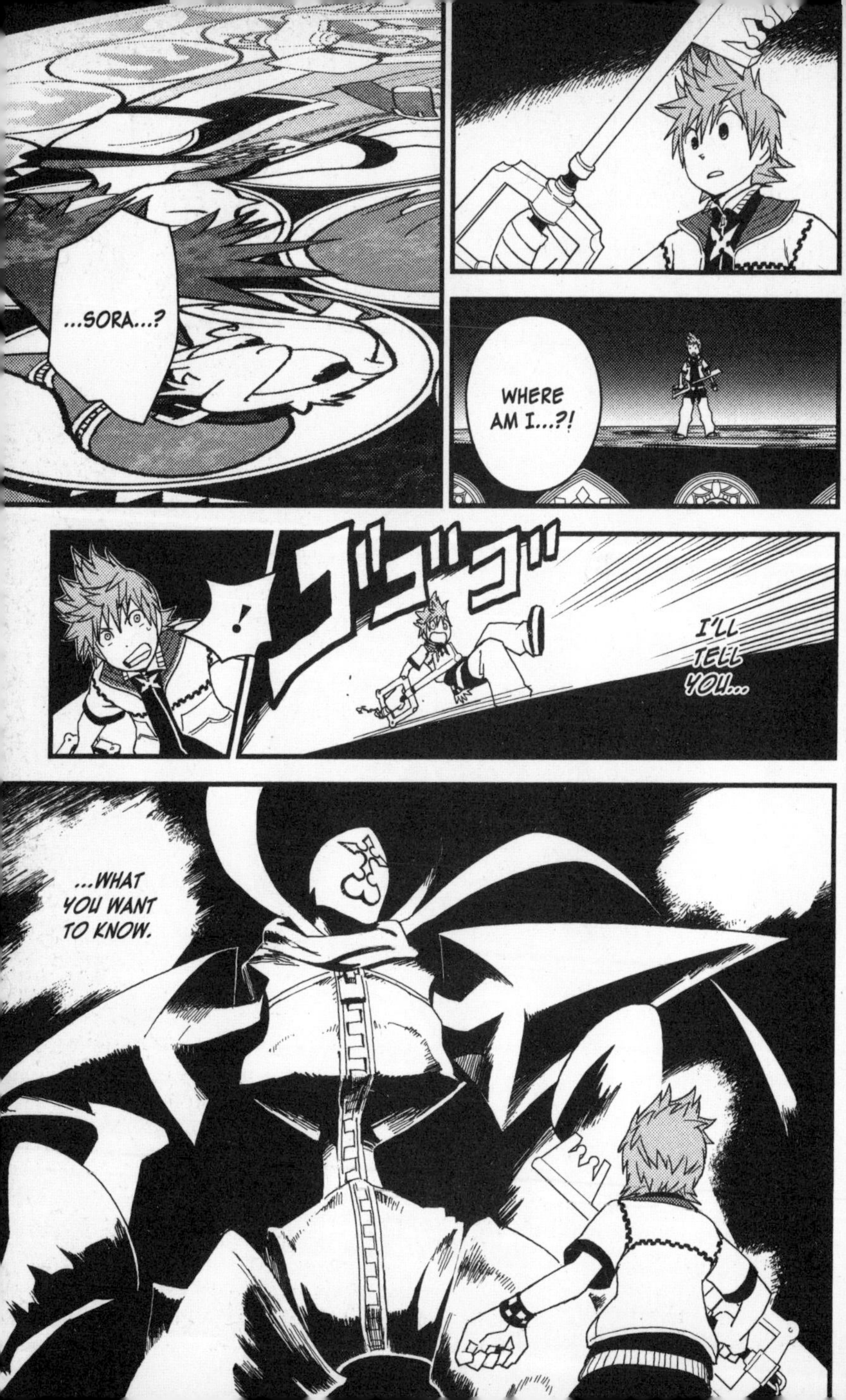
WHERE AM I...?!
...SORA...?
ゴゴゴ
I'LL TELL YOU...
!
...WHAT YOU WANT TO KNOW.

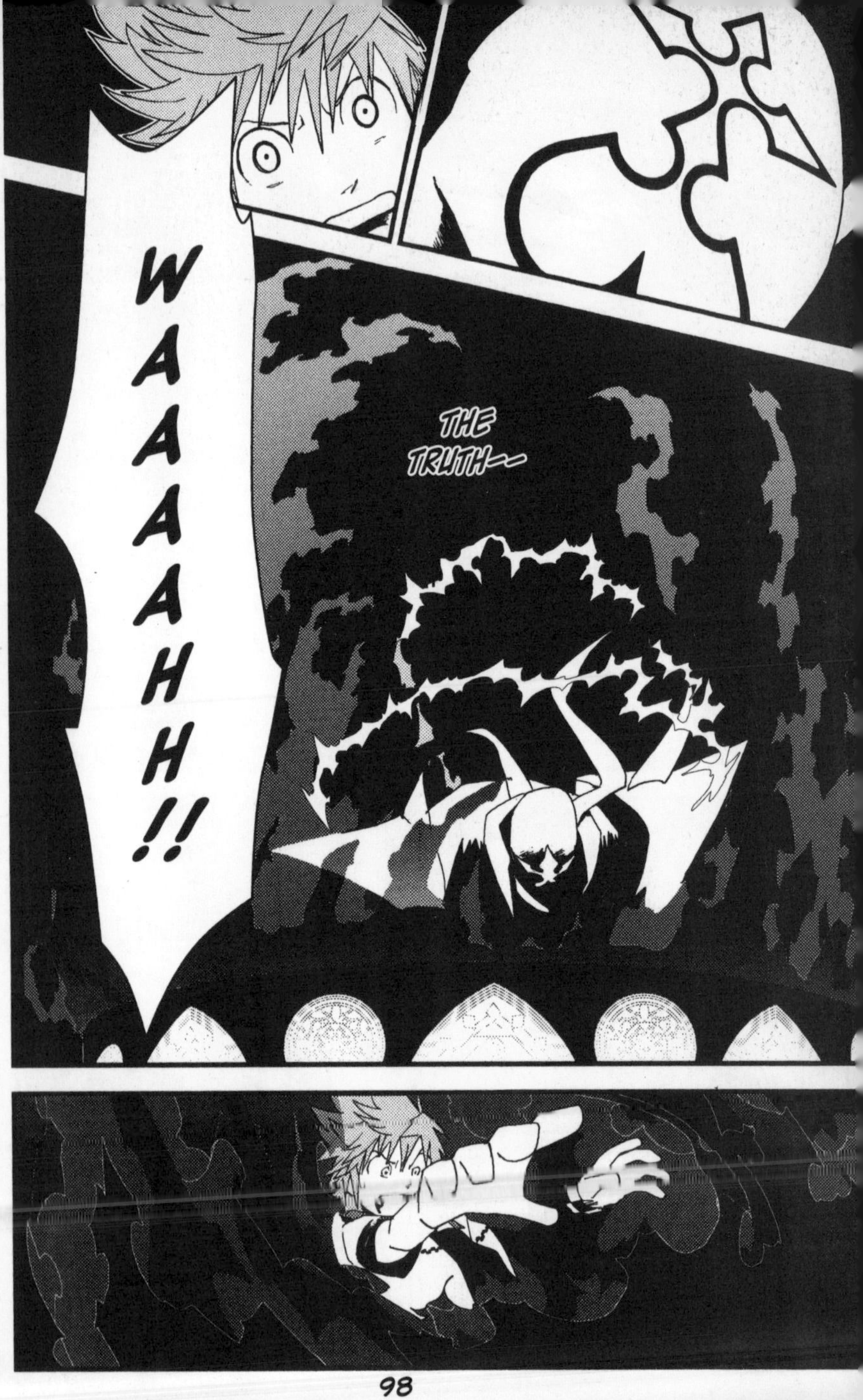
WAAAAHH!!
THE TRUTH--

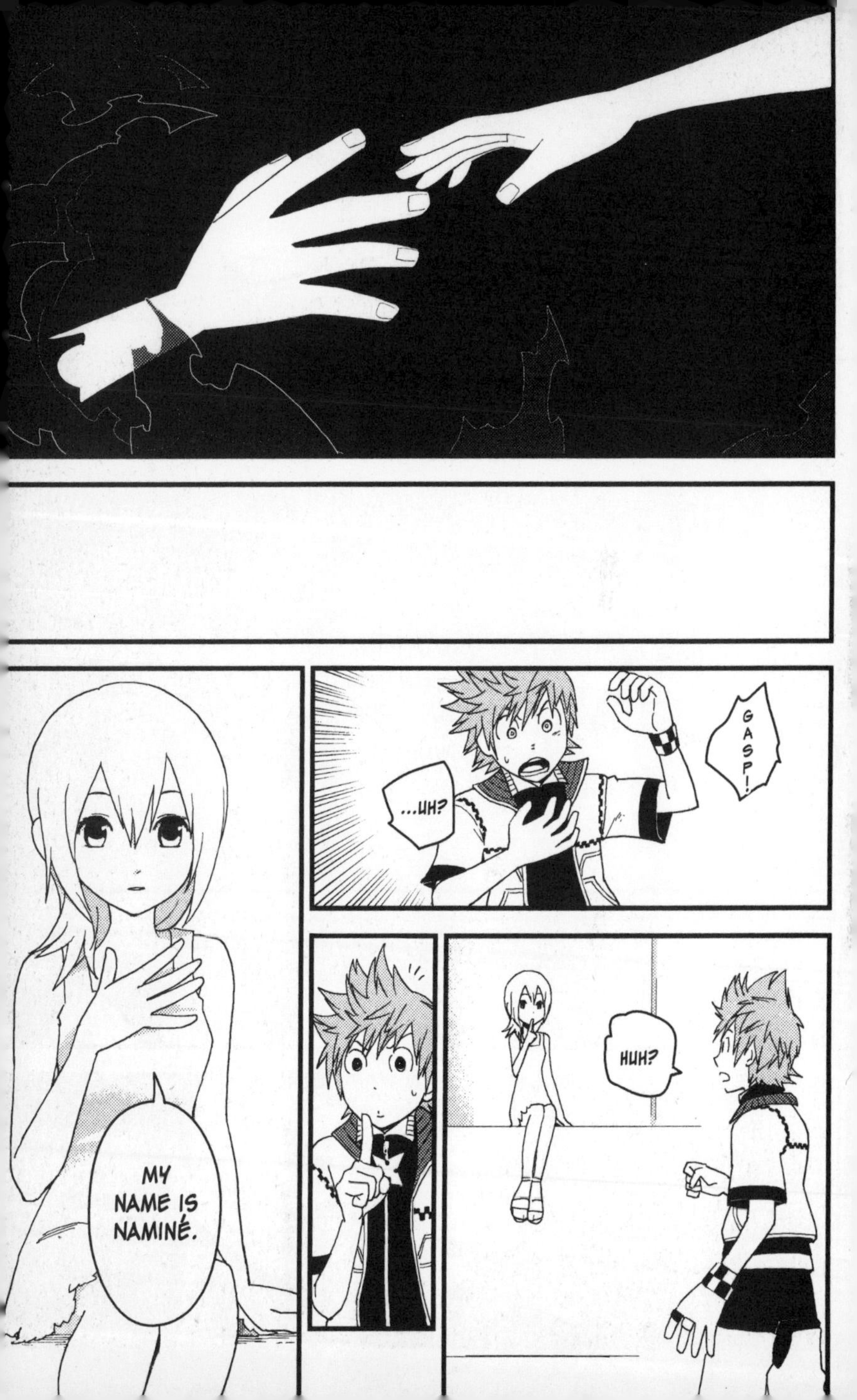
GASP!
...UH?
HUH?
MY NAME IS NAMINÉ.

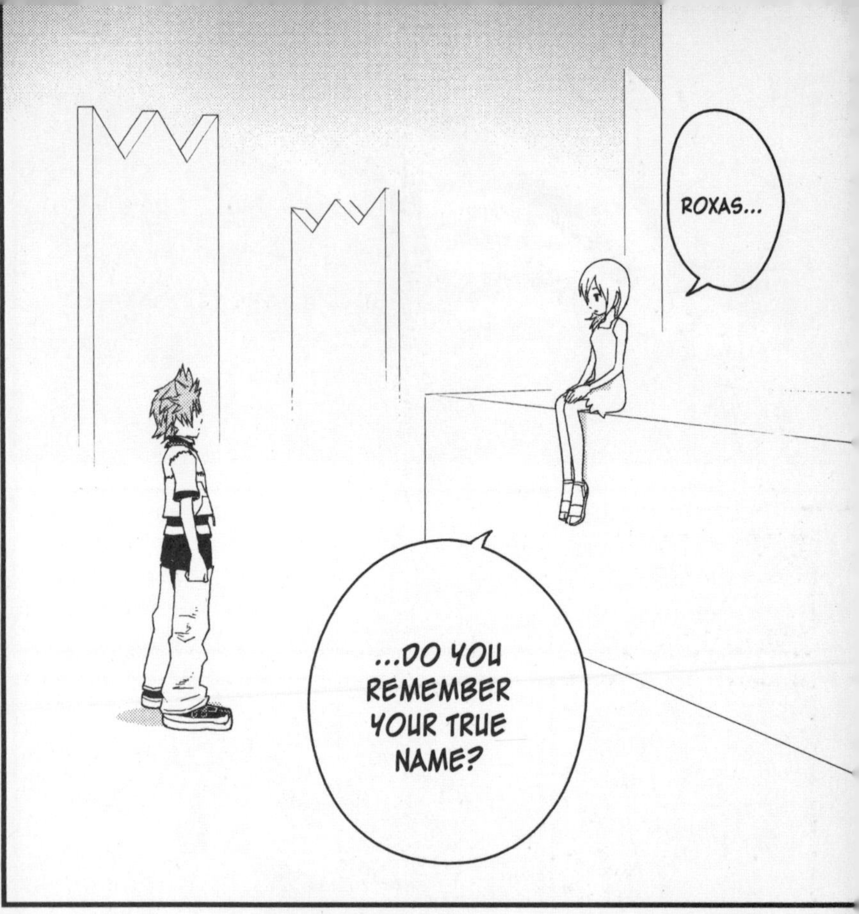
ROXAS...
...DO YOU REMEMBER YOUR TRUE NAME?
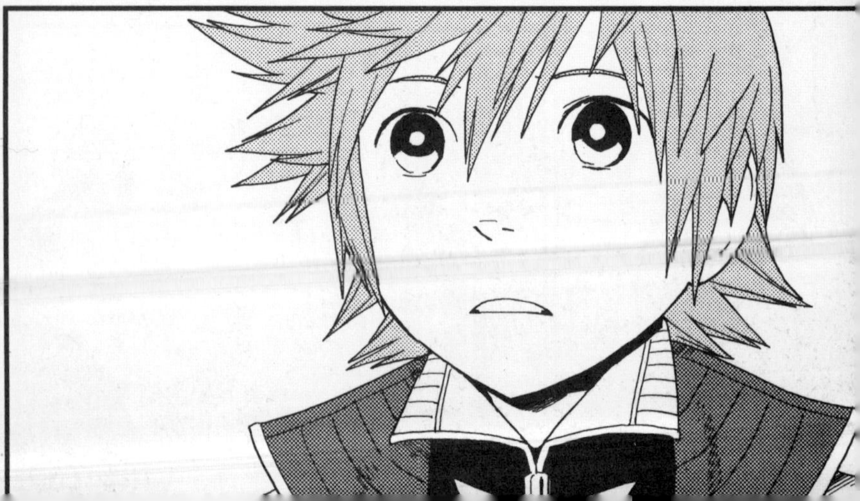

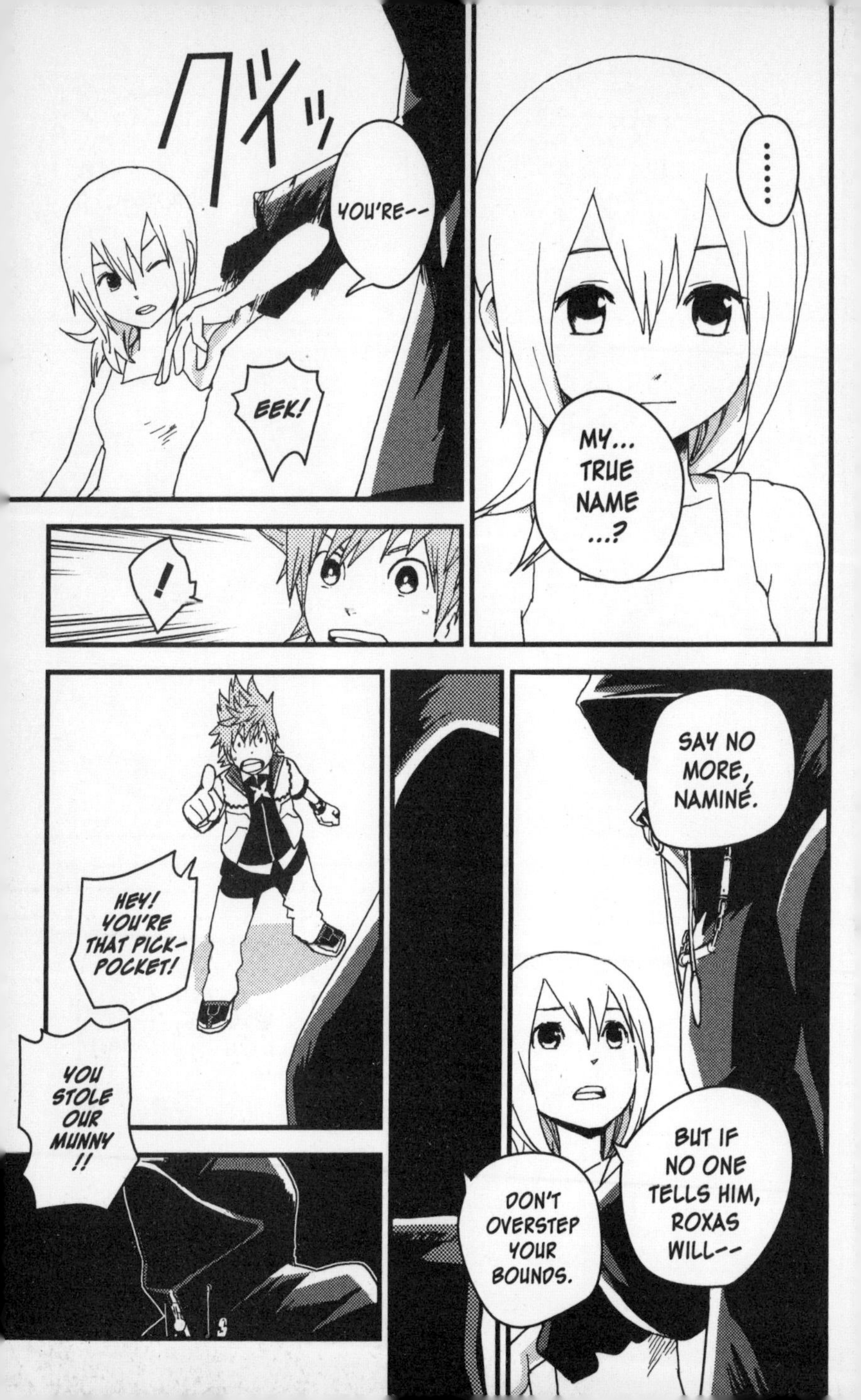
......
MY... TRUE NAME ...?
グイッ
YOU'RE--
EEK!
!
SAY NO MORE, NAMINÉ.
BUT IF NO ONE TELLS HIM, ROXAS WILL--
DON'T OVERSTEP YOUR BOUNDS.
HEY! YOU'RE THAT PICK-POCKET!
YOU STOLE OUR MUNNY !!

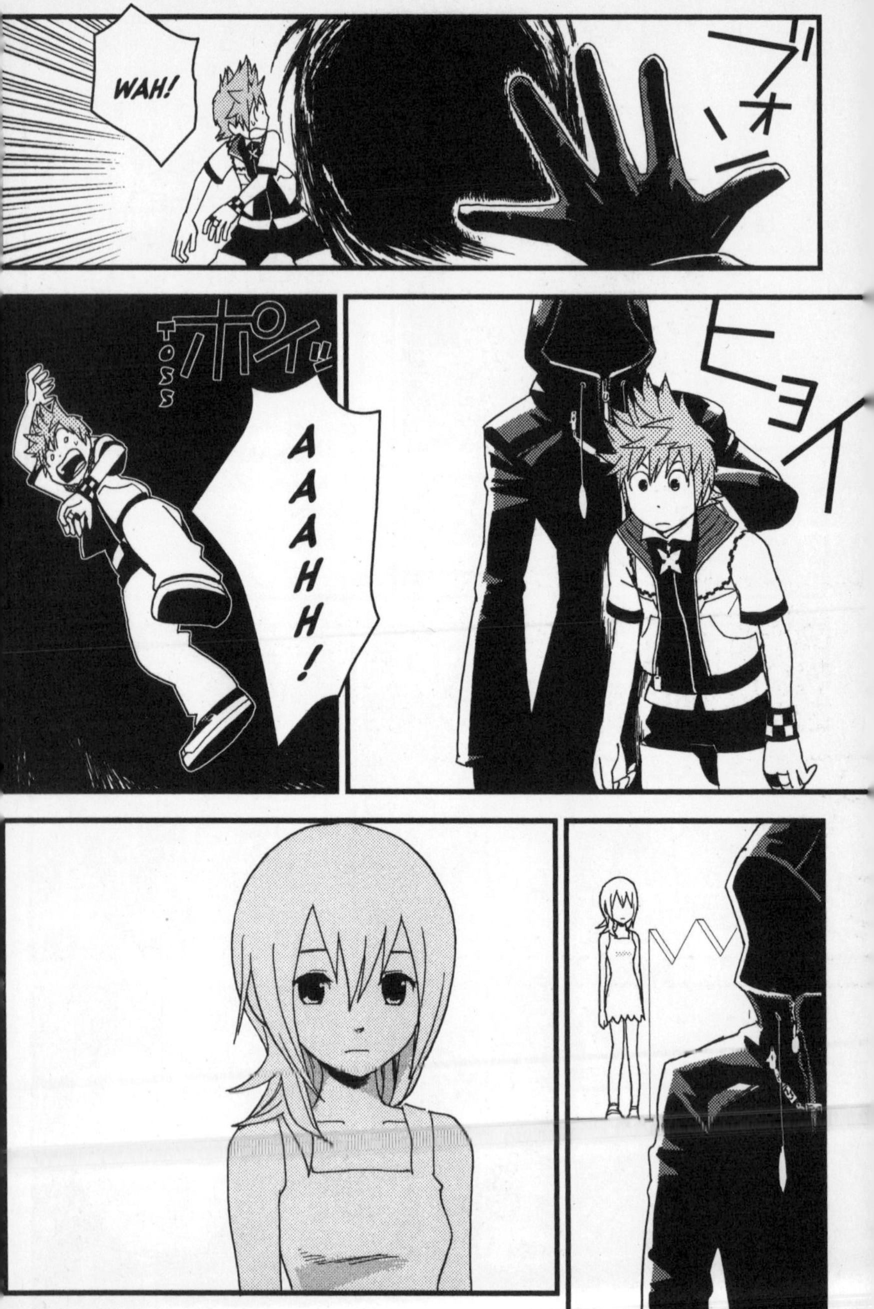
ブォン
WAH!
ヒョイ
ポイッ
TOSS
AAAAHH!

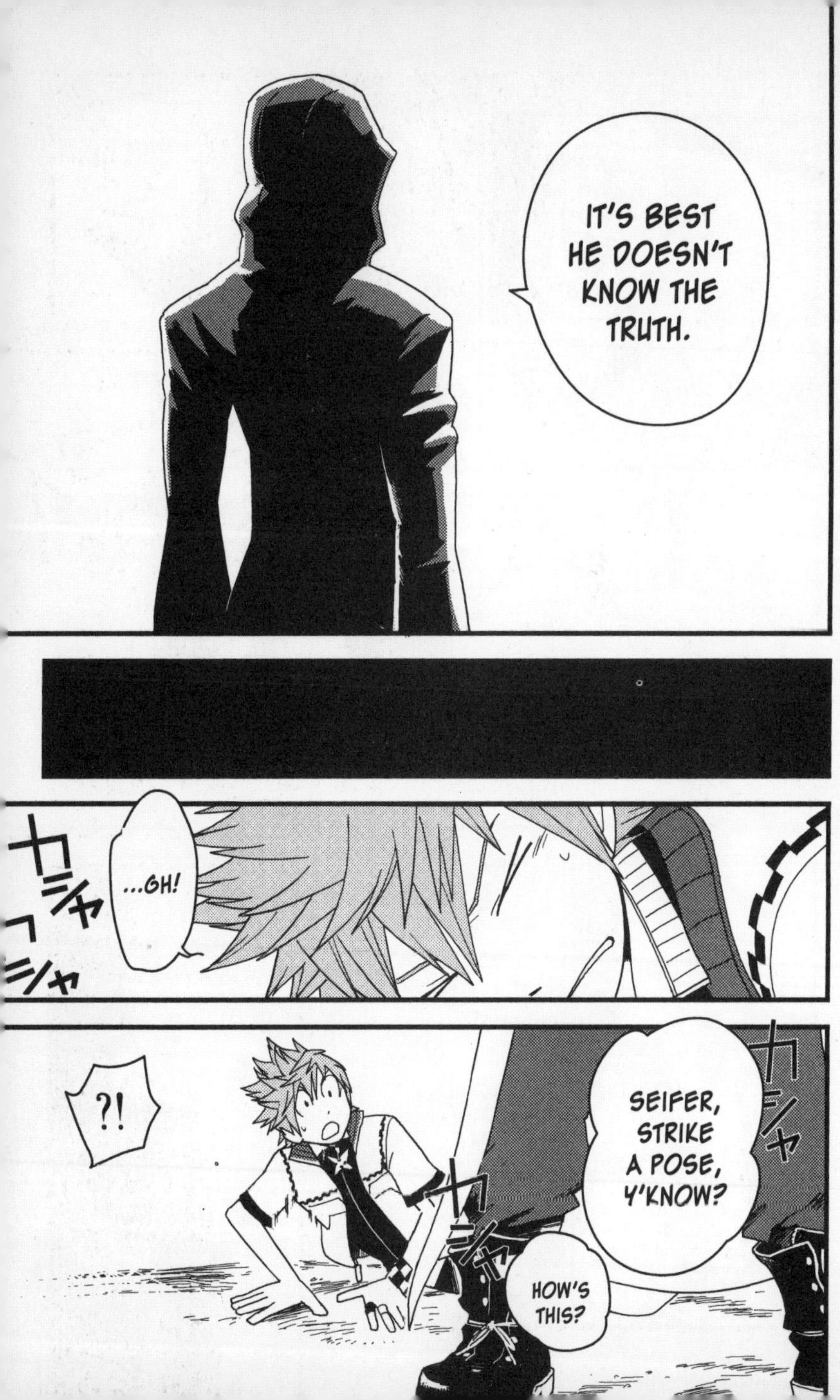
IT'S BEST HE DOESN'T KNOW THE TRUTH.
カシャッ
シャ
...GH!
カシャ
SEIFER, STRIKE A POSE, Y'KNOW?
カシャ
HOW'S THIS?
?!

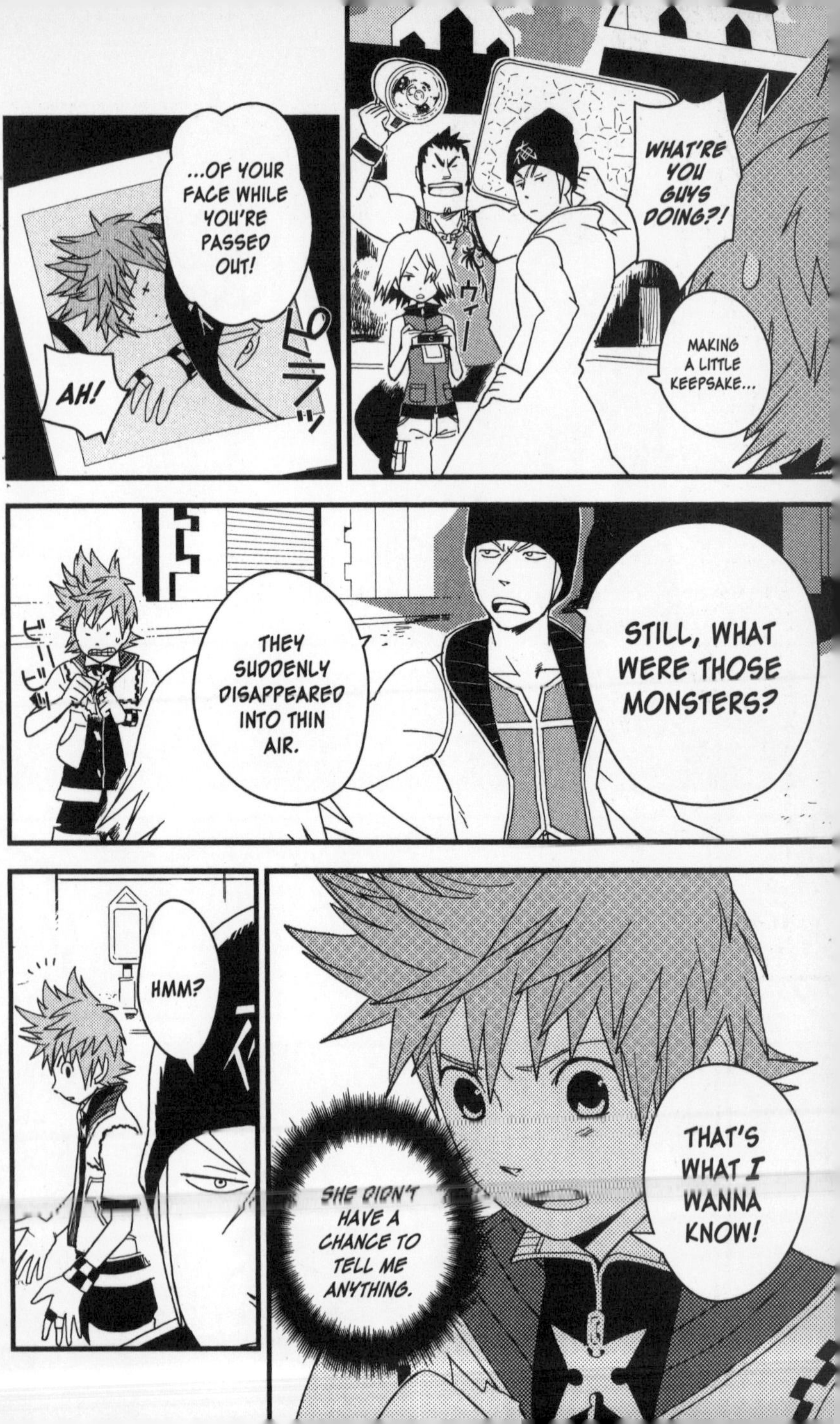
WHAT'RE YOU GUYS DOING?!
MAKING A LITTLE KEEPSAKE...
...OF YOUR FACE WHILE YOU'RE PASSED OUT!
AH!
STILL, WHAT WERE THOSE MONSTERS?
THEY SUDDENLY DISAPPEARED INTO THIN AIR.
THAT'S WHAT I WANNA KNOW!
SHE DIDN'T HAVE A CHANCE TO TELL ME ANYTHING.
HMM?

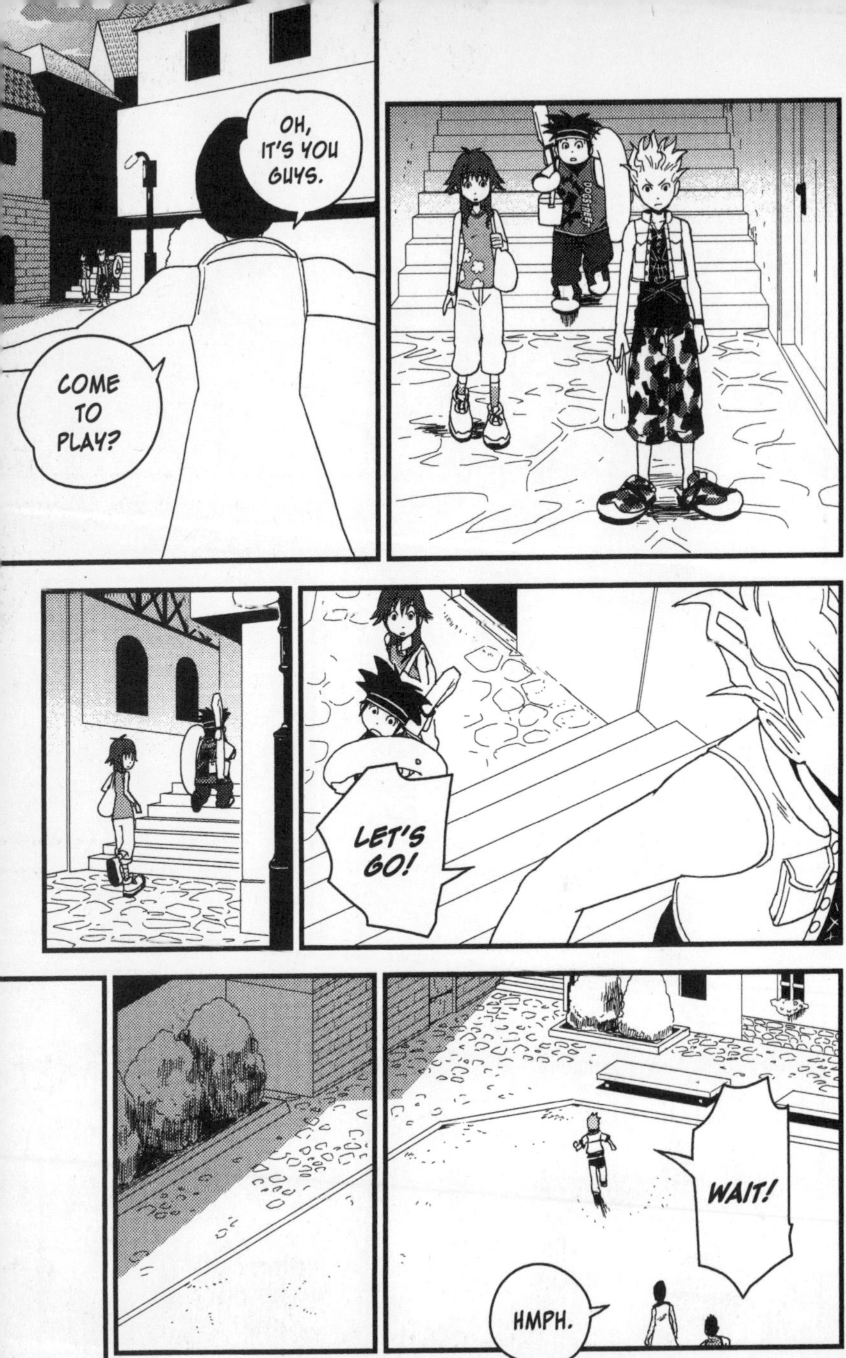
OH, IT'S YOU GUYS.
COME TO PLAY?
LET'S GO!
WAIT!
HMPH.

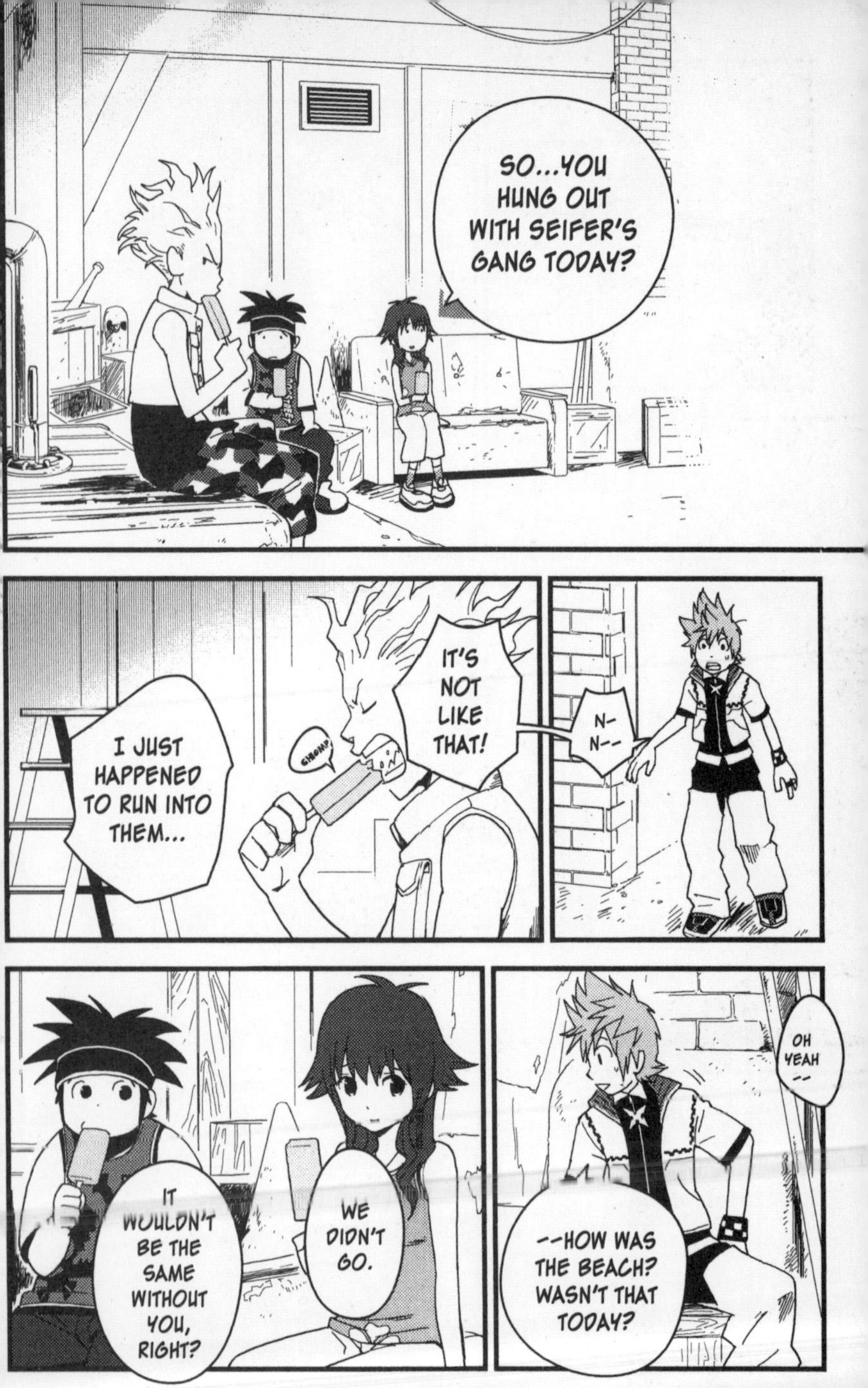
SO...YOU HUNG OUT WITH SEIFER'S GANG TODAY?
N- N--
IT'S NOT LIKE THAT!
I JUST HAPPENED TO RUN INTO THEM...
CHOMP
OH YEAH --
--HOW WAS THE BEACH? WASN'T THAT TODAY?
WE DIDN'T GO.
IT WOULDN'T BE THE SAME WITHOUT YOU, RIGHT?

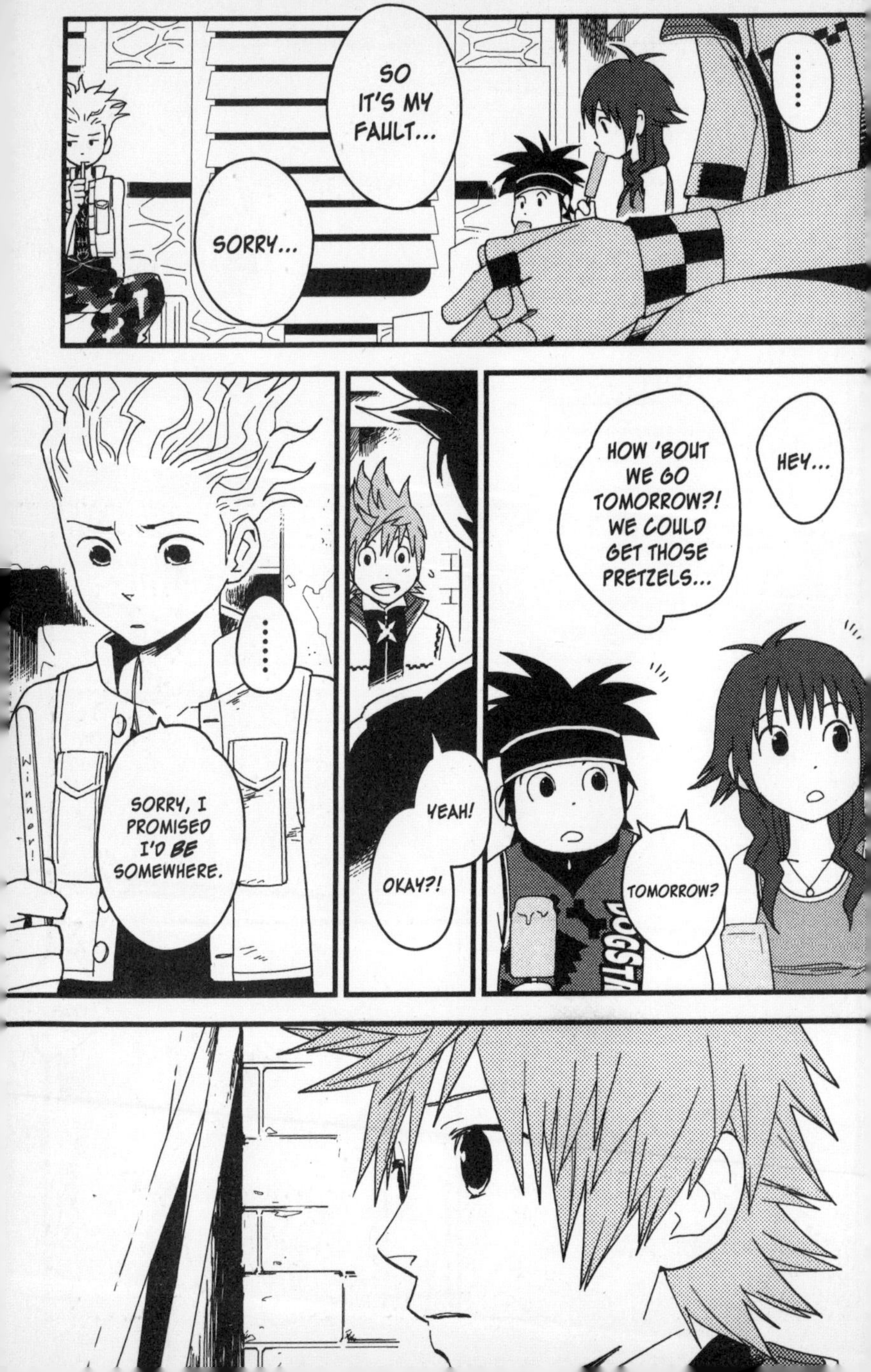
......
SO IT'S MY FAULT...
SORRY...
HEY...
HOW 'BOUT WE GO TOMORROW?! WE COULD GET THOSE PRETZELS...
TOMORROW?
YEAH!
OKAY?!
......
SORRY, I PROMISED I'D *BE* SOMEWHERE.
Winner!

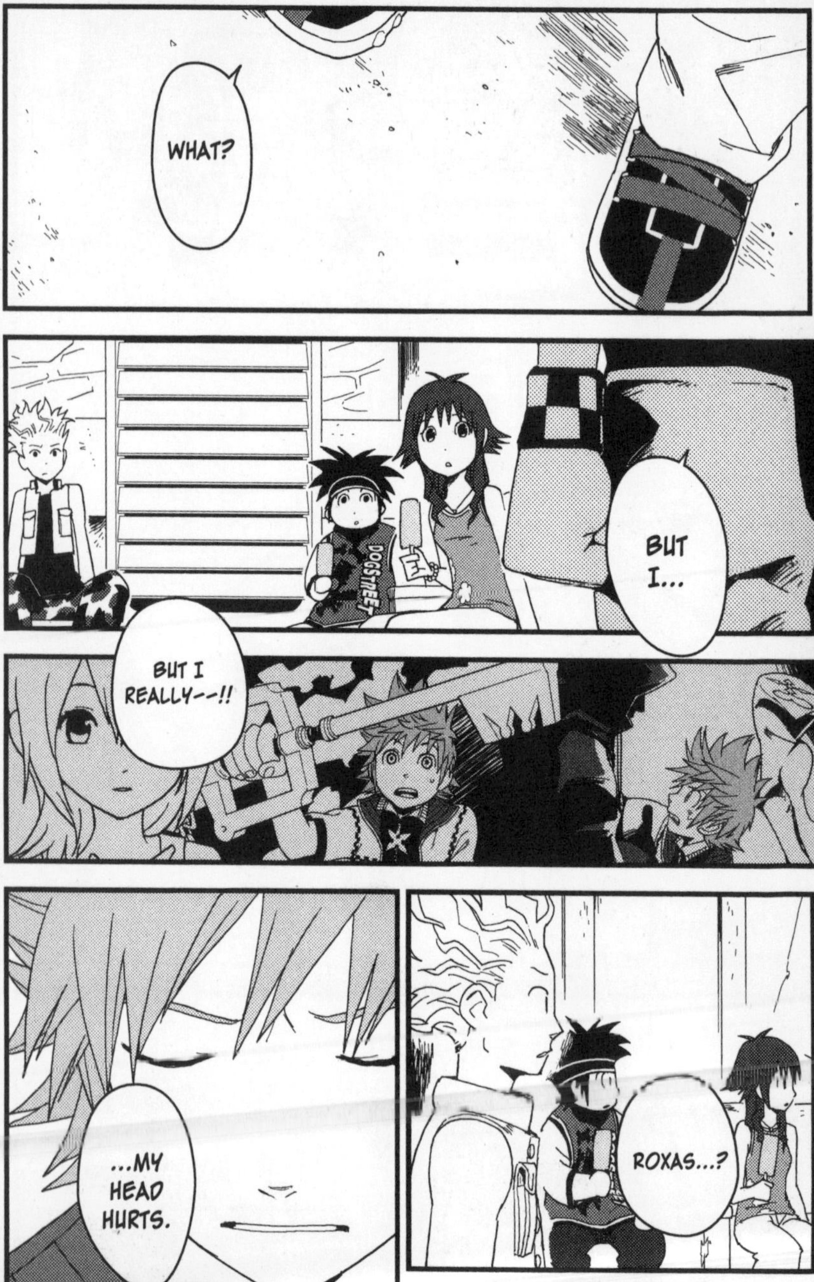
WHAT?
BUT I...
BUT I REALLY--!!
ROXAS...?
...MY HEAD HURTS.

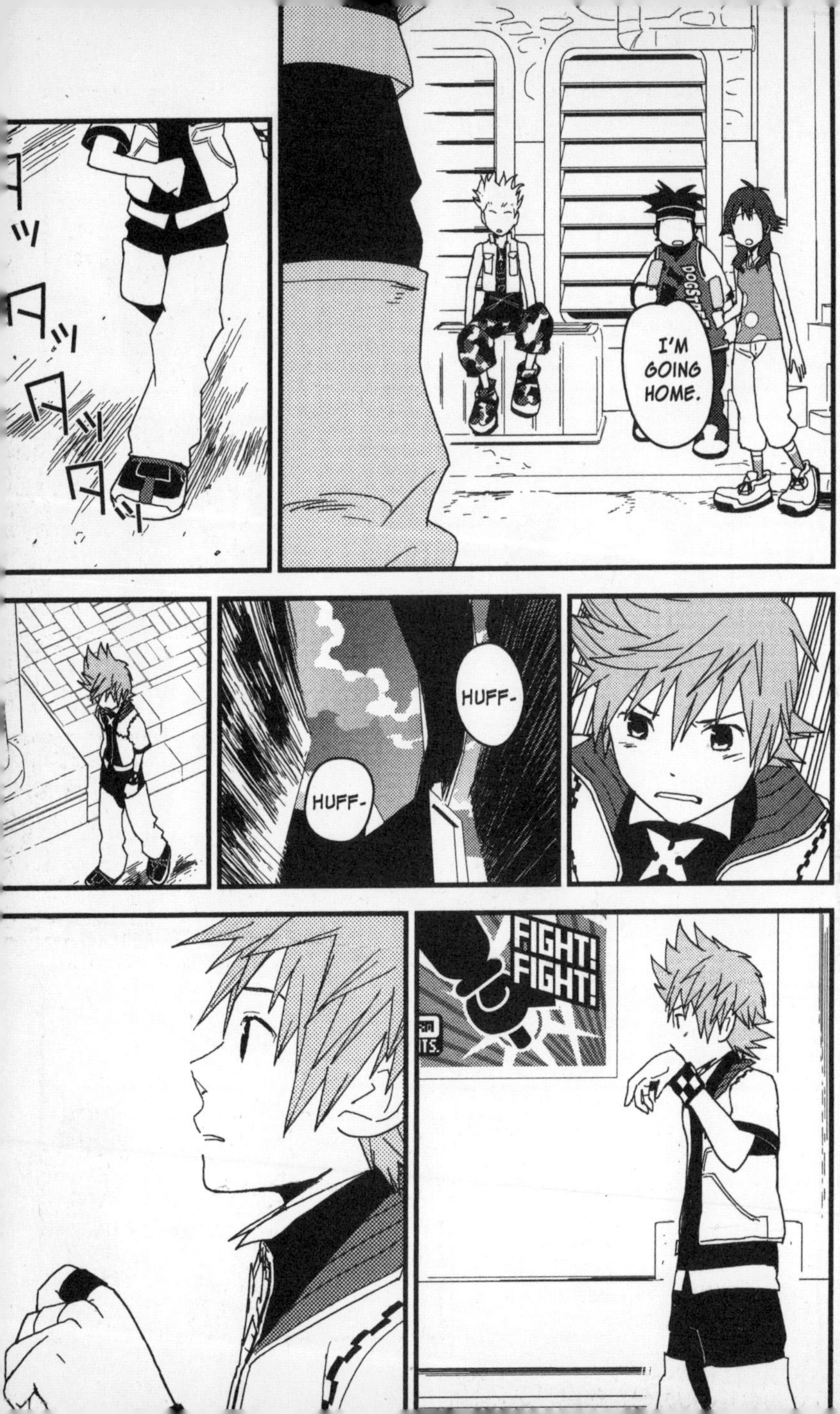
I'M GOING HOME.
HUFF-
HUFF-
FIGHT!
FIGHT!

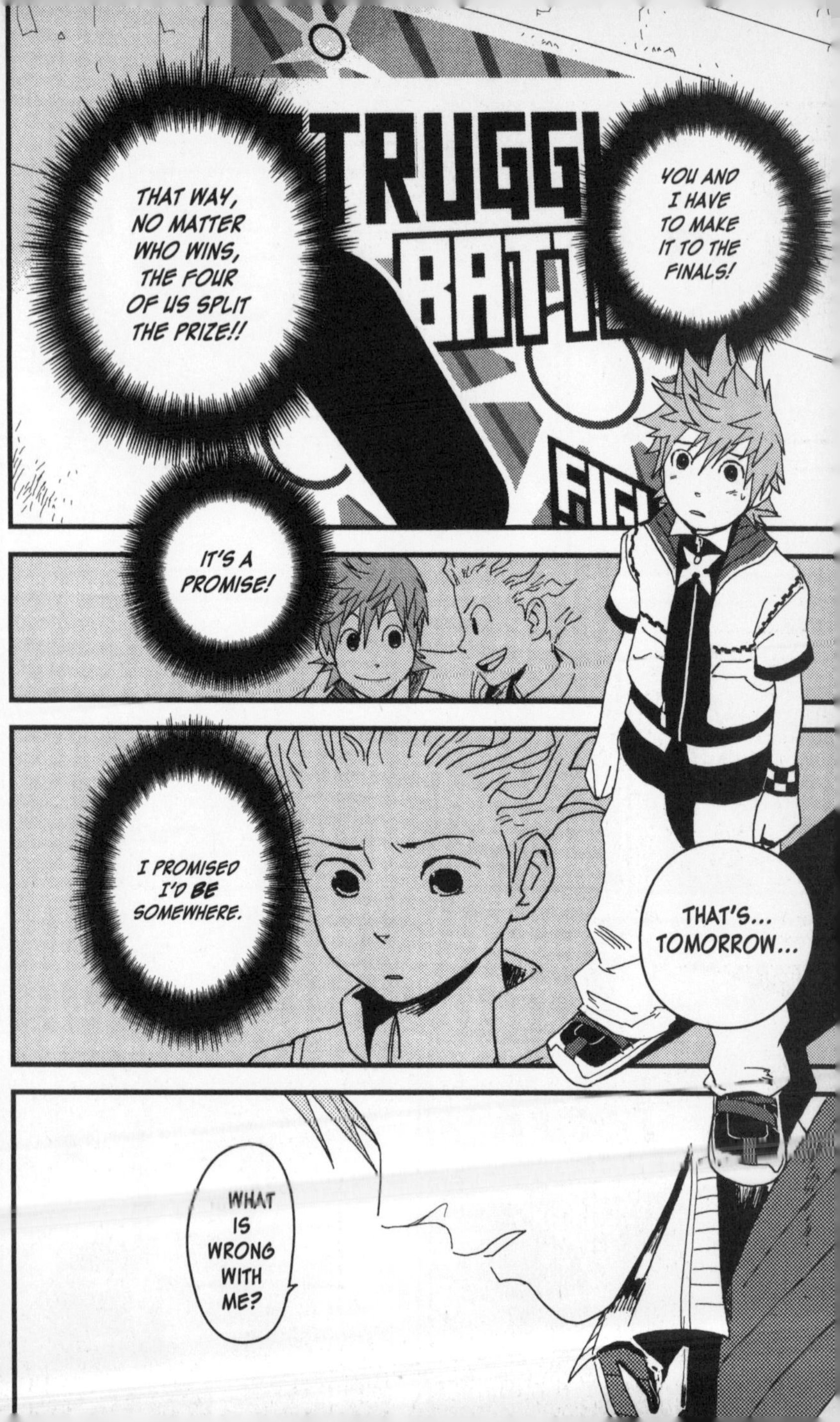
YOU AND I HAVE TO MAKE IT TO THE FINALS!
THAT WAY, NO MATTER WHO WINS, THE FOUR OF US SPLIT THE PRIZE!!
IT'S A PROMISE!
I PROMISED I'D BE SOMEWHERE.
THAT'S... TOMORROW...
WHAT IS WRONG WITH ME?

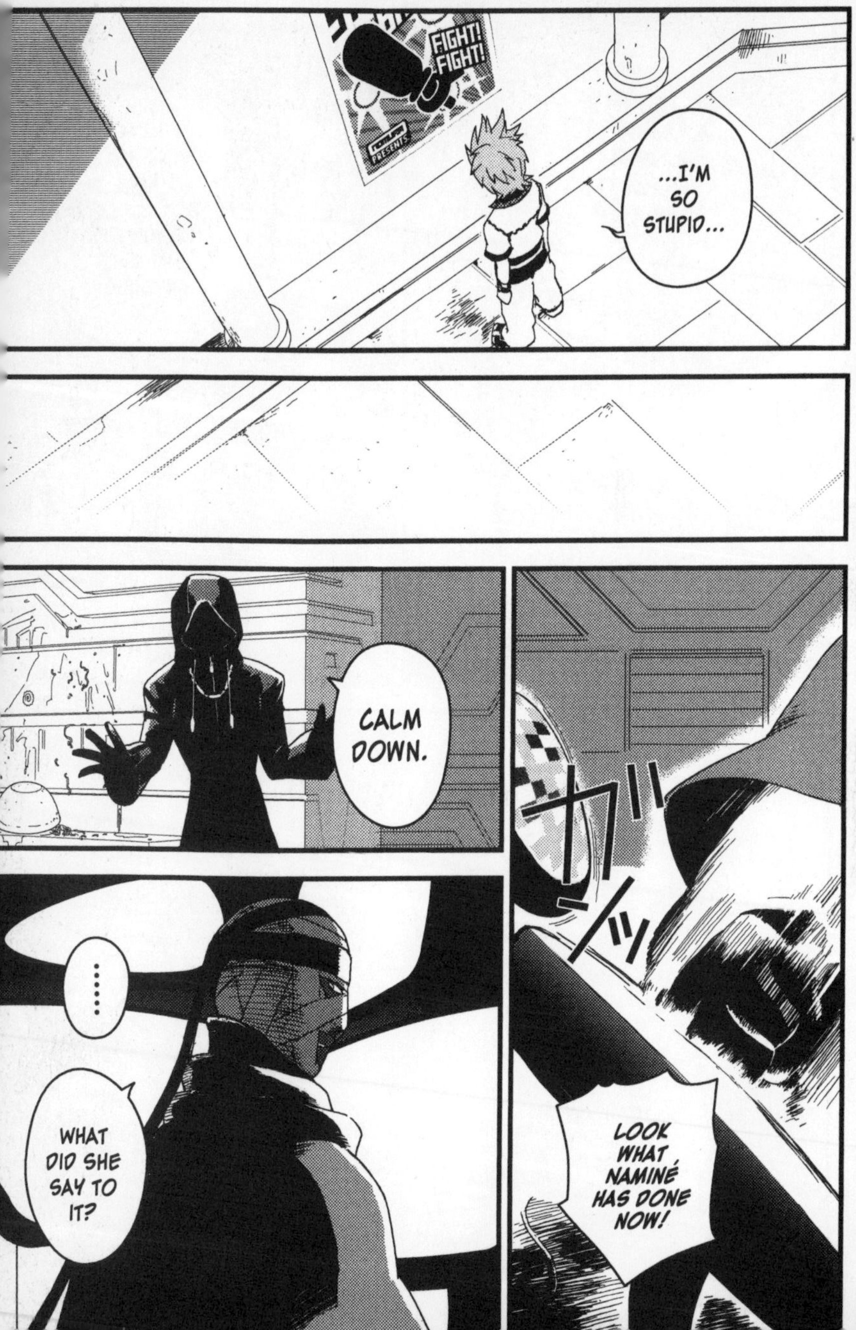
FIGHT! FIGHT!
PRESENTS
...I'M SO STUPID...
LOOK WHAT NAMINÉ HAS DONE NOW!
CALM DOWN.
......
WHAT DID SHE SAY TO IT?

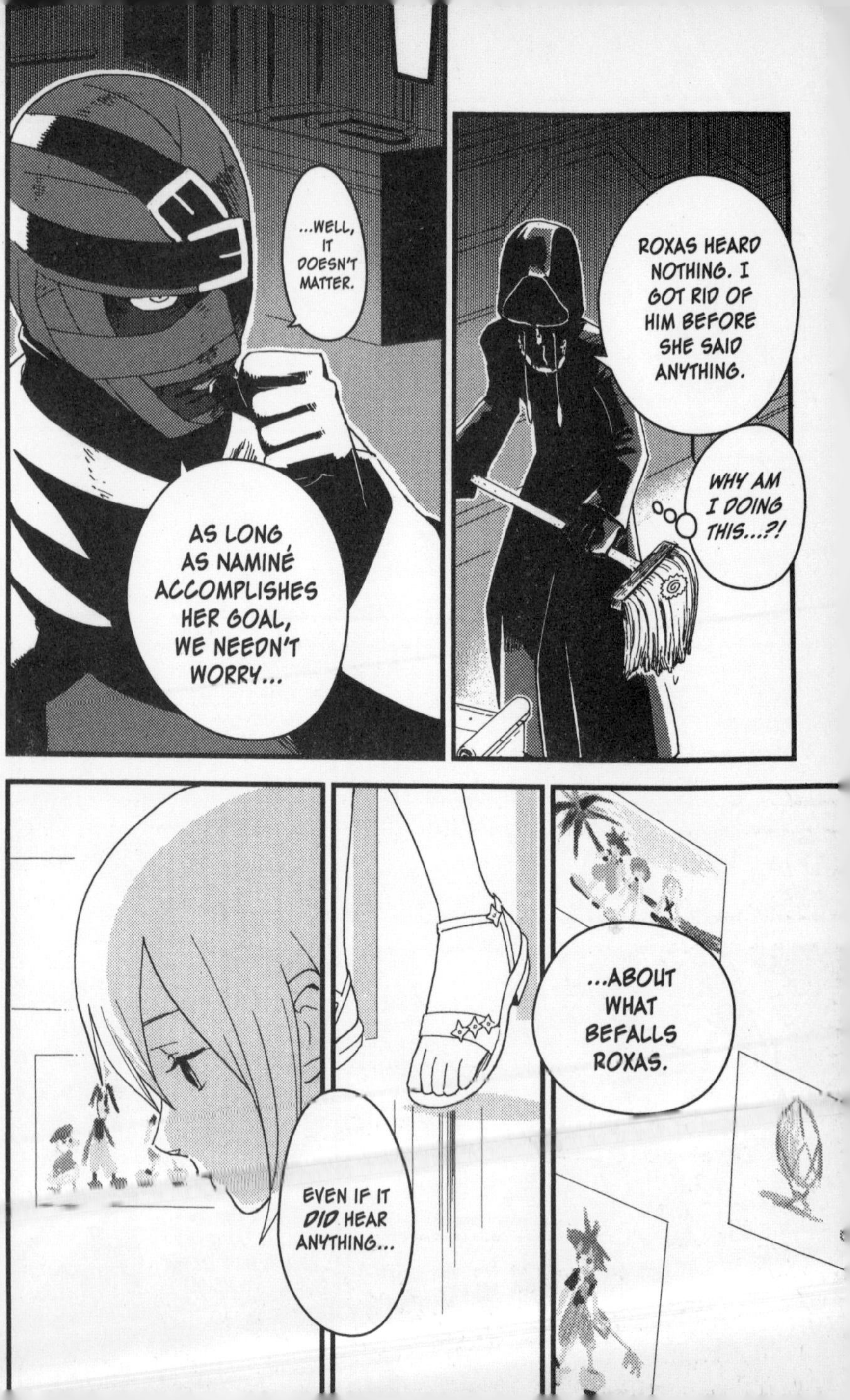
ROXAS HEARD NOTHING. I GOT RID OF HIM BEFORE SHE SAID ANYTHING.
WHY AM I DOING THIS...?!
...WELL, IT DOESN'T MATTER.
AS LONG AS NAMINÉ ACCOMPLISHES HER GOAL, WE NEEDN'T WORRY...
...ABOUT WHAT BEFALLS ROXAS.
EVEN IF IT *DID* HEAR ANYTHING...

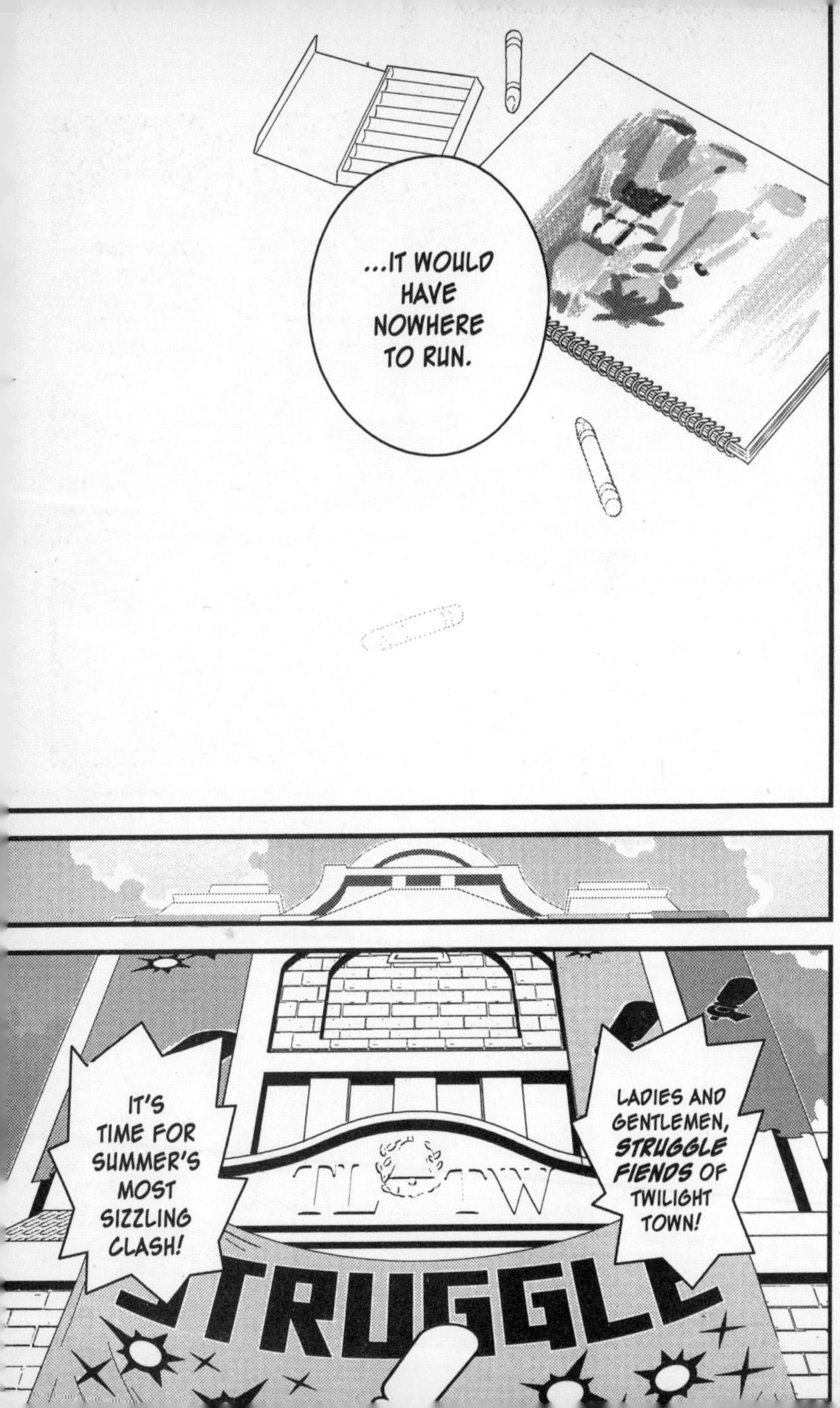
...IT WOULD HAVE NOWHERE TO RUN.
LADIES AND GENTLEMEN, STRUGGLE FIENDS OF TWILIGHT TOWN!
IT'S TIME FOR SUMMER'S MOST SIZZLING CLASH!

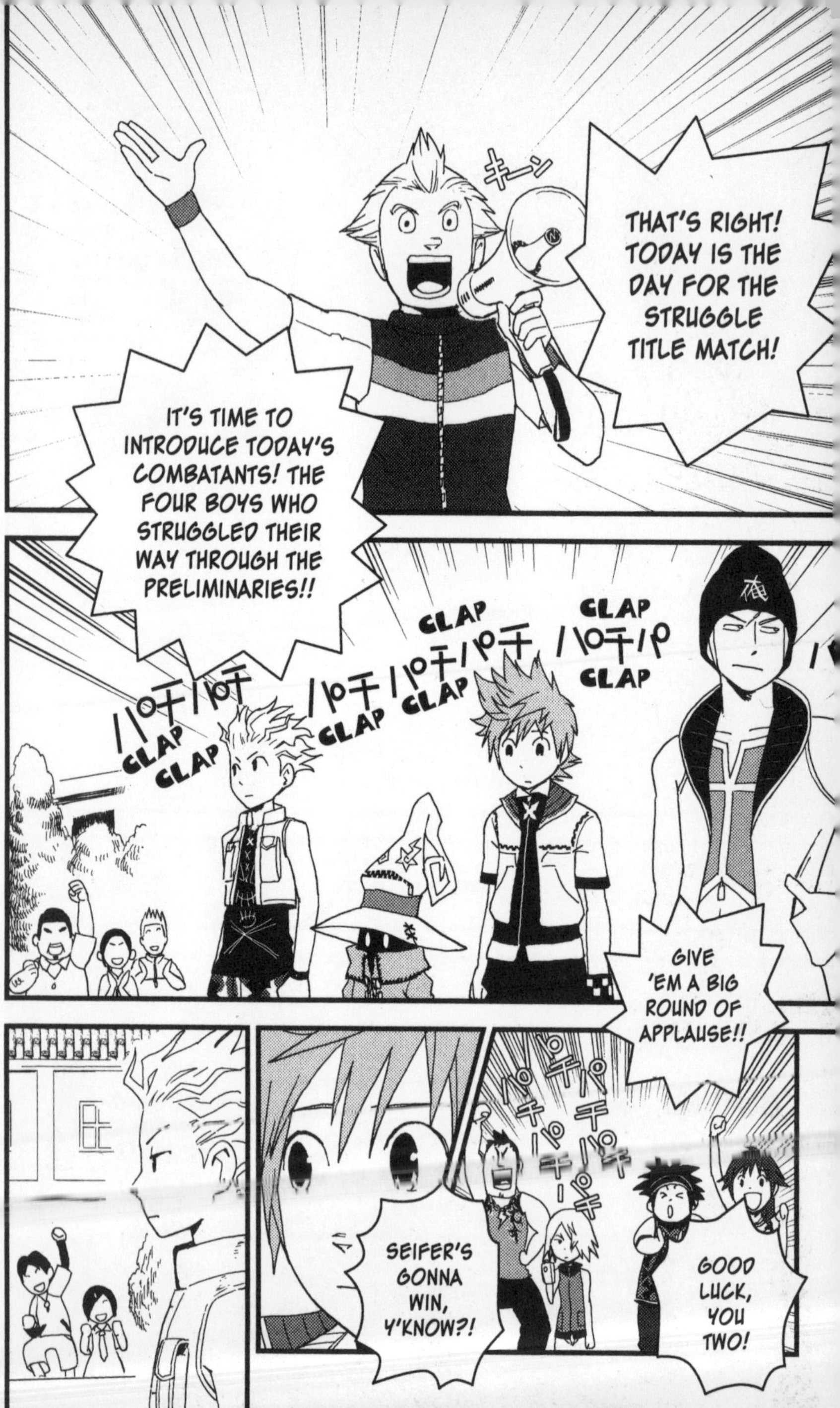

THAT'S RIGHT! TODAY IS THE DAY FOR THE STRUGGLE TITLE MATCH!
キーン
IT'S TIME TO INTRODUCE TODAY'S COMBATANTS! THE FOUR BOYS WHO STRUGGLED THEIR WAY THROUGH THE PRELIMINARIES!!
パチパチ
CLAP
CLAP
パチパチ
CLAP
CLAP
パチパチ
CLAP
CLAP
パチパチ
CLAP
CLAP
GIVE 'EM A BIG ROUND OF APPLAUSE!!
GOOD LUCK, YOU TWO!
SEIFER'S GONNA WIN, Y'KNOW?!

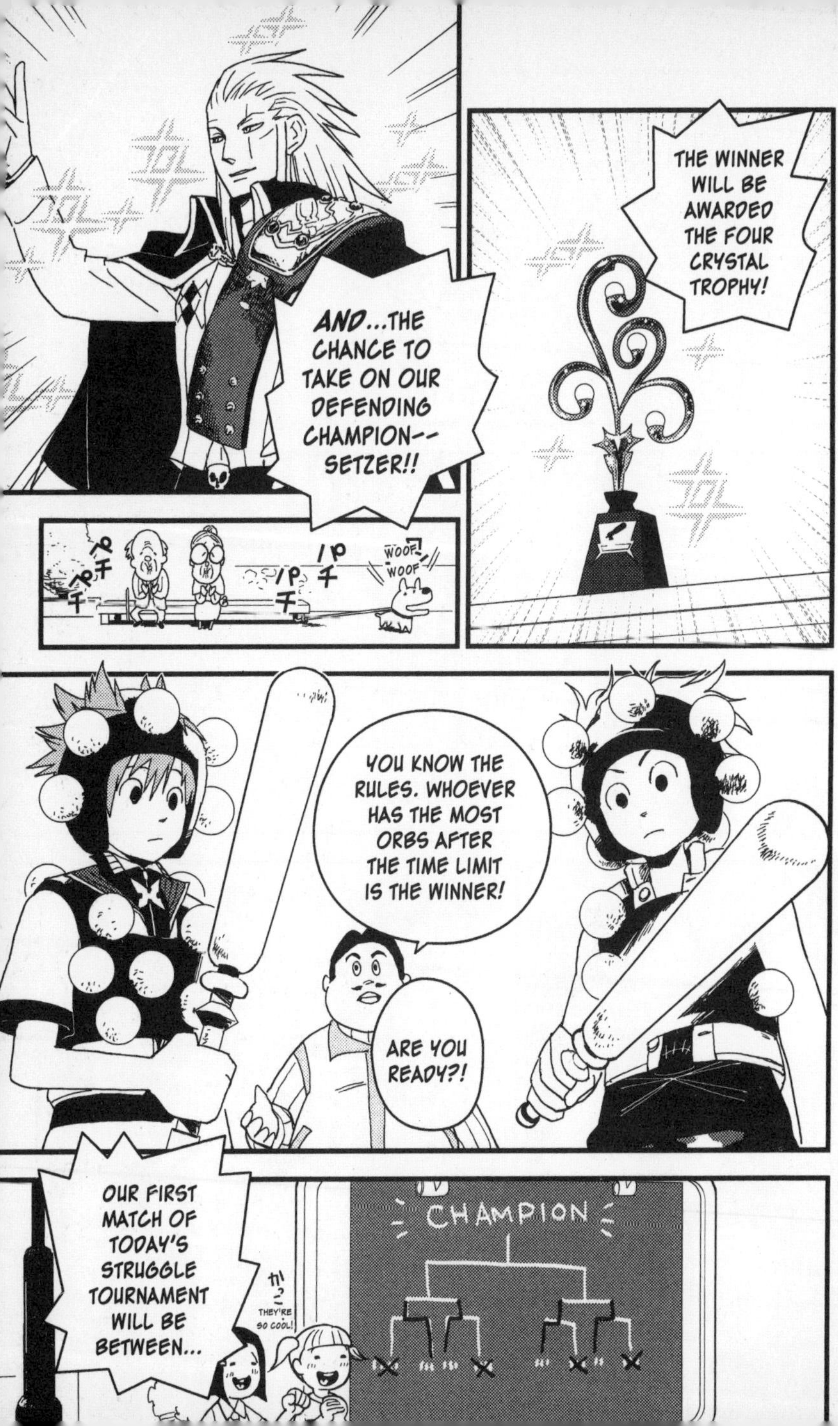

THE WINNER WILL BE AWARDED THE FOUR CRYSTAL TROPHY!
AND...THE CHANCE TO TAKE ON OUR DEFENDING CHAMPION--SETZER!!
WOOF WOOF
YOU KNOW THE RULES. WHOEVER HAS THE MOST ORBS AFTER THE TIME LIMIT IS THE WINNER!
ARE YOU READY?!
CHAMPION
THEY'RE SO COOL!
OUR FIRST MATCH OF TODAY'S STRUGGLE TOURNAMENT WILL BE BETWEEN...

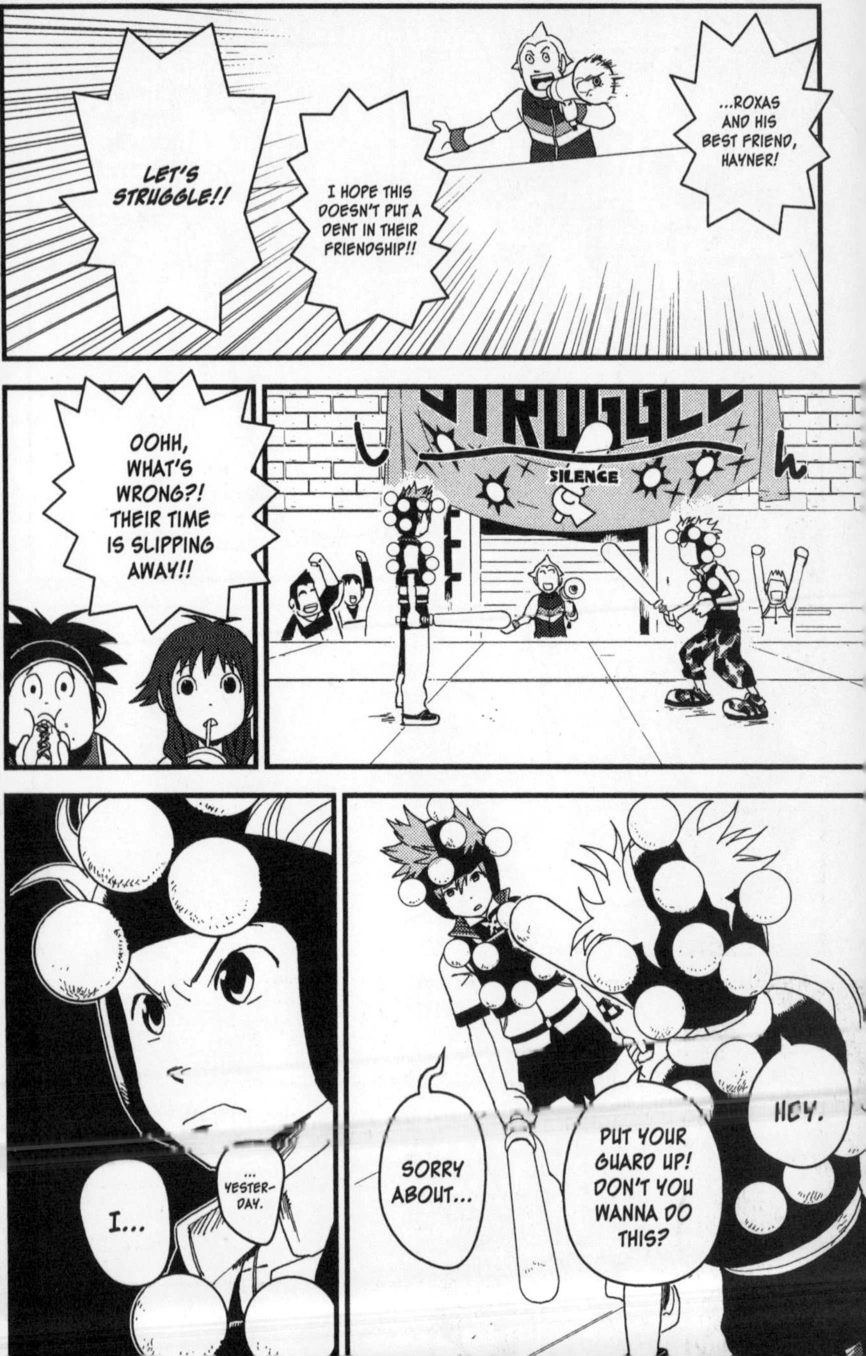
...ROXAS AND HIS BEST FRIEND, HAYNER!
I HOPE THIS DOESN'T PUT A DENT IN THEIR FRIENDSHIP!!
LET'S STRUGGLE!!
SILENCE
OOHH, WHAT'S WRONG?! THEIR TIME IS SLIPPING AWAY!!
HEY.
PUT YOUR GUARD UP! DON'T YOU WANNA DO THIS?
SORRY ABOUT...
...YESTER-DAY.
I...

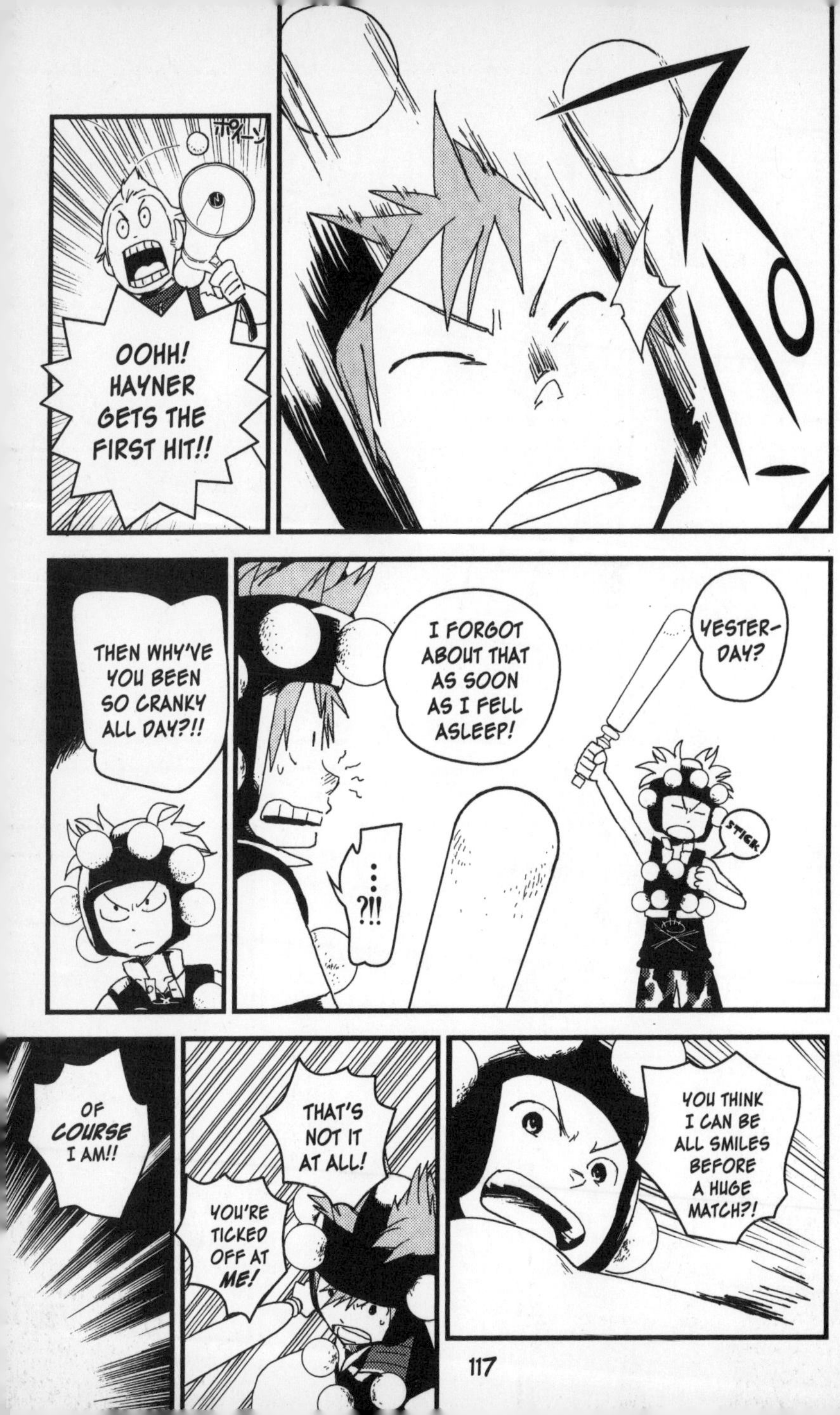
ポイーン
OOHH! HAYNER GETS THE FIRST HIT!!
YESTER-DAY?
STICK
I FORGOT ABOUT THAT AS SOON AS I FELL ASLEEP!
...?!!
THEN WHY'VE YOU BEEN SO CRANKY ALL DAY?!!
YOU THINK I CAN BE ALL SMILES BEFORE A HUGE MATCH?!
THAT'S NOT IT AT ALL!
YOU'RE TICKED OFF AT ME!
OF COURSE I AM!!

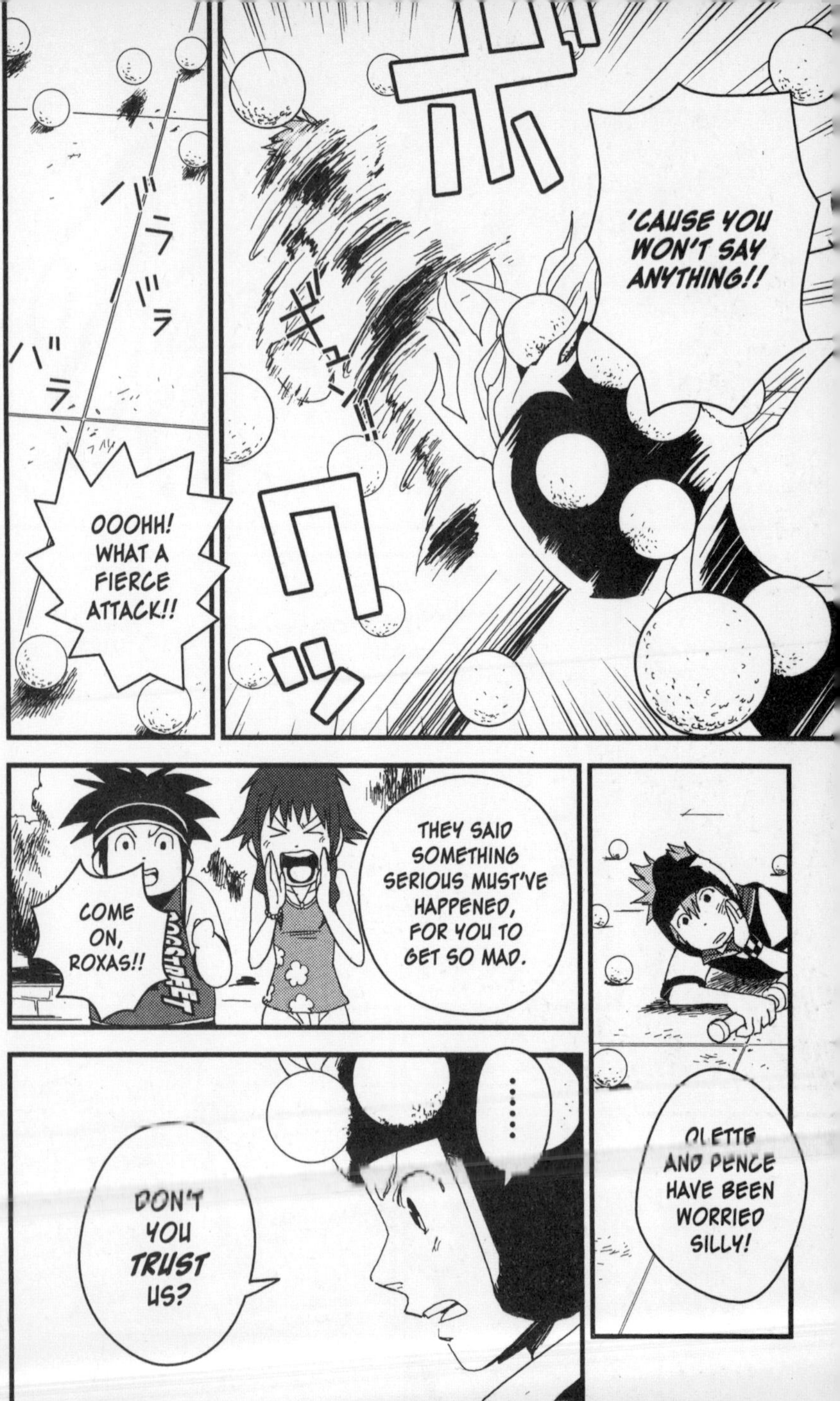
'CAUSE YOU WON'T SAY ANYTHING!!
OOOHH! WHAT A FIERCE ATTACK!!
OLETTE AND PENCE HAVE BEEN WORRIED SILLY!
THEY SAID SOMETHING SERIOUS MUST'VE HAPPENED, FOR YOU TO GET SO MAD.
COME ON, ROXAS!!
......
DON'T YOU TRUST US?

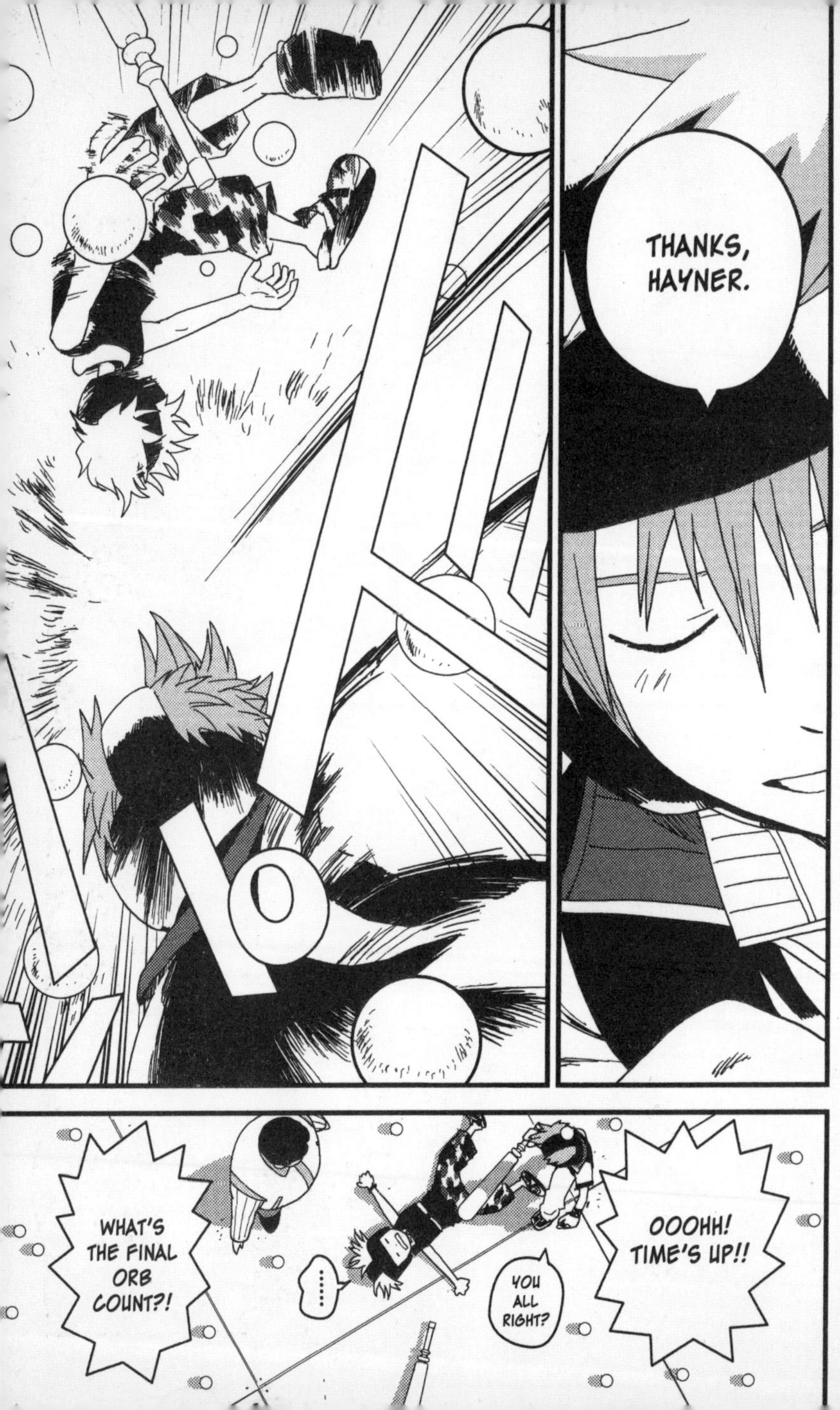
THANKS, HAYNER.
OOOHH! TIME'S UP!!
YOU ALL RIGHT?
......
WHAT'S THE FINAL ORB COUNT?!

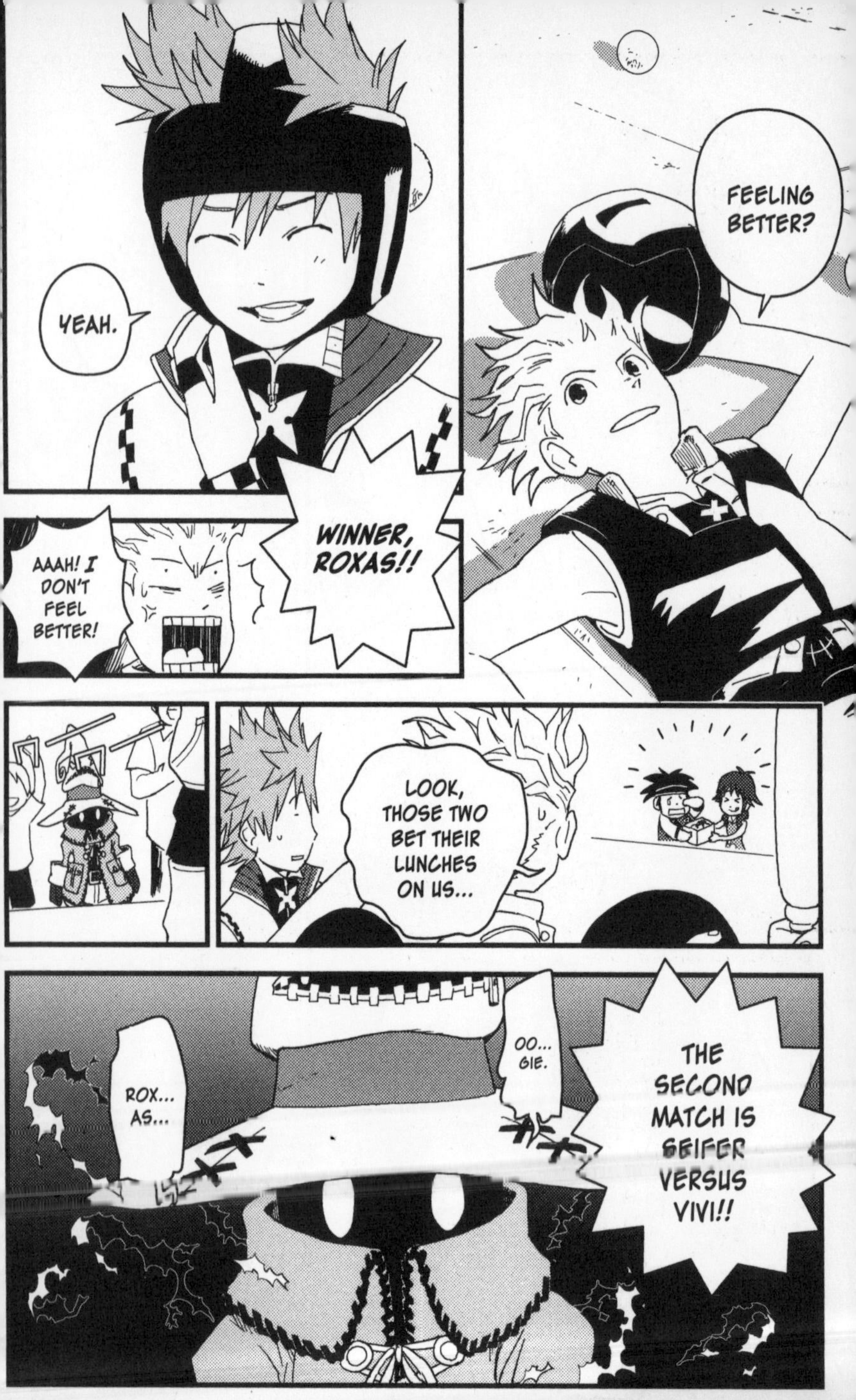
FEELING BETTER?
YEAH.
WINNER, ROXAS!!
AAAH! I DON'T FEEL BETTER!
LOOK, THOSE TWO BET THEIR LUNCHES ON US...
THE SECOND MATCH IS SEIFER VERSUS VIVI!!
OO... GIE.
ROX... AS...

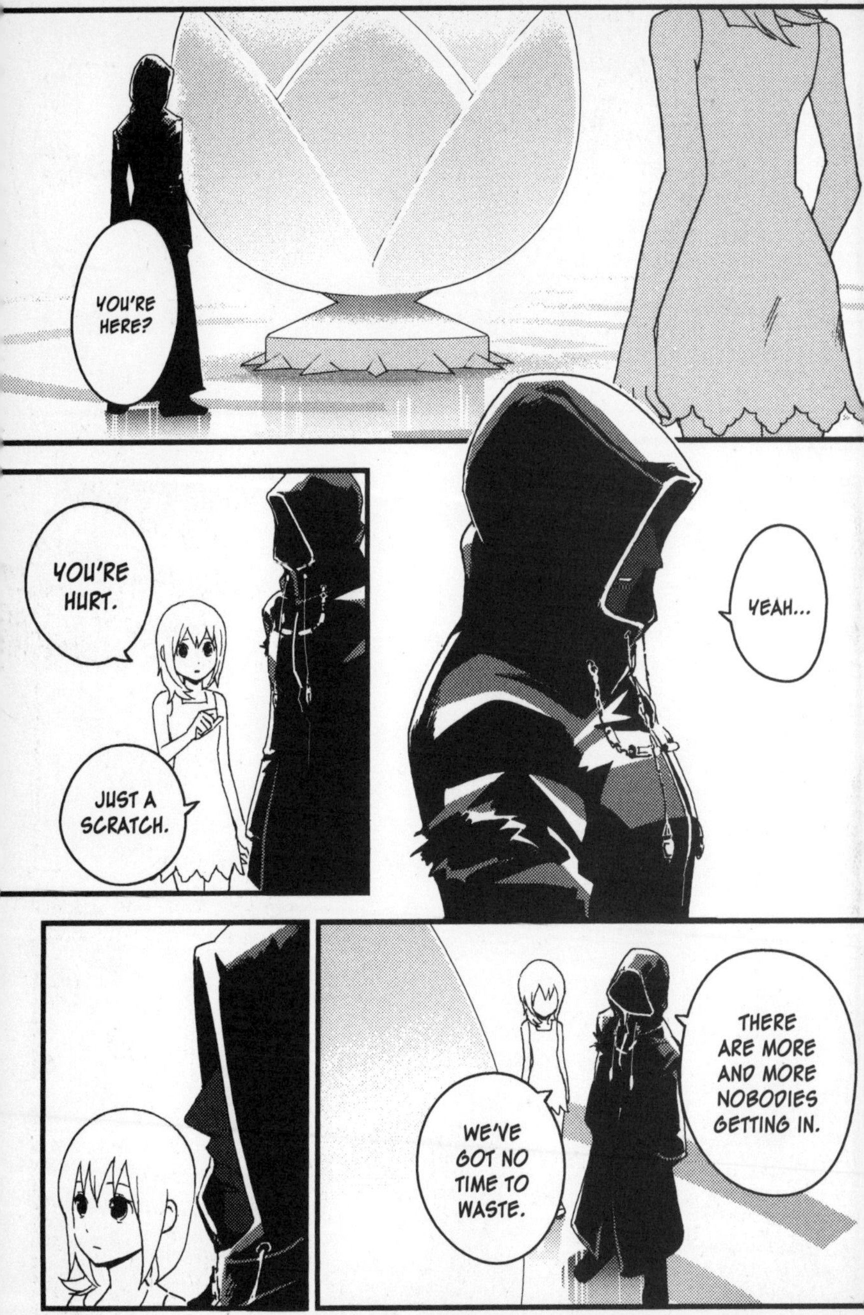
YOU'RE HERE?
YEAH...
YOU'RE HURT.
JUST A SCRATCH.
THERE ARE MORE AND MORE NOBODIES GETTING IN.
WE'VE GOT NO TIME TO WASTE.

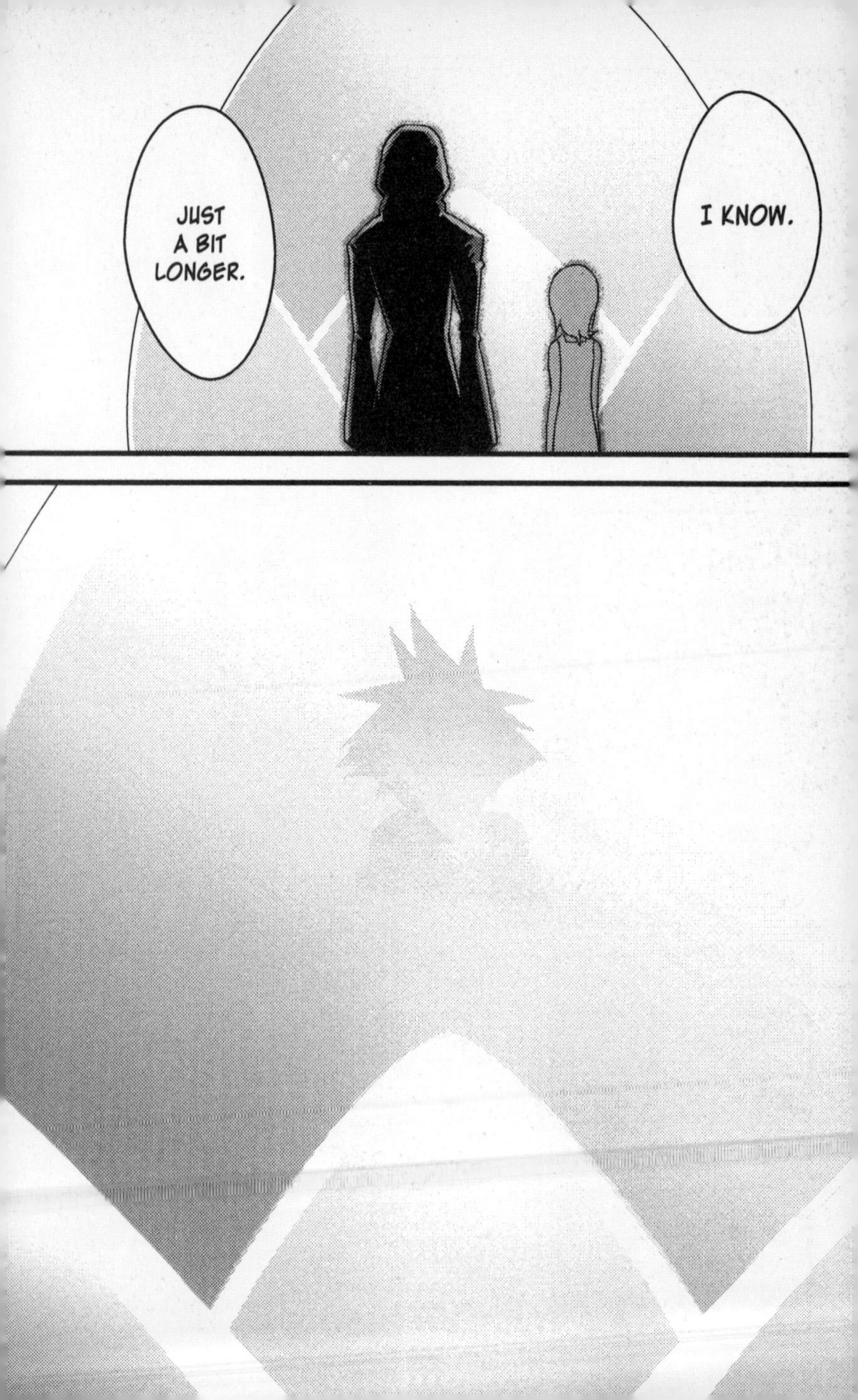
I KNOW.
JUST A BIT LONGER.

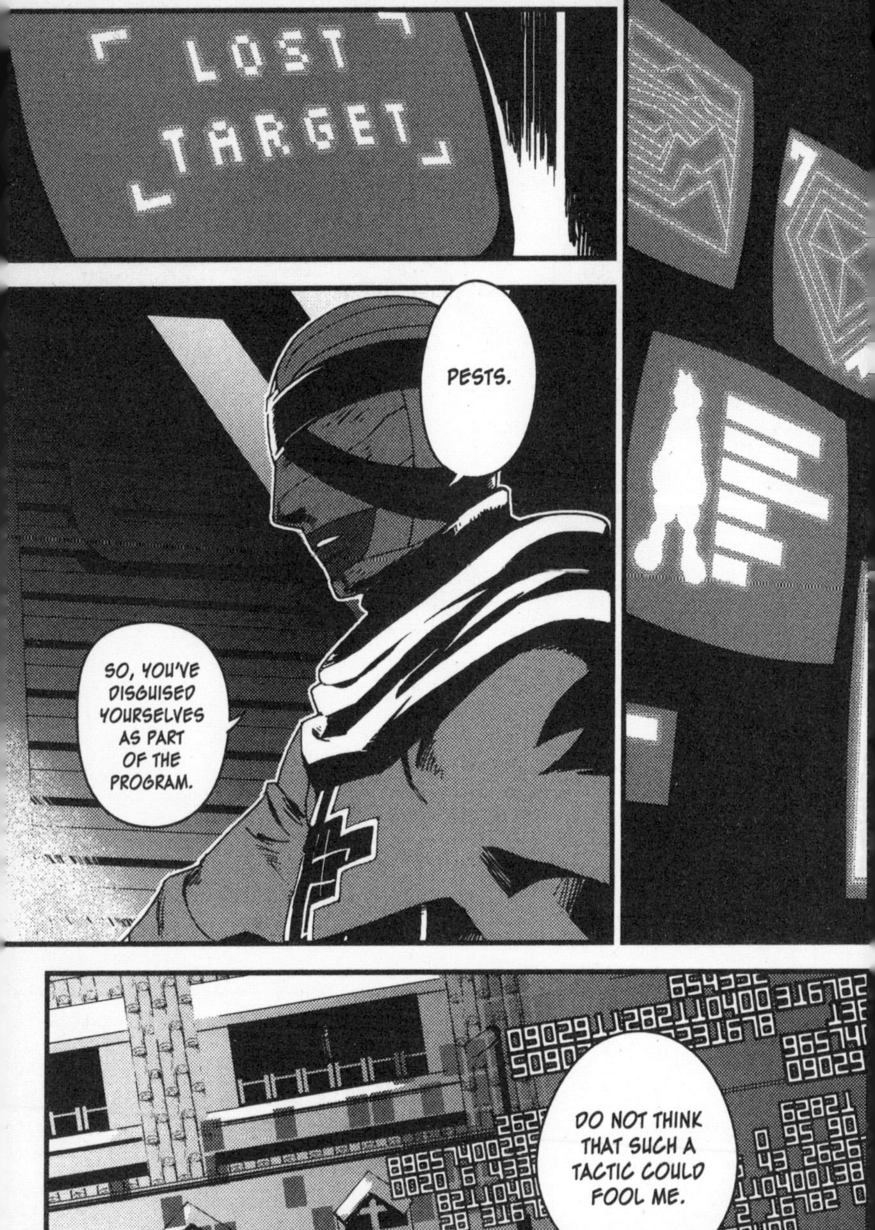
LOST TARGET
PESTS.
SO, YOU'VE DISGUISED YOURSELVES AS PART OF THE PROGRAM.
DO NOT THINK THAT SUCH A TACTIC COULD FOOL ME.

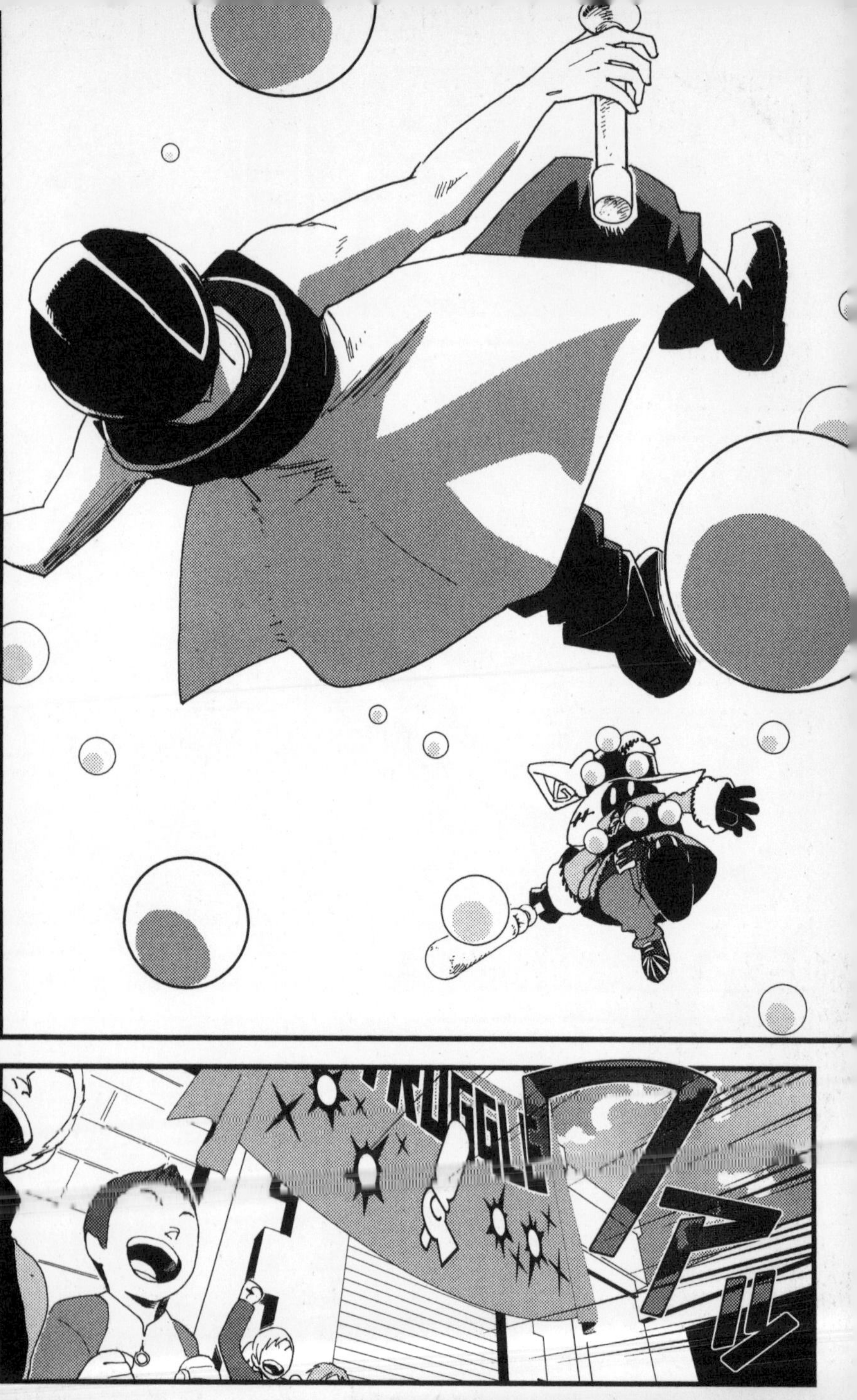
NUGGLE
ワァッ

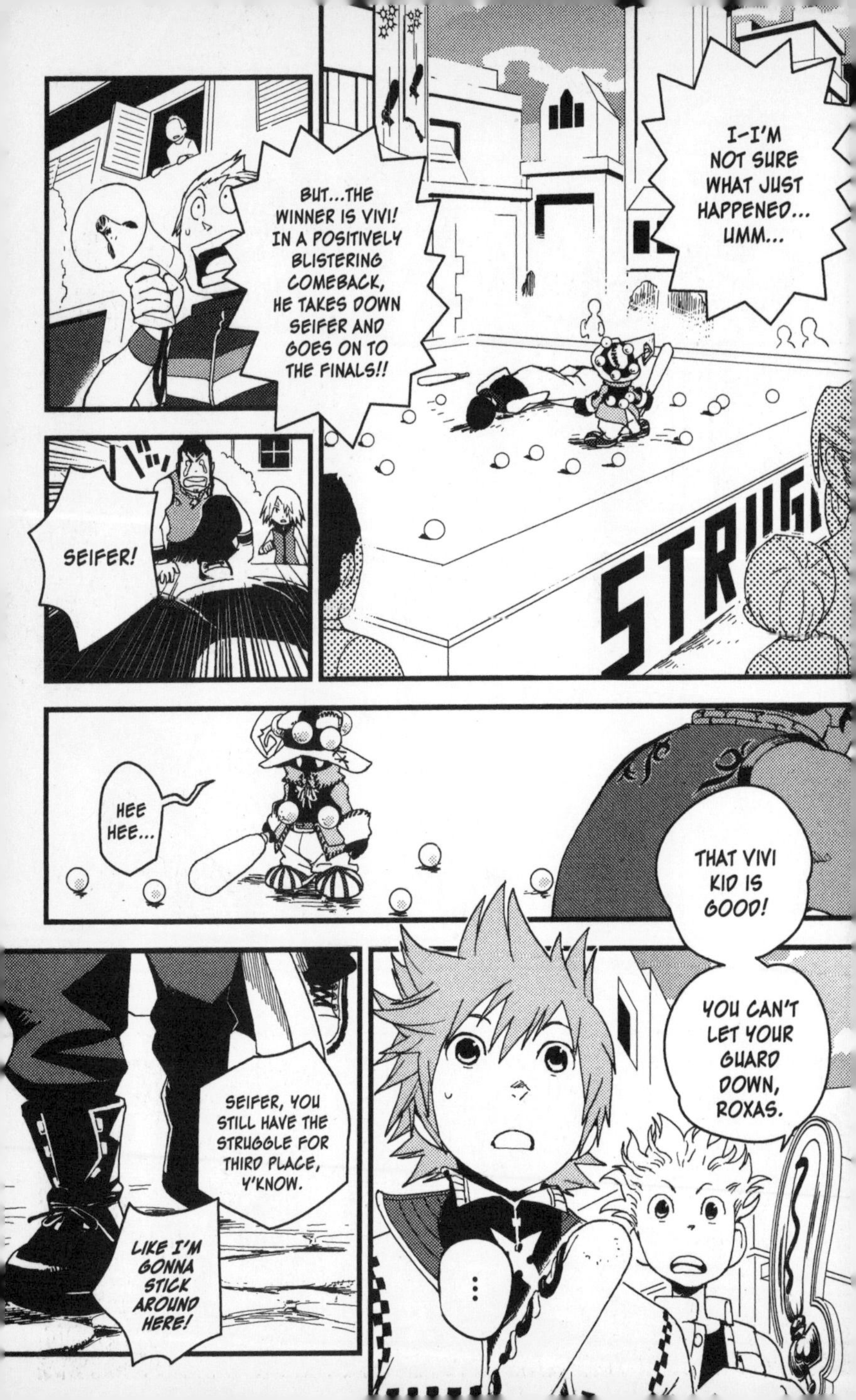

I-I'M NOT SURE WHAT JUST HAPPENED... UMM...
BUT...THE WINNER IS VIVI! IN A POSITIVELY BLISTERING COMEBACK, HE TAKES DOWN SEIFER AND GOES ON TO THE FINALS!!
SEIFER!
HEE HEE...
THAT VIVI KID IS GOOD!
YOU CAN'T LET YOUR GUARD DOWN, ROXAS.
...
SEIFER, YOU STILL HAVE THE STRUGGLE FOR THIRD PLACE, Y'KNOW.
LIKE I'M GONNA STICK AROUND HERE!

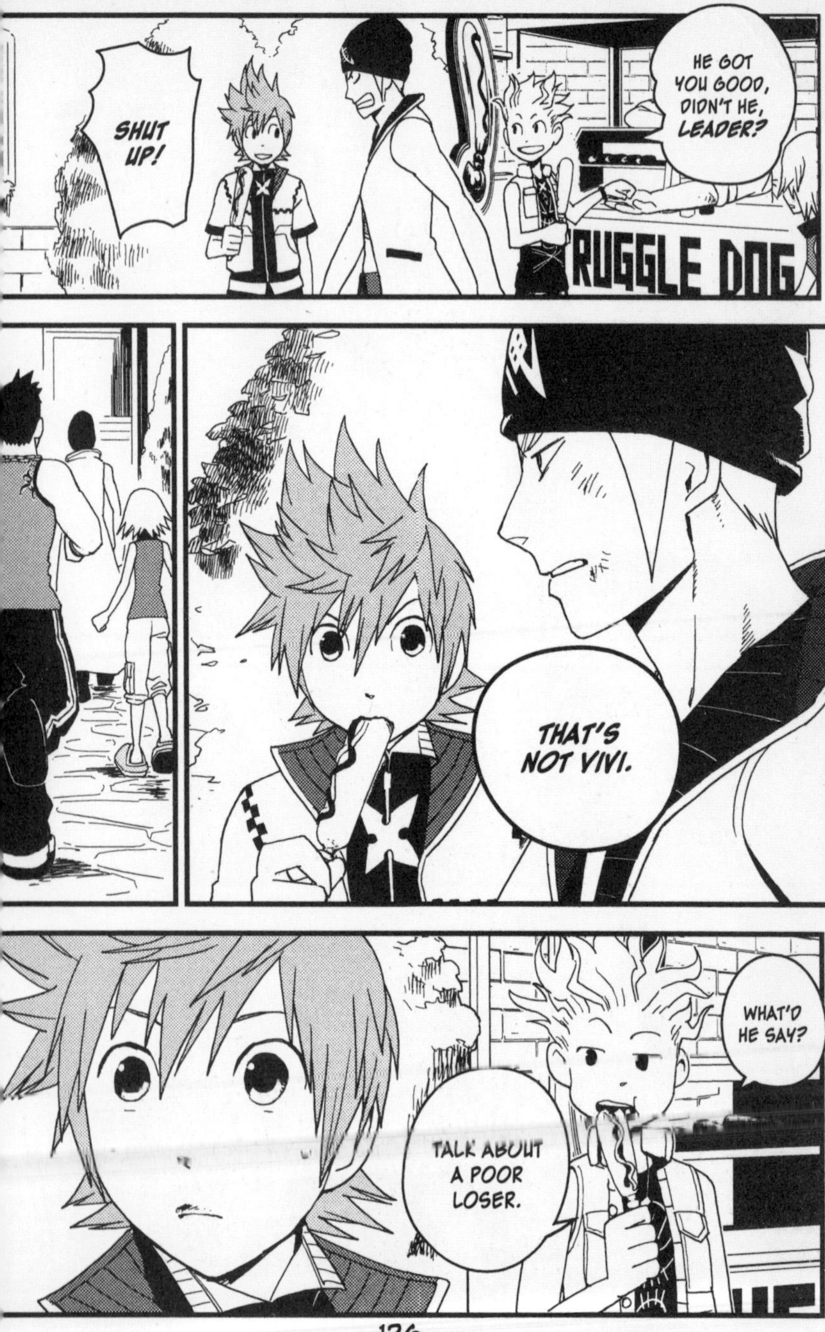
HE GOT YOU GOOD, DIDN'T HE, LEADER?
RUGGLE DOG
SHUT UP!
THAT'S NOT VIVI.
WHAT'D HE SAY?
TALK ABOUT A POOR LOSER.

Chapter 5: No. XIII

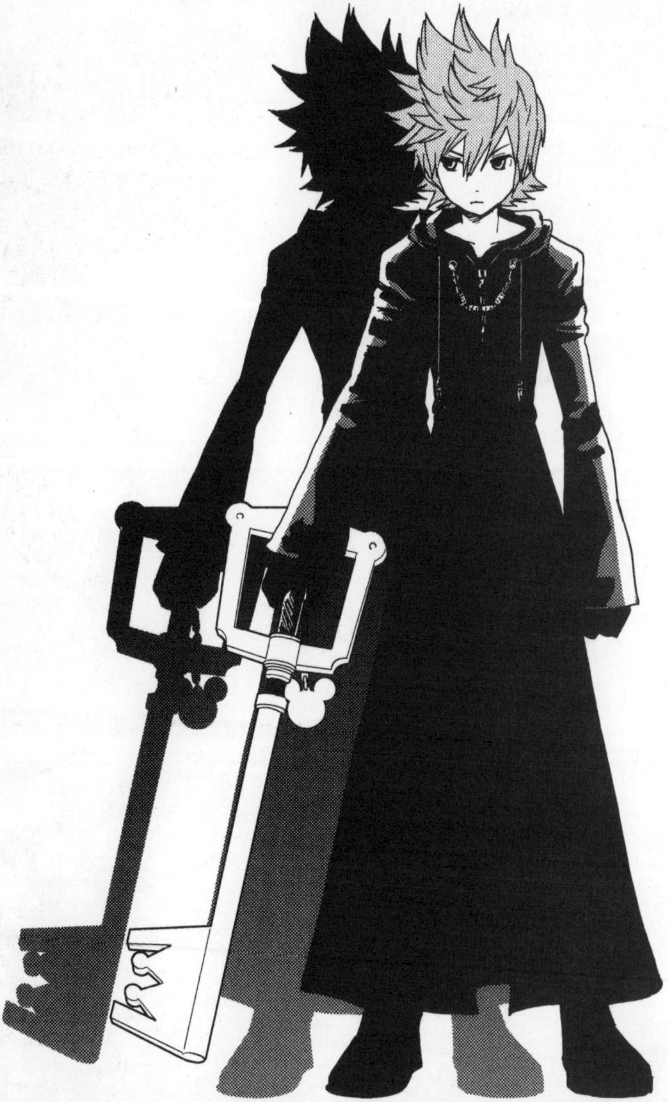

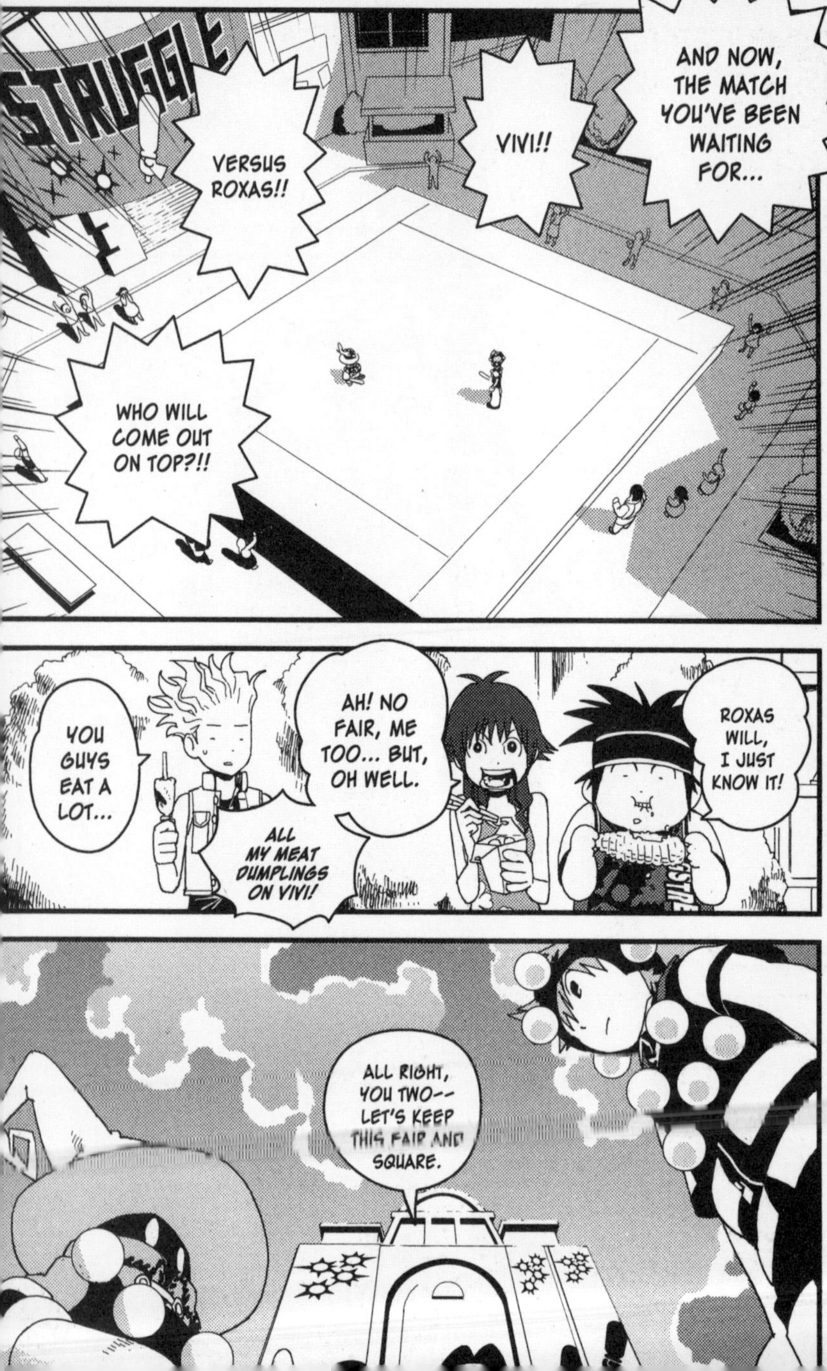

AND NOW, THE MATCH YOU'VE BEEN WAITING FOR...
VIVI!!
VERSUS ROXAS!!
STRUGGLE
WHO WILL COME OUT ON TOP?!!
ROXAS WILL, I JUST KNOW IT!
AH! NO FAIR, ME TOO... BUT, OH WELL.
ALL MY MEAT DUMPLINGS ON VIVI!
YOU GUYS EAT A LOT...
ALL RIGHT, YOU TWO-- LET'S KEEP THIS FAIR AND SQUARE.

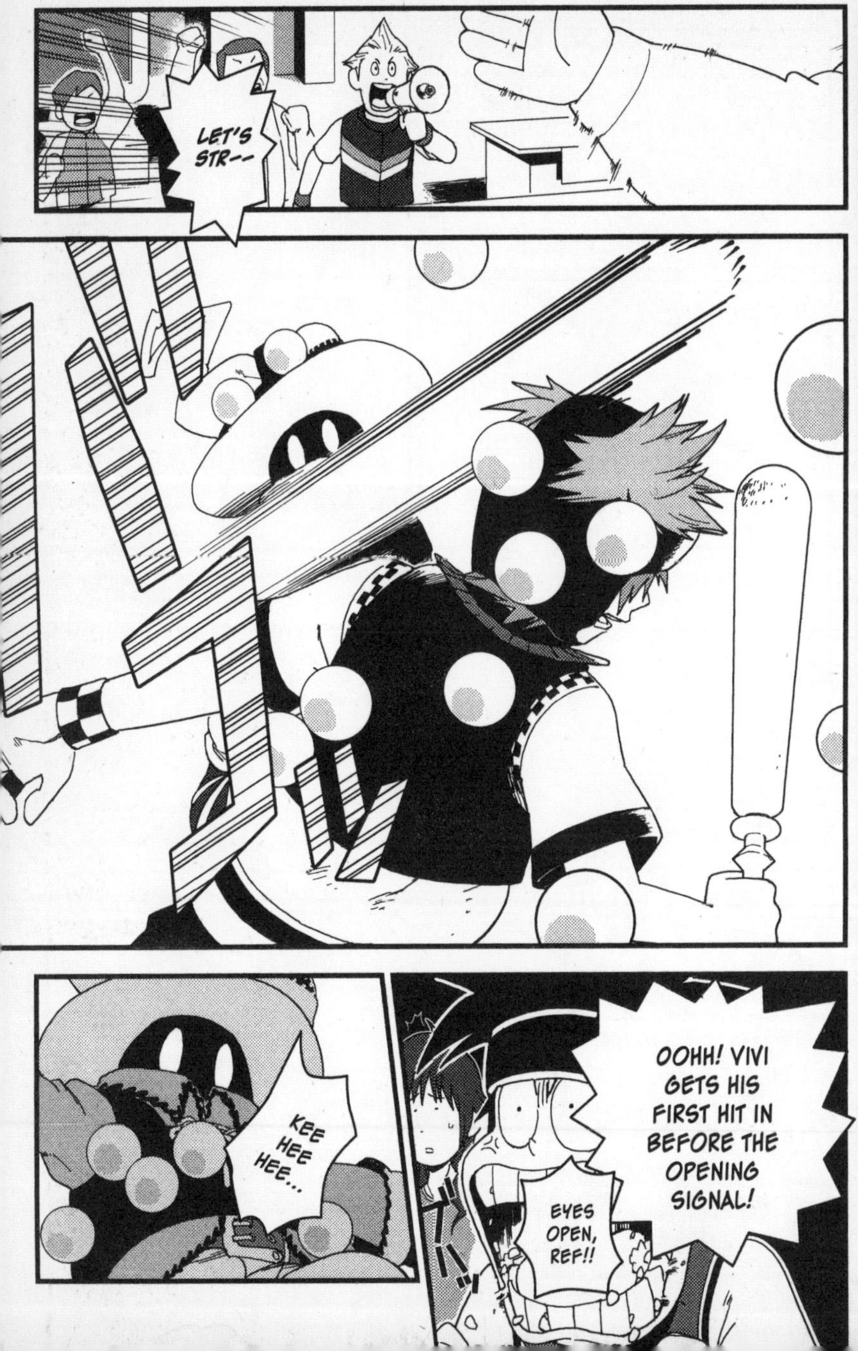
LET'S STR--
OOHH! VIVI GETS HIS FIRST HIT IN BEFORE THE OPENING SIGNAL!
EYES OPEN, REF!!
KEE HEE HEE...

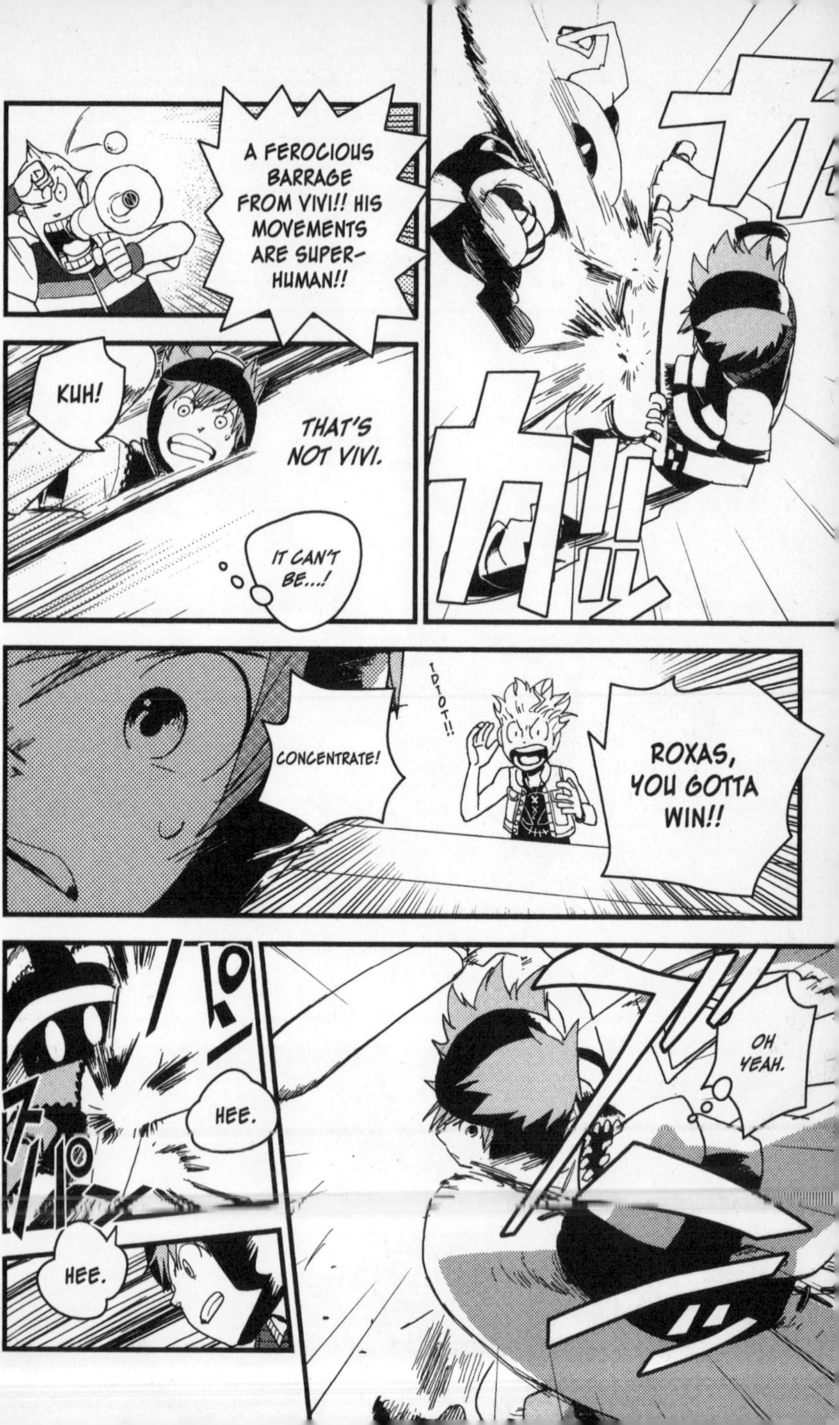
A FEROCIOUS BARRAGE FROM VIVI!! HIS MOVEMENTS ARE SUPER-HUMAN!!
KUH!
THAT'S NOT VIVI.
IT CAN'T BE...!
ROXAS, YOU GOTTA WIN!!
IDIOT!!
CONCENTRATE!
OH YEAH.
HEE.
HEE.

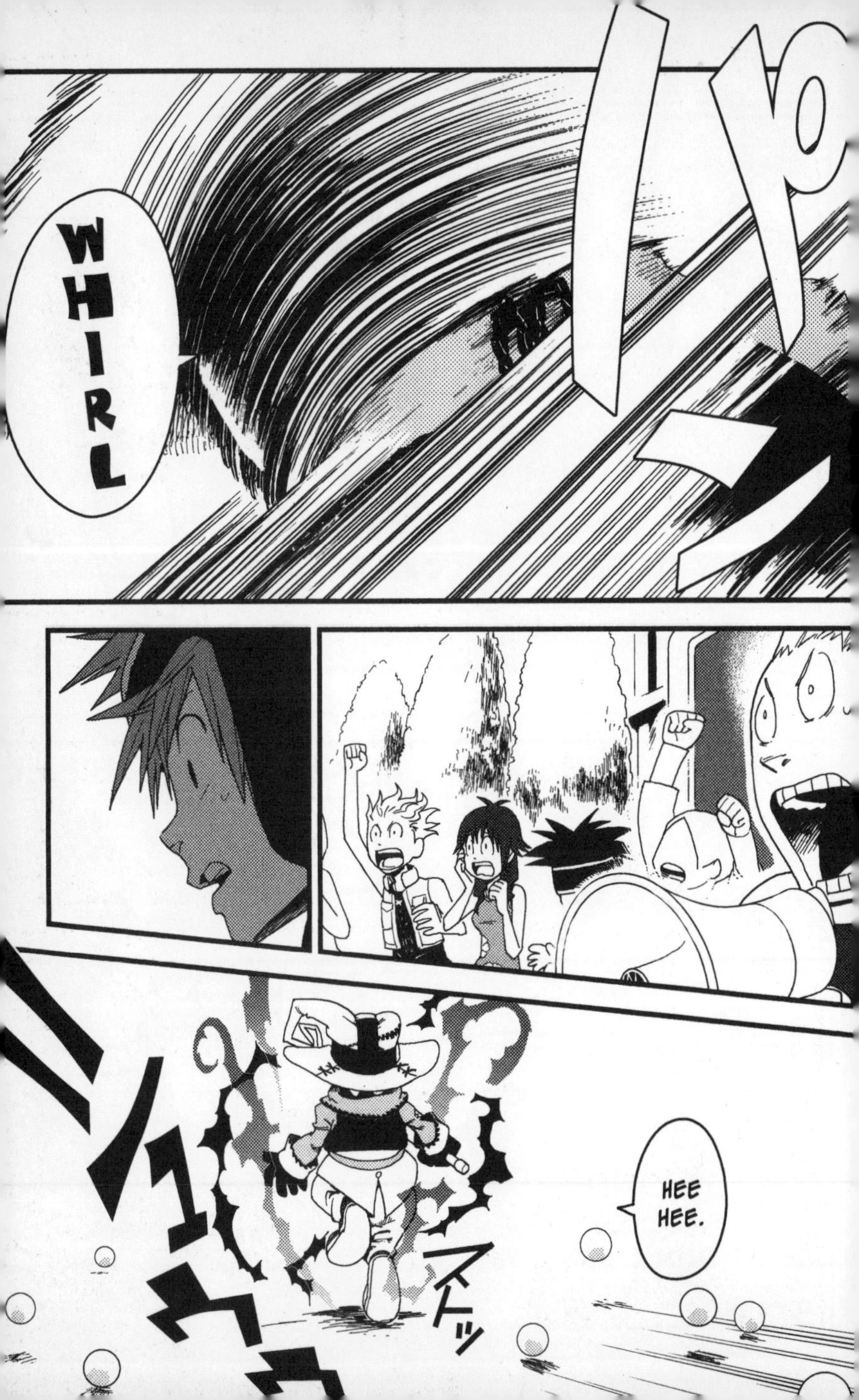
WHIRL
HEE HEE.
ストッ

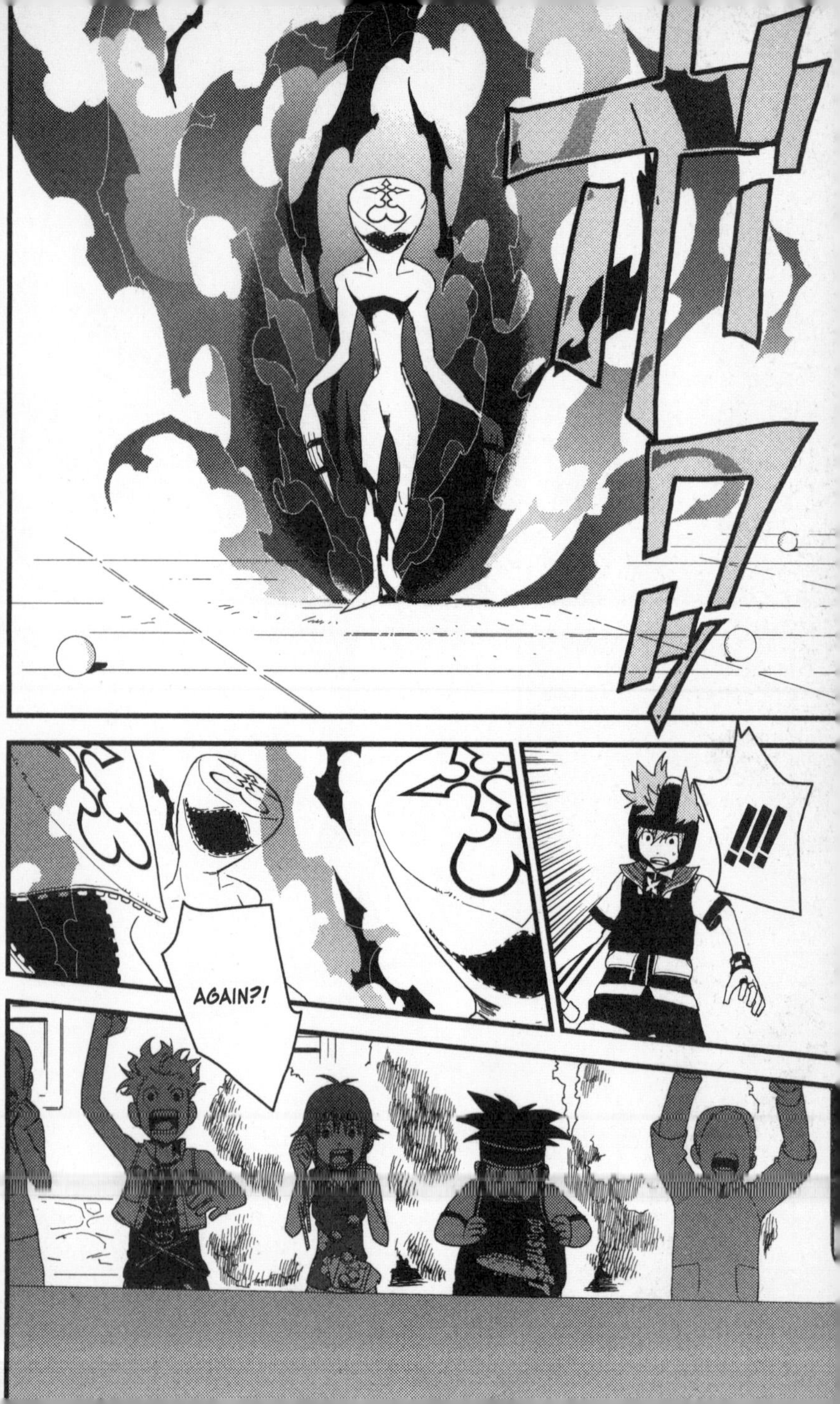
!!!
AGAIN?!

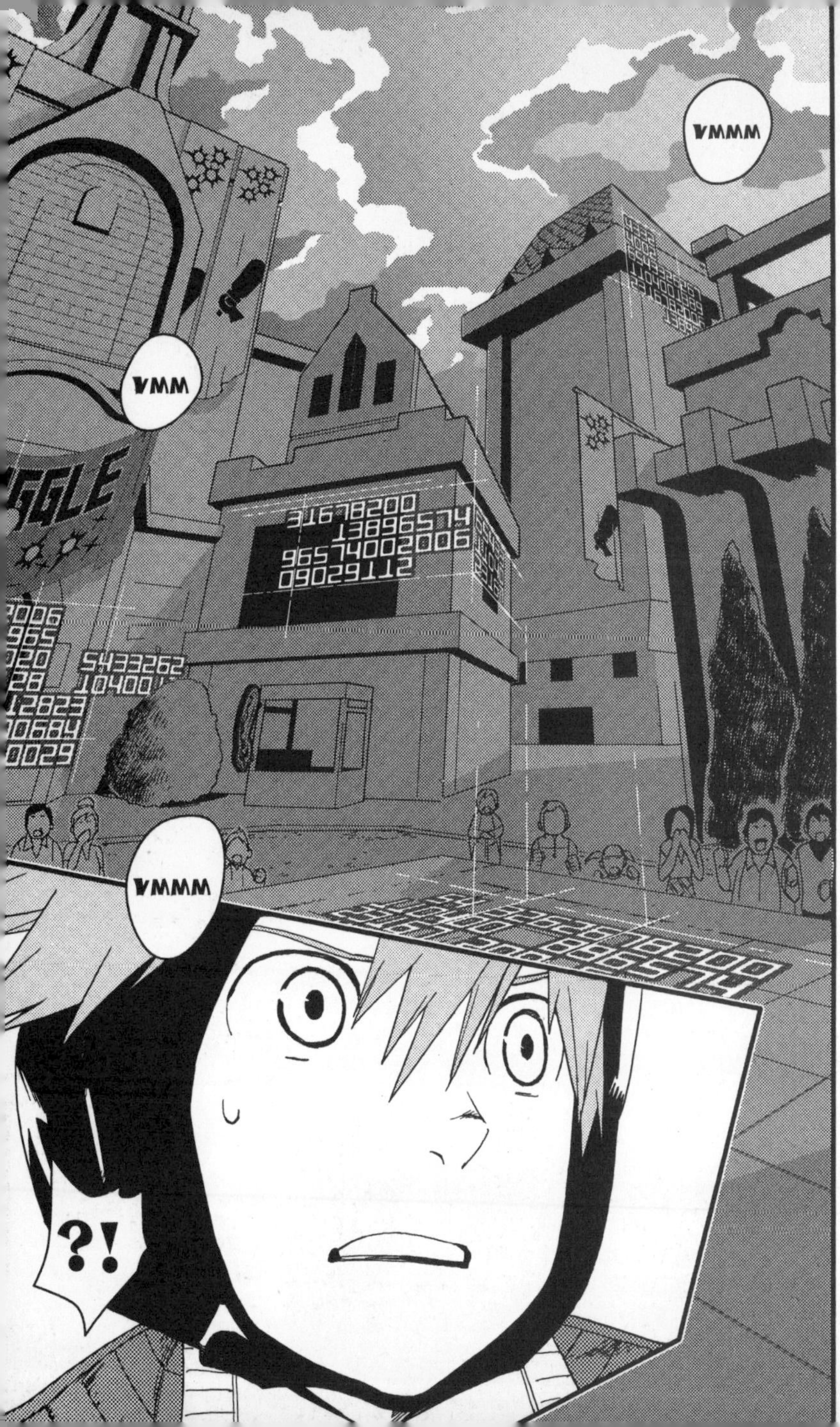
VMMM
VMM
GGLE
VMMM
?!

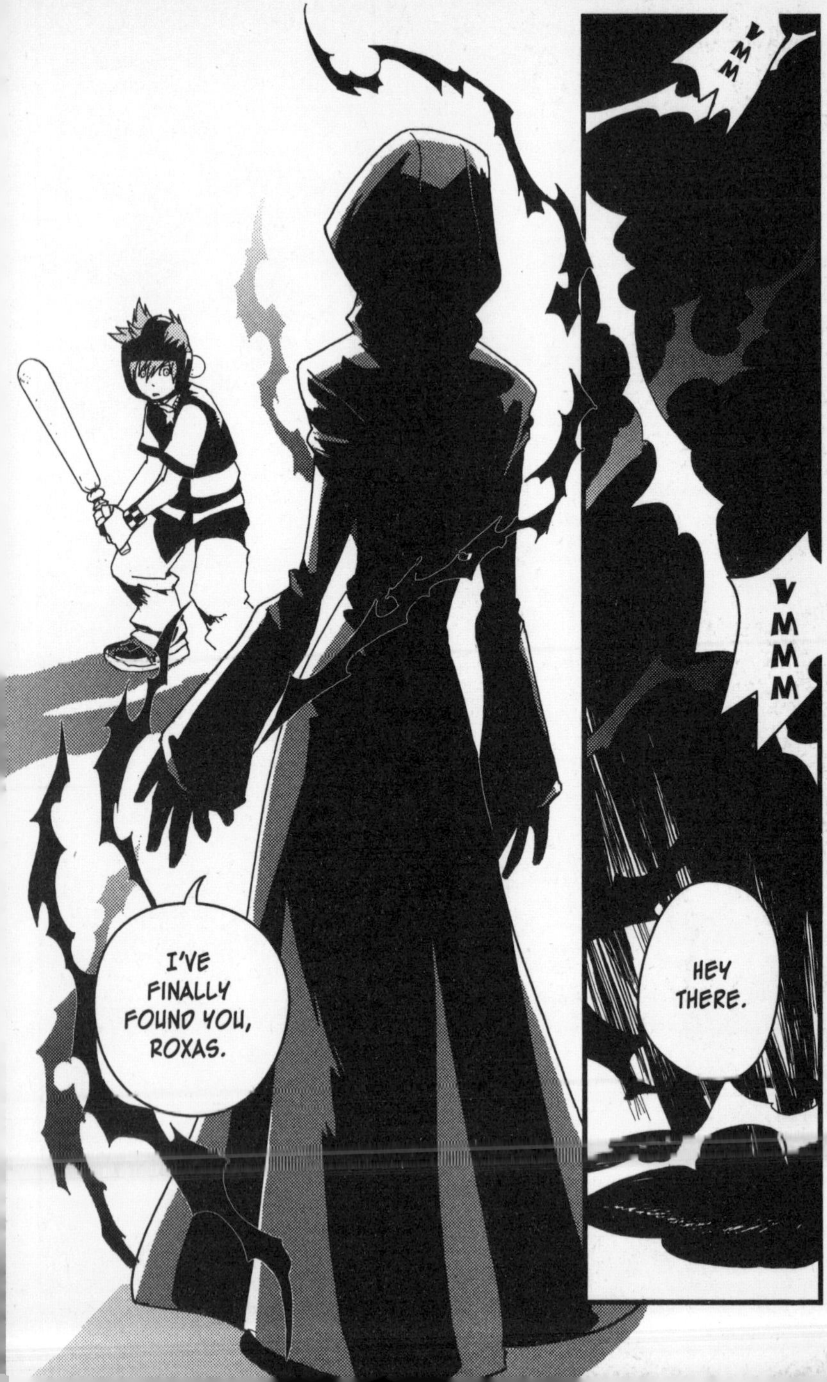
VMMM
HEY THERE.
I'VE FINALLY FOUND YOU, ROXAS.

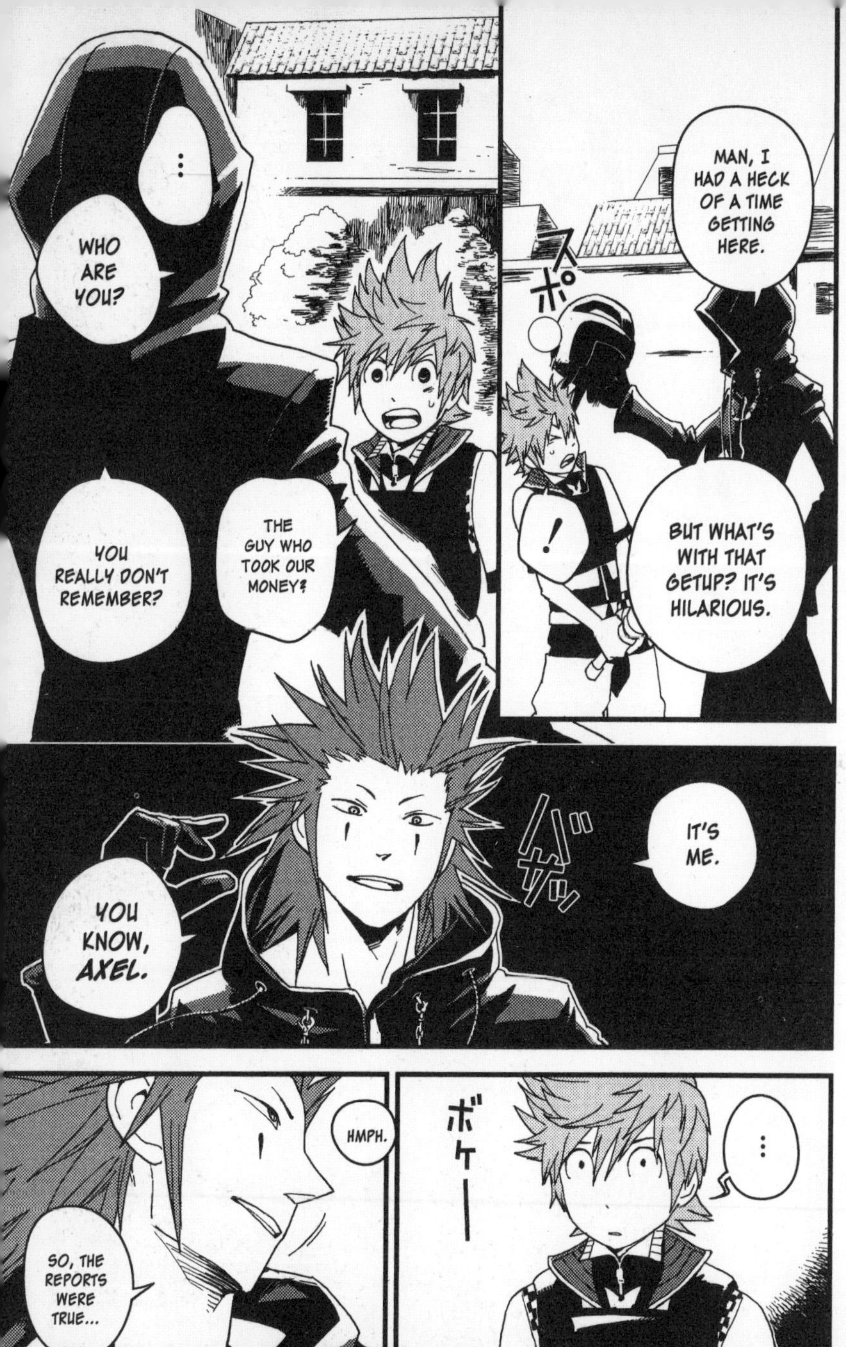
MAN, I HAD A HECK OF A TIME GETTING HERE.
スポ
!
BUT WHAT'S WITH THAT GETUP? IT'S HILARIOUS.
...
WHO ARE YOU?
THE GUY WHO TOOK OUR MONEY?
YOU REALLY DON'T REMEMBER?
IT'S ME.
バサッ
YOU KNOW, AXEL.
ボケー
...
HMPH.
SO, THE REPORTS WERE TRUE...

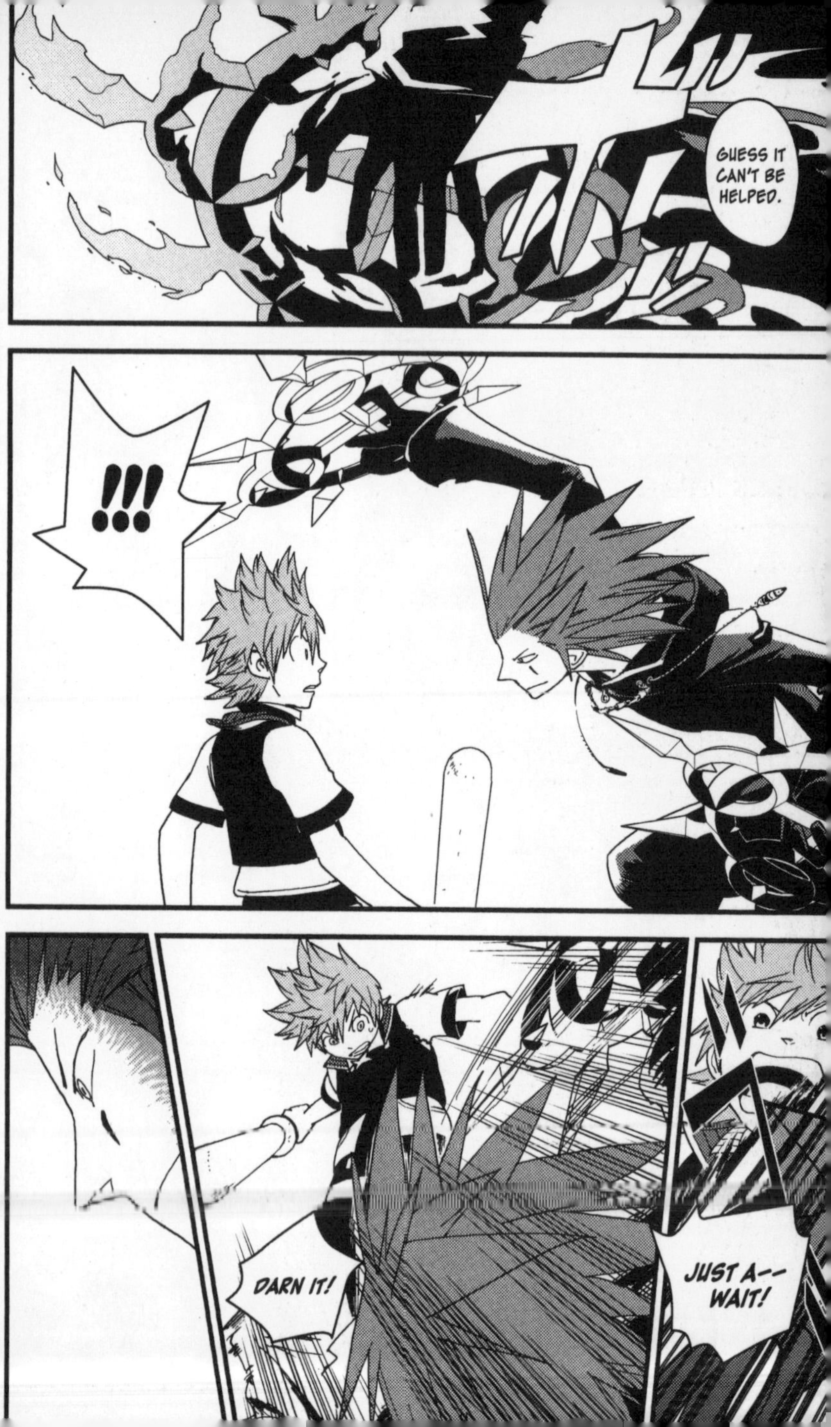
GUESS IT CAN'T BE HELPED.
!!!
JUST A-- WAIT!
DARN IT!

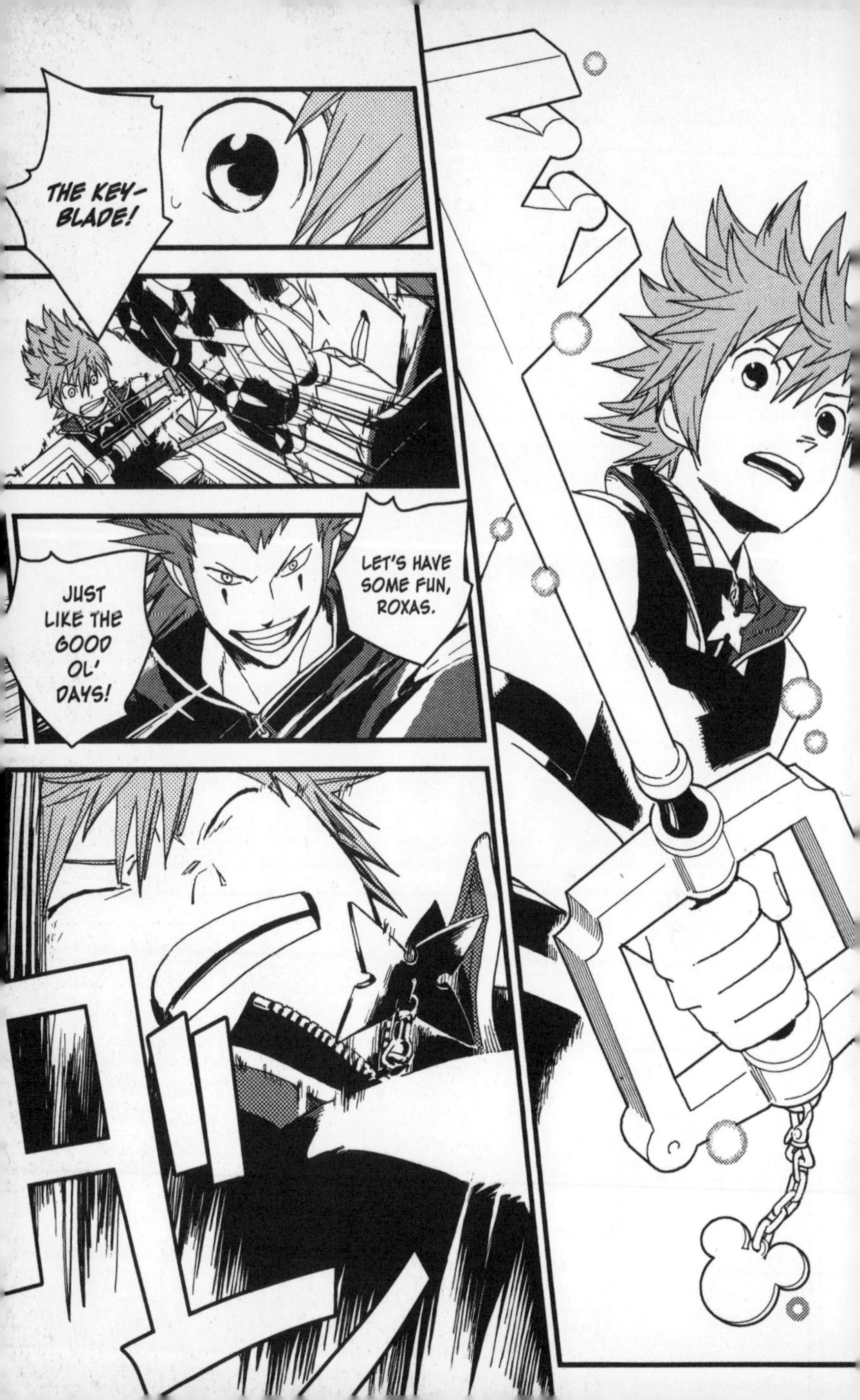
THE KEY-BLADE!
LET'S HAVE SOME FUN, ROXAS.
JUST LIKE THE GOOD OL' DAYS!

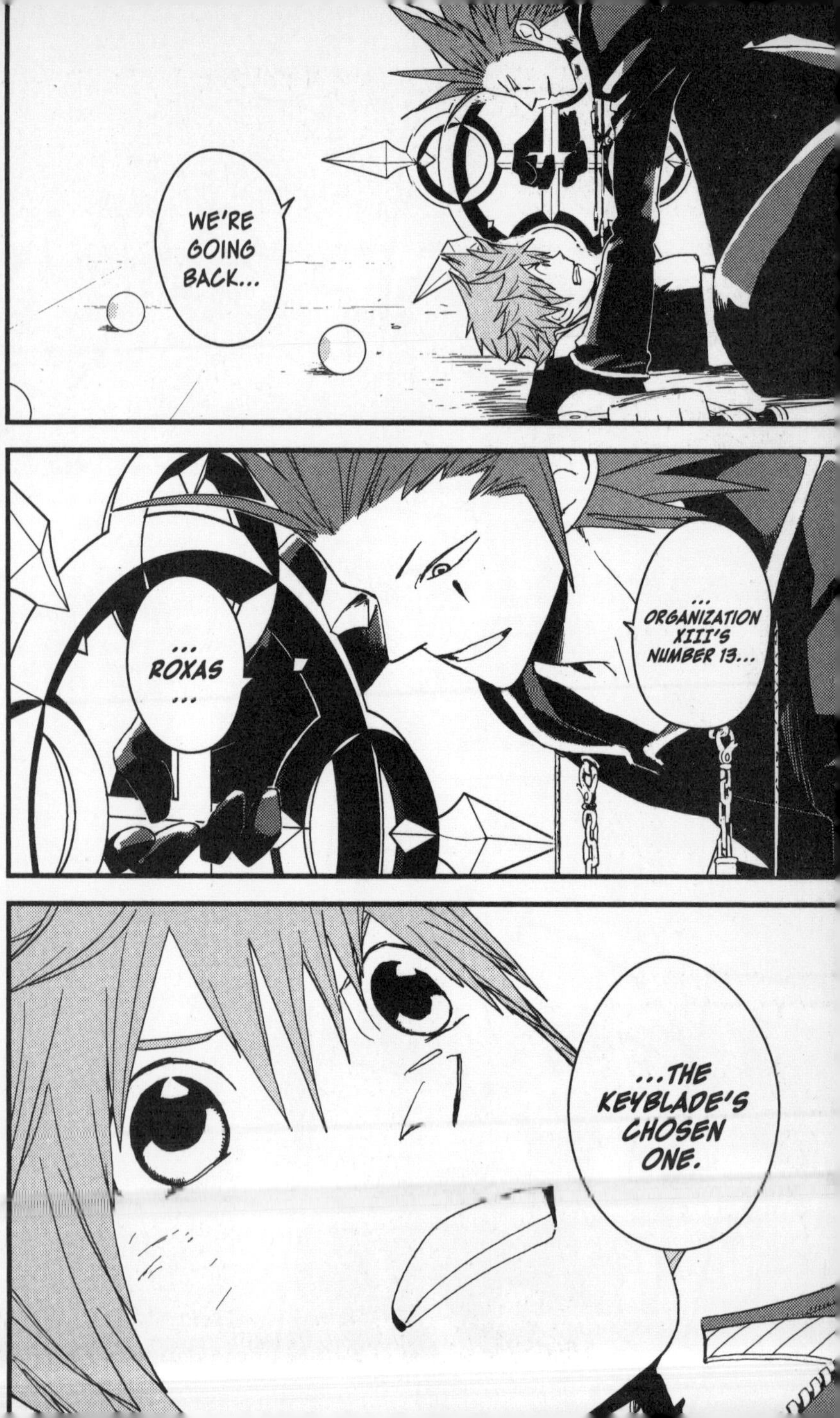
WE'RE GOING BACK...
...ORGANIZATION XIII'S NUMBER 13...
...ROXAS...
...THE KEYBLADE'S CHOSEN ONE.

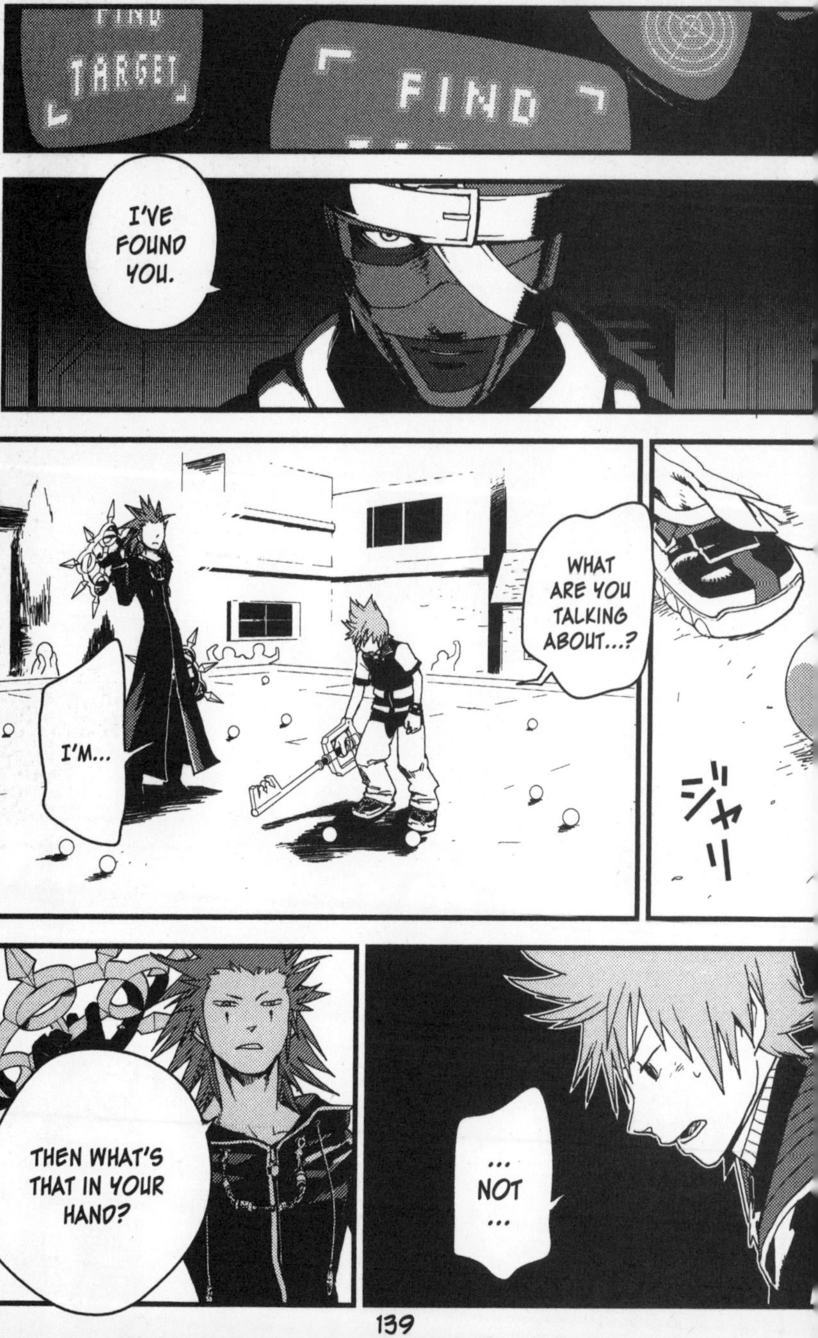
FIND
TARGET
I'VE FOUND YOU.
ジャリ
WHAT ARE YOU TALKING ABOUT...?
I'M...
... NOT ...
THEN WHAT'S THAT IN YOUR HAND?

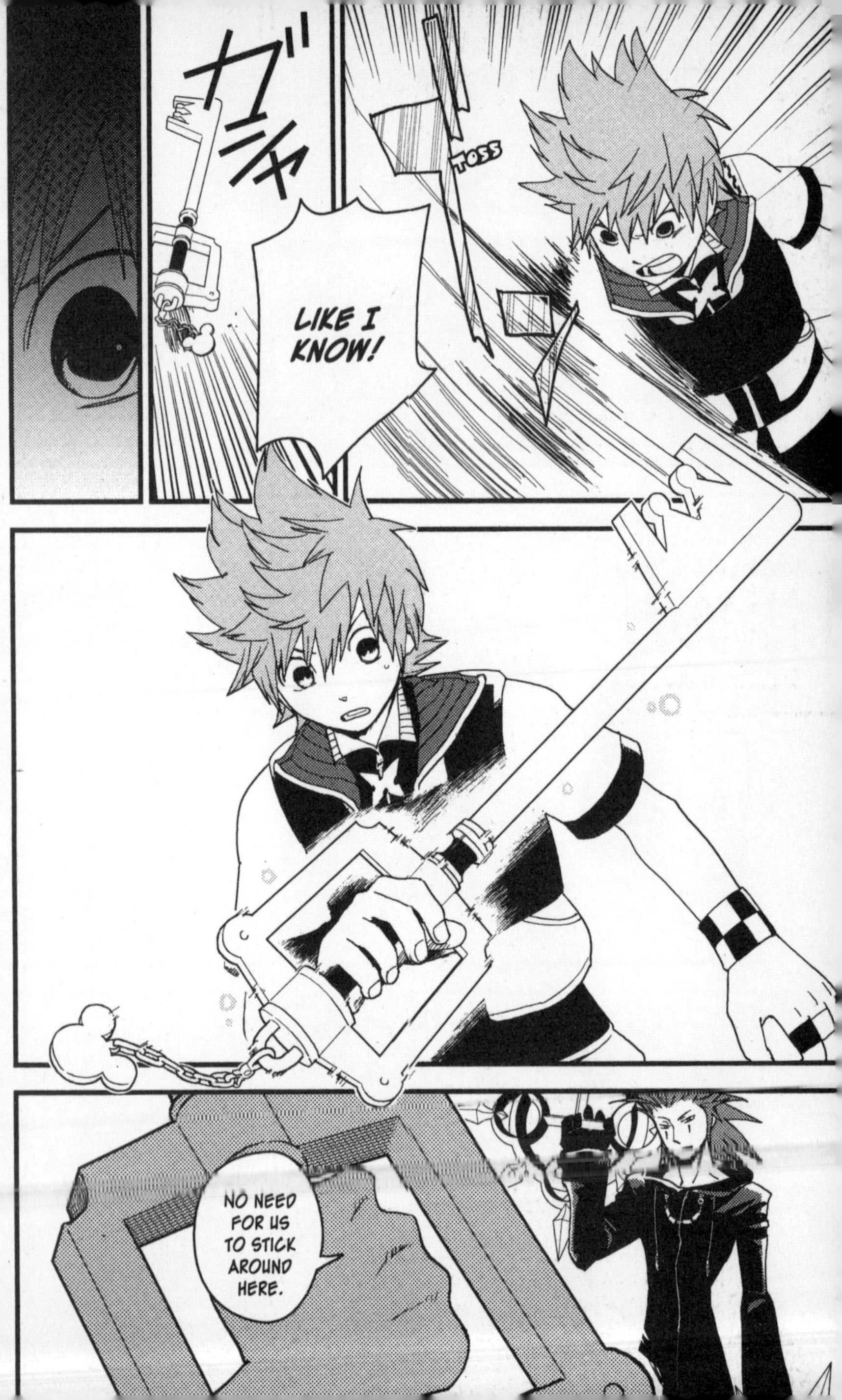
TOSS
LIKE I KNOW!
ガシャ
NO NEED FOR US TO STICK AROUND HERE.

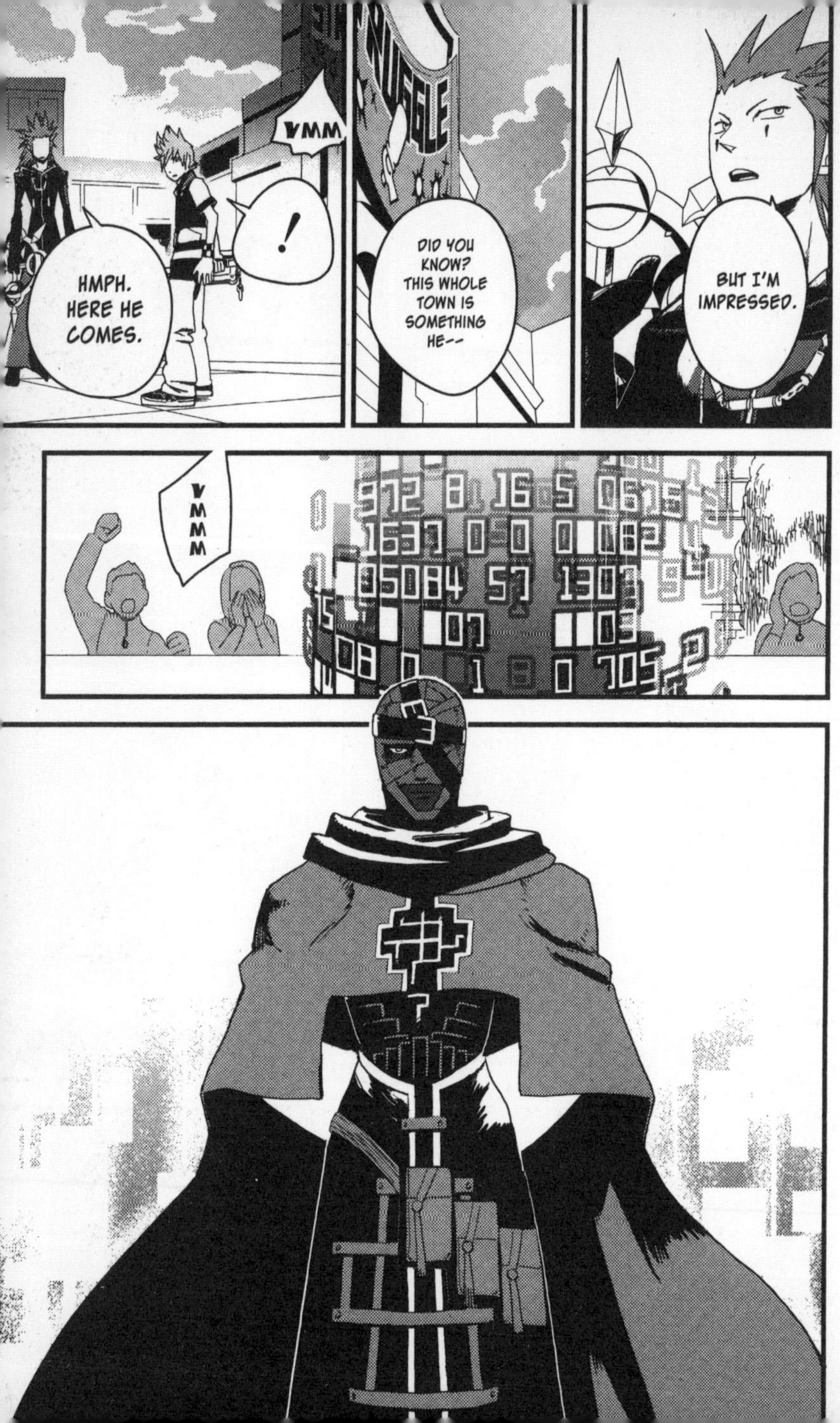
BUT I'M IMPRESSED.
DID YOU KNOW? THIS WHOLE TOWN IS SOMETHING HE--
VMM
!
HMPH. HERE HE COMES.
VMMM

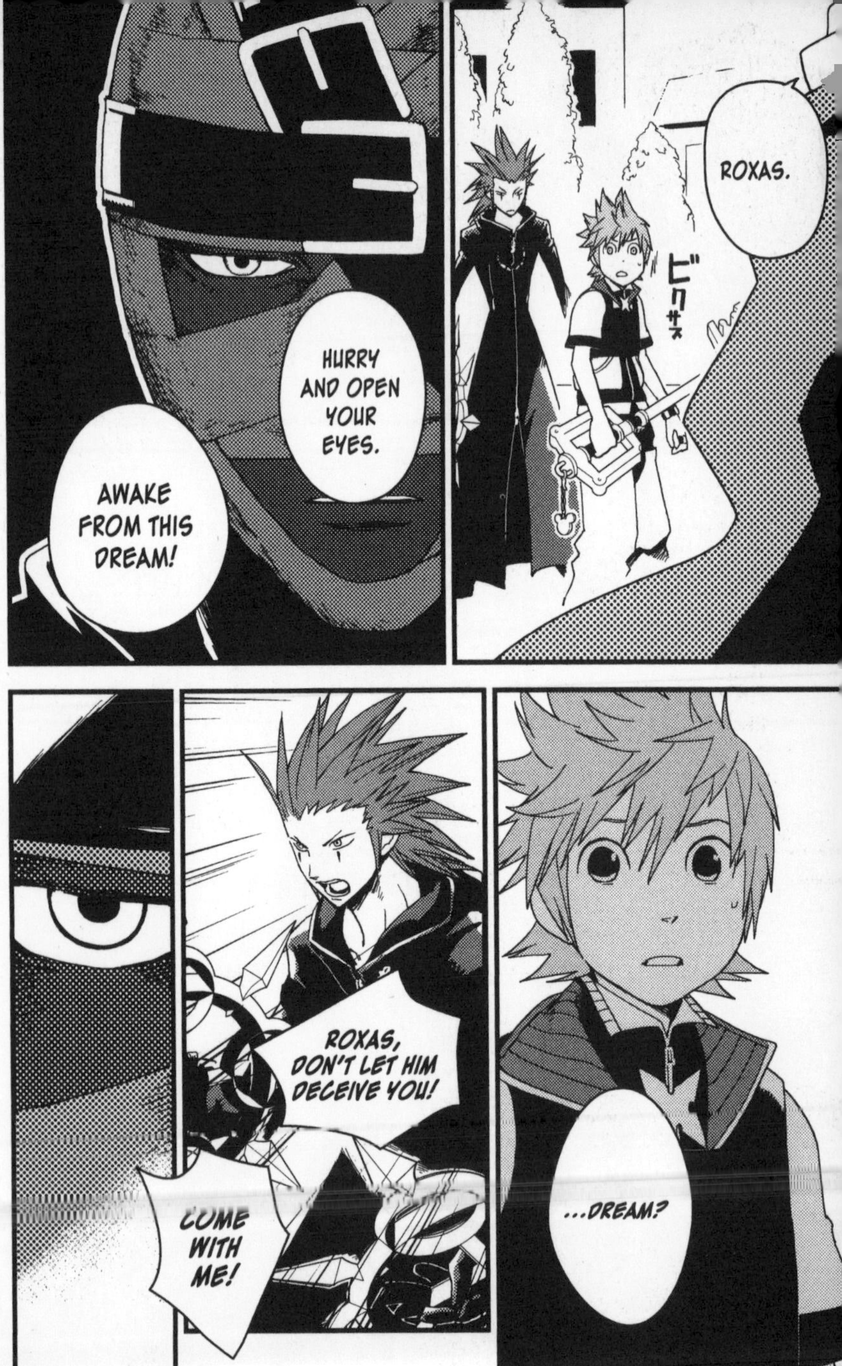

ROXAS.
ビク
HURRY AND OPEN YOUR EYES.
AWAKE FROM THIS DREAM!
...DREAM?
ROXAS, DON'T LET HIM DECEIVE YOU!
COME WITH ME!

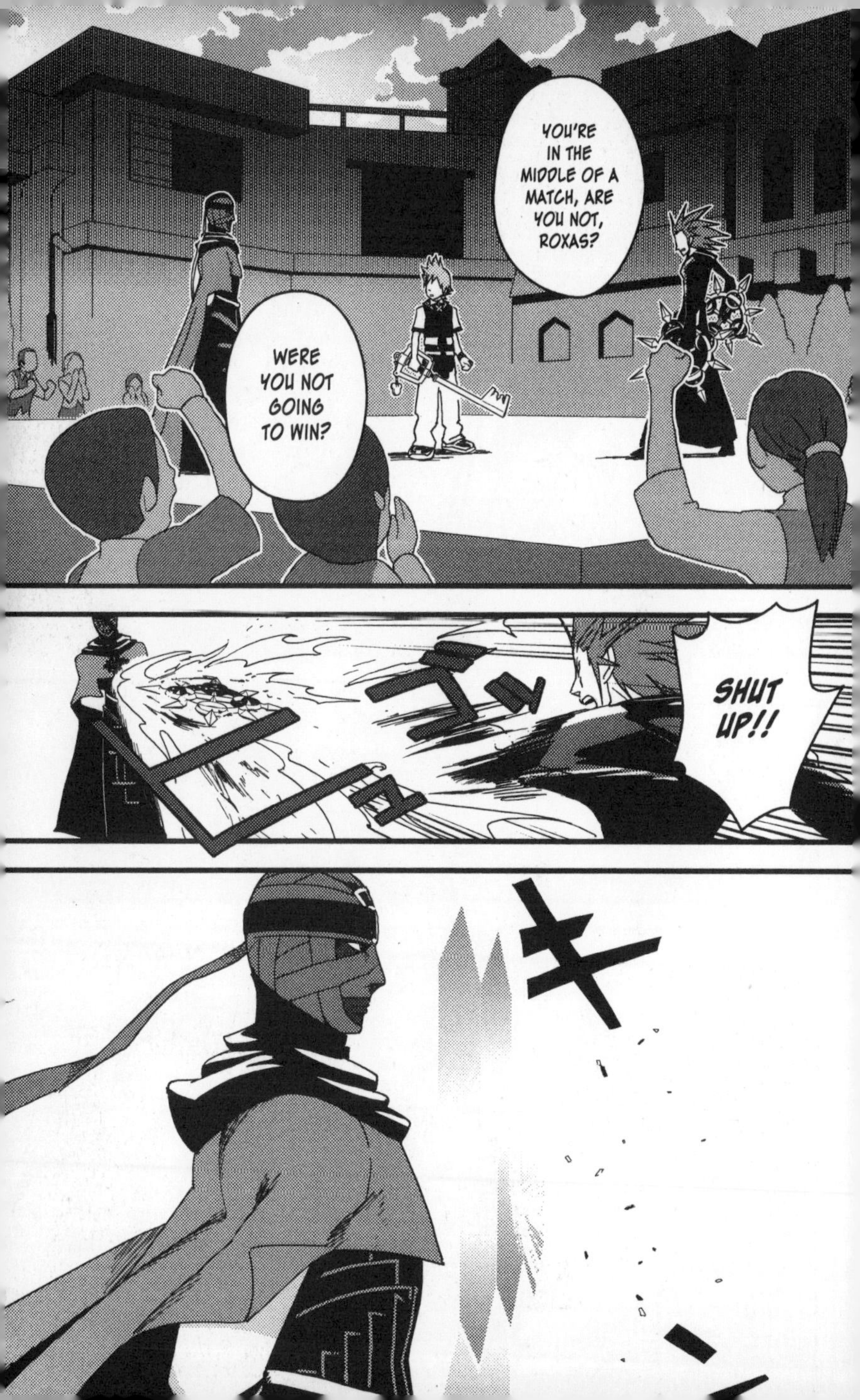
YOU'RE IN THE MIDDLE OF A MATCH, ARE YOU NOT, ROXAS?
WERE YOU NOT GOING TO WIN?
SHUT UP!!

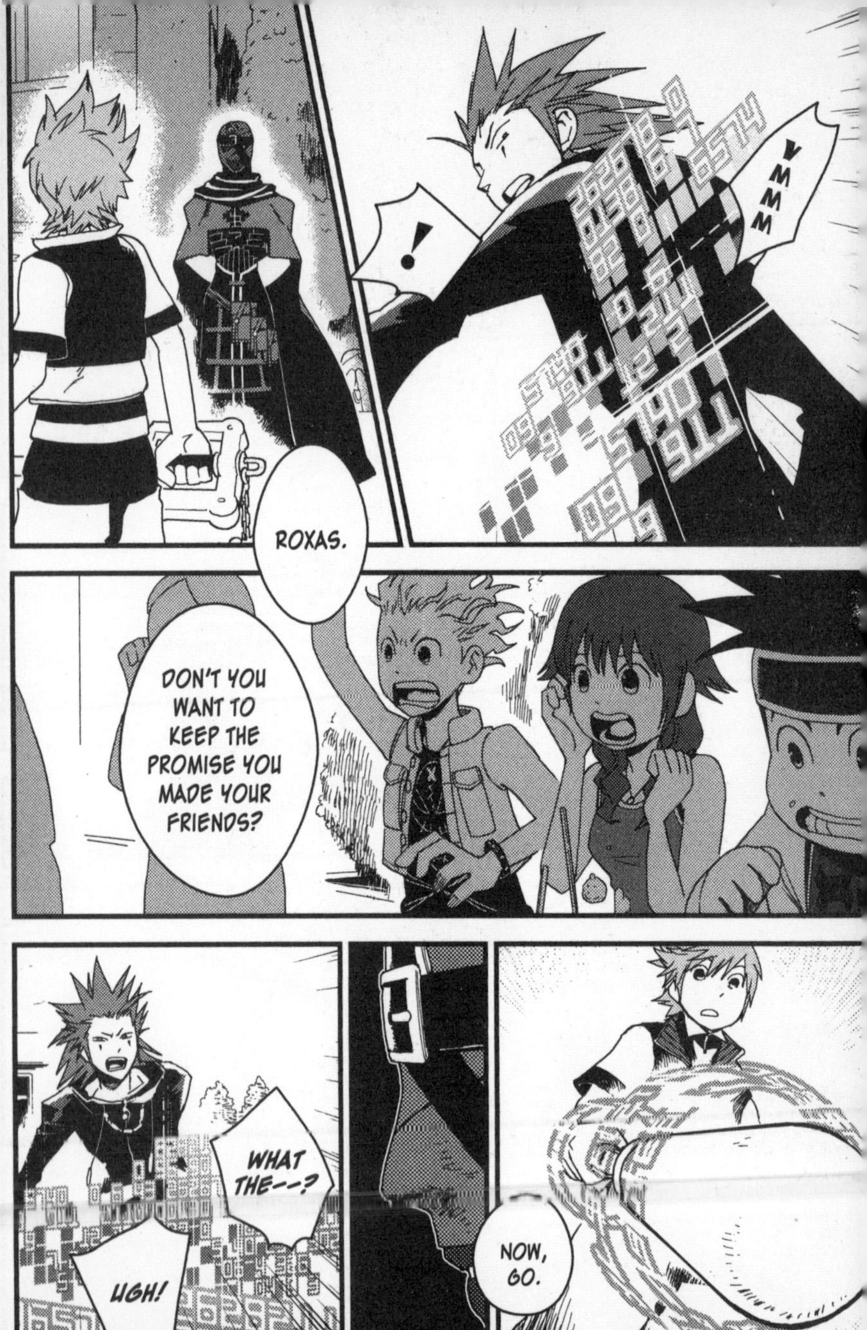
VMMM
!
ROXAS.
DON'T YOU WANT TO KEEP THE PROMISE YOU MADE YOUR FRIENDS?
NOW, GO.
WHAT THE--?
UGH!

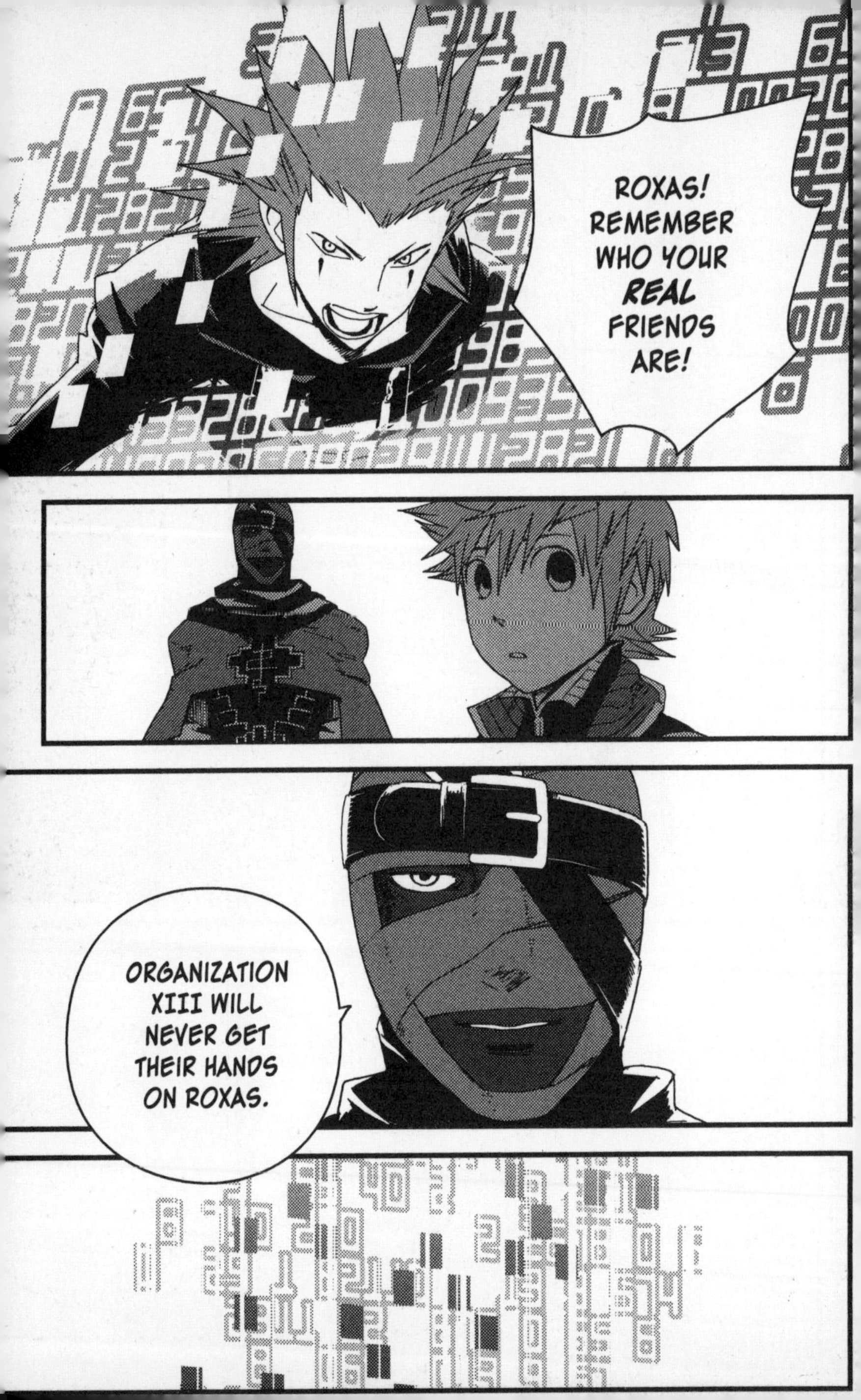
ROXAS! REMEMBER WHO YOUR *REAL* FRIENDS ARE!
ORGANIZATION XIII WILL NEVER GET THEIR HANDS ON ROXAS.

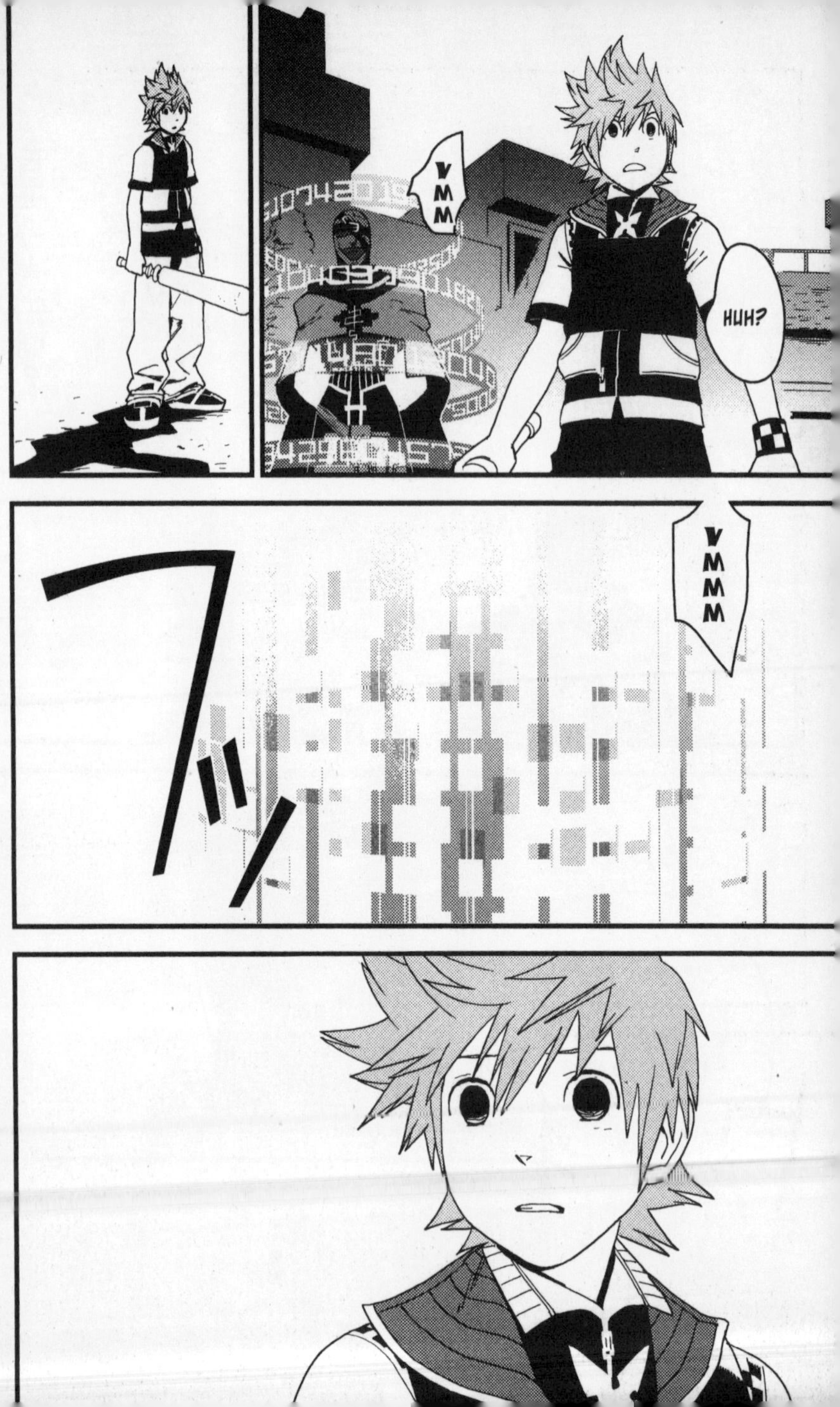
VMM
HUH?
VMMM

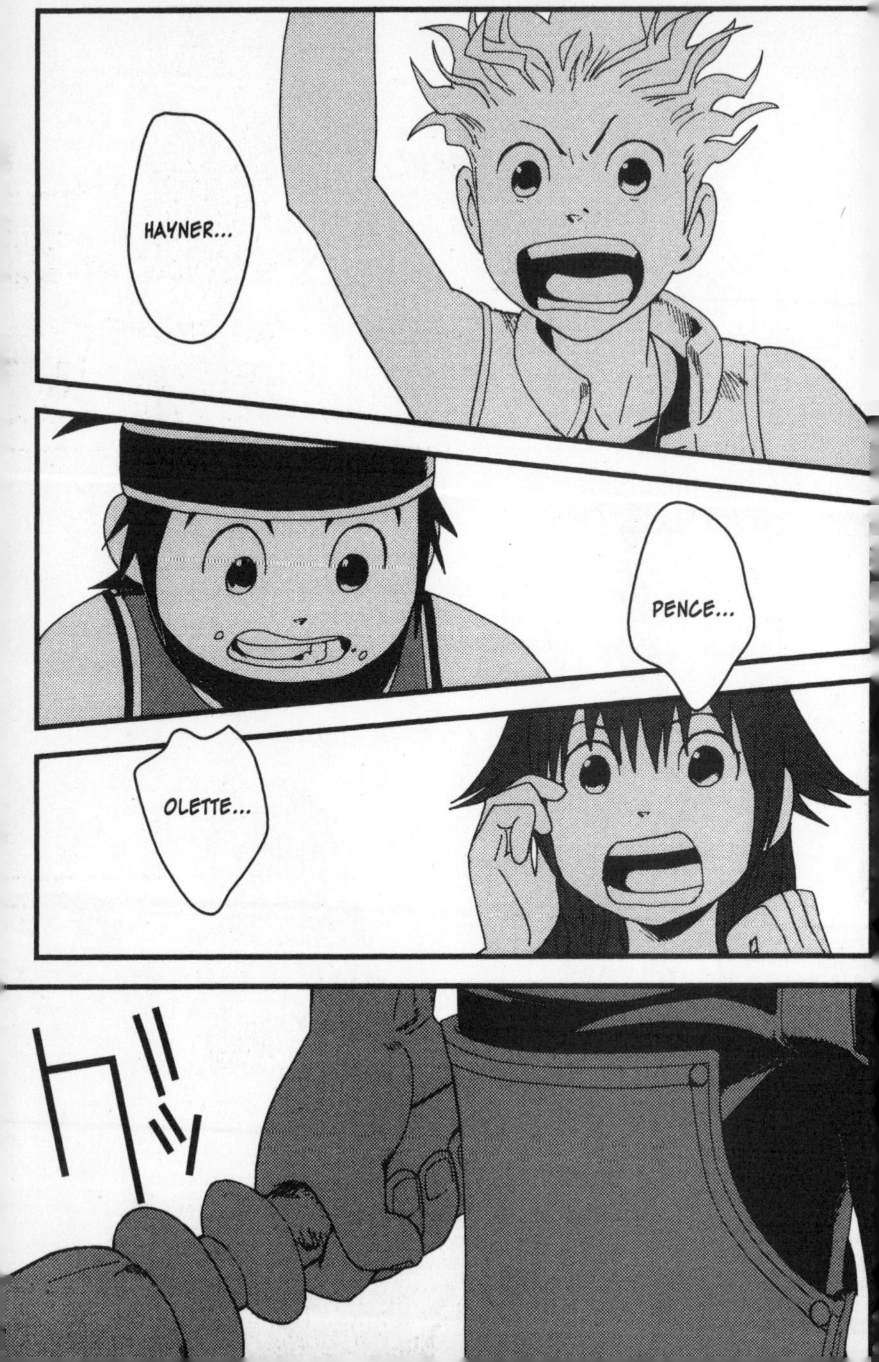
HAYNER...
PENCE...
OLETTE...
ガッ

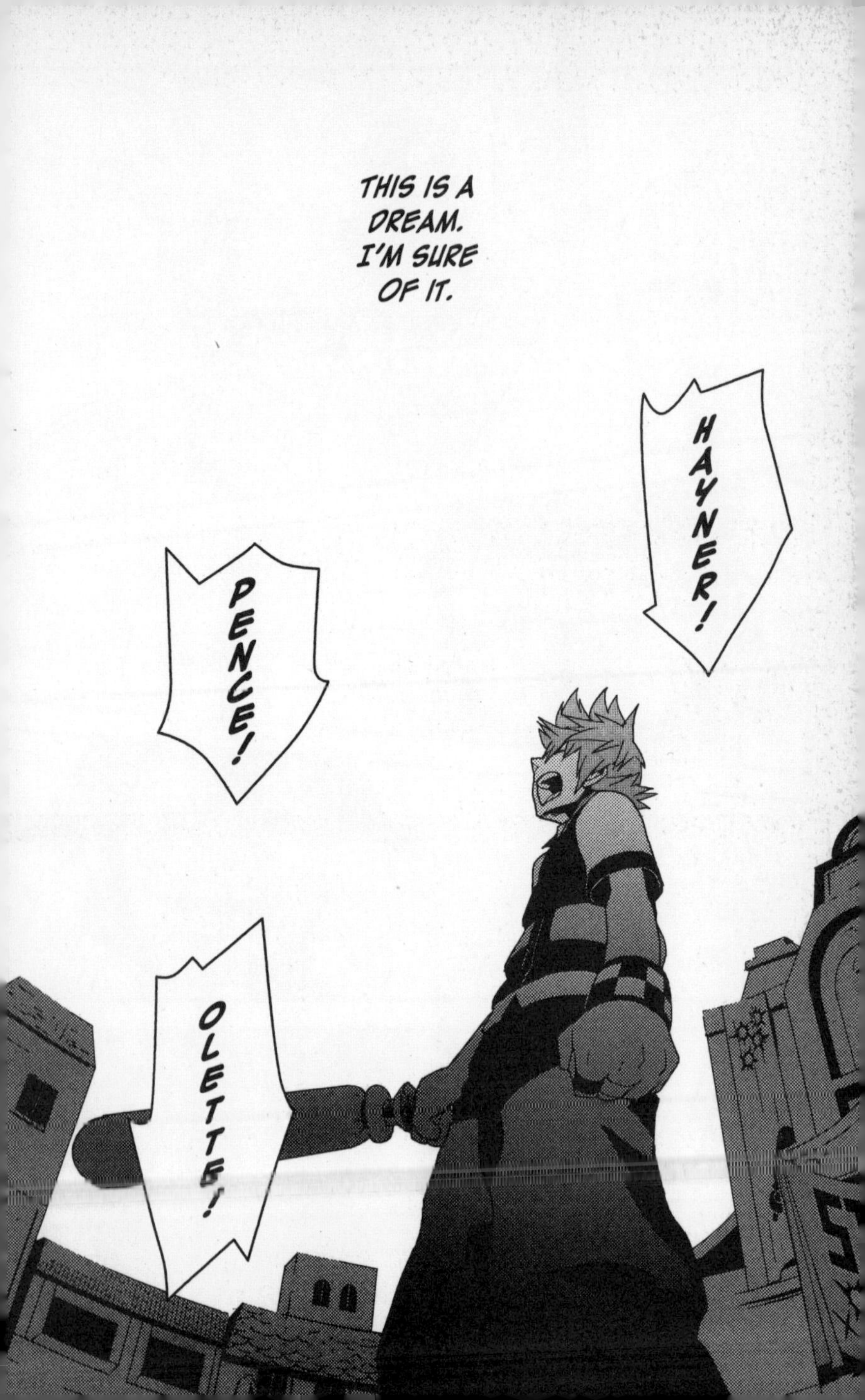
THIS IS A DREAM. I'M SURE OF IT.
HAYNER!
PENCE!
OLETTE!

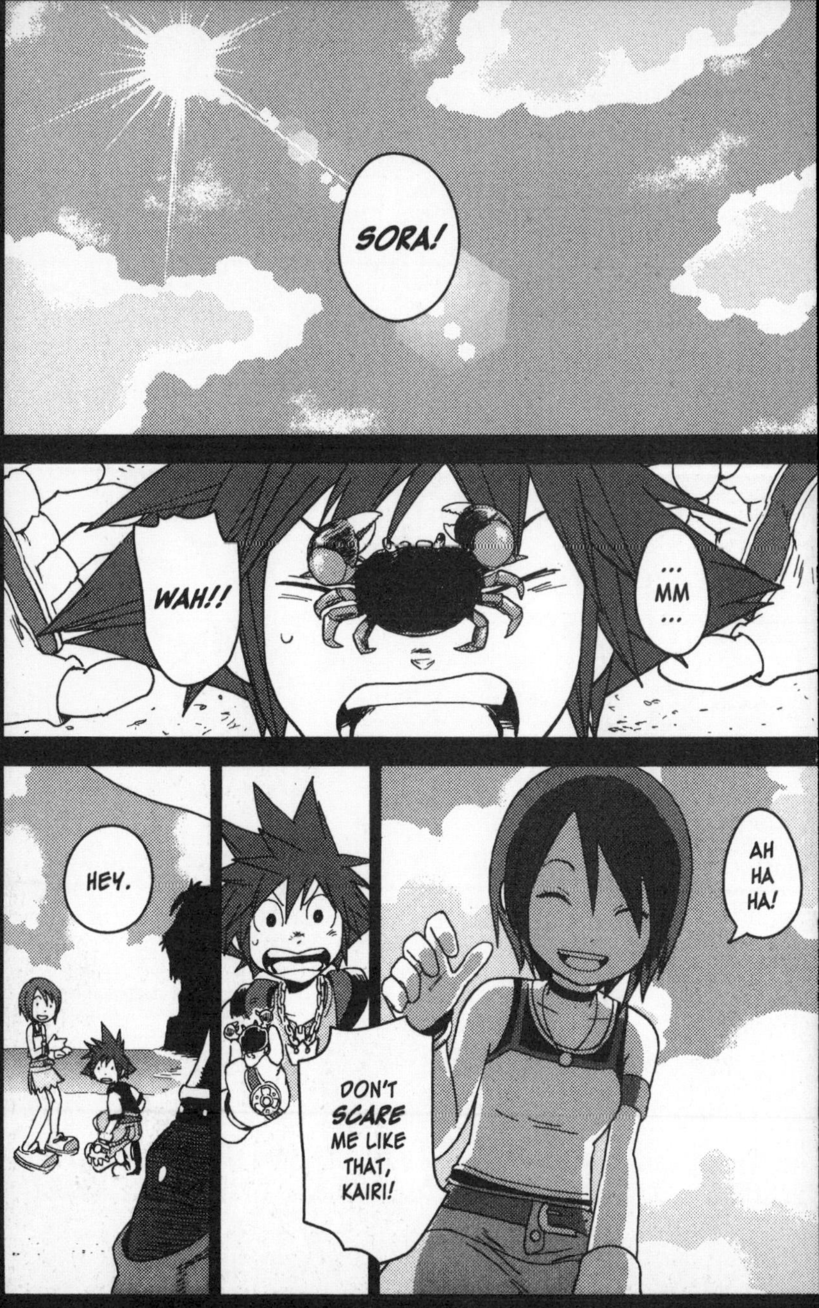
SORA!
...MM...
WAH!!
AH HA HA!
DON'T SCARE ME LIKE THAT, KAIRI!
HEY.

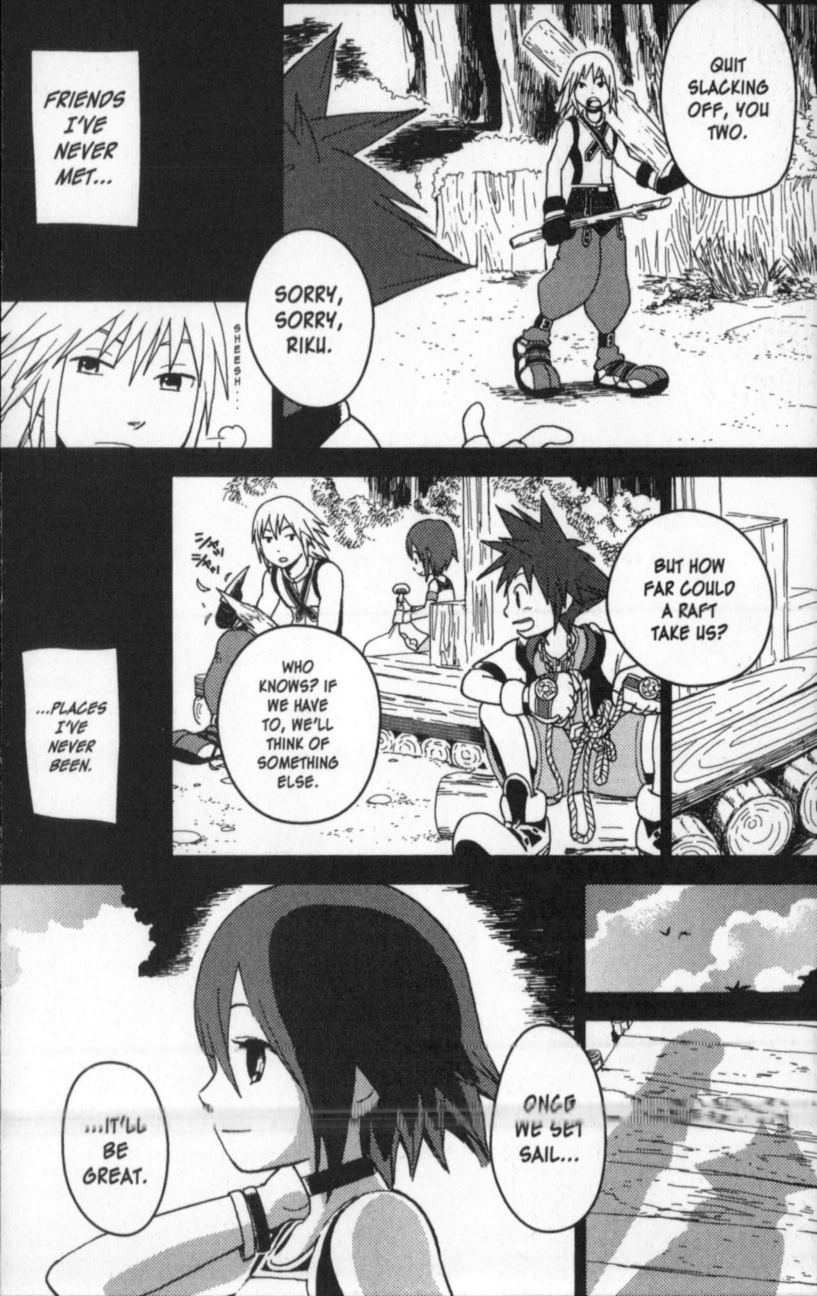
QUIT SLACKING OFF, YOU TWO.
SORRY, SORRY, RIKU.
SHEESH...
FRIENDS I'VE NEVER MET...
BUT HOW FAR COULD A RAFT TAKE US?
WHO KNOWS? IF WE HAVE TO, WE'LL THINK OF SOMETHING ELSE.
...PLACES I'VE NEVER BEEN.
ONCE WE SET SAIL...
...IT'LL BE GREAT.

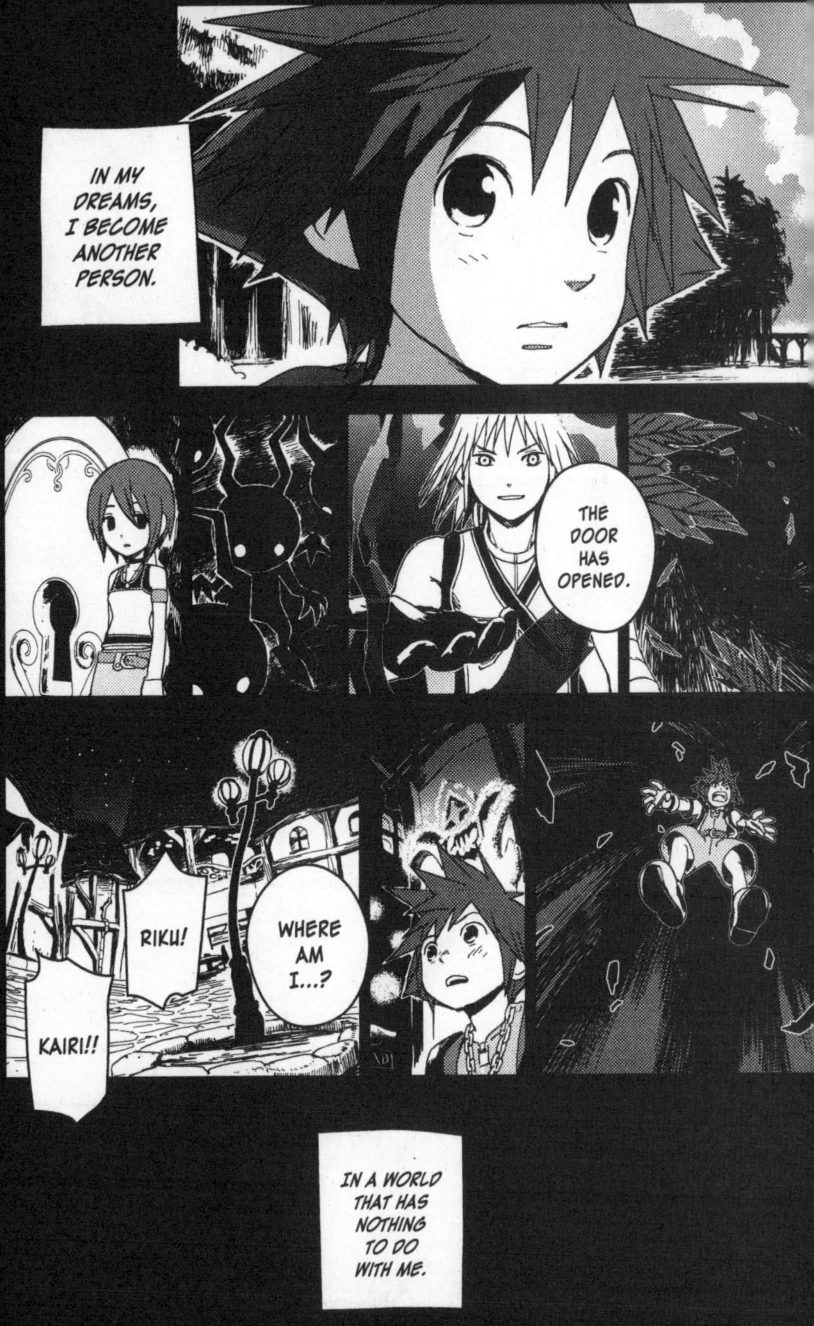
IN MY DREAMS, I BECOME ANOTHER PERSON.
THE DOOR HAS OPENED.
WHERE AM I...?
RIKU!
KAIRI!!
IN A WORLD THAT HAS NOTHING TO DO WITH ME.

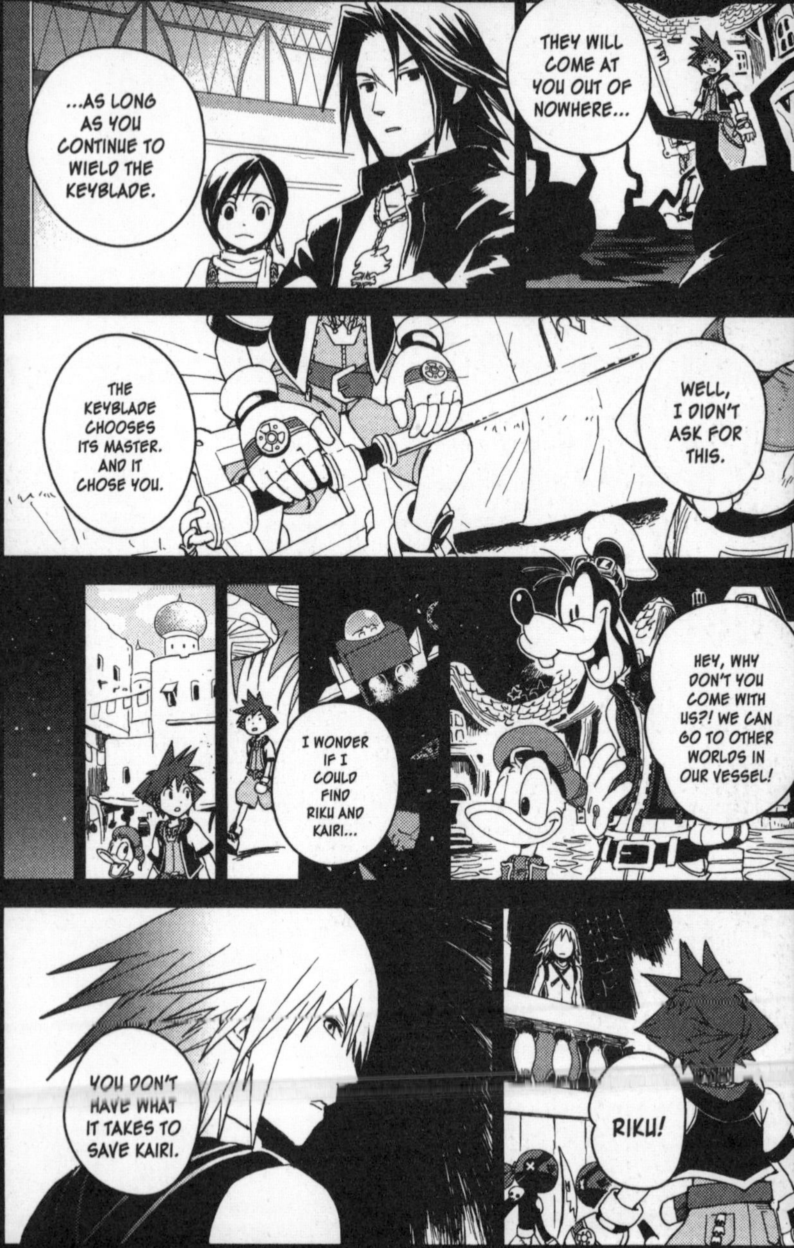
THEY WILL COME AT YOU OUT OF NOWHERE...
...AS LONG AS YOU CONTINUE TO WIELD THE KEYBLADE.
WELL, I DIDN'T ASK FOR THIS.
THE KEYBLADE CHOOSES ITS MASTER. AND IT CHOSE YOU.
HEY, WHY DON'T YOU COME WITH US?! WE CAN GO TO OTHER WORLDS IN OUR VESSEL!
I WONDER IF I COULD FIND RIKU AND KAIRI...
RIKU!
YOU DON'T HAVE WHAT IT TAKES TO SAVE KAIRI.

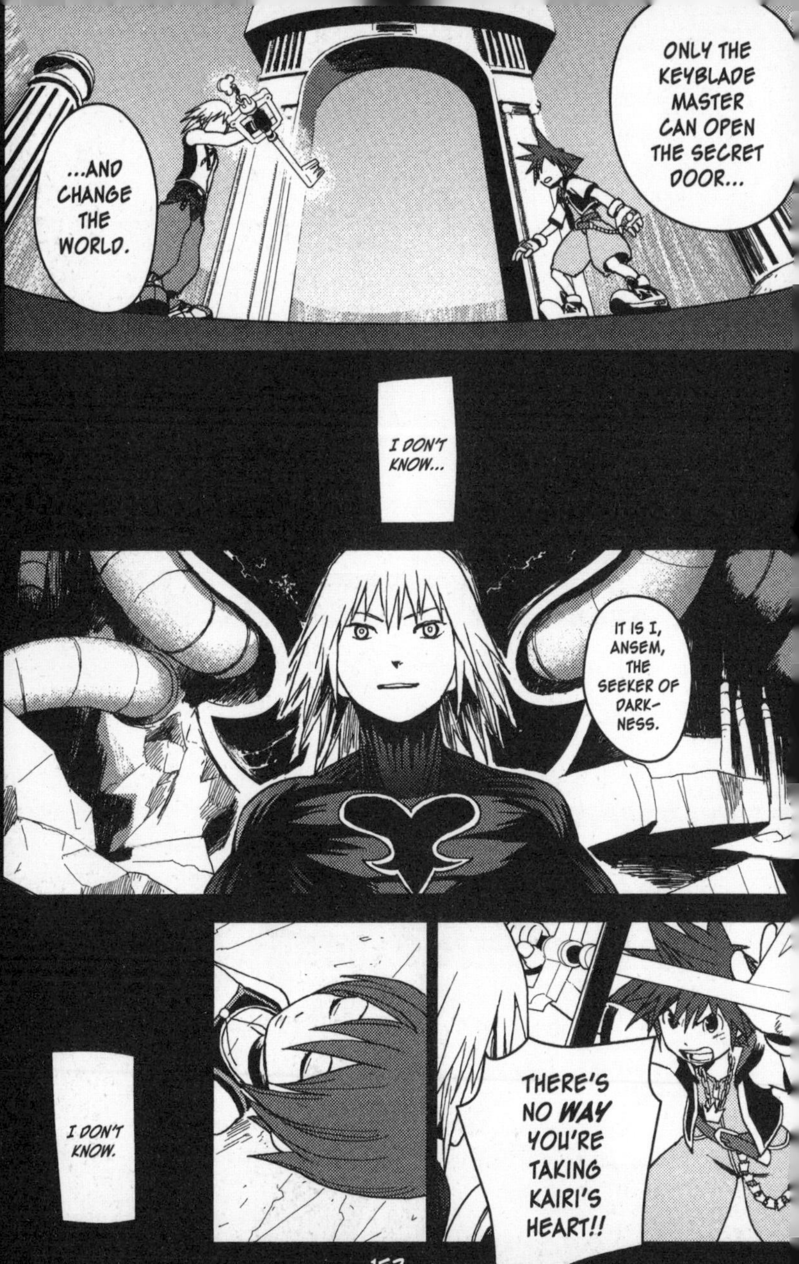
ONLY THE KEYBLADE MASTER CAN OPEN THE SECRET DOOR...
...AND CHANGE THE WORLD.
I DON'T KNOW...
IT IS I, ANSEM, THE SEEKER OF DARK-NESS.
THERE'S NO WAY YOU'RE TAKING KAIRI'S HEART!!
I DON'T KNOW.

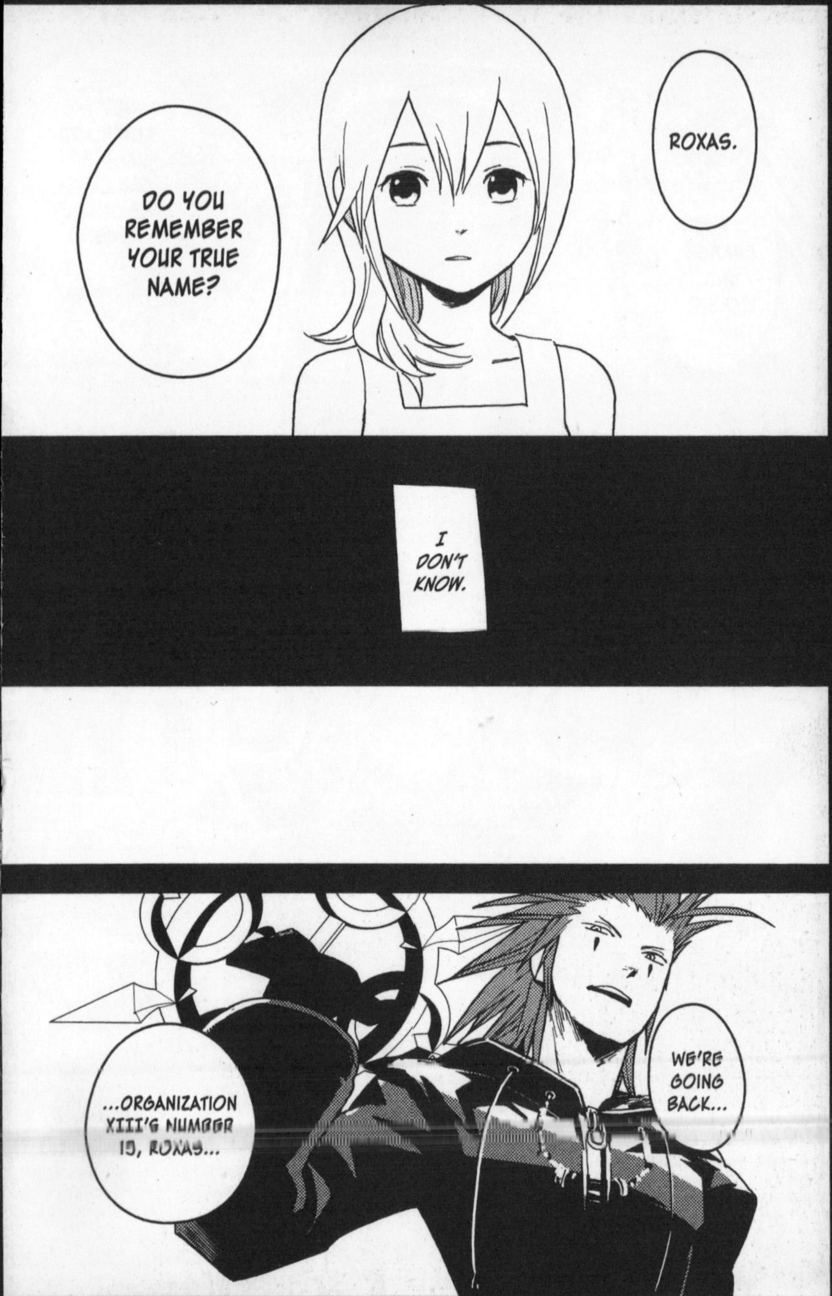
ROXAS.
DO YOU REMEMBER YOUR TRUE NAME?
I DON'T KNOW.
WE'RE GOING BACK...
...ORGANIZATION XIII'S NUMBER 13, ROXAS...

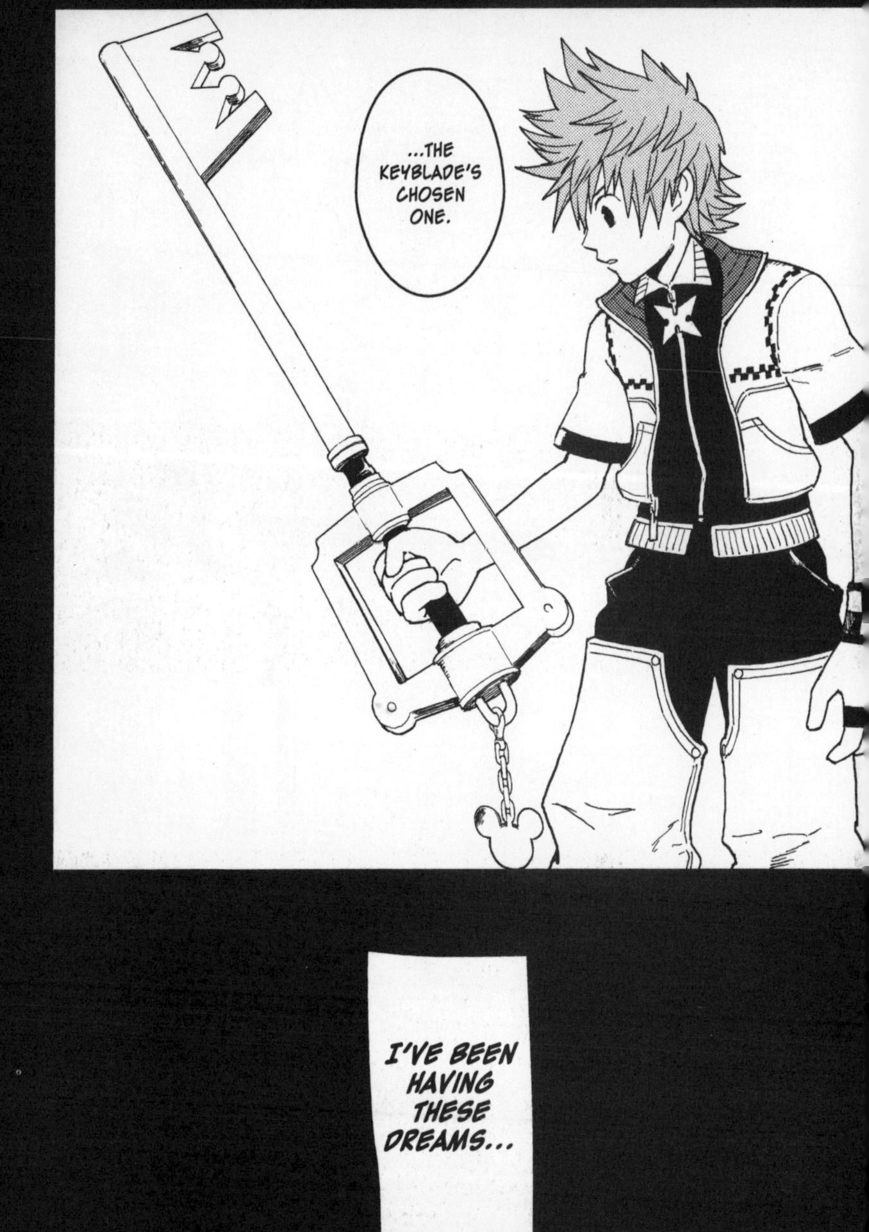
...THE KEYBLADE'S CHOSEN ONE.
I'VE BEEN HAVING THESE DREAMS...

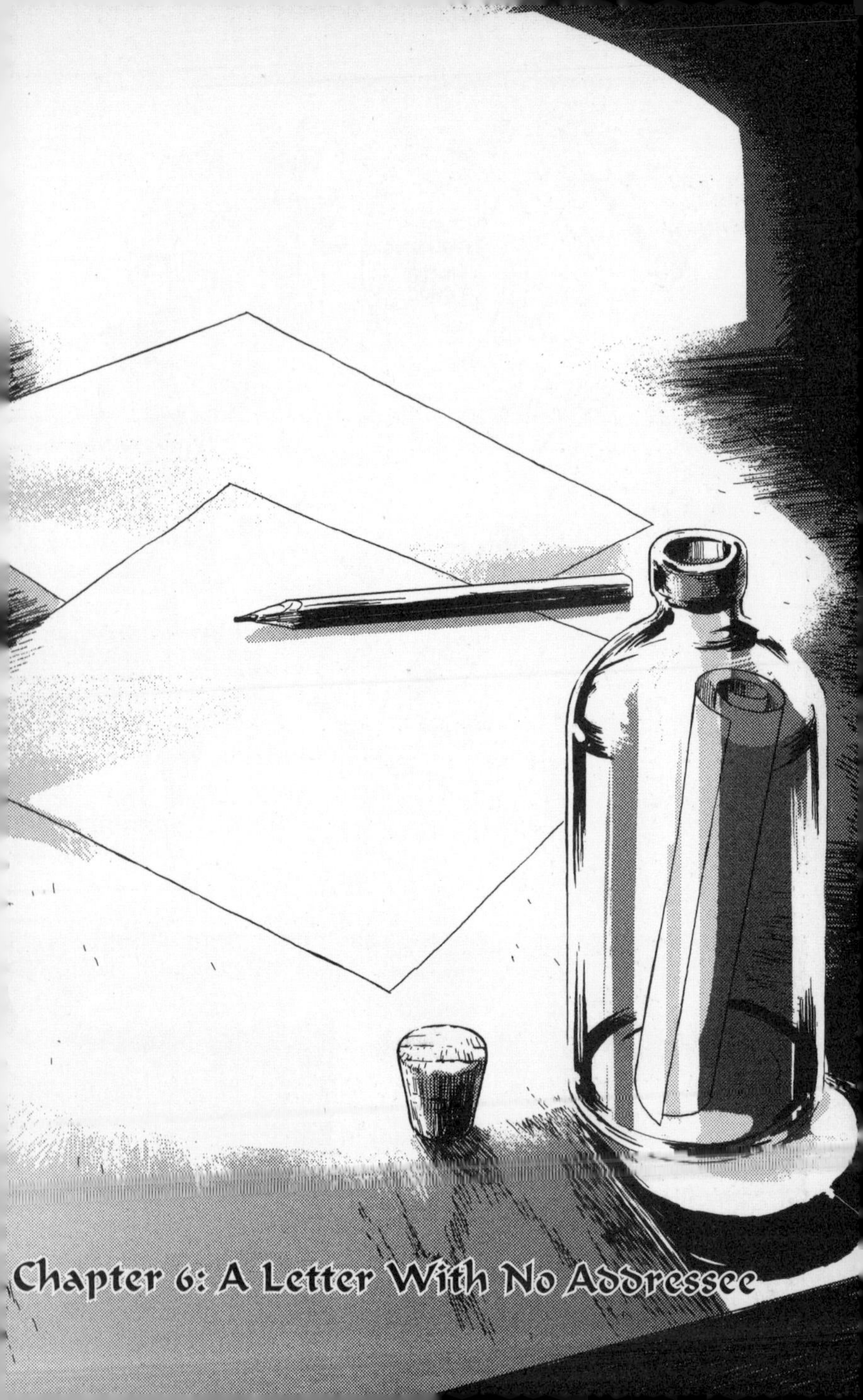
Chapter 6: A Letter With No Addressee

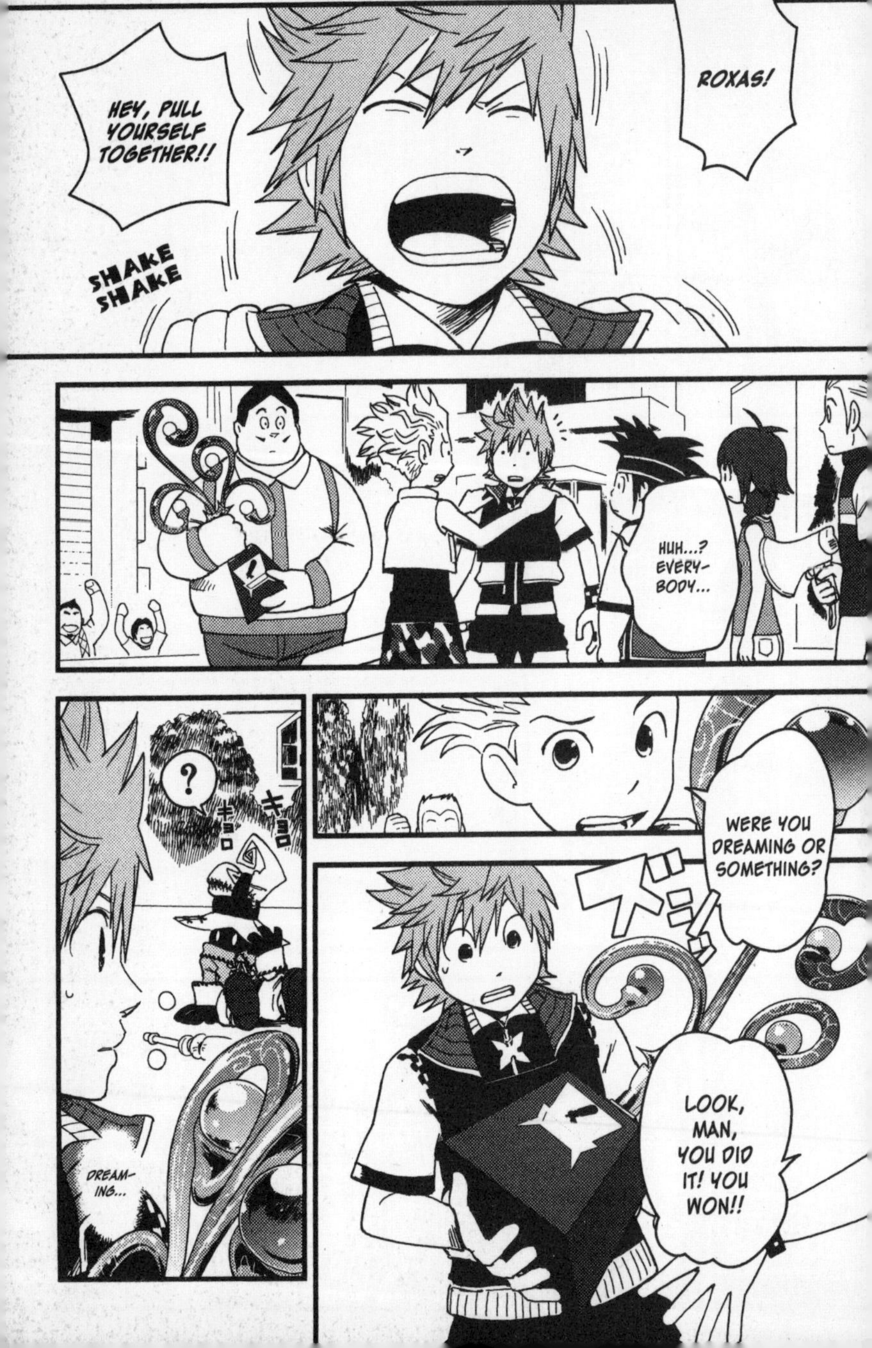
ROXAS!
HEY, PULL YOURSELF TOGETHER!!
SHAKE SHAKE
HUH...? EVERY-BODY...
WERE YOU DREAMING OR SOMETHING?
ズシッ
LOOK, MAN, YOU DID IT! YOU WON!!
?
キョロ キョロ
DREAM-ING...

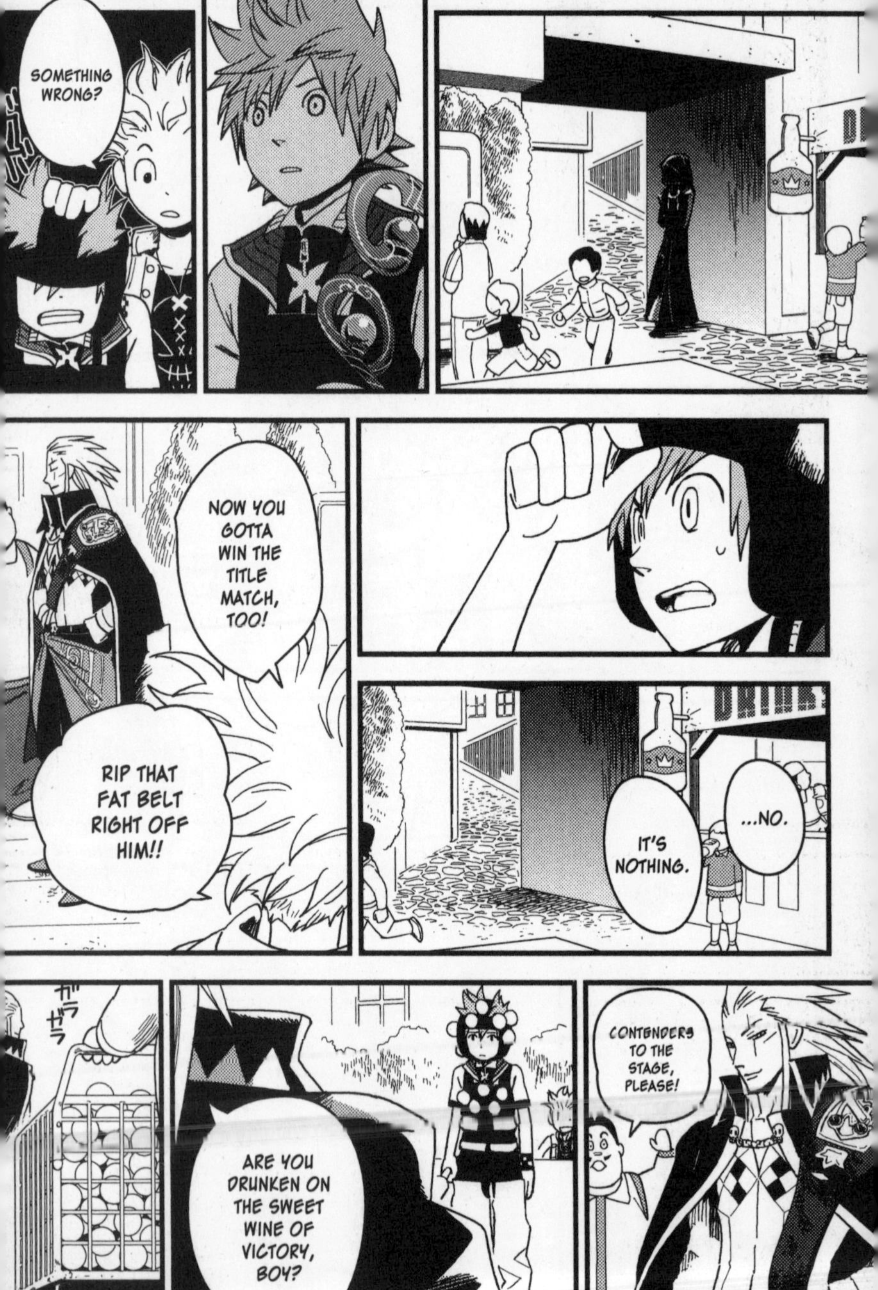
SOMETHING WRONG?
...NO.
IT'S NOTHING.
NOW YOU GOTTA WIN THE TITLE MATCH, TOO!
RIP THAT FAT BELT RIGHT OFF HIM!!
CONTENDERS TO THE STAGE, PLEASE!
ARE YOU DRUNKEN ON THE SWEET WINE OF VICTORY, BOY?

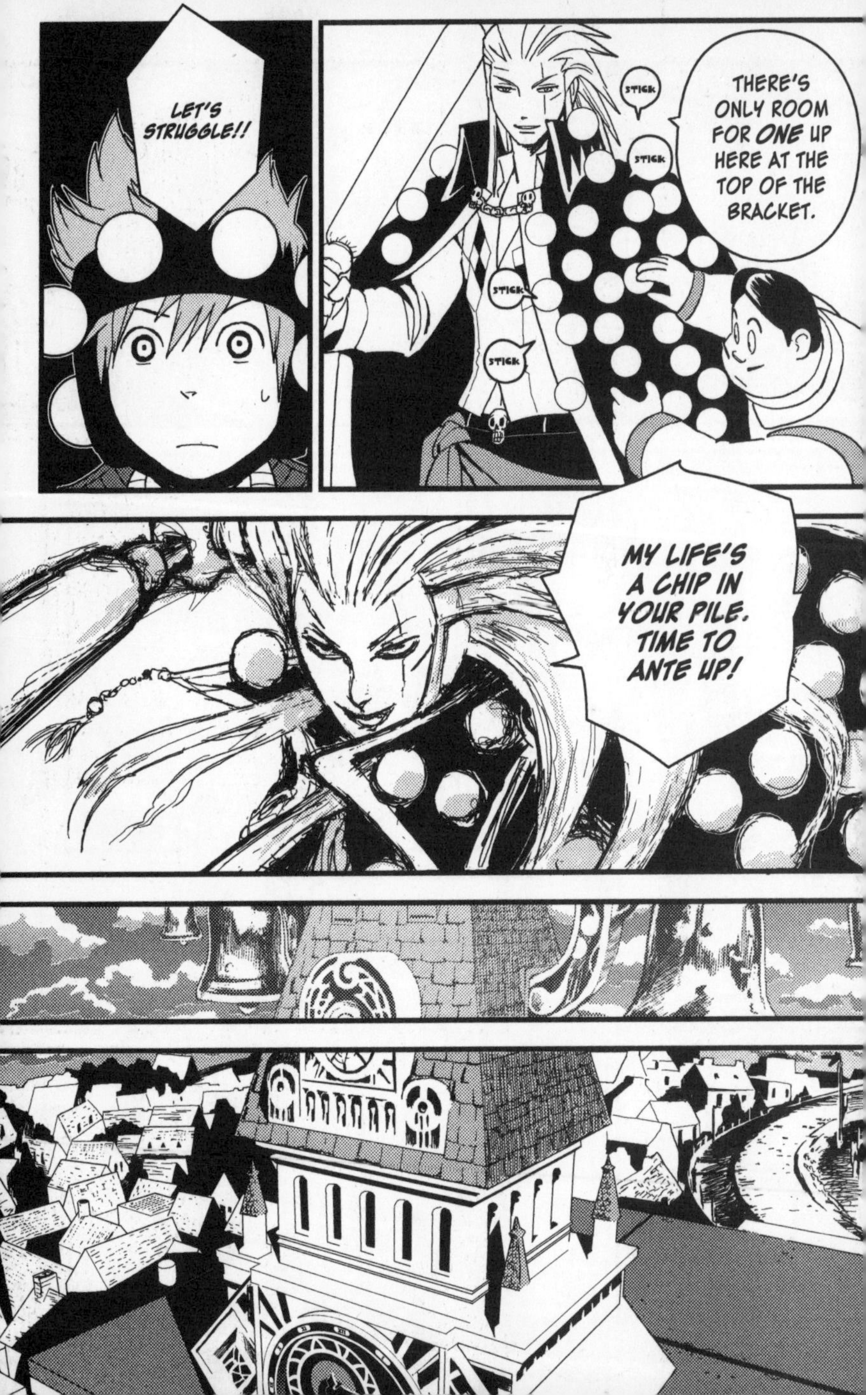
THERE'S ONLY ROOM FOR ONE UP HERE AT THE TOP OF THE BRACKET.
STICK
STICK
STICK
STICK
LET'S STRUGGLE!!
MY LIFE'S A CHIP IN YOUR PILE. TIME TO ANTE UP!

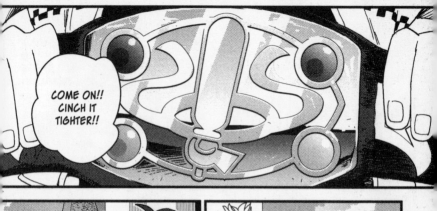

COME ON!! CINCH IT TIGHTER!!

LOOKS GOOD ON YOU, NEW CHAMPION!

PFT! AH HA HA!

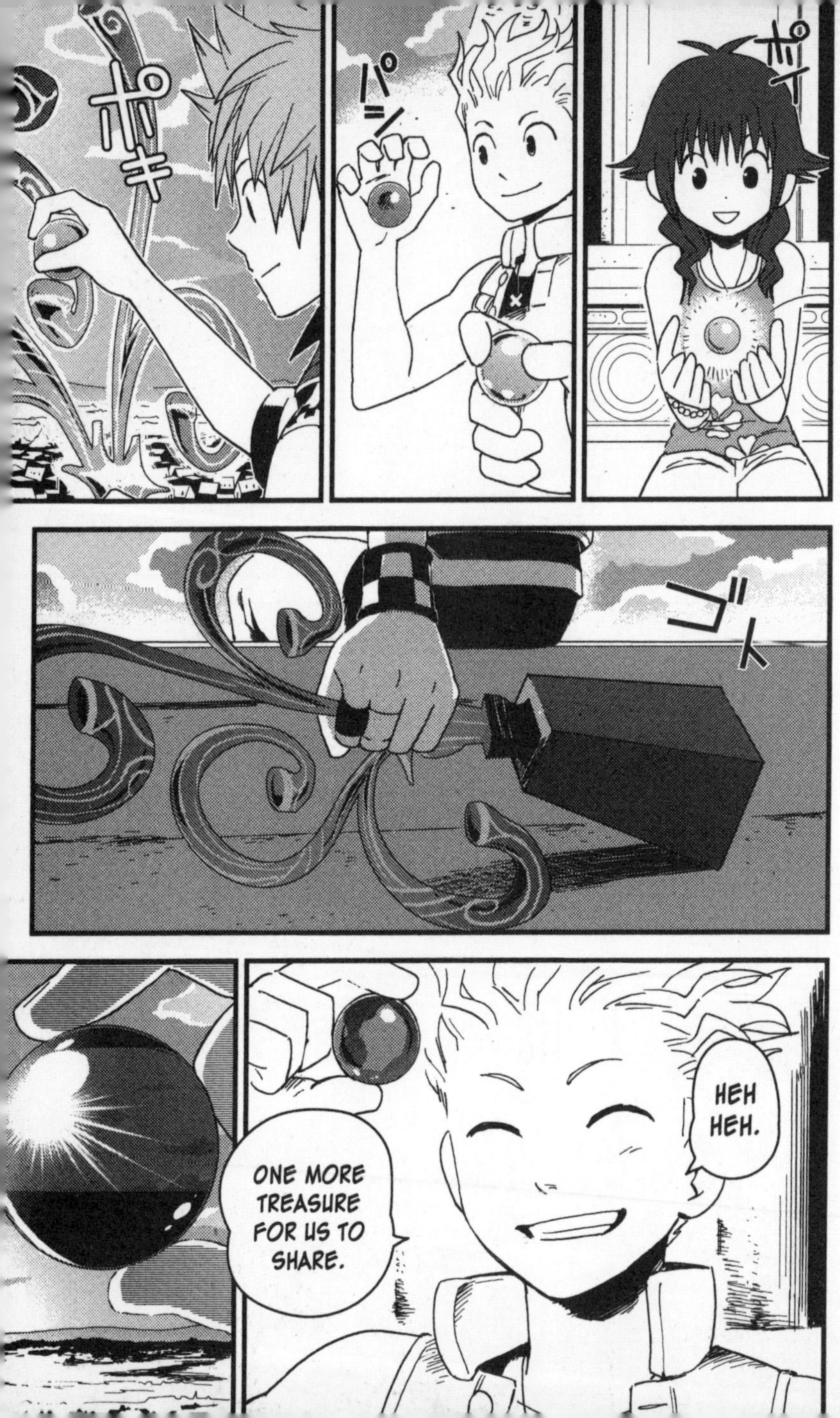
ポイ
パシ
ポキ
ゴト
HEH HEH.
ONE MORE TREASURE FOR US TO SHARE.

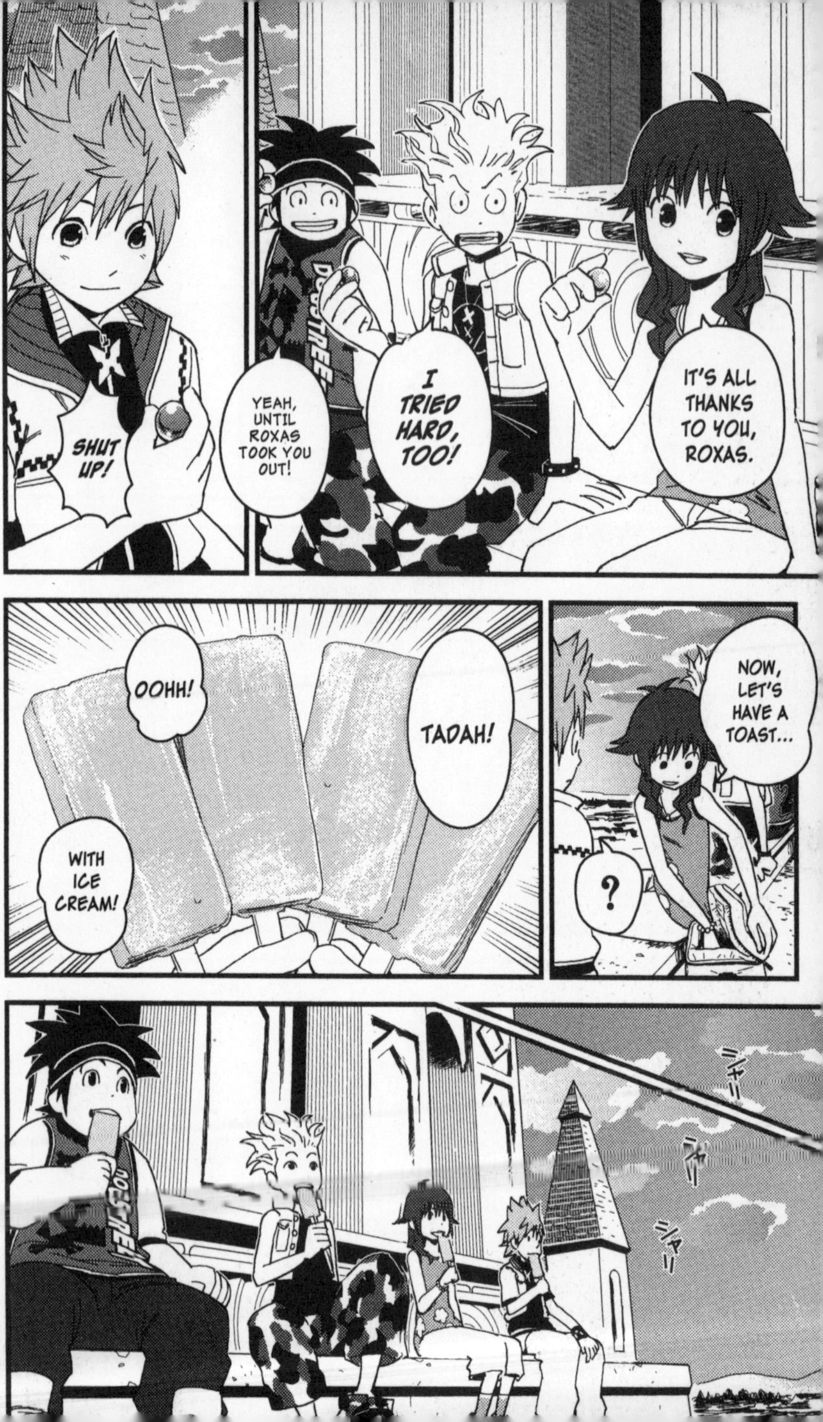
IT'S ALL THANKS TO YOU, ROXAS.
I TRIED HARD, TOO!
YEAH, UNTIL ROXAS TOOK YOU OUT!
SHUT UP!
NOW, LET'S HAVE A TOAST...
?
TADAH!
OOHH!
WITH ICE CREAM!

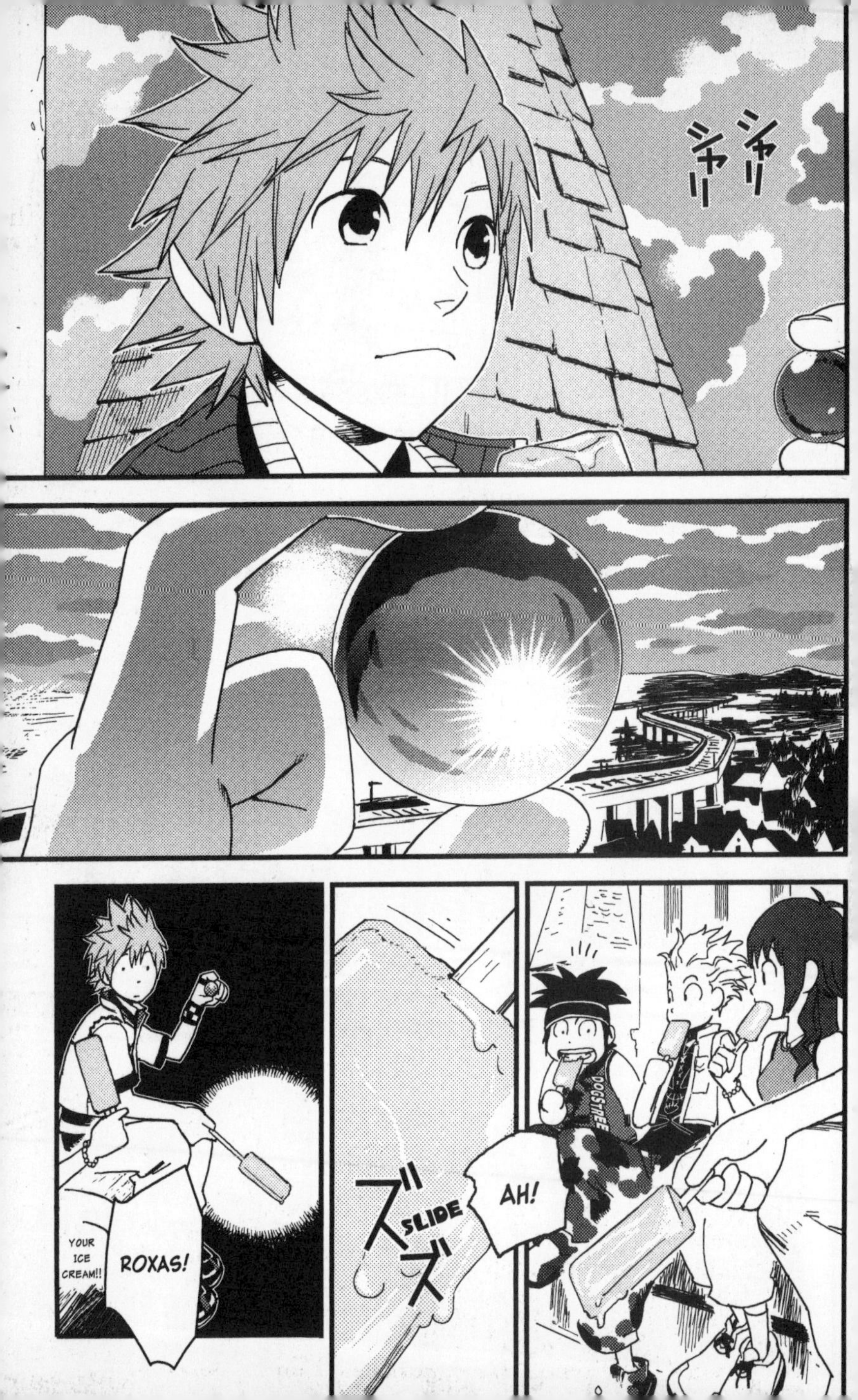
シャリ
シャリー
AH!
ズズ
SLIDE
ROXAS!
YOUR ICE CREAM!!

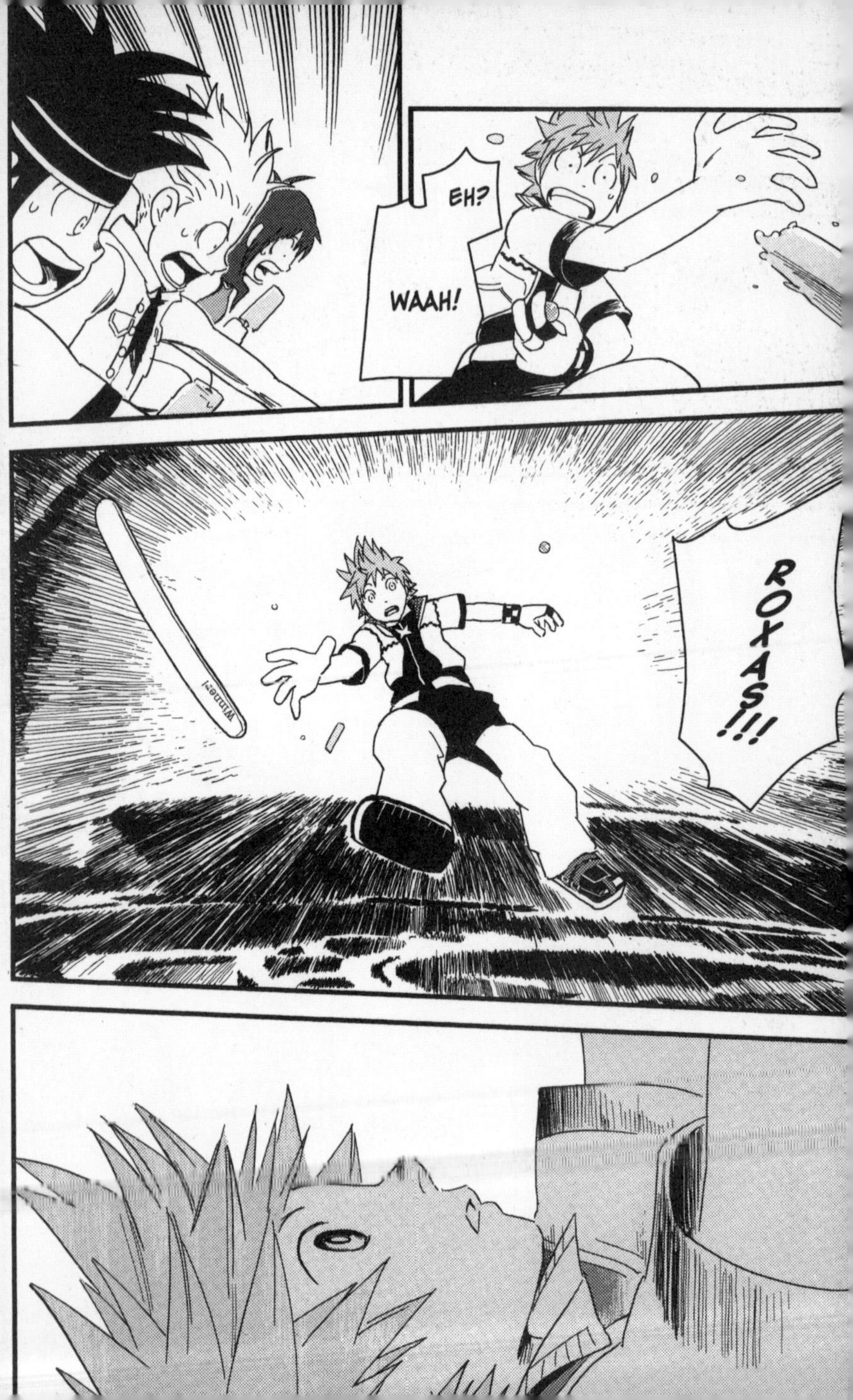
EH?
WAAH!
ROXAS!!!
Winner!

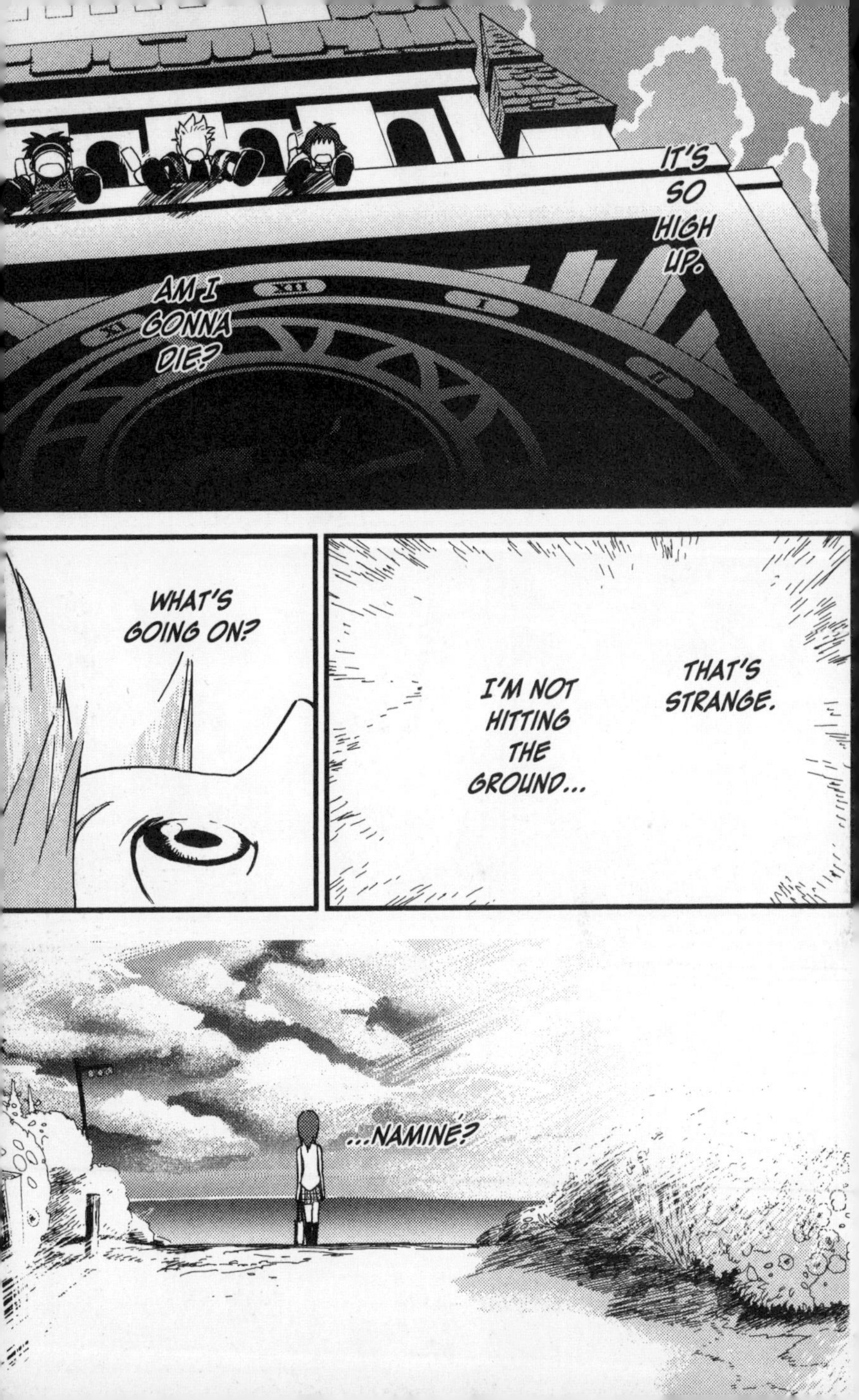
IT'S SO HIGH UP.
AM I GONNA DIE?
THAT'S STRANGE.
I'M NOT HITTING THE GROUND...
WHAT'S GOING ON?
...NAMINE?

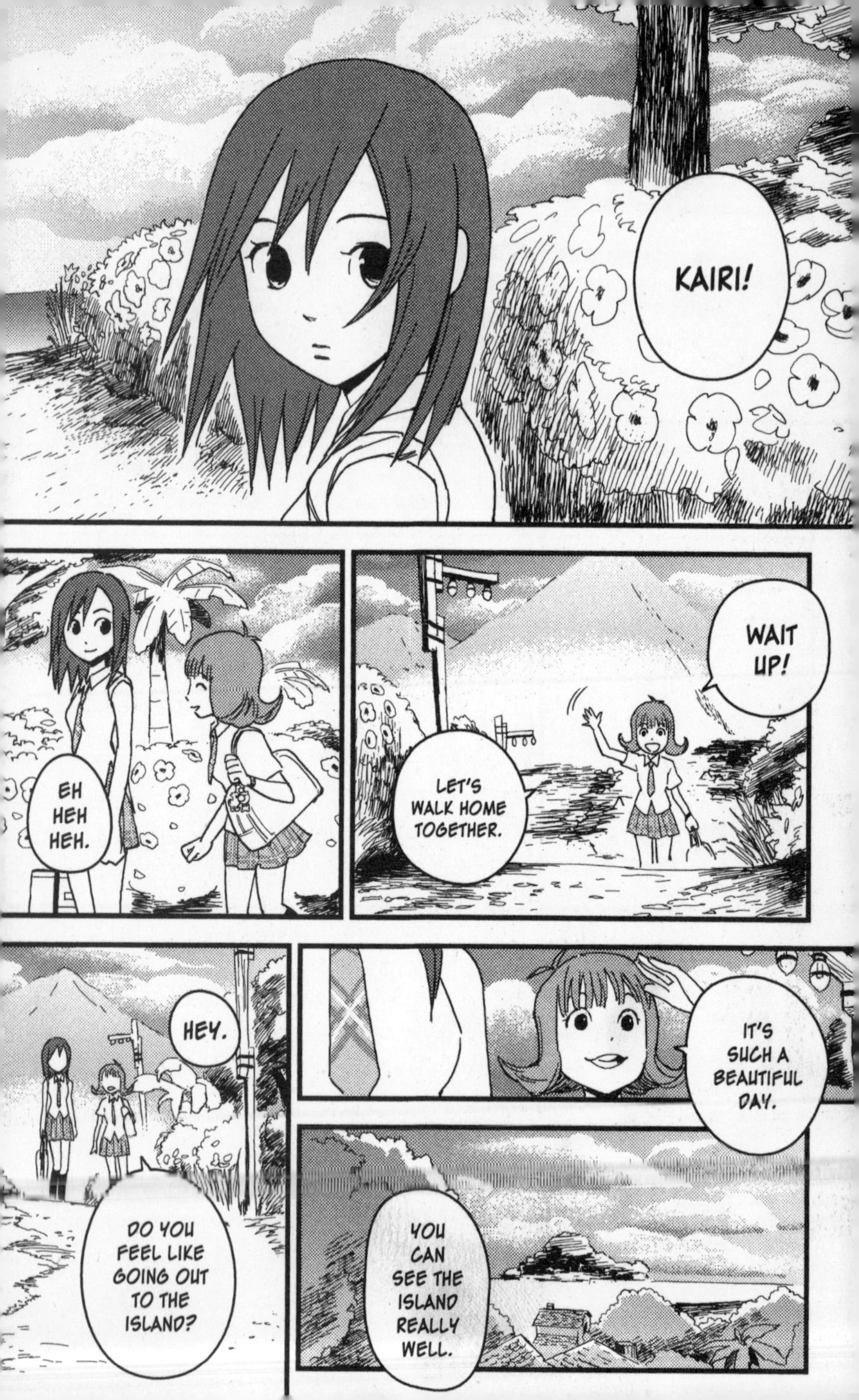
KAIRI!
WAIT UP!
LET'S WALK HOME TOGETHER.
EH HEH HEH.
IT'S SUCH A BEAUTIFUL DAY.
YOU CAN SEE THE ISLAND REALLY WELL.
HEY.
DO YOU FEEL LIKE GOING OUT TO THE ISLAND?

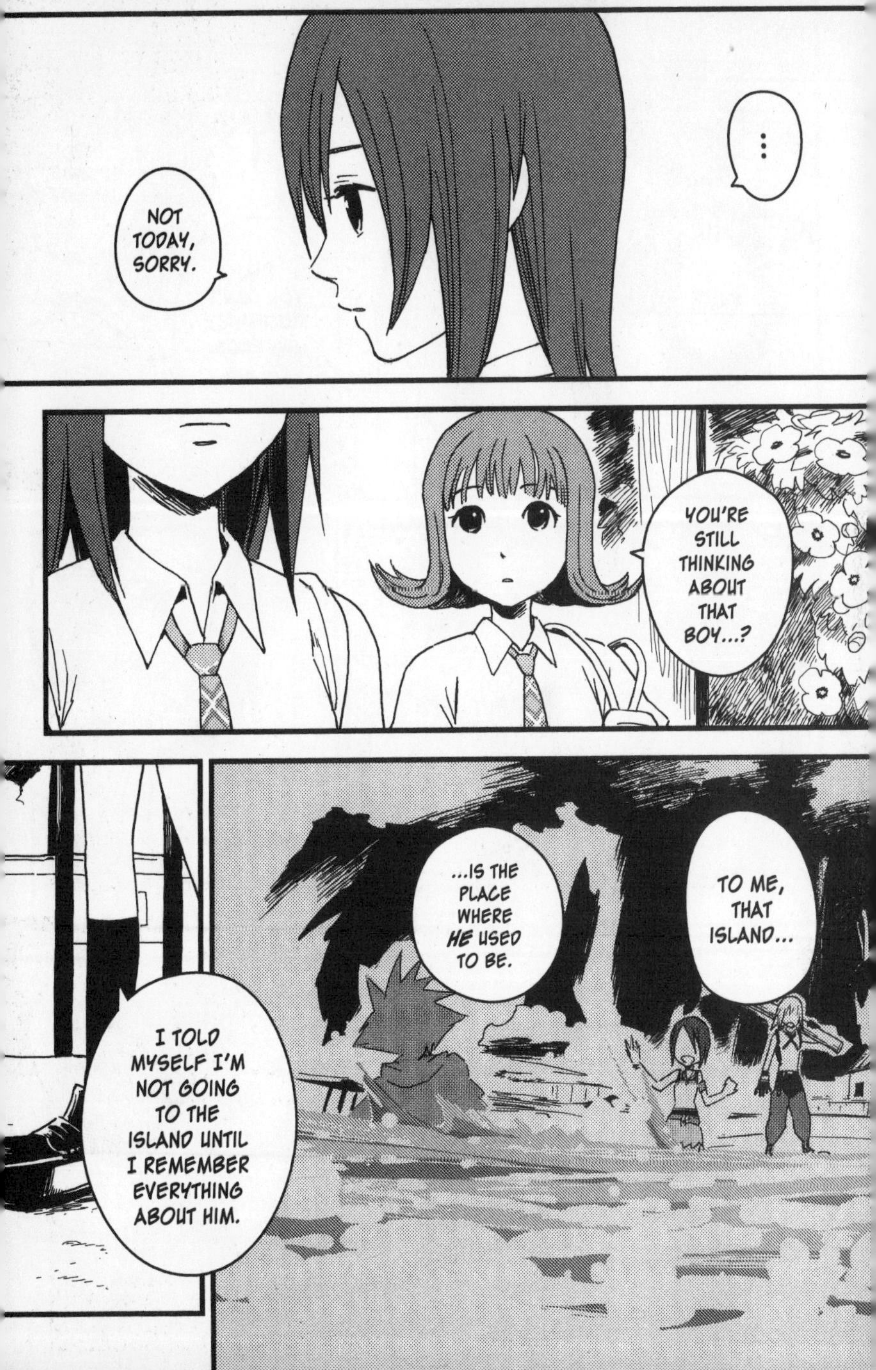
...
NOT TODAY, SORRY.
YOU'RE STILL THINKING ABOUT THAT BOY...?
TO ME, THAT ISLAND...
...IS THE PLACE WHERE *HE* USED TO BE.
I TOLD MYSELF I'M NOT GOING TO THE ISLAND UNTIL I REMEMBER EVERYTHING ABOUT HIM.

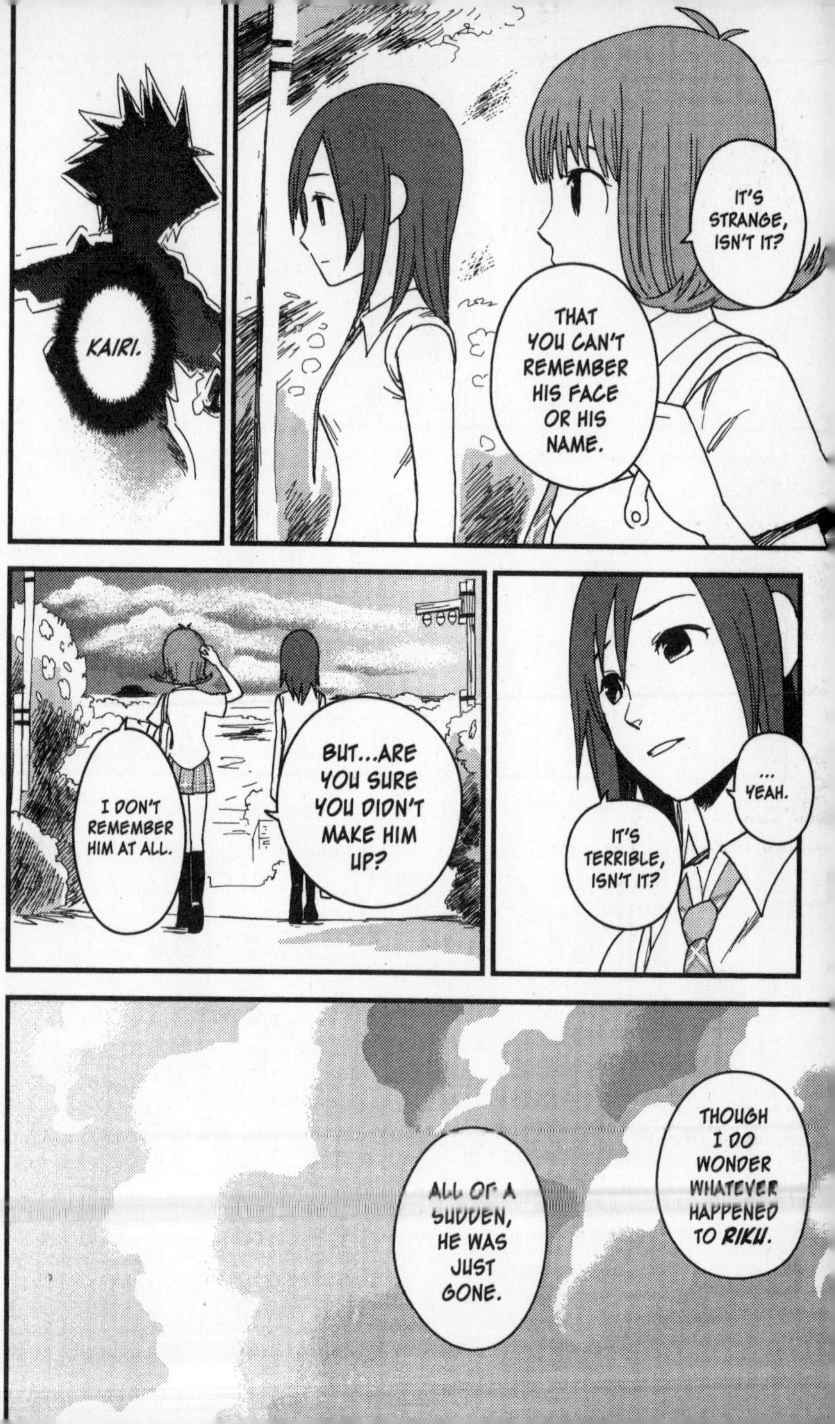

IT'S STRANGE, ISN'T IT?
THAT YOU CAN'T REMEMBER HIS FACE OR HIS NAME.
KAIRI.
... YEAH.
IT'S TERRIBLE, ISN'T IT?
BUT...ARE YOU SURE YOU DIDN'T MAKE HIM UP?
I DON'T REMEMBER HIM AT ALL.
THOUGH I DO WONDER WHATEVER HAPPENED TO *RIKU*.
ALL OF A SUDDEN, HE WAS JUST GONE.

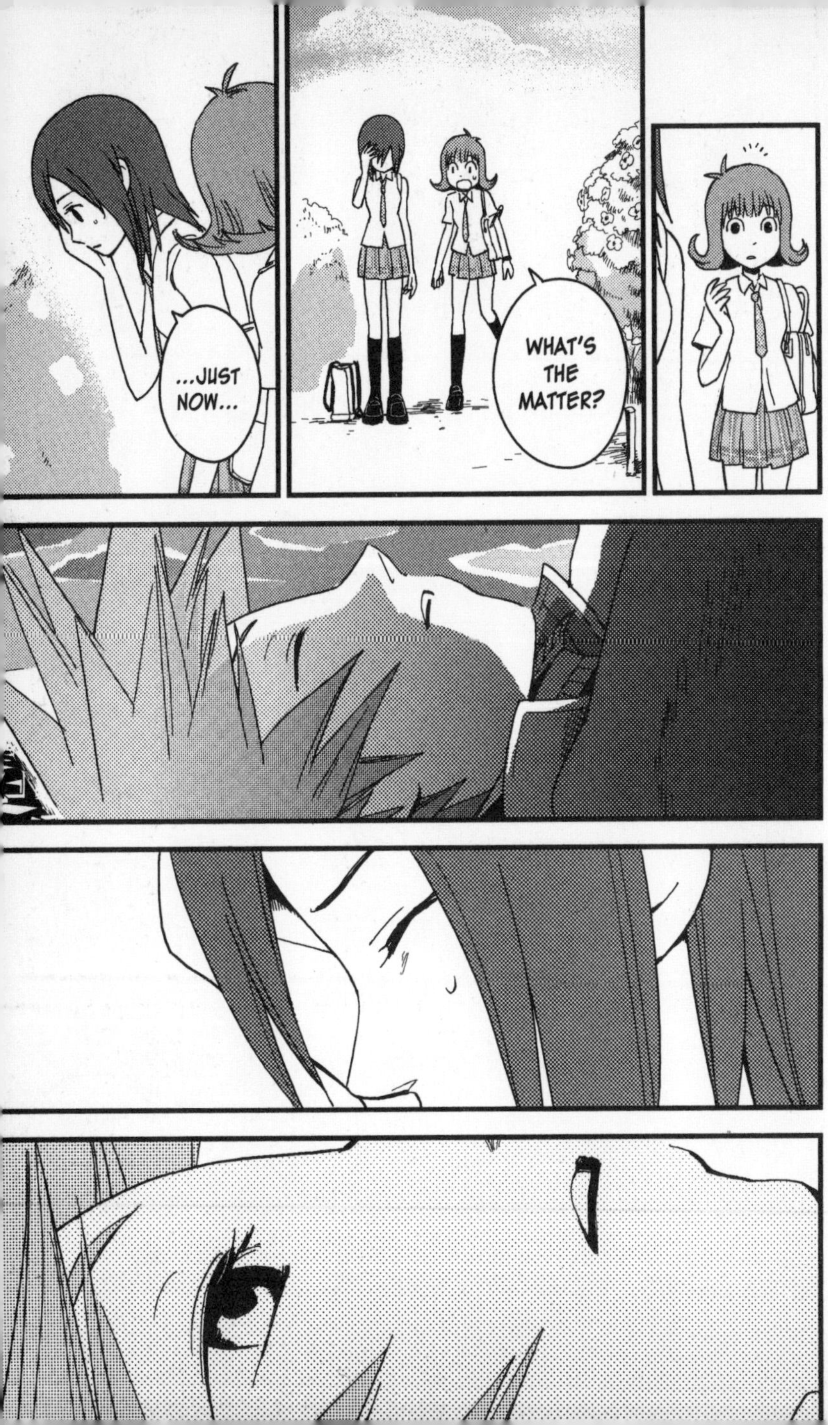
WHAT'S THE MATTER?
...JUST NOW...

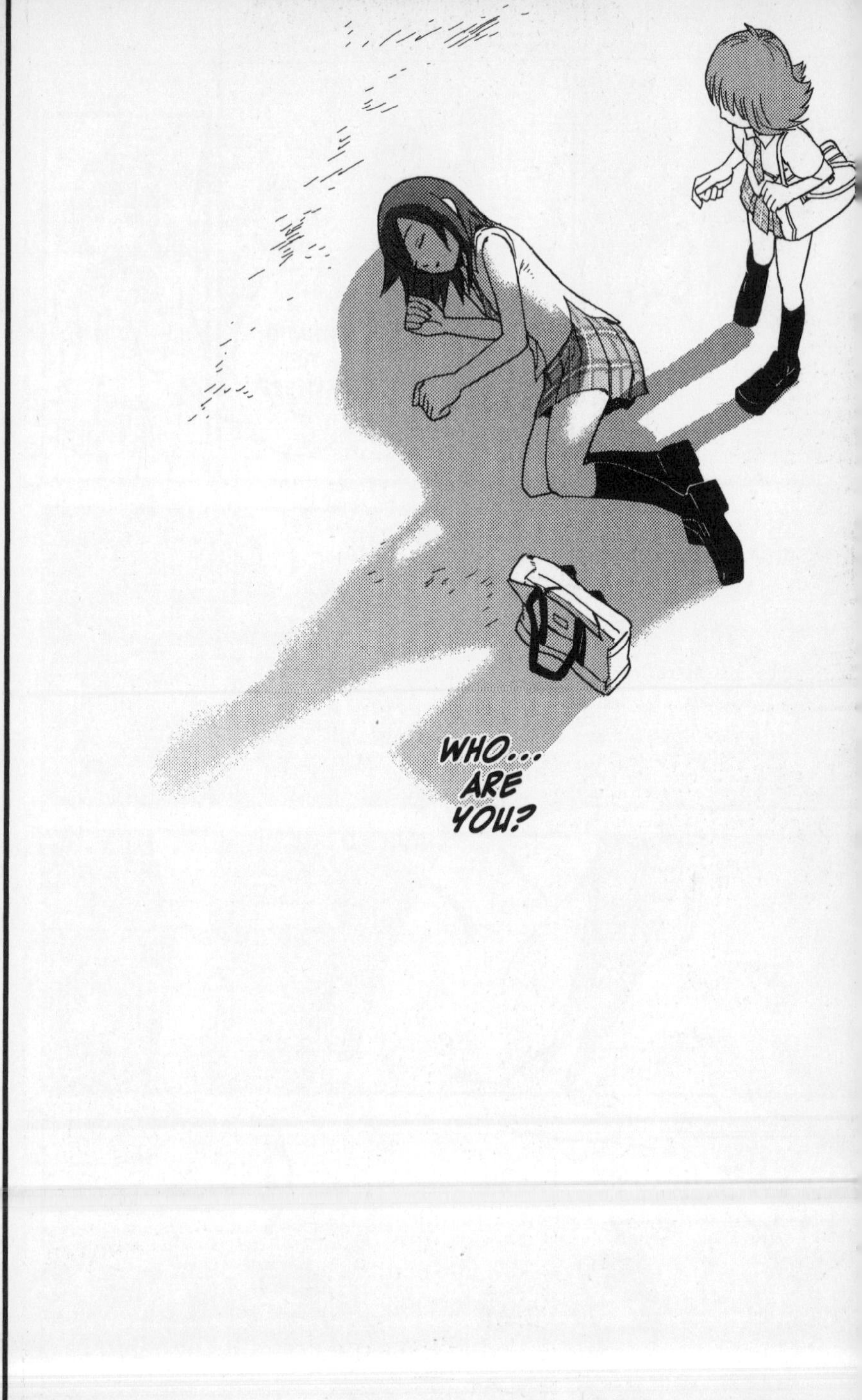
WHO... ARE YOU?

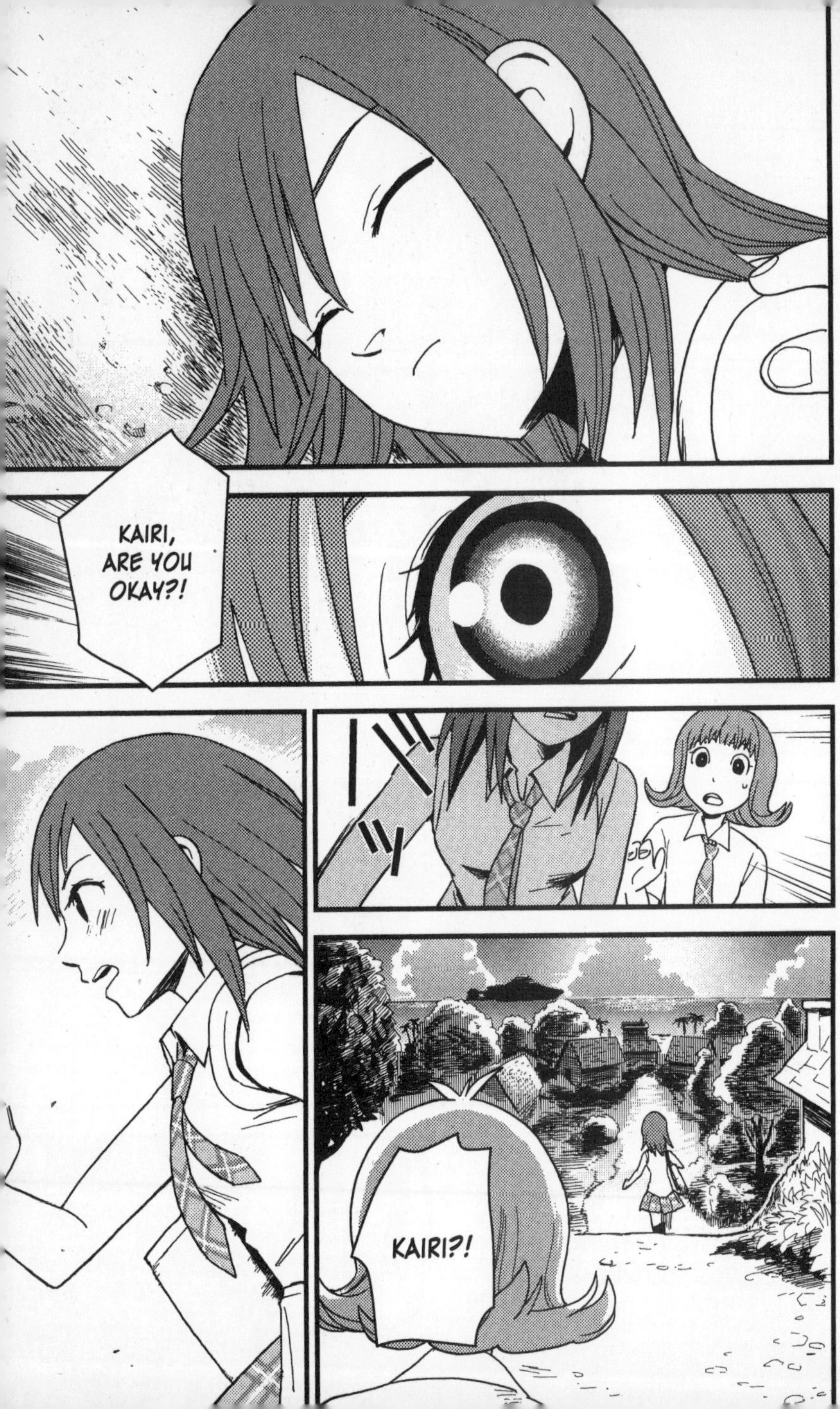
KAIRI, ARE YOU OKAY?!
KAIRI?!

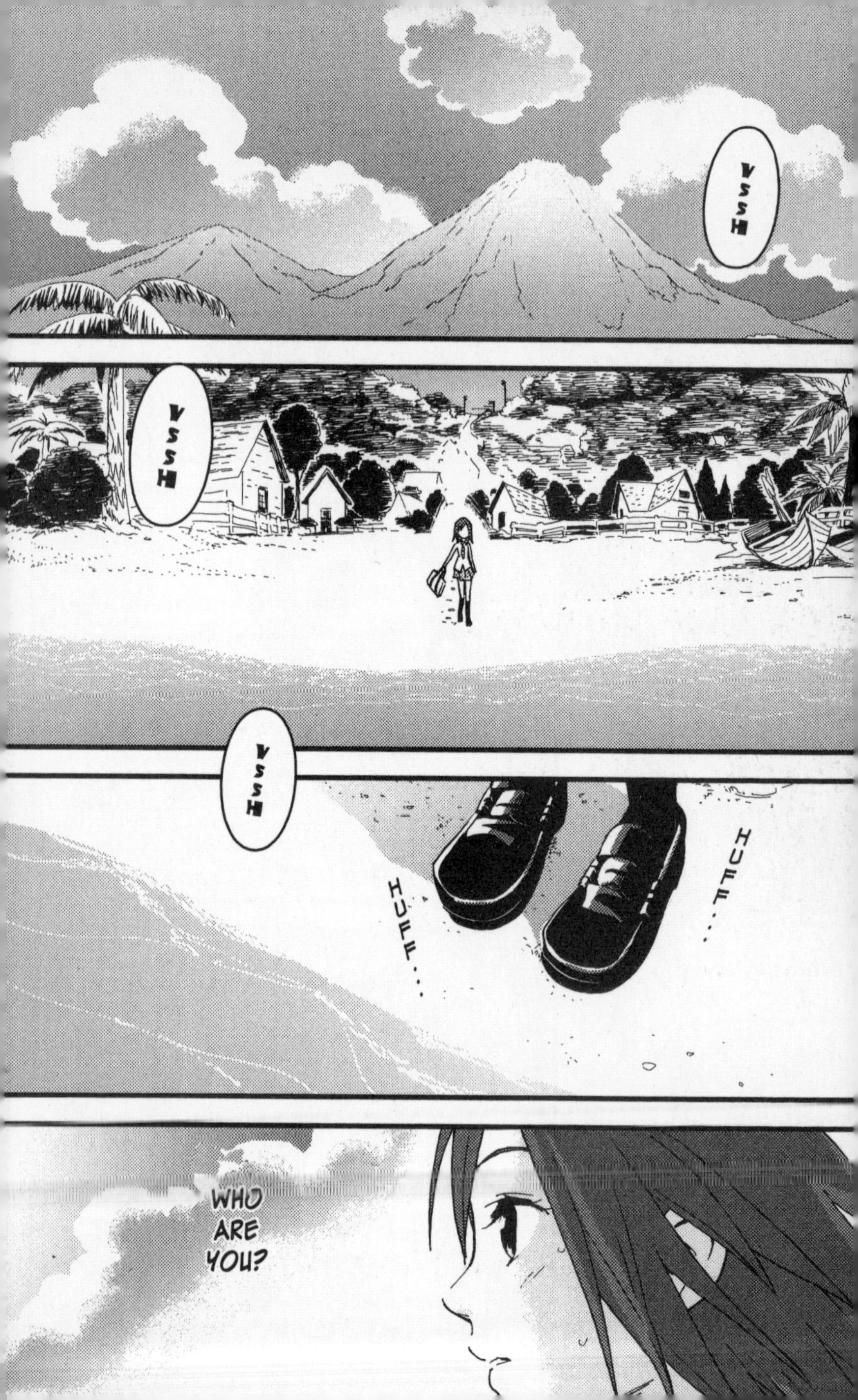
VSSH
VSSH
VSSH
HUFF...
HUFF...
WHO ARE YOU?

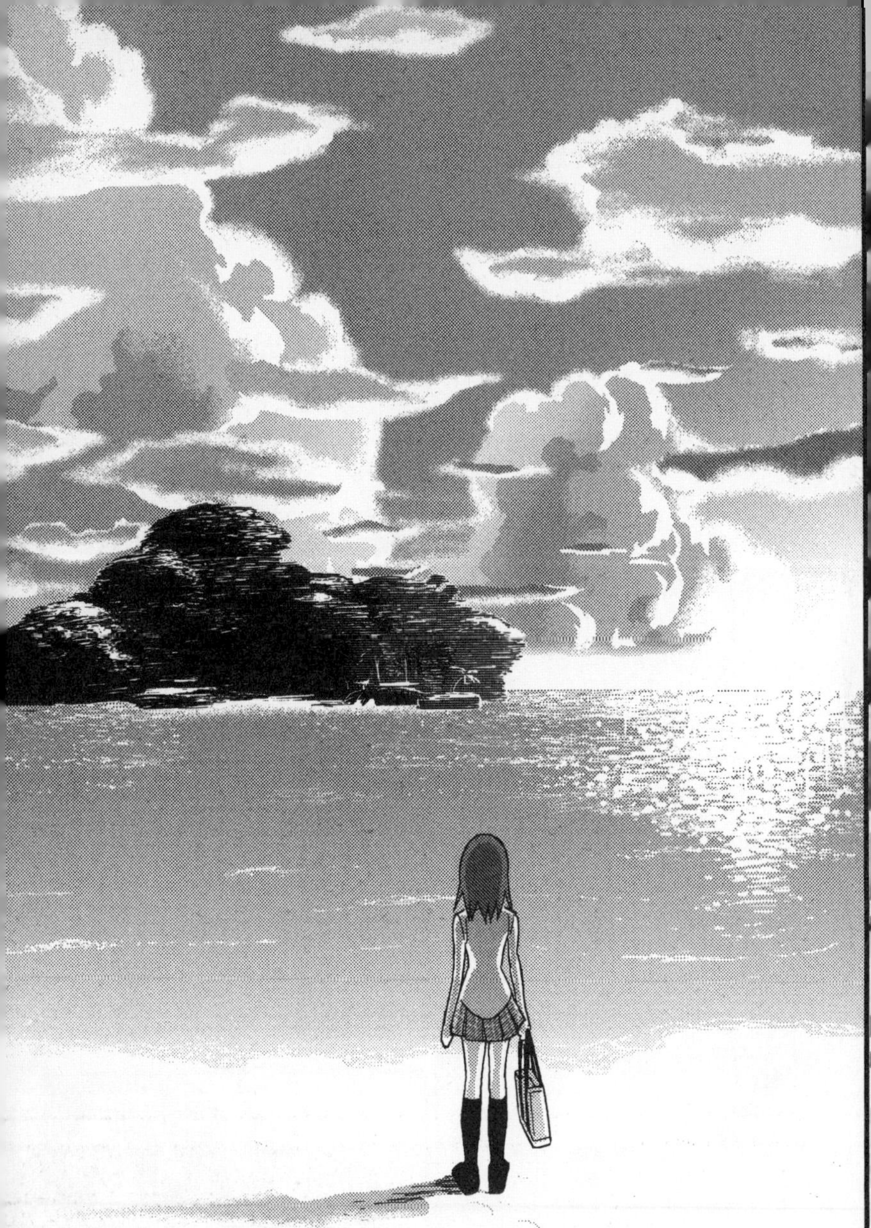

Chapter 7: What I Want to Ask Is...

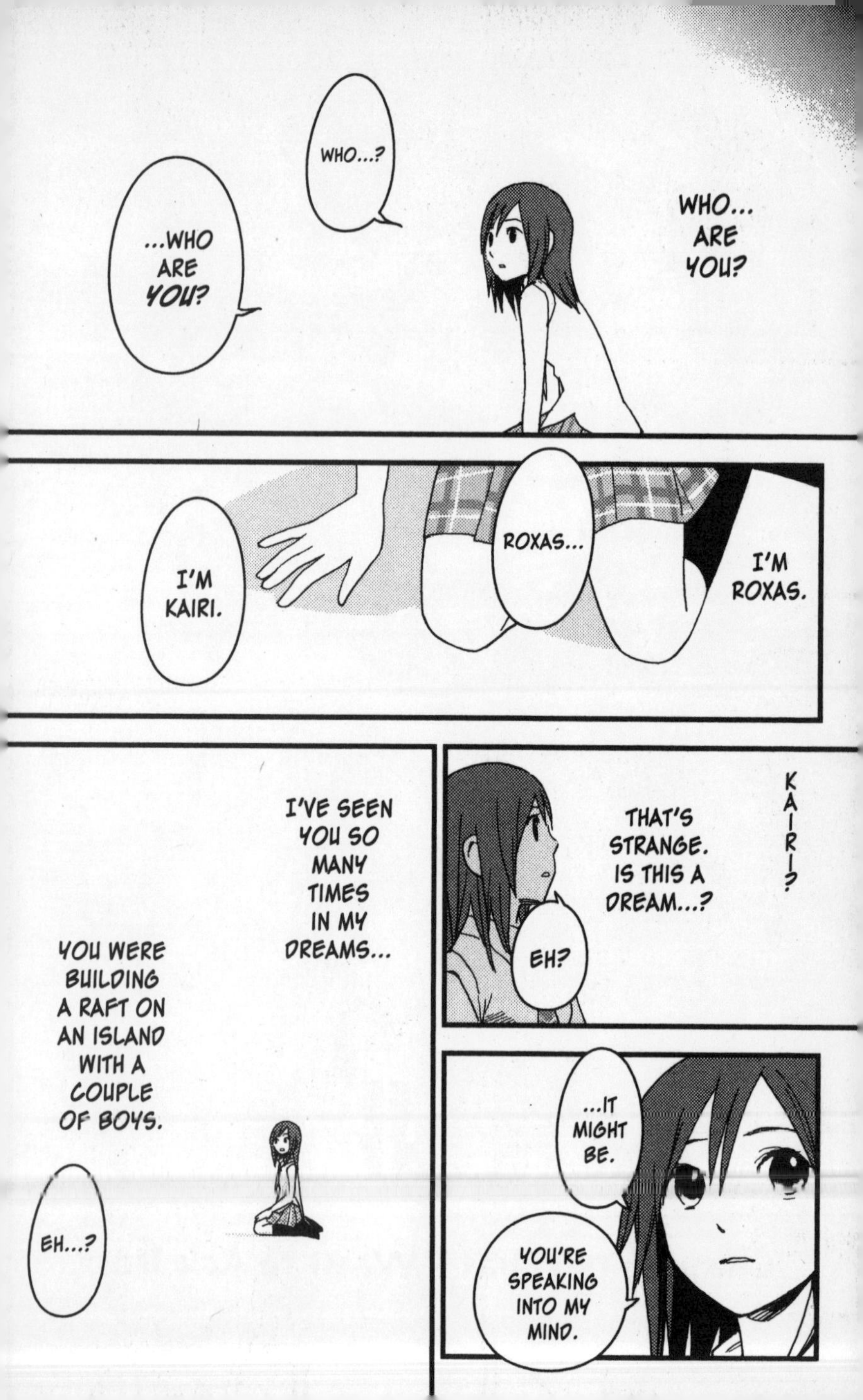
WHO... ARE YOU?
WHO...?
...WHO ARE YOU?
I'M ROXAS.
ROXAS...
I'M KAIRI.
KAIRI?
THAT'S STRANGE. IS THIS A DREAM...?
EH?
...IT MIGHT BE.
YOU'RE SPEAKING INTO MY MIND.
I'VE SEEN YOU SO MANY TIMES IN MY DREAMS...
YOU WERE BUILDING A RAFT ON AN ISLAND WITH A COUPLE OF BOYS.
EH...?

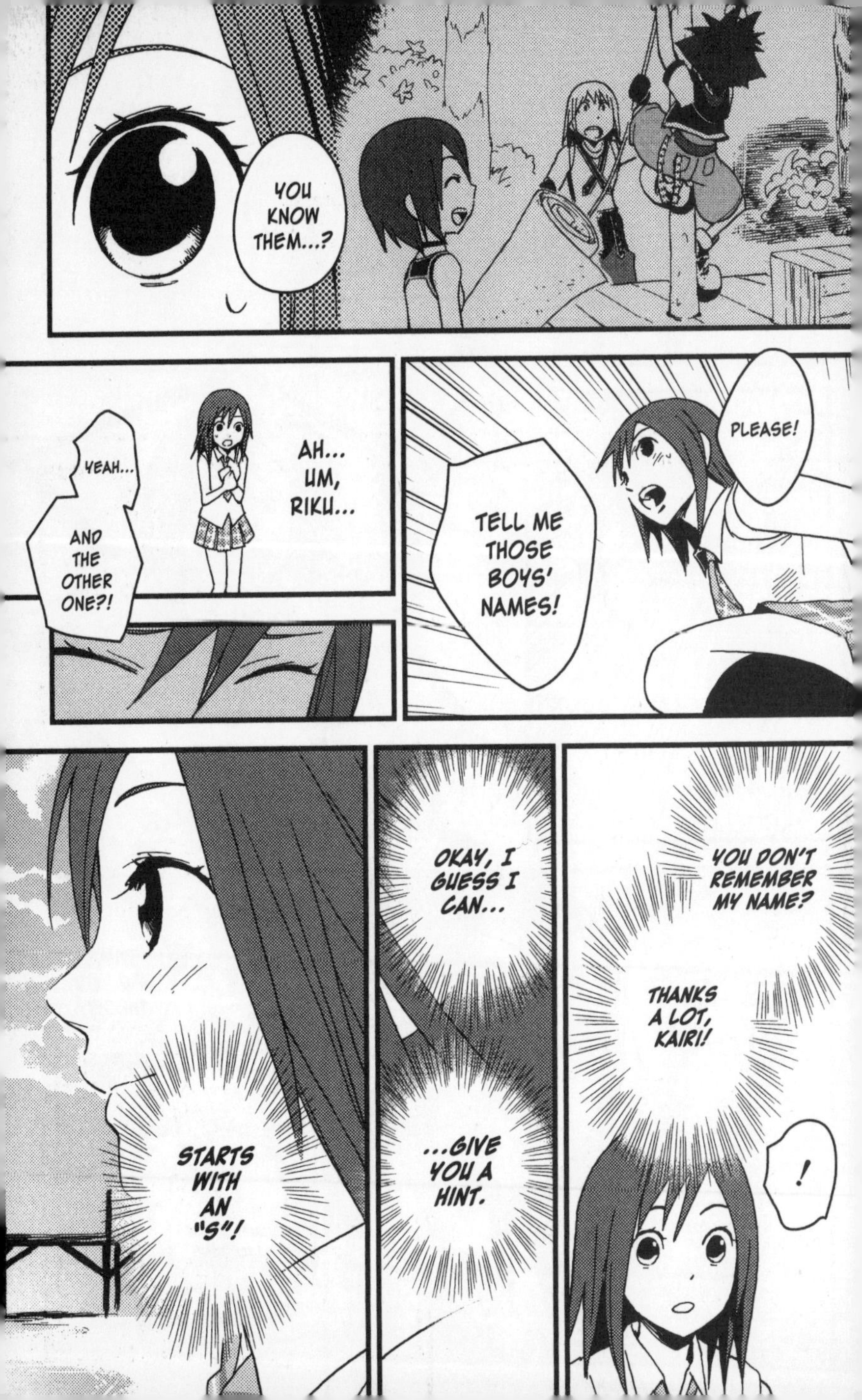

YOU KNOW THEM...?
PLEASE!
TELL ME THOSE BOYS' NAMES!
AH... UM, RIKU...
YEAH...
AND THE OTHER ONE?!
YOU DON'T REMEMBER MY NAME?
THANKS A LOT, KAIRI!
!
OKAY, I GUESS I CAN...
...GIVE YOU A HINT.
STARTS WITH AN "S"!

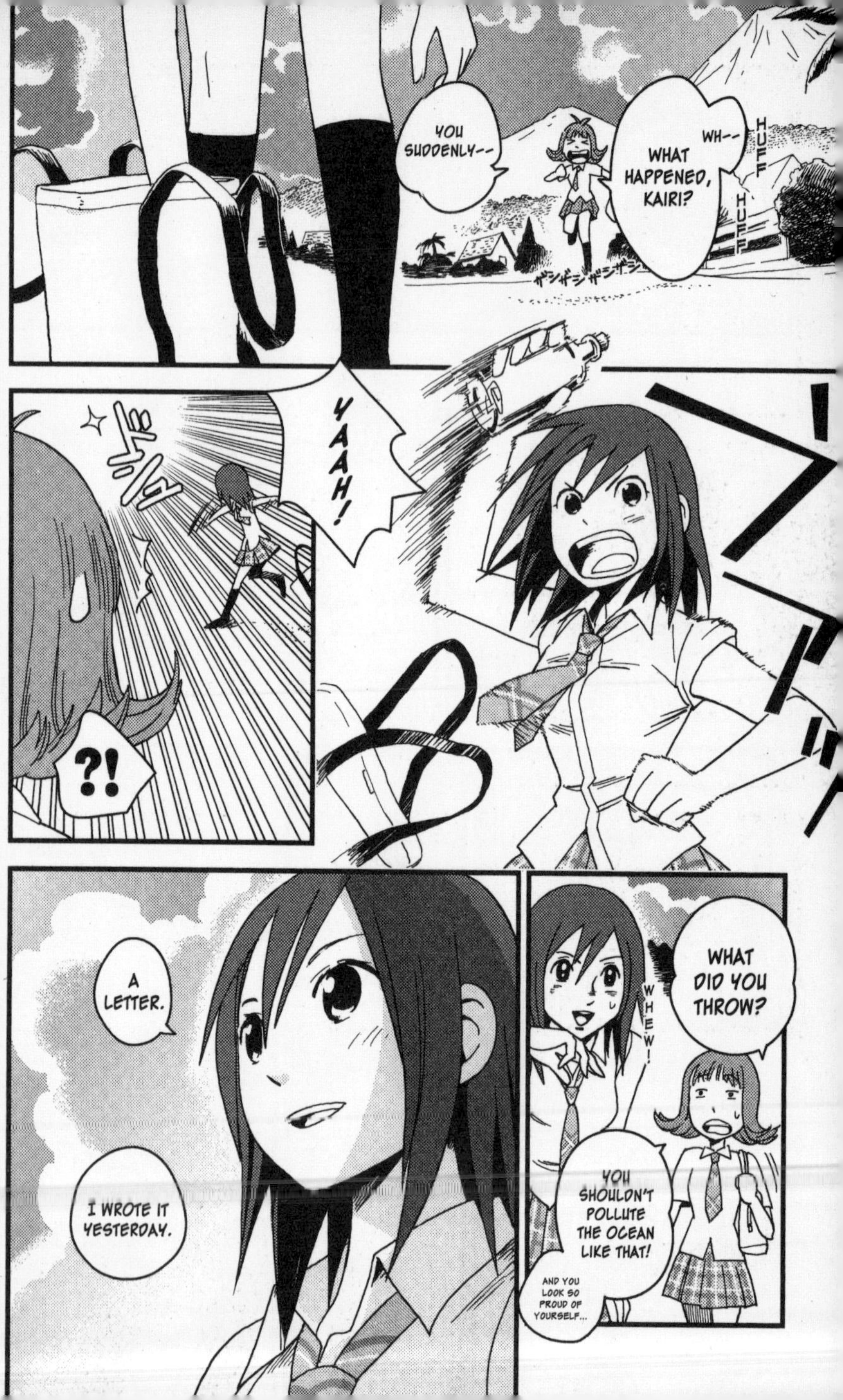
HUFF HUFF
WH-- WHAT HAPPENED, KAIRI?
YOU SUDDENLY--
YAAAH!
?!
WHAT DID YOU THROW?
WHEW!
YOU SHOULDN'T POLLUTE THE OCEAN LIKE THAT!
AND YOU LOOK SO PROUD OF YOURSELF...
A LETTER.
I WROTE IT YESTERDAY.

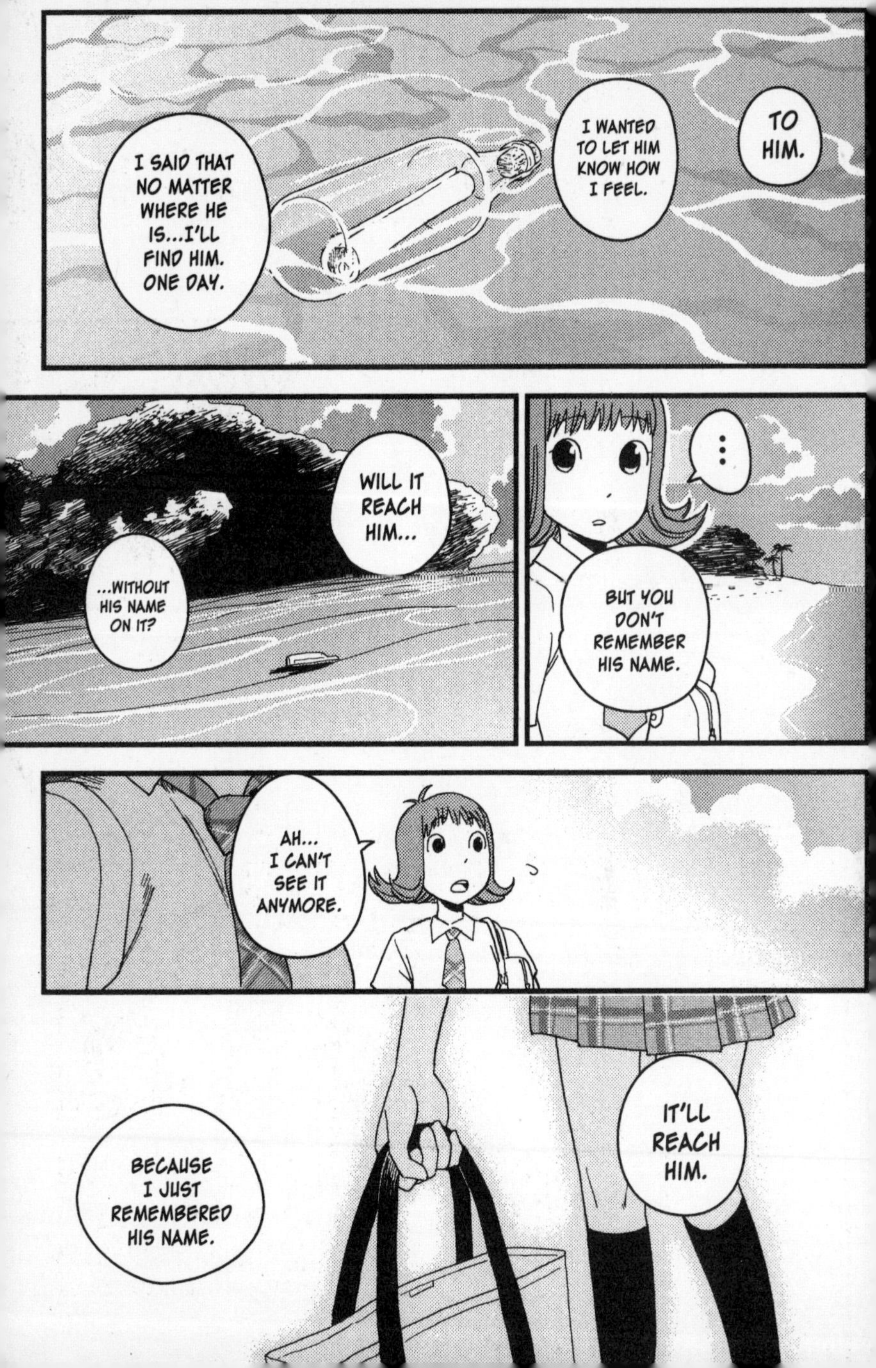
TO HIM.
I WANTED TO LET HIM KNOW HOW I FEEL.
I SAID THAT NO MATTER WHERE HE IS...I'LL FIND HIM. ONE DAY.
...
BUT YOU DON'T REMEMBER HIS NAME.
WILL IT REACH HIM...
...WITHOUT HIS NAME ON IT?
AH... I CAN'T SEE IT ANYMORE.
IT'LL REACH HIM.
BECAUSE I JUST REMEMBERED HIS NAME.

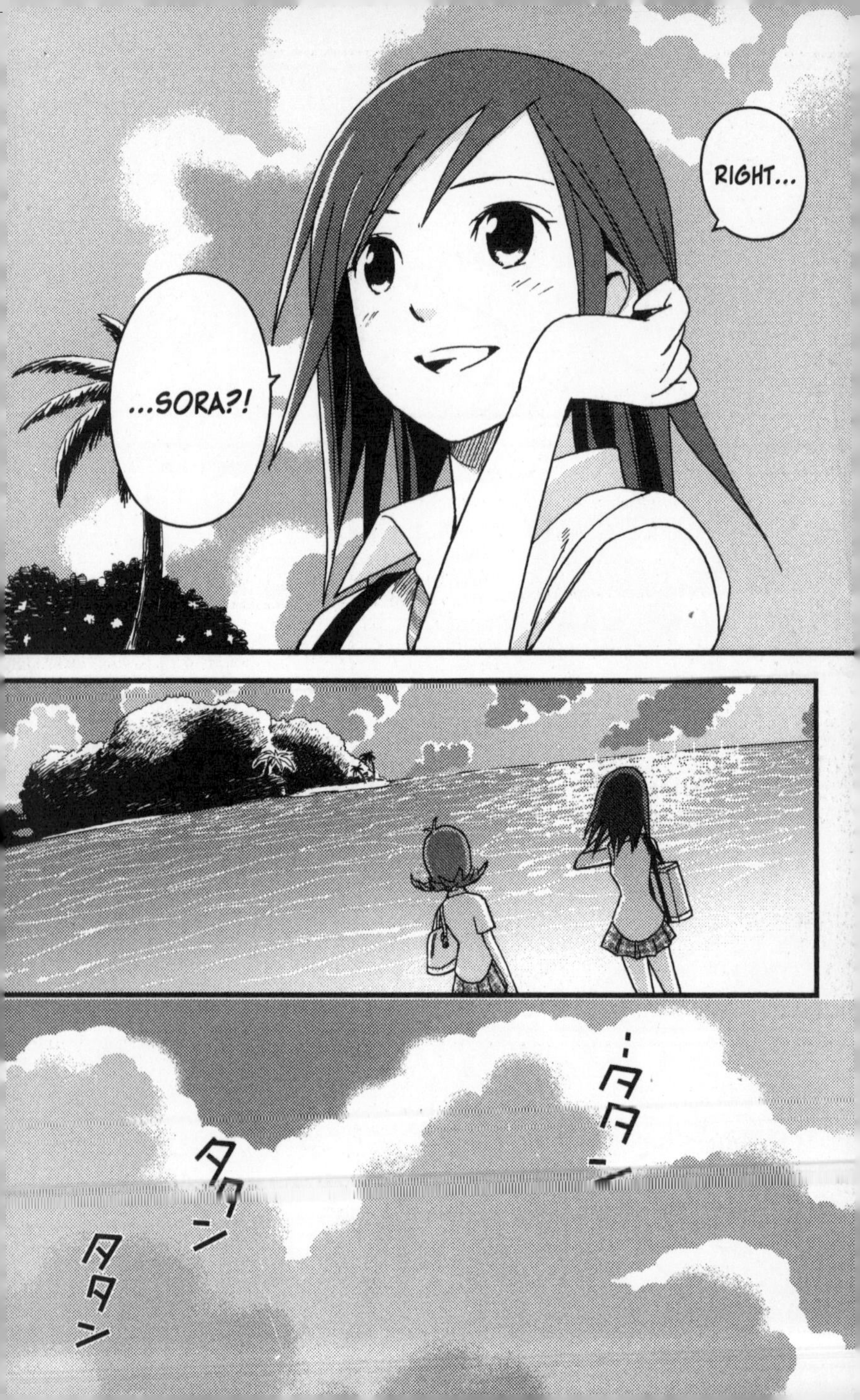
RIGHT...
...SORA?!
タタ—
タタン
タタン

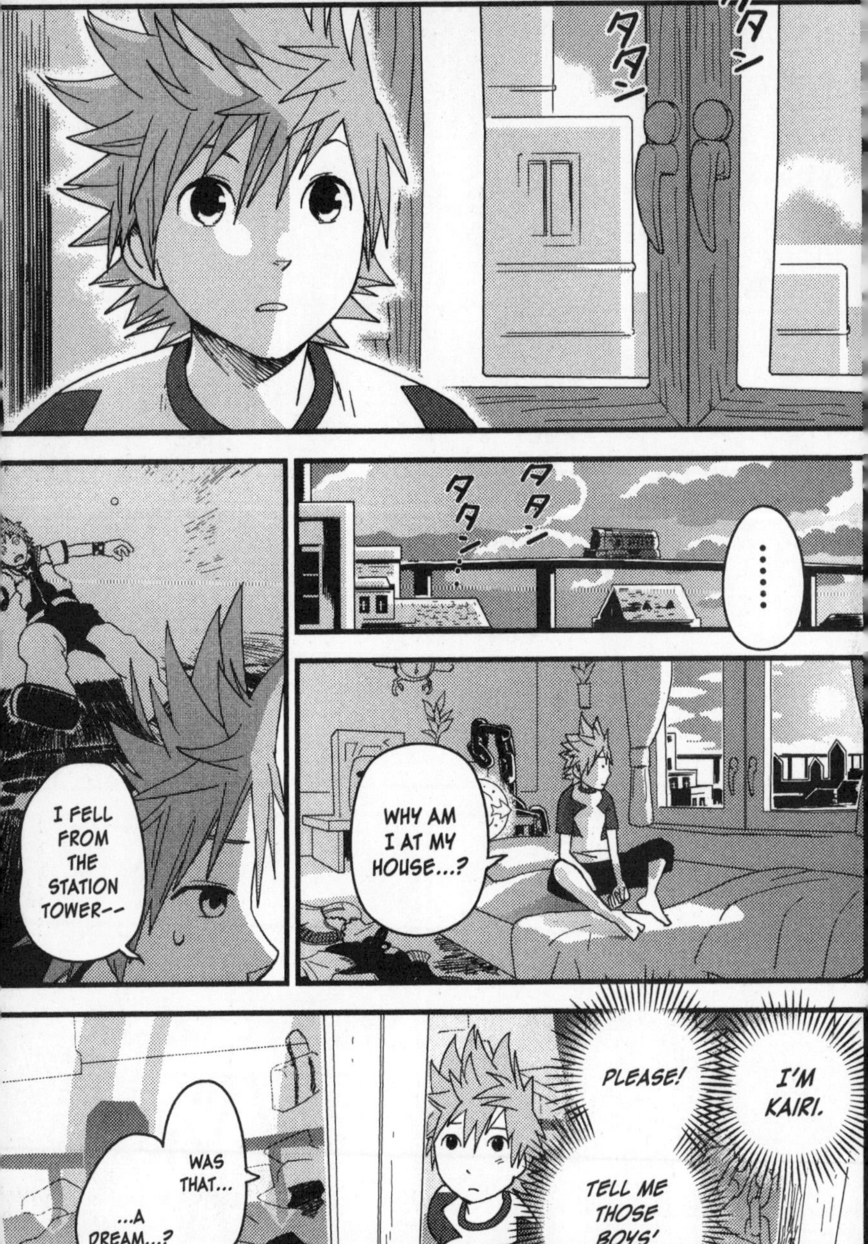
タタン
タタン
タタン
タタン
......
WHY AM I AT MY HOUSE...?
I FELL FROM THE STATION TOWER--
I'M KAIRI.
PLEASE!
TELL ME THOSE BOYS' NAMES!
WAS THAT...
...A DREAM...?

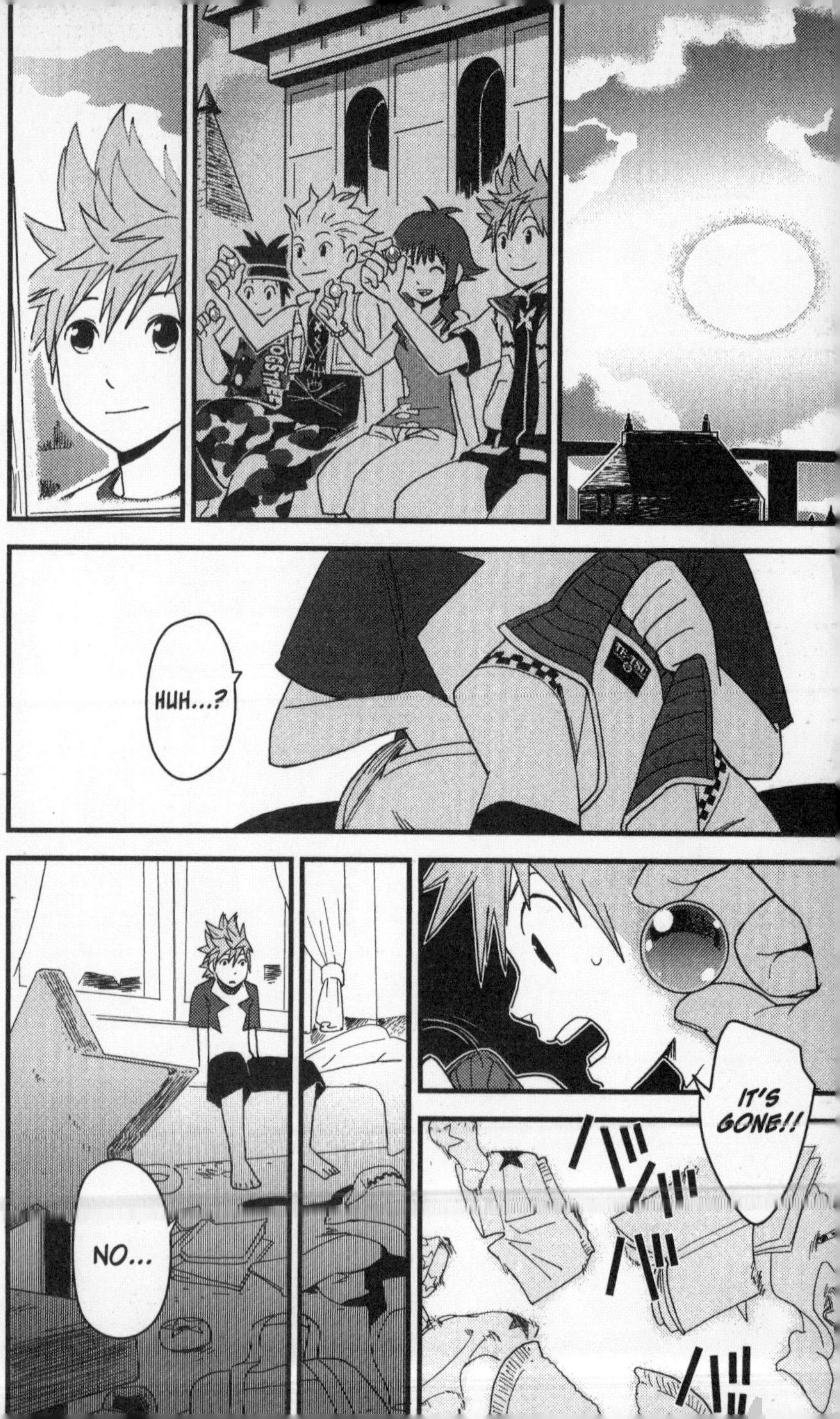
HUH...?
IT'S GONE!!
NO...

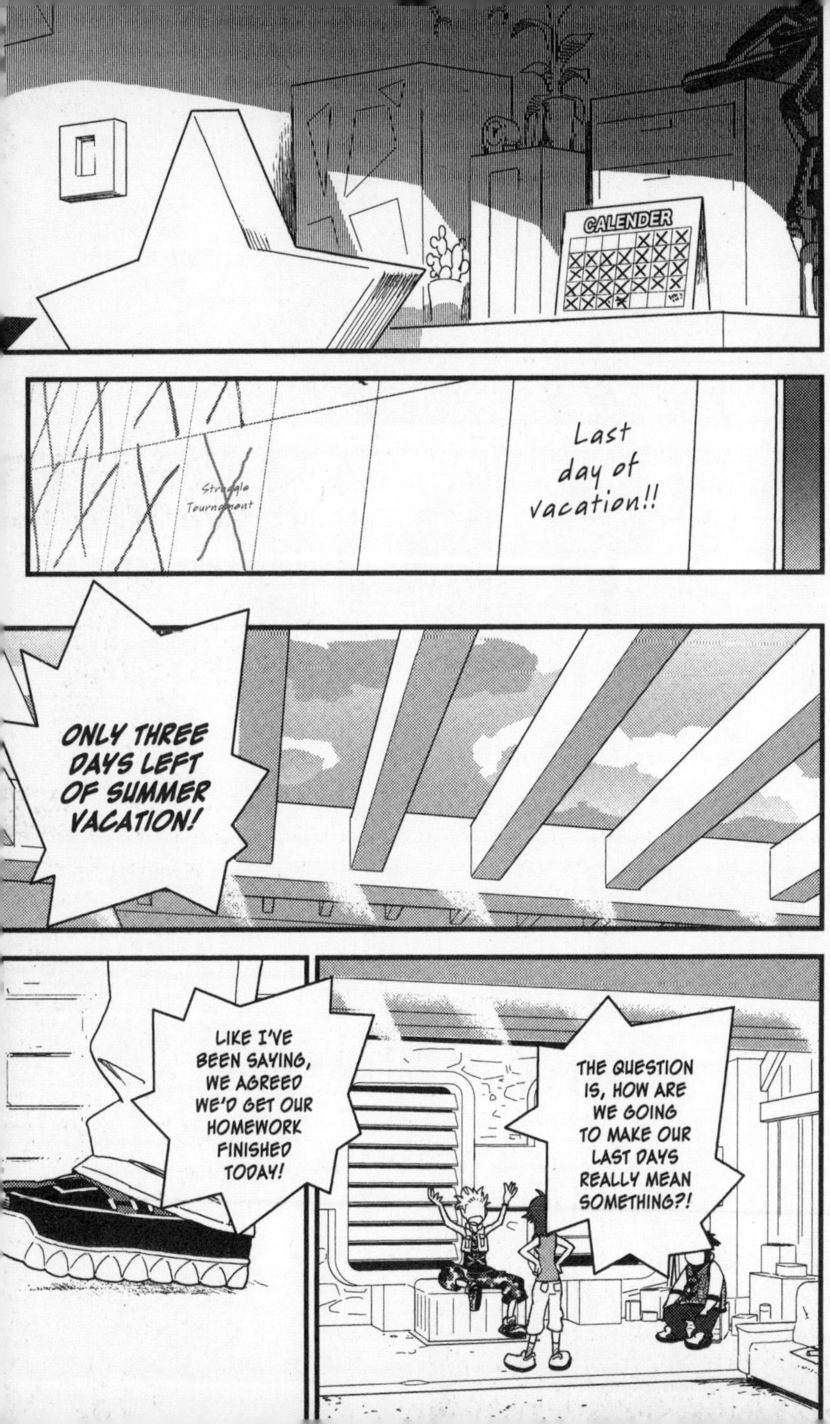
CALENDER
Last day of vacation!!
Struggle Tournament
ONLY THREE DAYS LEFT OF SUMMER VACATION!
THE QUESTION IS, HOW ARE WE GOING TO MAKE OUR LAST DAYS REALLY MEAN SOMETHING?!
LIKE I'VE BEEN SAYING, WE AGREED WE'D GET OUR HOMEWORK FINISHED TODAY!

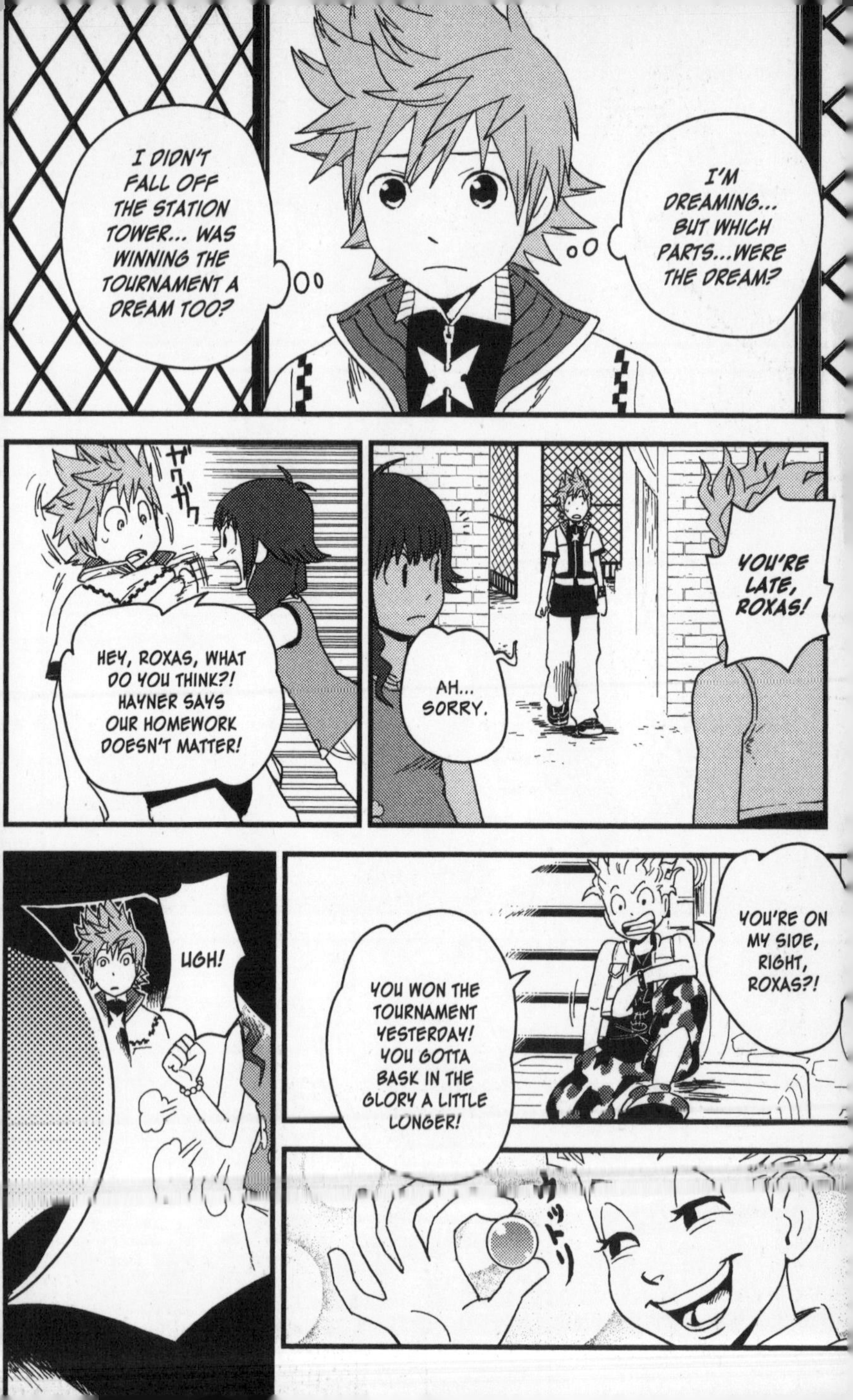
I'M DREAMING... BUT WHICH PARTS...WERE THE DREAM?
I DIDN'T FALL OFF THE STATION TOWER... WAS WINNING THE TOURNAMENT A DREAM TOO?
YOU'RE LATE, ROXAS!
AH... SORRY.
HEY, ROXAS, WHAT DO YOU THINK?! HAYNER SAYS OUR HOMEWORK DOESN'T MATTER!
YOU'RE ON MY SIDE, RIGHT, ROXAS?!
YOU WON THE TOURNAMENT YESTERDAY! YOU GOTTA BASK IN THE GLORY A LITTLE LONGER!
UGH!

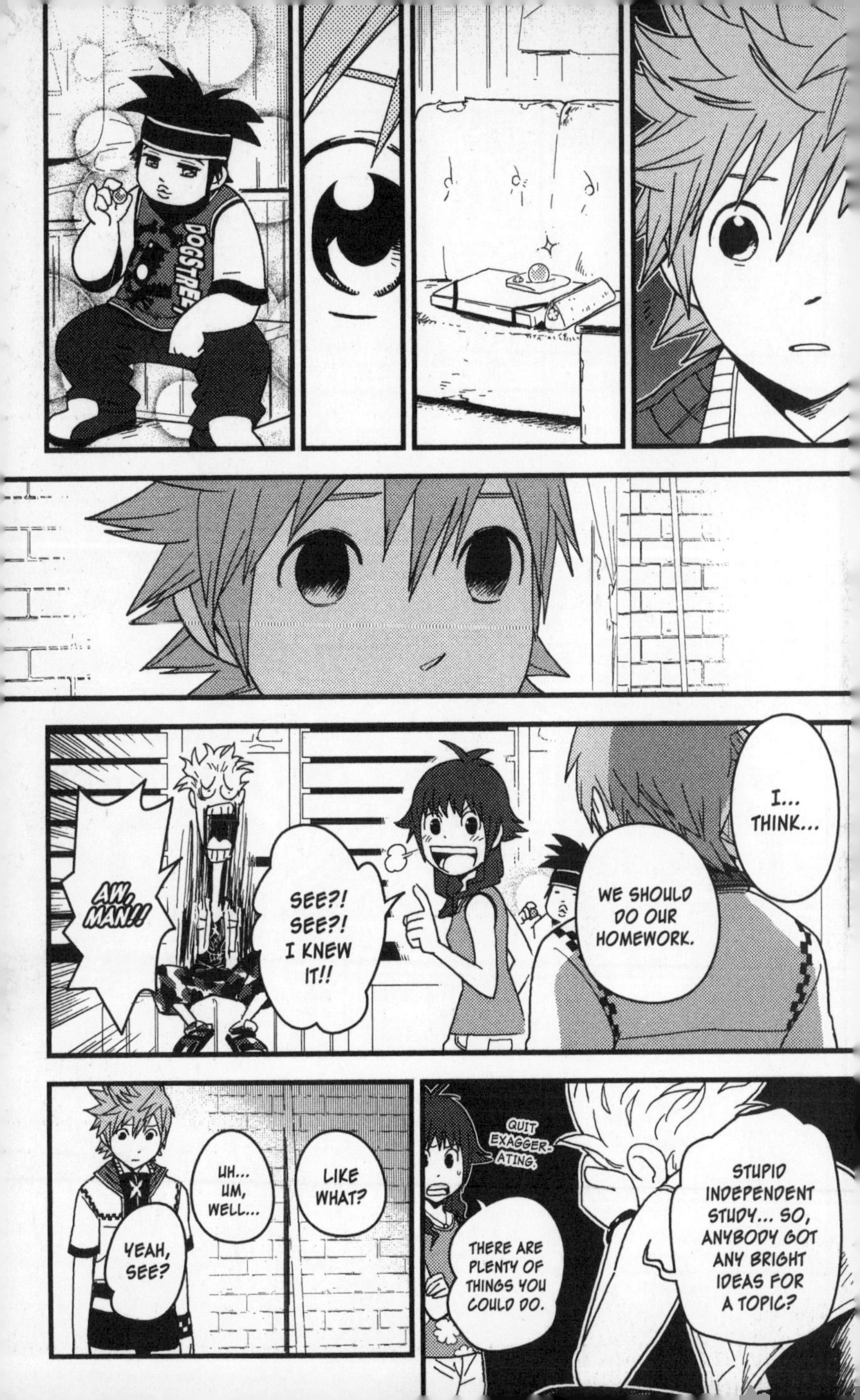
I... THINK...
WE SHOULD DO OUR HOMEWORK.
SEE?! SEE?! I KNEW IT!!
AW, MAN!!
STUPID INDEPENDENT STUDY... SO, ANYBODY GOT ANY BRIGHT IDEAS FOR A TOPIC?
QUIT EXAGGER-ATING.
THERE ARE PLENTY OF THINGS YOU COULD DO.
LIKE WHAT?
UH... UM, WELL...
YEAH, SEE?

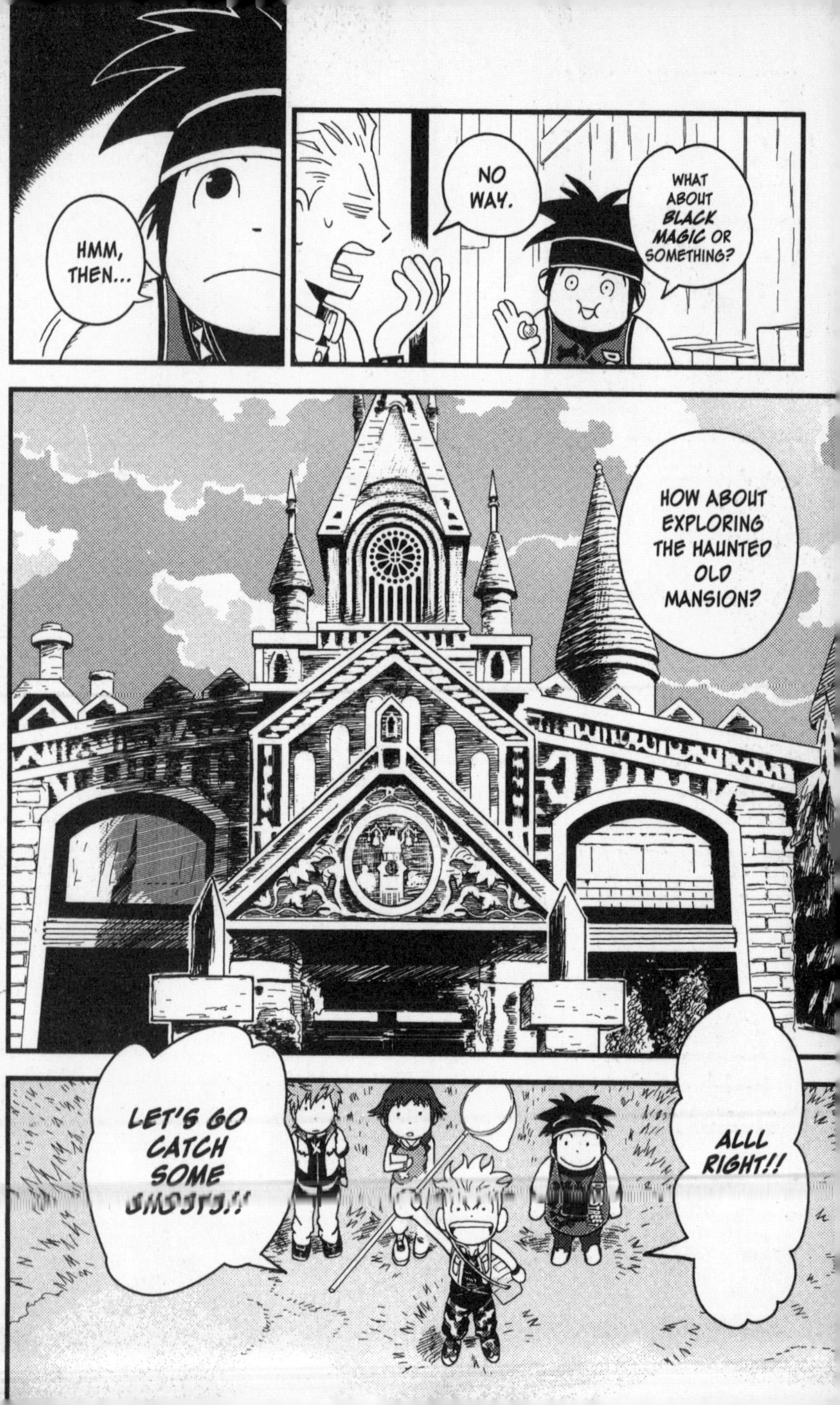
WHAT ABOUT BLACK MAGIC OR SOMETHING?
NO WAY.
HMM, THEN...
HOW ABOUT EXPLORING THE HAUNTED OLD MANSION?
LET'S GO CATCH SOME
ALLL RIGHT!!

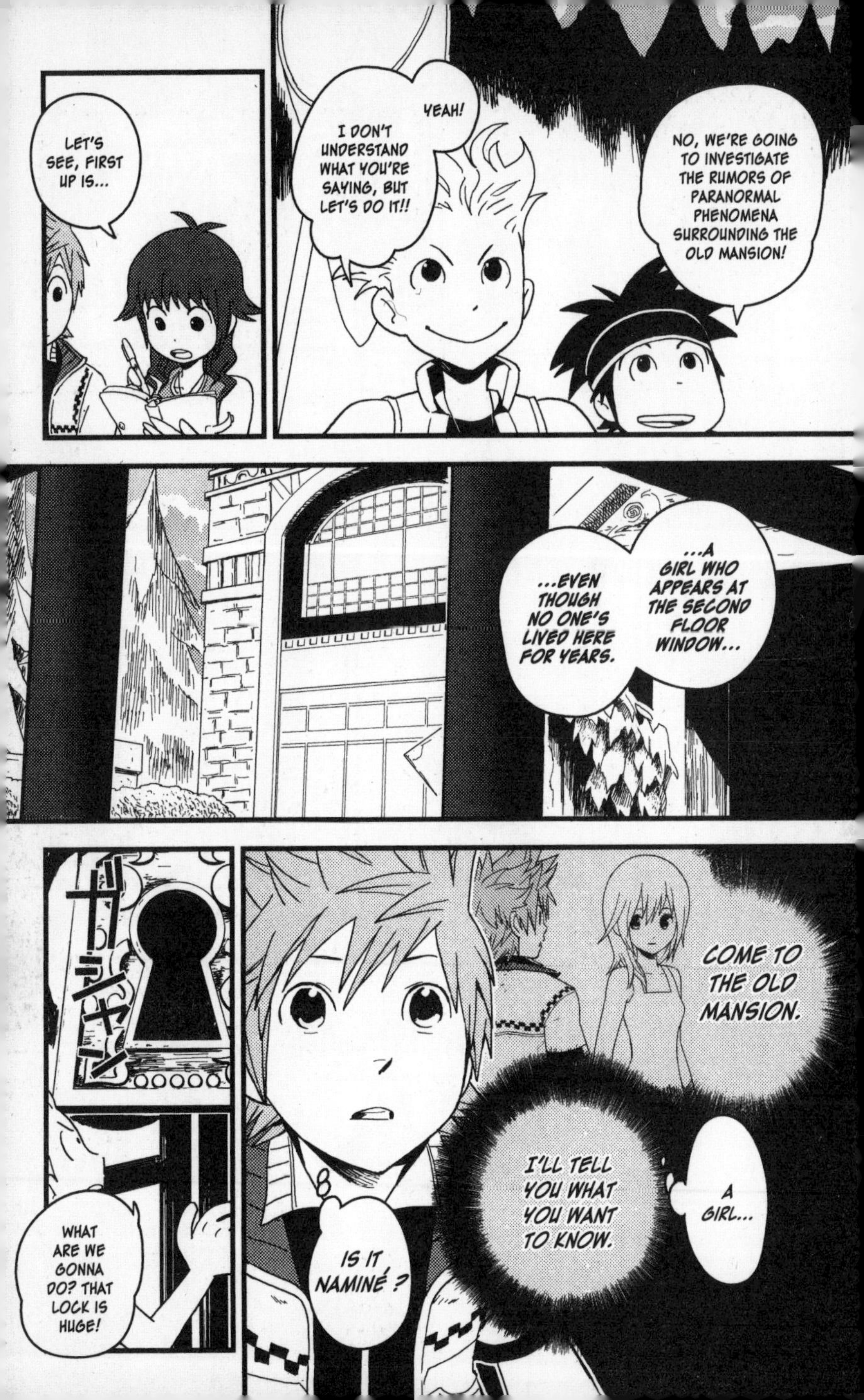
NO, WE'RE GOING TO INVESTIGATE THE RUMORS OF PARANORMAL PHENOMENA SURROUNDING THE OLD MANSION!
YEAH!
I DON'T UNDERSTAND WHAT YOU'RE SAYING, BUT LET'S DO IT!!
LET'S SEE, FIRST UP IS...
...A GIRL WHO APPEARS AT THE SECOND FLOOR WINDOW...
...EVEN THOUGH NO ONE'S LIVED HERE FOR YEARS.
COME TO THE OLD MANSION.
A GIRL...
I'LL TELL YOU WHAT YOU WANT TO KNOW.
IS IT NAMINÉ ?
WHAT ARE WE GONNA DO? THAT LOCK IS HUGE!

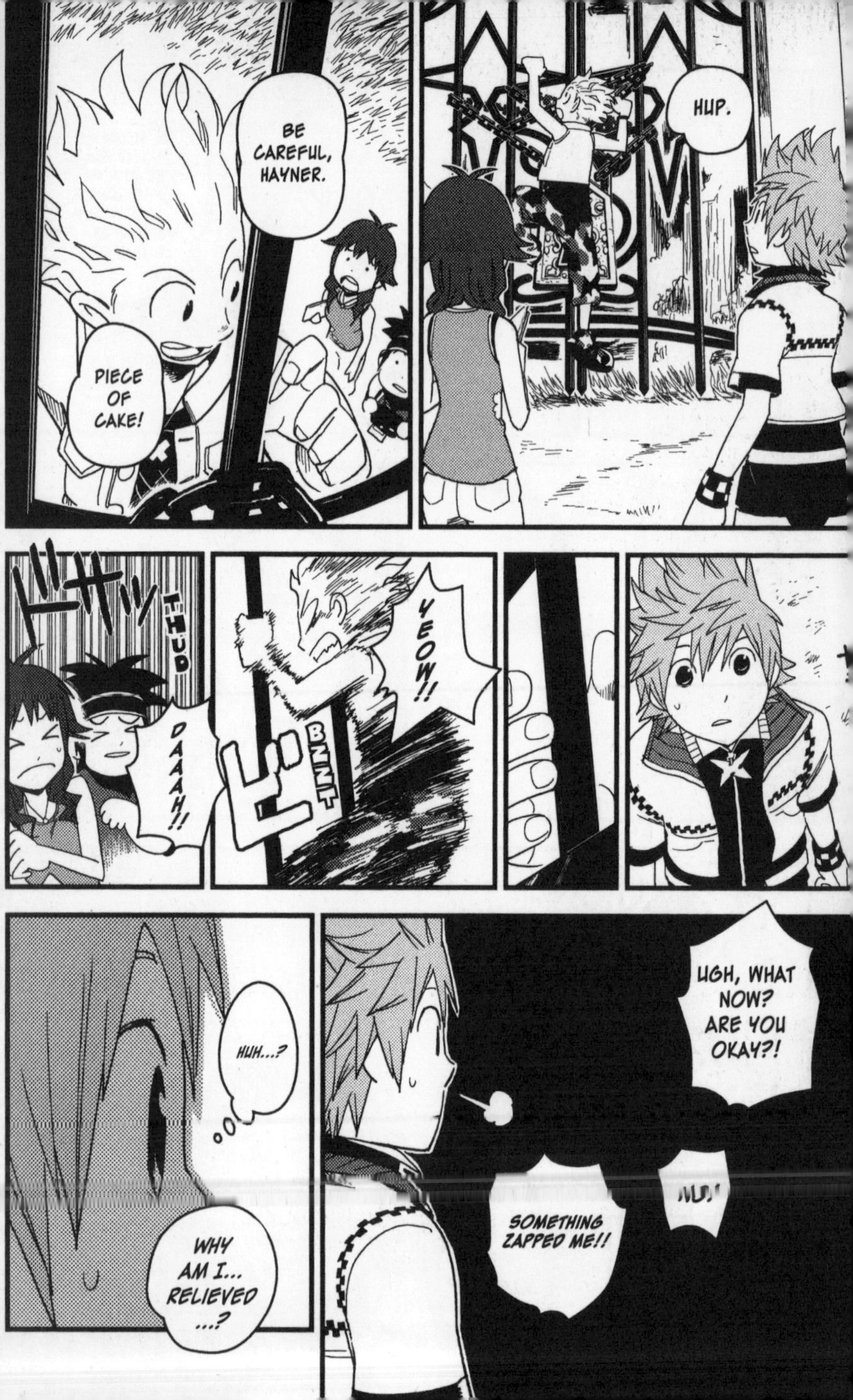
HUP.
BE CAREFUL, HAYNER.
PIECE OF CAKE!
YEOW!!
BZZT
THUD
DAAAH!!
UGH, WHAT NOW? ARE YOU OKAY?!
SOMETHING ZAPPED ME!!
HUH...?
WHY AM I... RELIEVED ...?

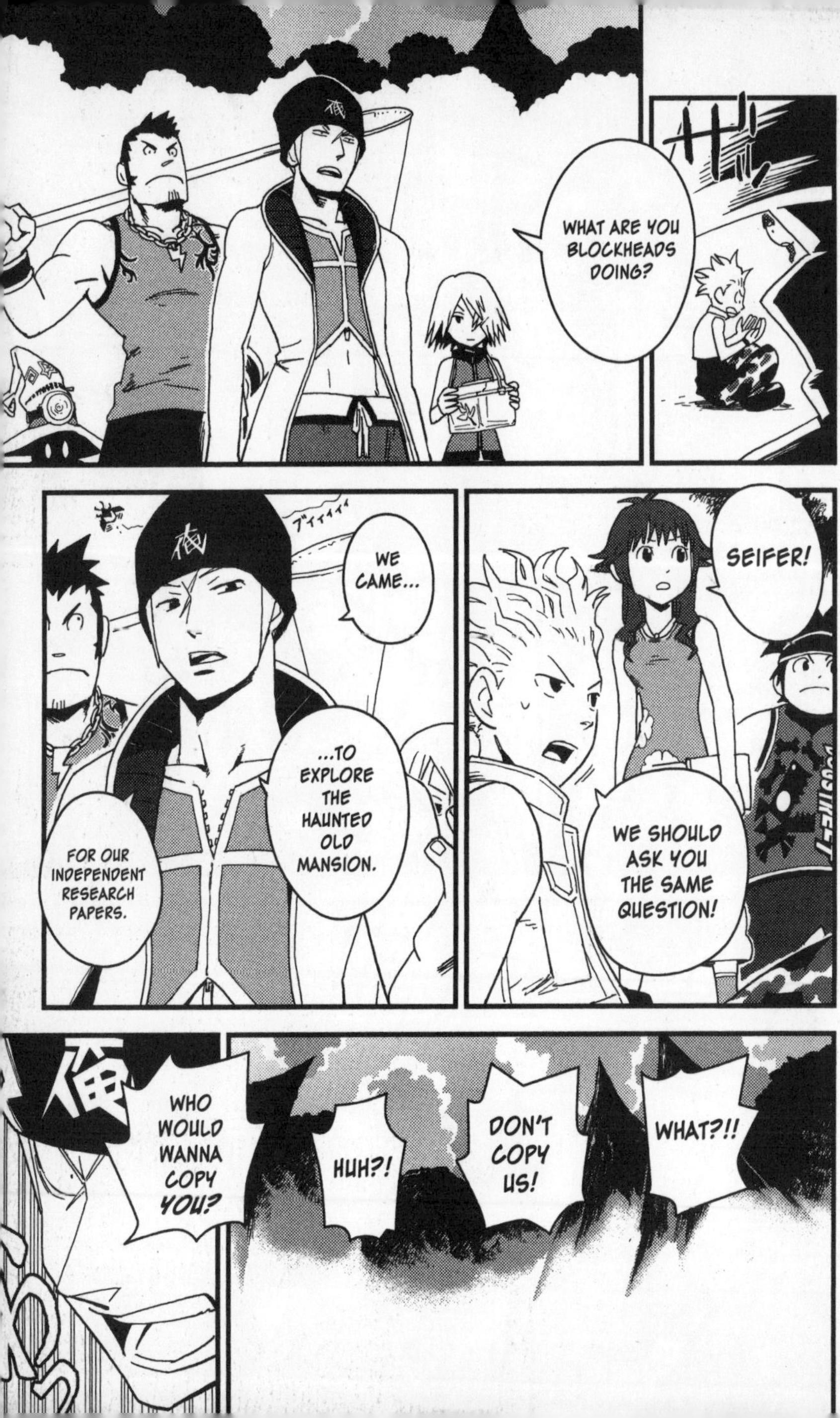
WHAT ARE YOU BLOCKHEADS DOING?
SEIFER!
WE SHOULD ASK YOU THE SAME QUESTION!
WE CAME...
...TO EXPLORE THE HAUNTED OLD MANSION.
FOR OUR INDEPENDENT RESEARCH PAPERS.
WHAT?!!
DON'T COPY US!
HUH?!
WHO WOULD WANNA COPY YOU?

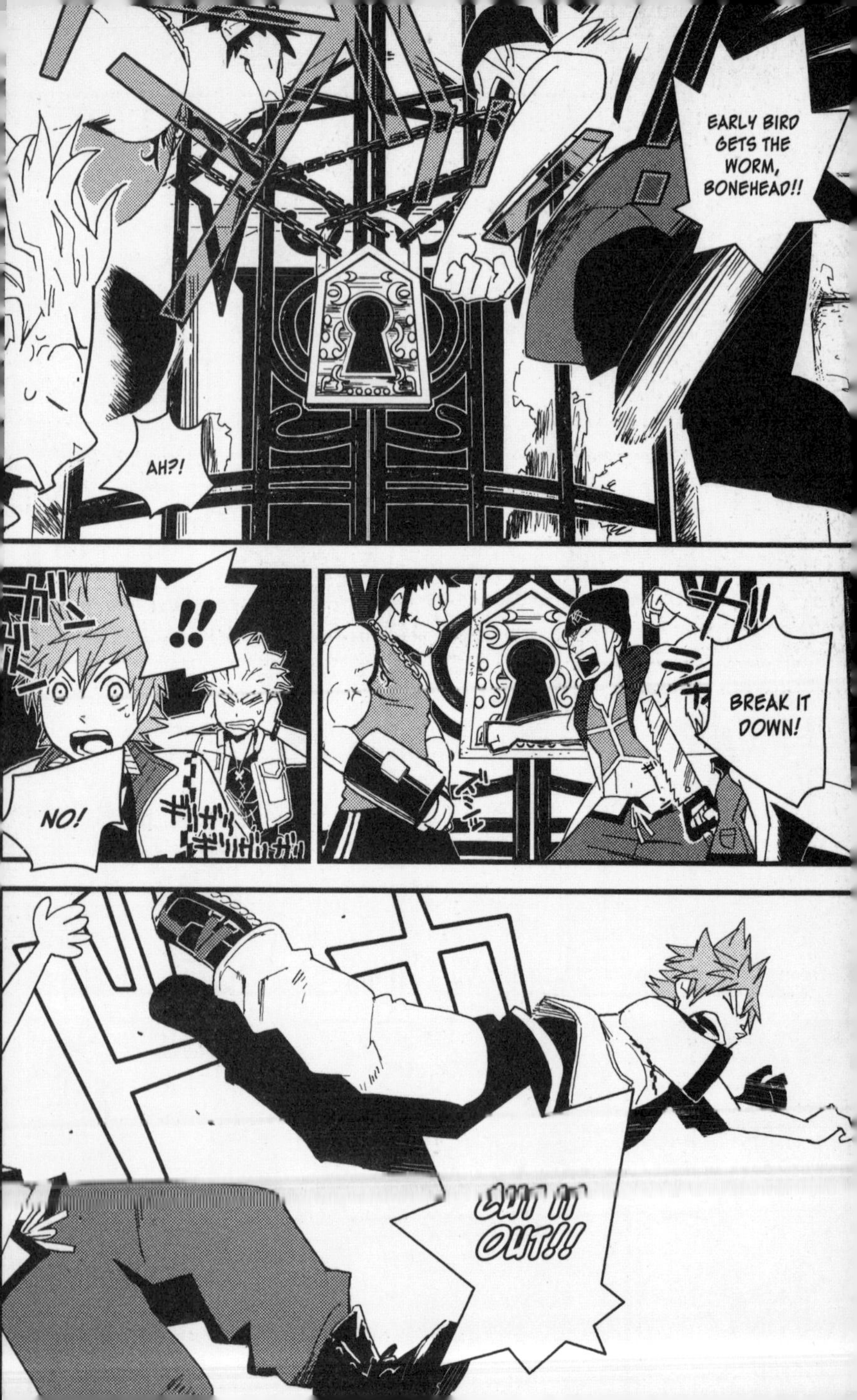
EARLY BIRD GETS THE WORM, BONEHEAD!!
AH?!
BREAK IT DOWN!
!!
NO!
CUT IT OUT!!

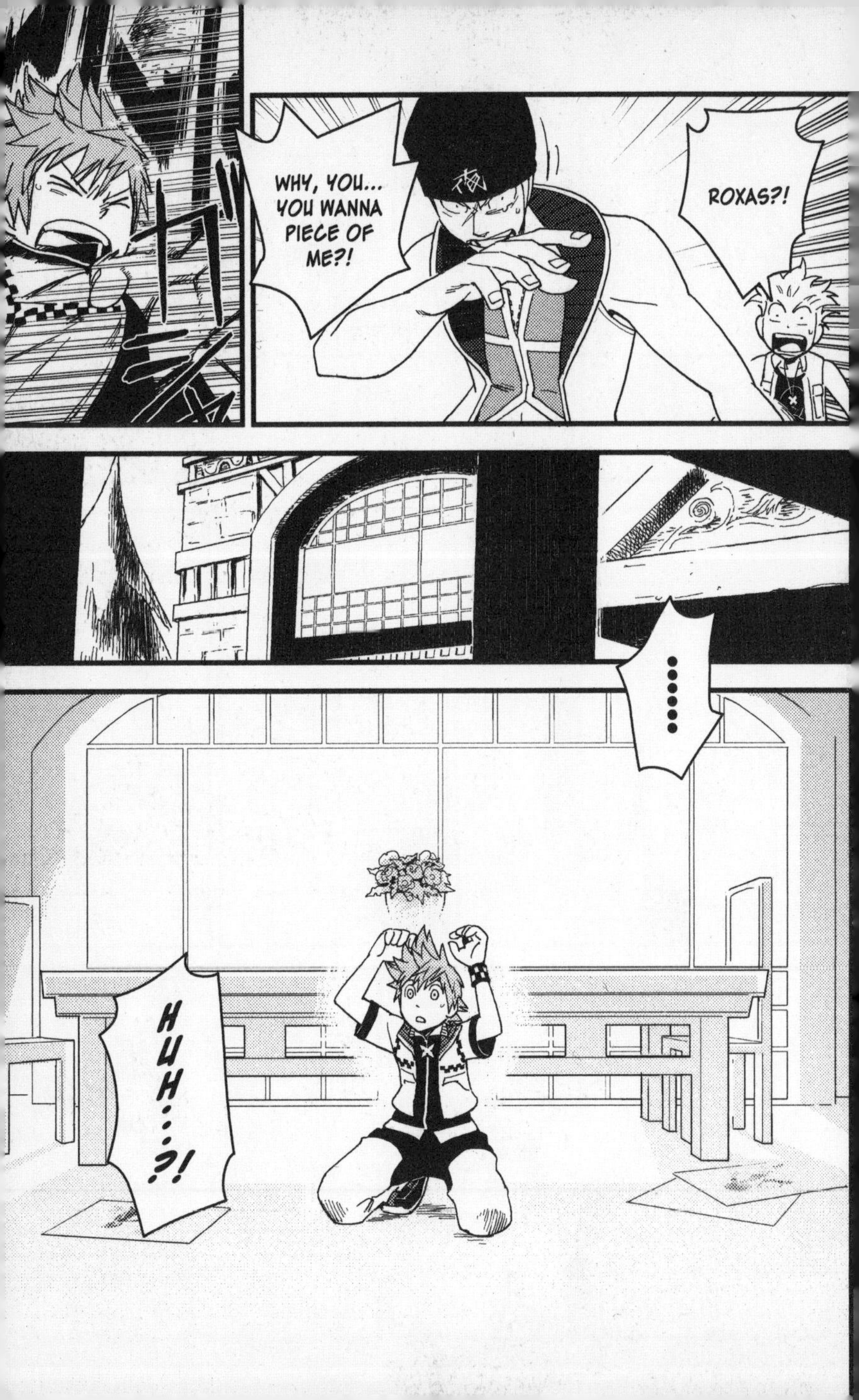
ROXAS?!
WHY, YOU... YOU WANNA PIECE OF ME?!
......
HUH...?!

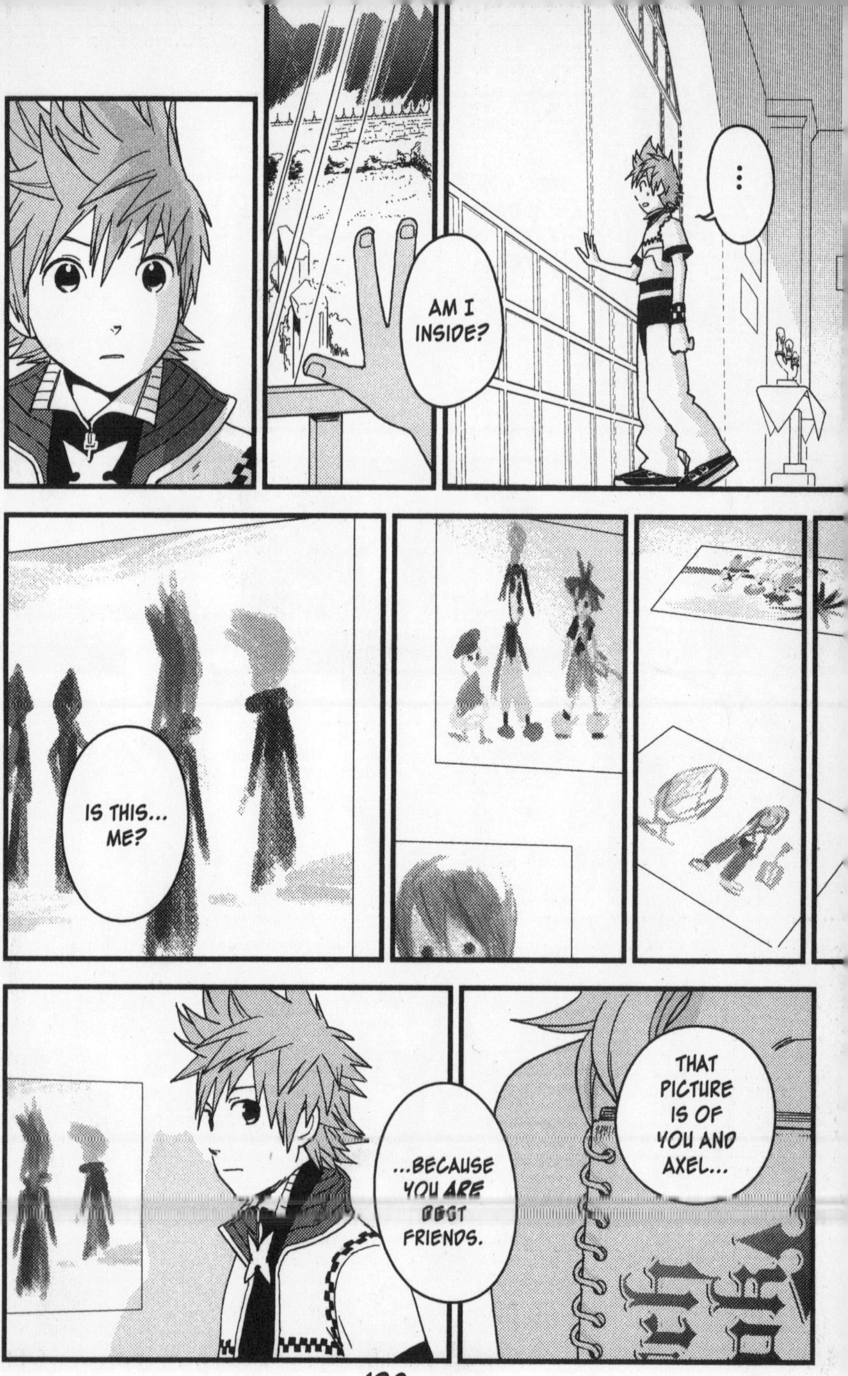
...
AM I INSIDE?
IS THIS... ME?
THAT PICTURE IS OF YOU AND AXEL...
...BECAUSE YOU ARE BEST FRIENDS.

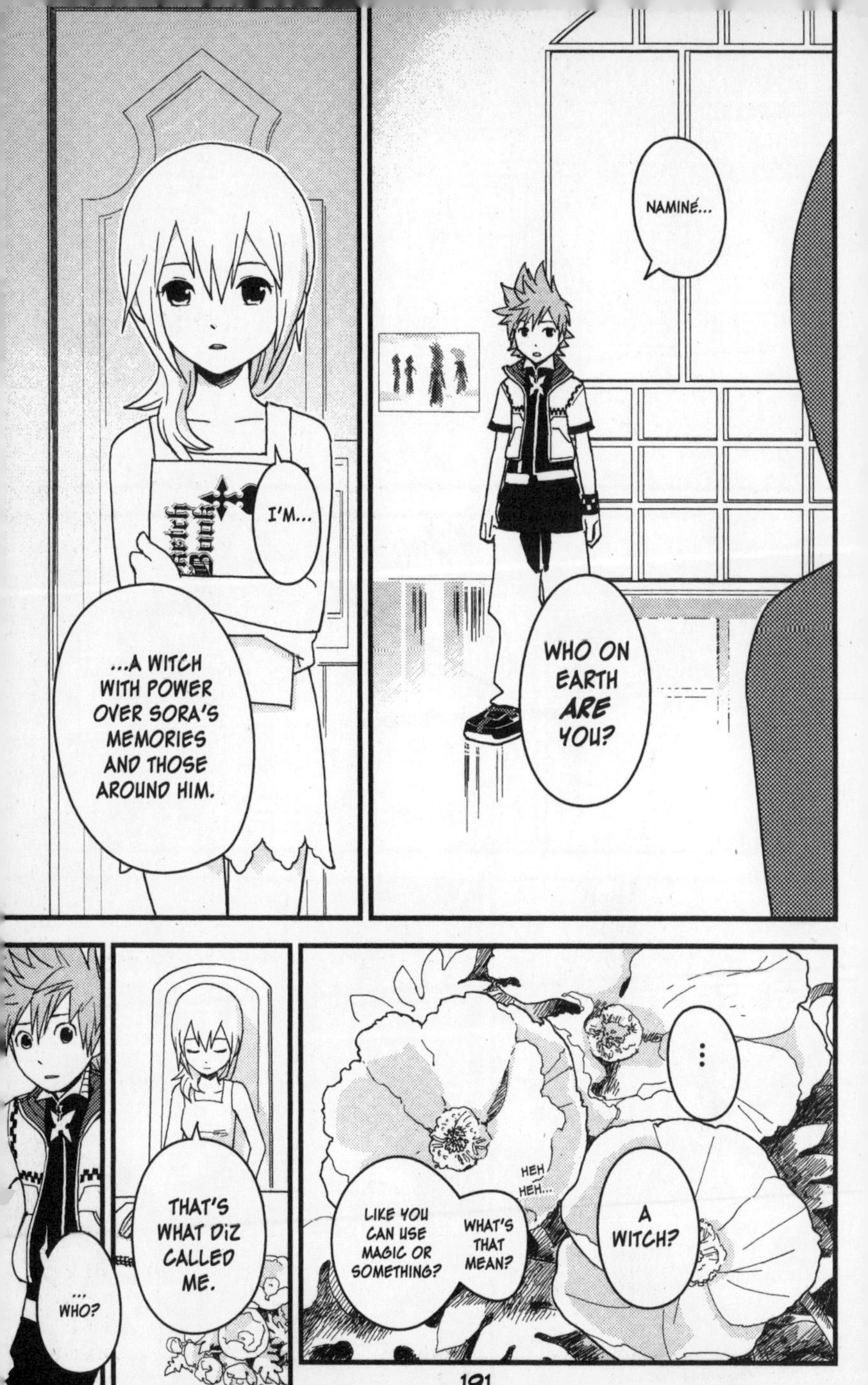
NAMINÉ...
WHO ON EARTH ARE YOU?
I'M...
...A WITCH WITH POWER OVER SORA'S MEMORIES AND THOSE AROUND HIM.
...
A WITCH?
HEH HEH...
WHAT'S THAT MEAN?
LIKE YOU CAN USE MAGIC OR SOMETHING?
THAT'S WHAT DiZ CALLED ME.
... WHO?

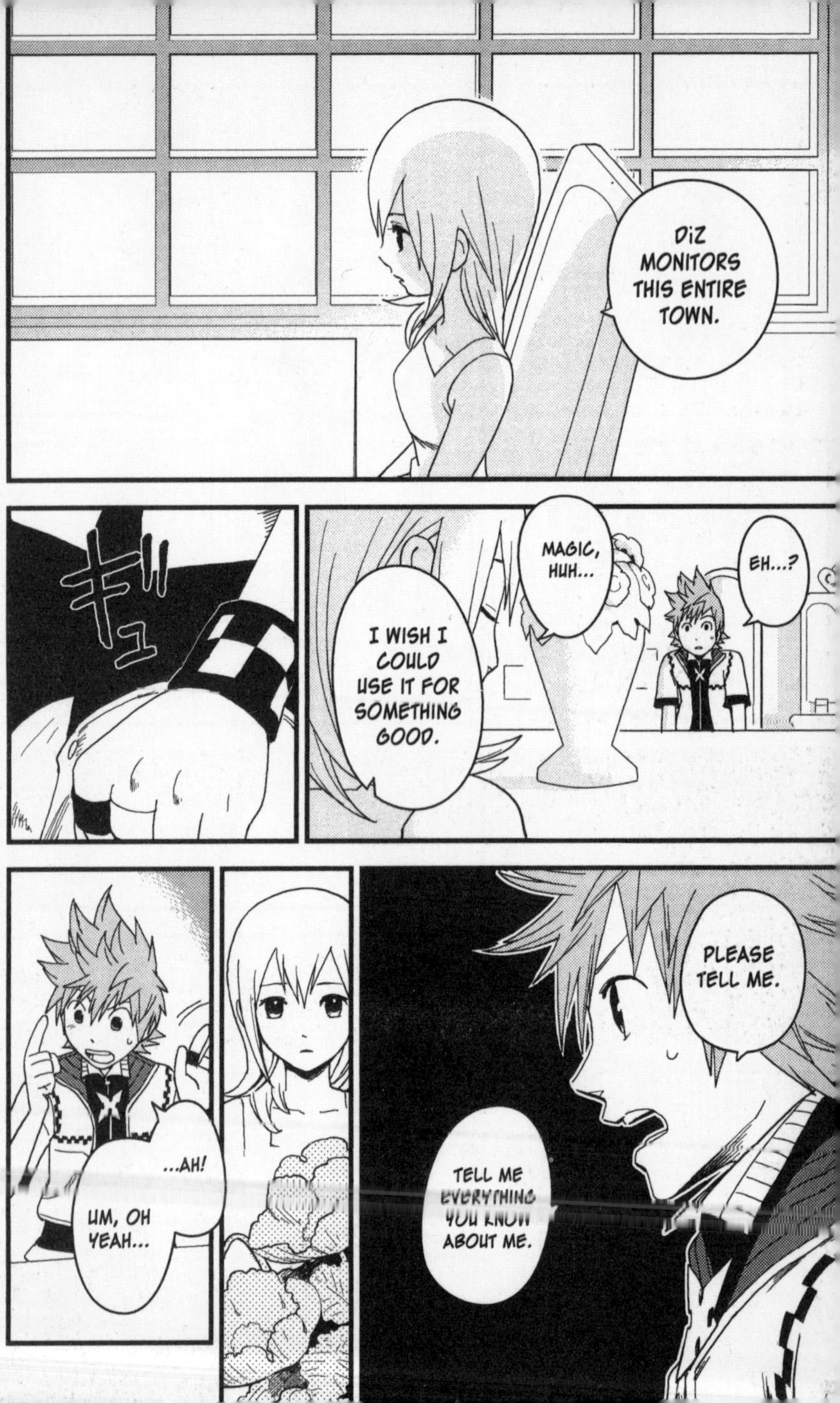
DiZ MONITORS THIS ENTIRE TOWN.
EH...?
MAGIC, HUH...
I WISH I COULD USE IT FOR SOMETHING GOOD.
ギュ
PLEASE TELL ME.
TELL ME EVERYTHING YOU KNOW ABOUT ME.
...AH!
UM, OH YEAH...

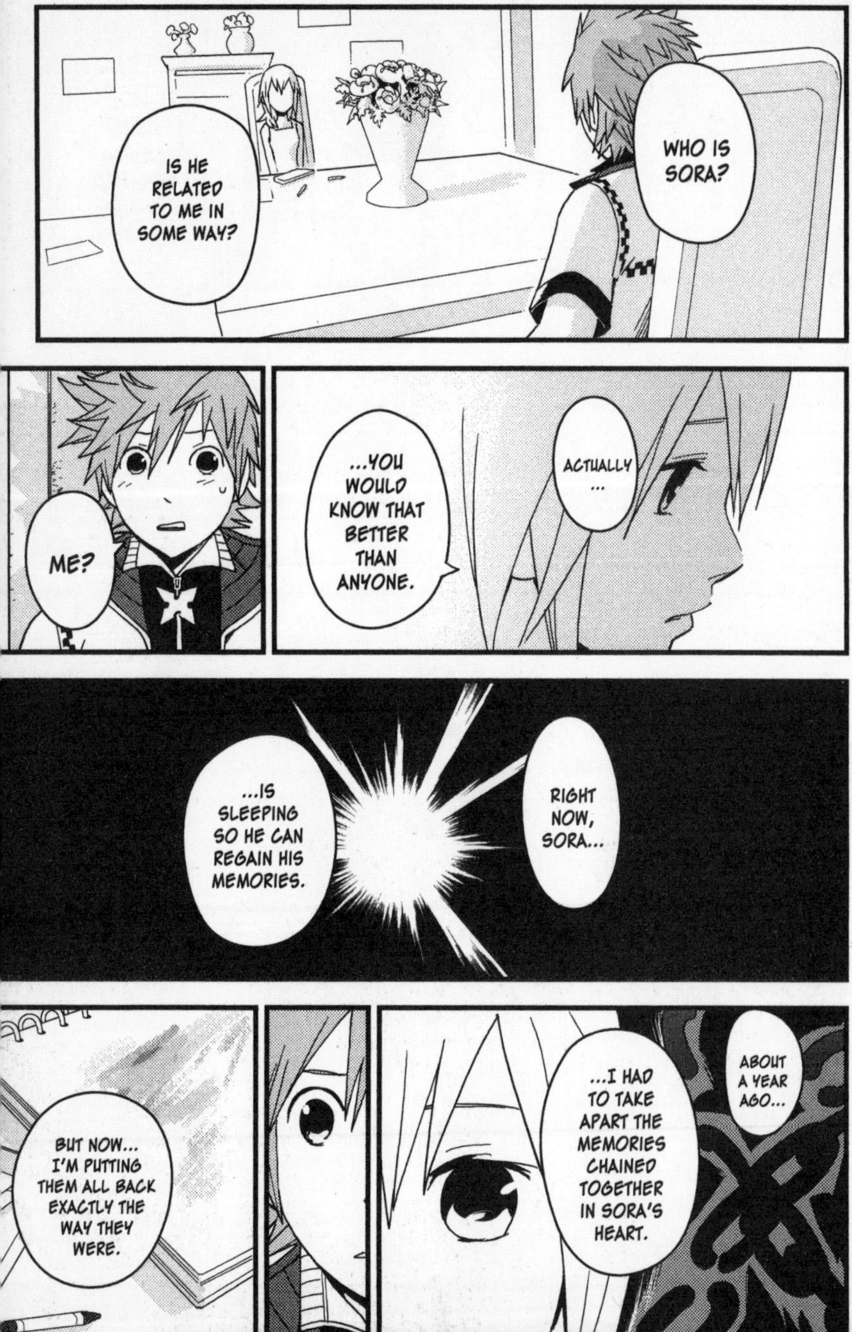
WHO IS SORA?
IS HE RELATED TO ME IN SOME WAY?
ACTUALLY...
...YOU WOULD KNOW THAT BETTER THAN ANYONE.
ME?
RIGHT NOW, SORA...
...IS SLEEPING SO HE CAN REGAIN HIS MEMORIES.
ABOUT A YEAR AGO...
...I HAD TO TAKE APART THE MEMORIES CHAINED TOGETHER IN SORA'S HEART.
BUT NOW... I'M PUTTING THEM ALL BACK EXACTLY THE WAY THEY WERE.

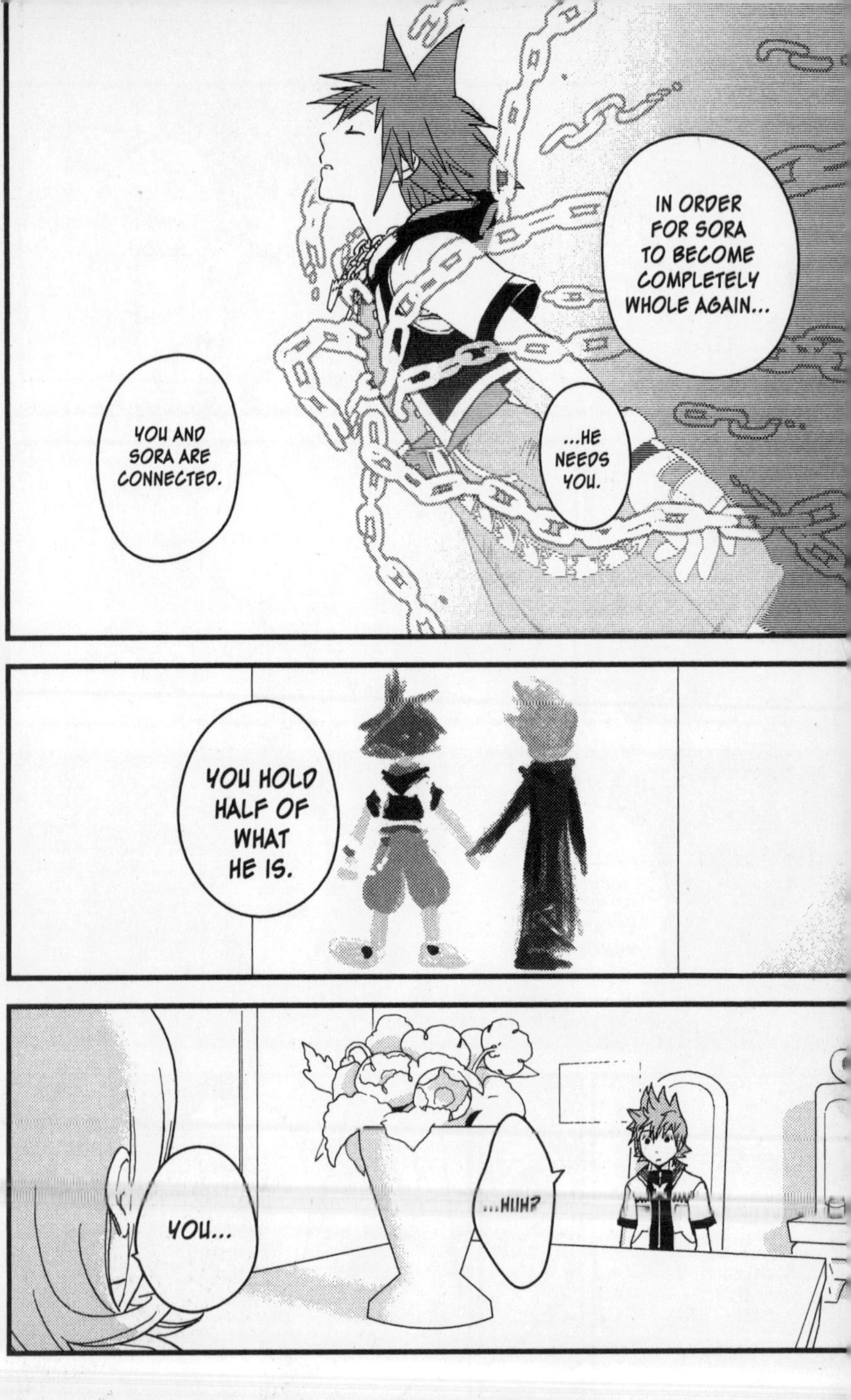
IN ORDER FOR SORA TO BECOME COMPLETELY WHOLE AGAIN...
...HE NEEDS YOU.
YOU AND SORA ARE CONNECTED.
YOU HOLD HALF OF WHAT HE IS.
...HUH?
YOU...

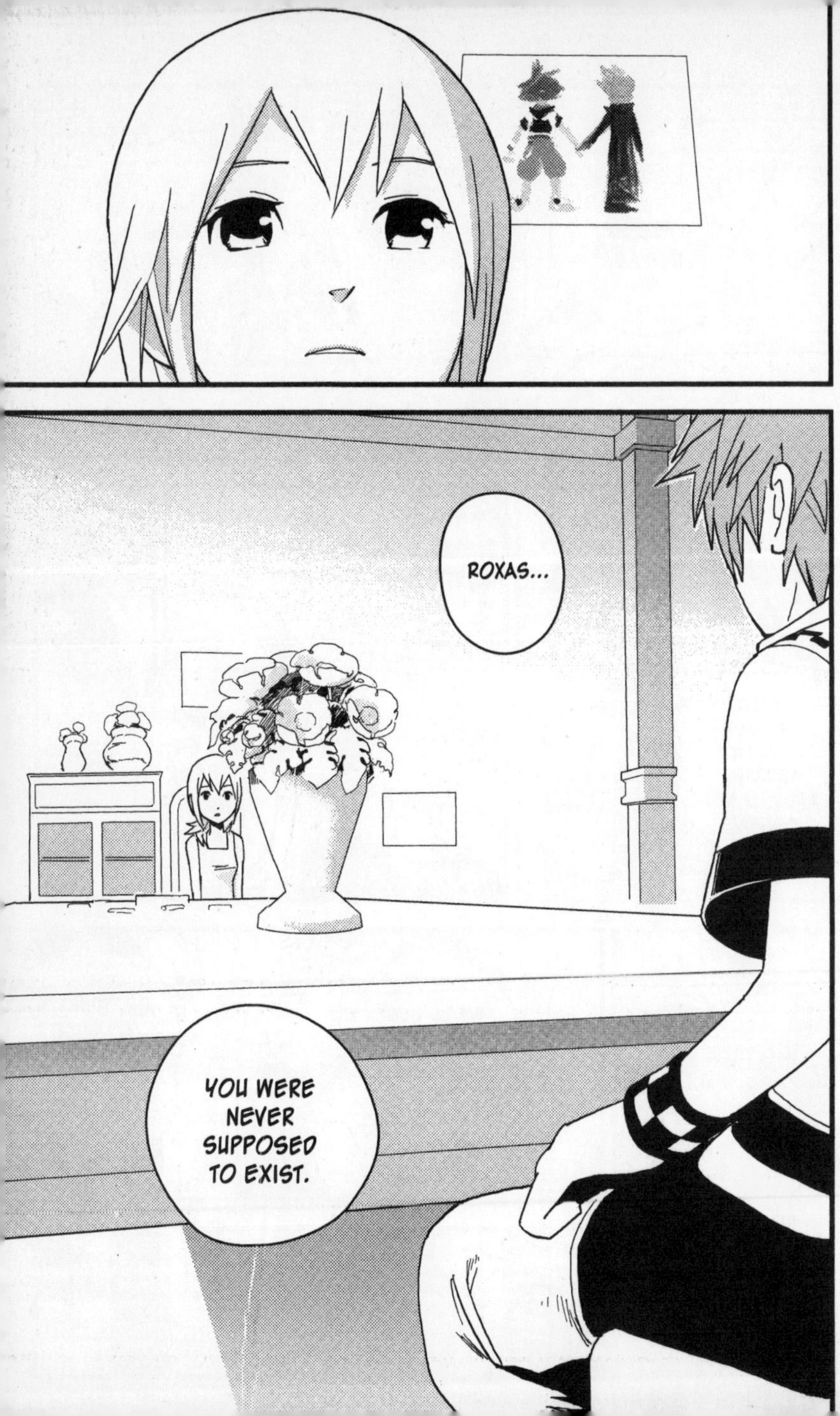
ROXAS...
YOU WERE NEVER SUPPOSED TO EXIST.

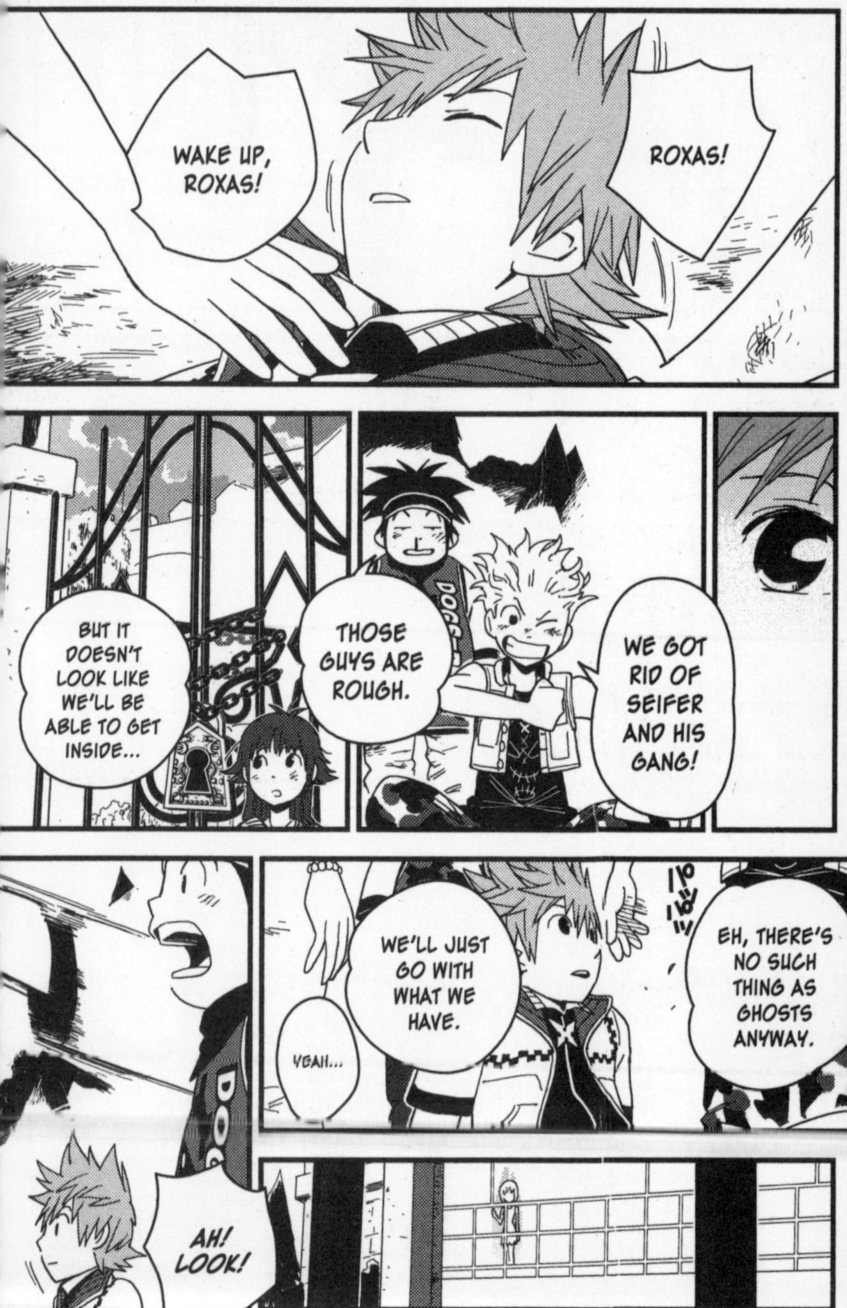
ROXAS!
WAKE UP, ROXAS!
WE GOT RID OF SEIFER AND HIS GANG!
THOSE GUYS ARE ROUGH.
BUT IT DOESN'T LOOK LIKE WE'LL BE ABLE TO GET INSIDE...
EH, THERE'S NO SUCH THING AS GHOSTS ANYWAY.
WE'LL JUST GO WITH WHAT WE HAVE.
YEAH...
AH! LOOK!

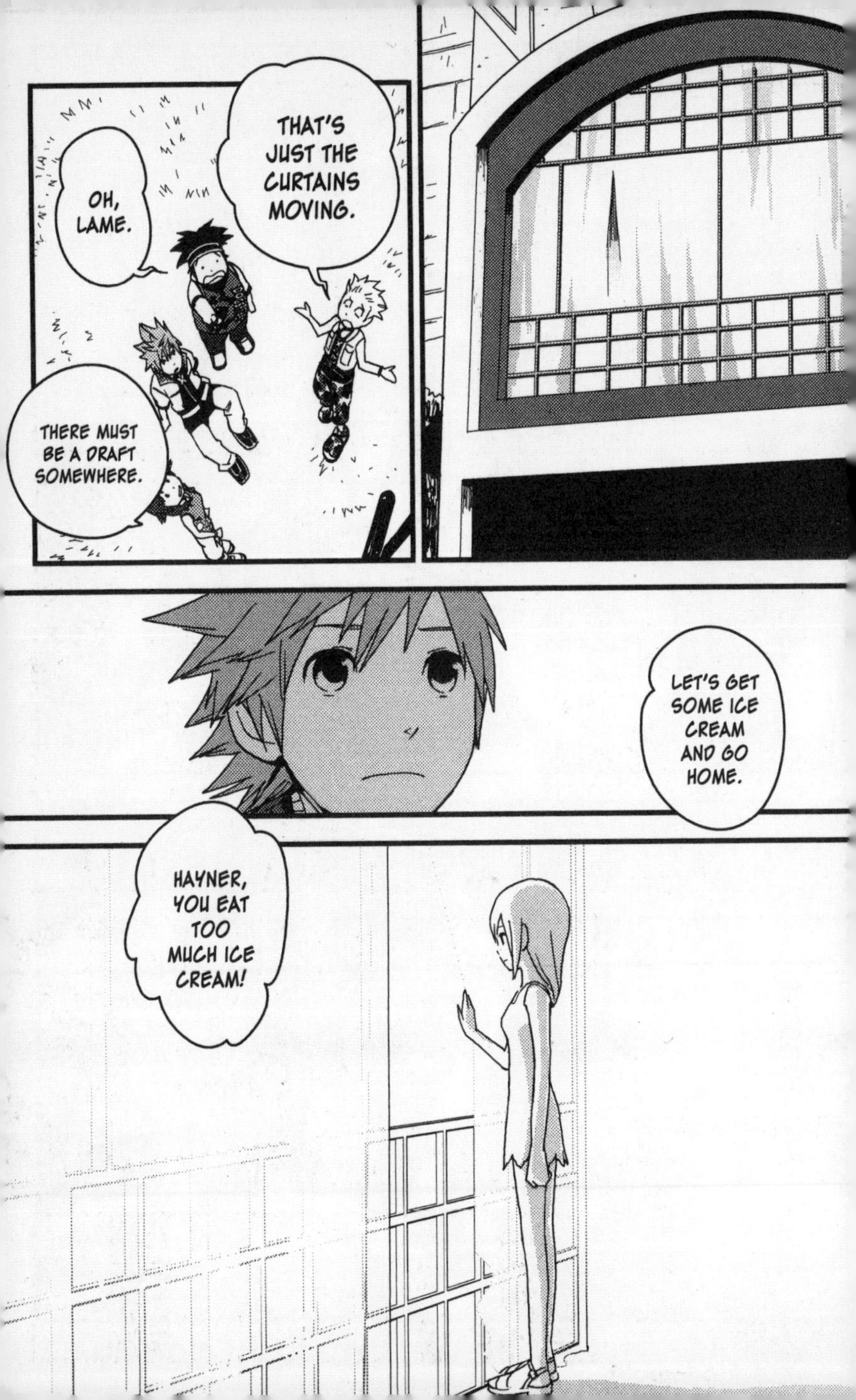
THAT'S JUST THE CURTAINS MOVING.
OH, LAME.
THERE MUST BE A DRAFT SOMEWHERE.
LET'S GET SOME ICE CREAM AND GO HOME.
HAYNER, YOU EAT TOO MUCH ICE CREAM!

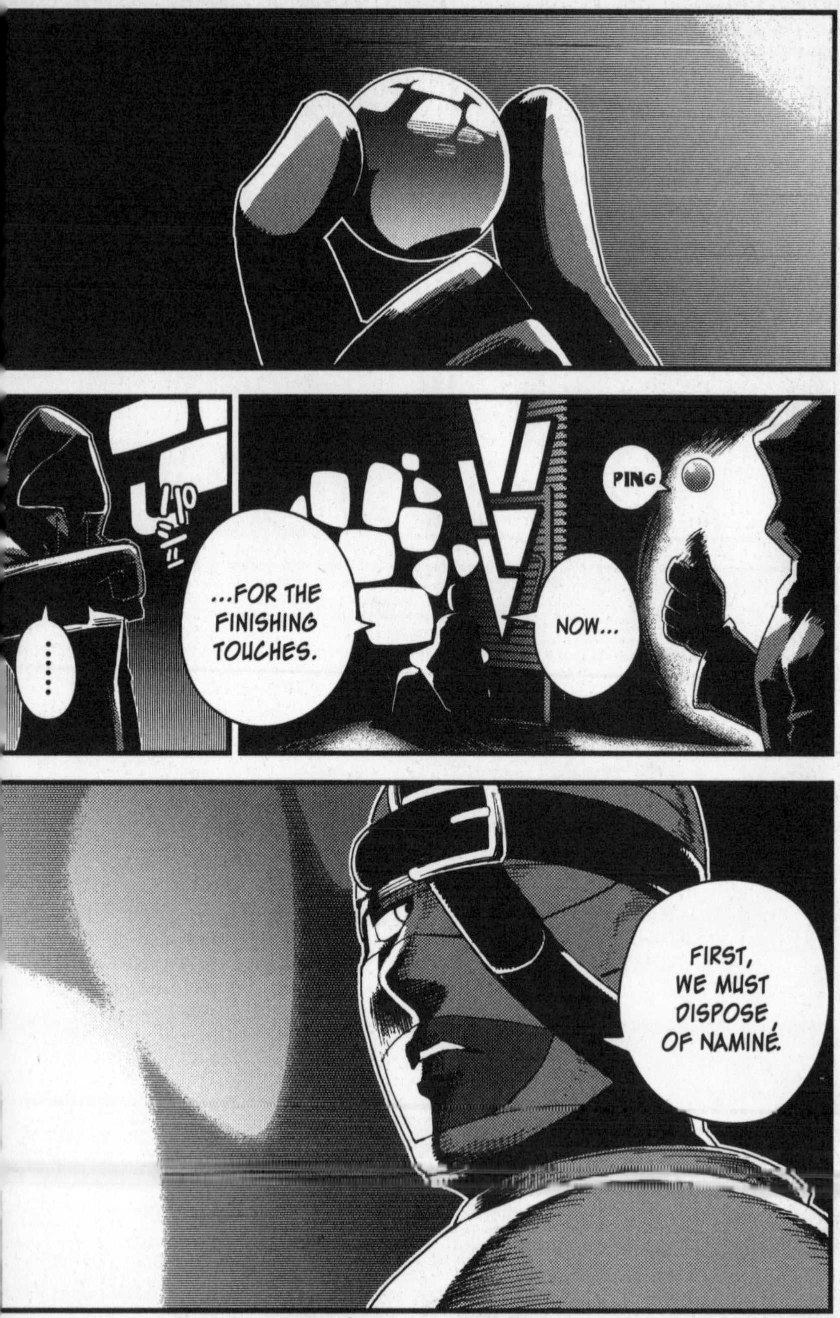
PING
NOW...
...FOR THE FINISHING TOUCHES.
......
FIRST, WE MUST DISPOSE OF NAMINÉ.

To be continued in volume 2

DISNEY · SQUARE ENIX

KINGDOM HEARTS II

What Dreams May Come...

Will Roxas finally learn the true nature
of his connection to his dream-self, Sora?
And what about Naminé? Will she
be able to reveal the truth to Roxas
before the ominous character
DiZ "disposes" of her?
And what about Axel? Just whose
side is he on, anyway?

To find out the answers to these
questions, and more, you'll have
to return for the next fantastic
volume of KINGDOM HEARTS II!

KINGDOM HEARTS II CHARACTER FILE

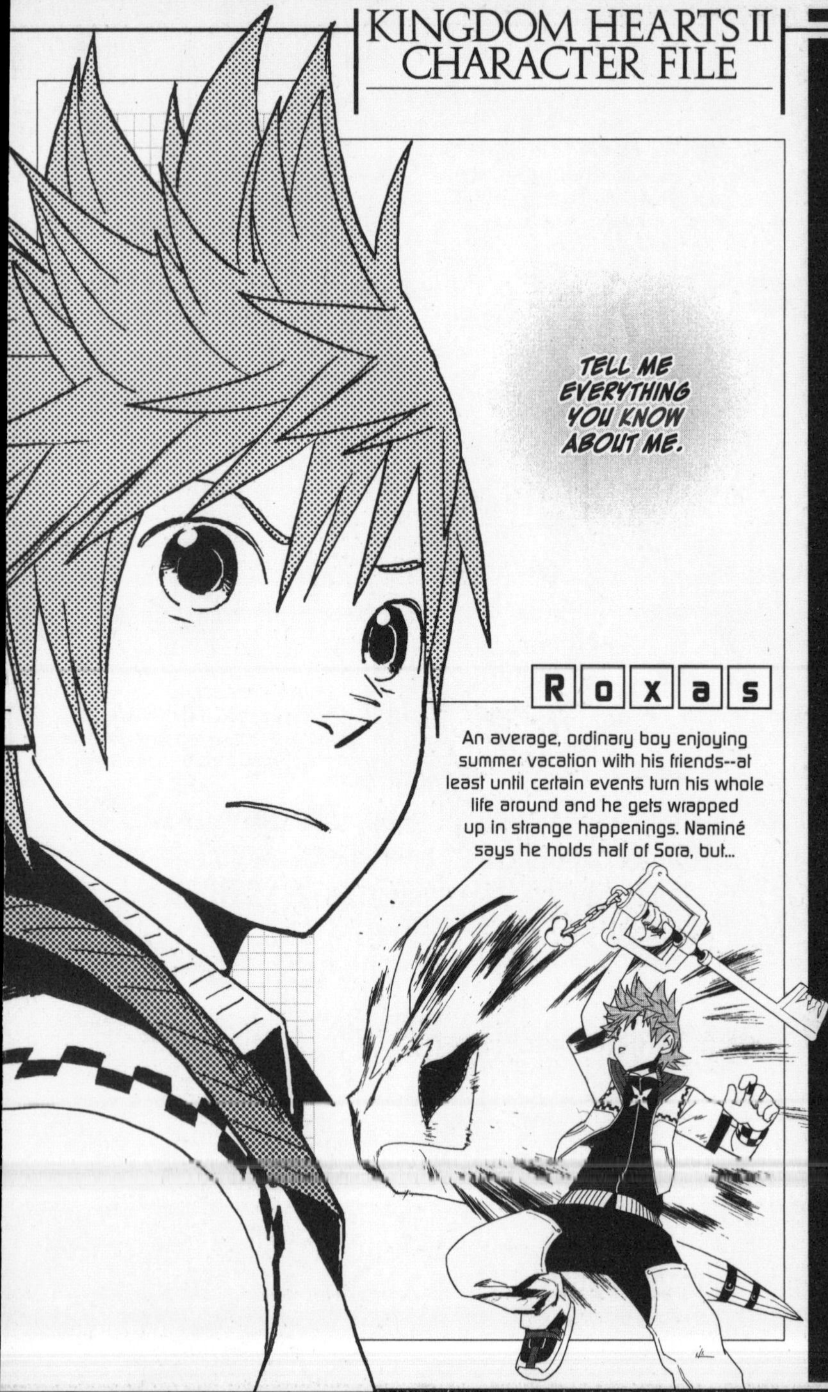
TELL ME EVERYTHING YOU KNOW ABOUT ME.

Roxas

An average, ordinary boy enjoying summer vacation with his friends--at least until certain events turn his whole life around and he gets wrapped up in strange happenings. Naminé says he holds half of Sora, but...

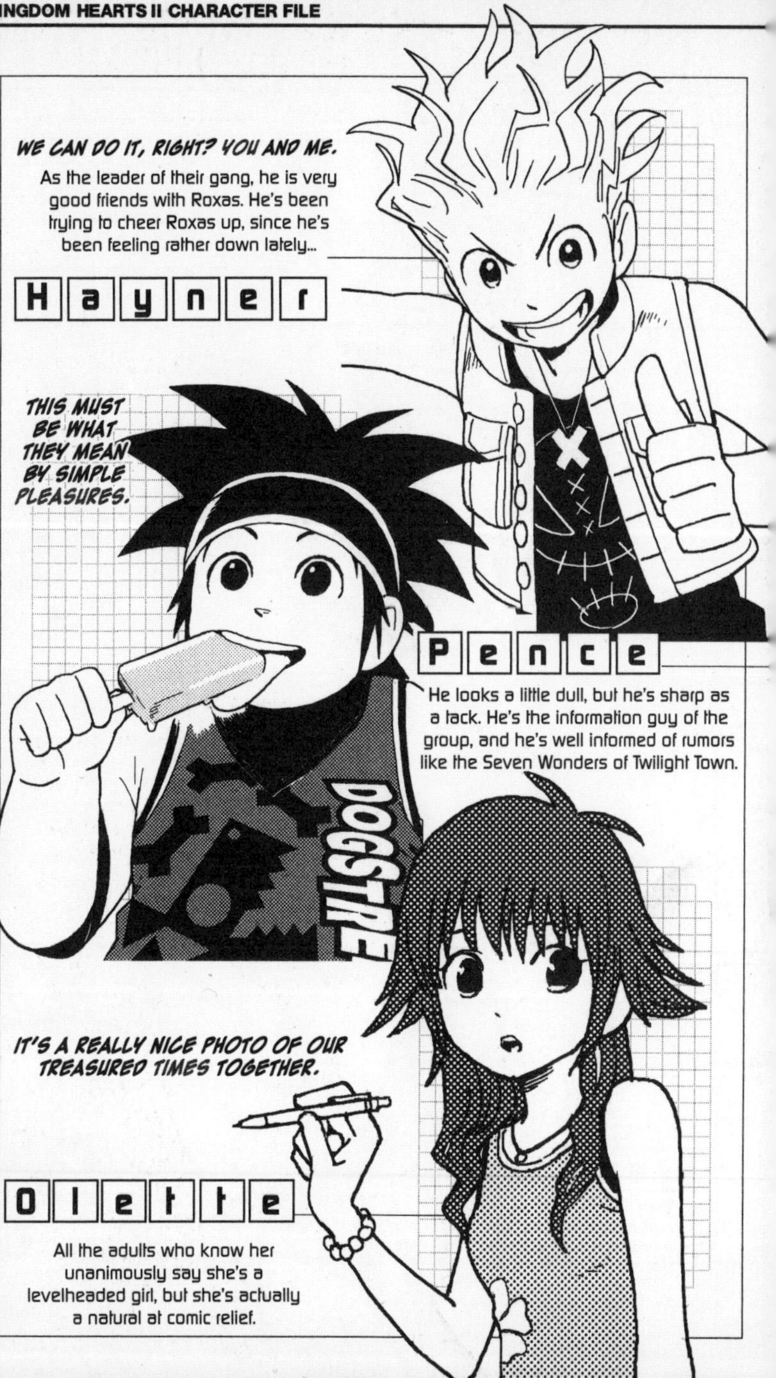

WE CAN DO IT, RIGHT? YOU AND ME.

As the leader of their gang, he is very good friends with Roxas. He's been trying to cheer Roxas up, since he's been feeling rather down lately...

Hayner

THIS MUST BE WHAT THEY MEAN BY SIMPLE PLEASURES.

Pence

He looks a little dull, but he's sharp as a tack. He's the information guy of the group, and he's well informed of rumors like the Seven Wonders of Twilight Town.

IT'S A REALLY NICE PHOTO OF OUR TREASURED TIMES TOGETHER.

Olette

All the adults who know her unanimously say she's a levelheaded girl, but she's actually a natural at comic relief.

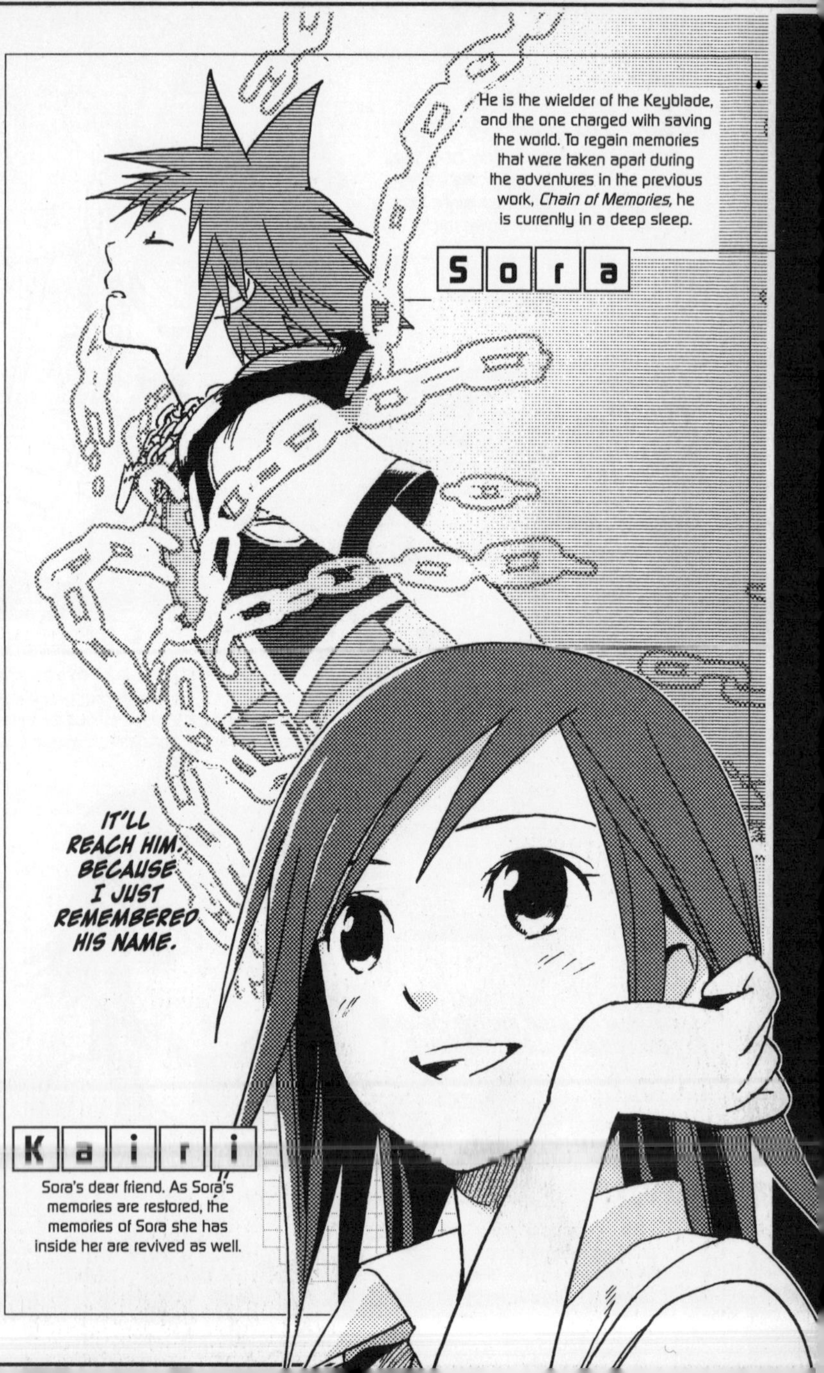
He is the wielder of the Keyblade, and the one charged with saving the world. To regain memories that were taken apart during the adventures in the previous work, *Chain of Memories,* he is currently in a deep sleep.
Sora
IT'LL REACH HIM. BECAUSE I JUST REMEMBERED HIS NAME.
Kairi
Sora's dear friend. As Sora's memories are restored, the memories of Sora she has inside her are revived as well.

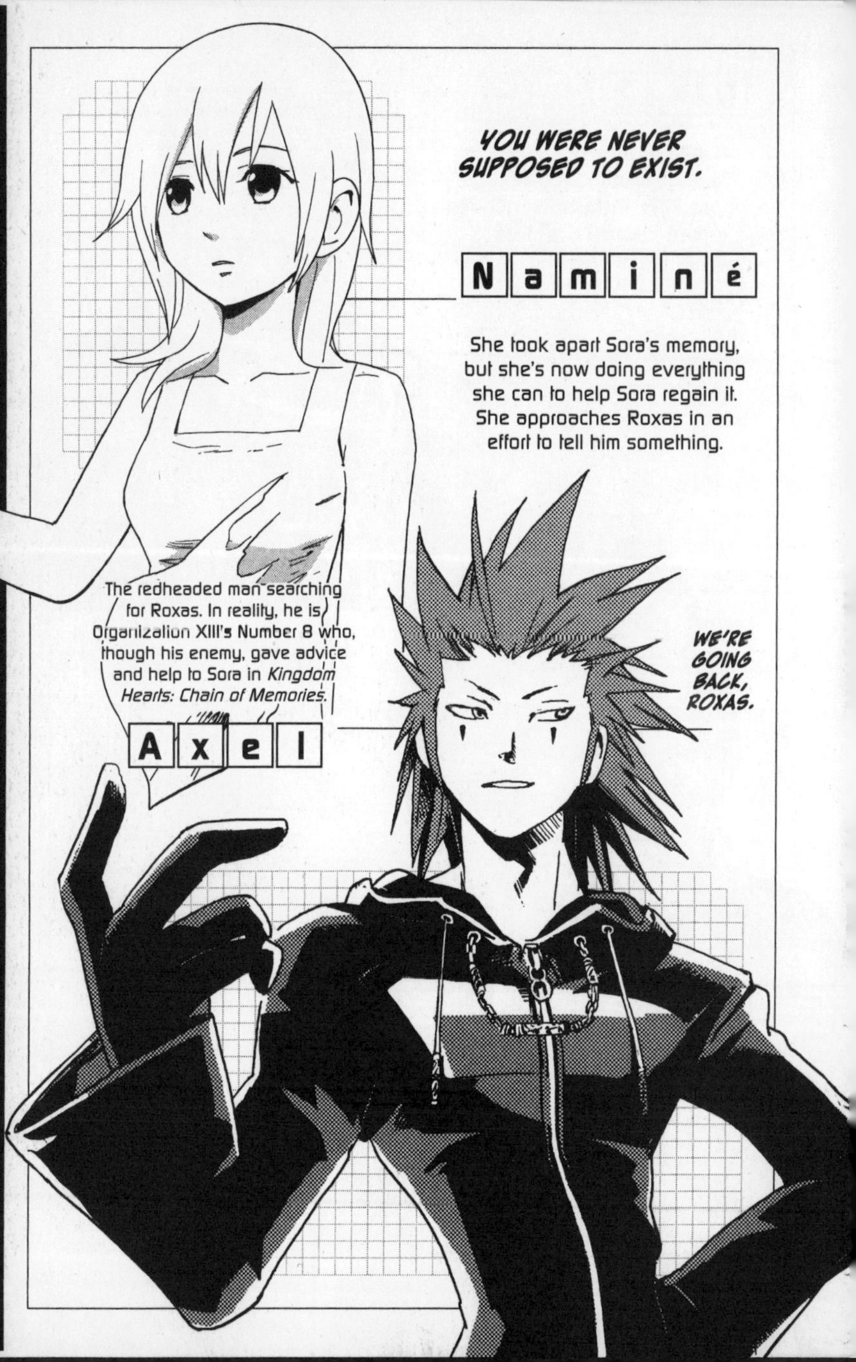
YOU WERE NEVER SUPPOSED TO EXIST.
Naminé
She took apart Sora's memory, but she's now doing everything she can to help Sora regain it. She approaches Roxas in an effort to tell him something.
WE'RE GOING BACK, ROXAS.
The redheaded man searching for Roxas. In reality, he is Organization XIII's Number 8 who, though his enemy, gave advice and help to Sora in *Kingdom Hearts: Chain of Memories.*
Axel

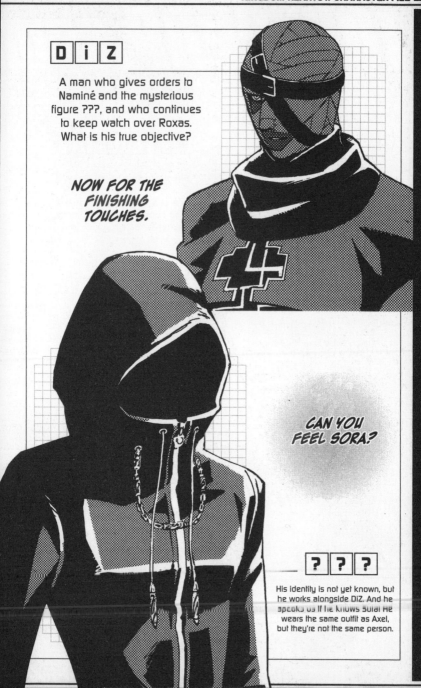

D i Z

A man who gives orders to Naminé and the mysterious figure ???, and who continues to keep watch over Roxas. What is his true objective?

NOW FOR THE FINISHING TOUCHES.

CAN YOU FEEL SORA?

? ? ?

His identity is not yet known, but he works alongside DiZ. And he speaks as if he knows Sora. He wears the same outfit as Axel, but they're not the same person.

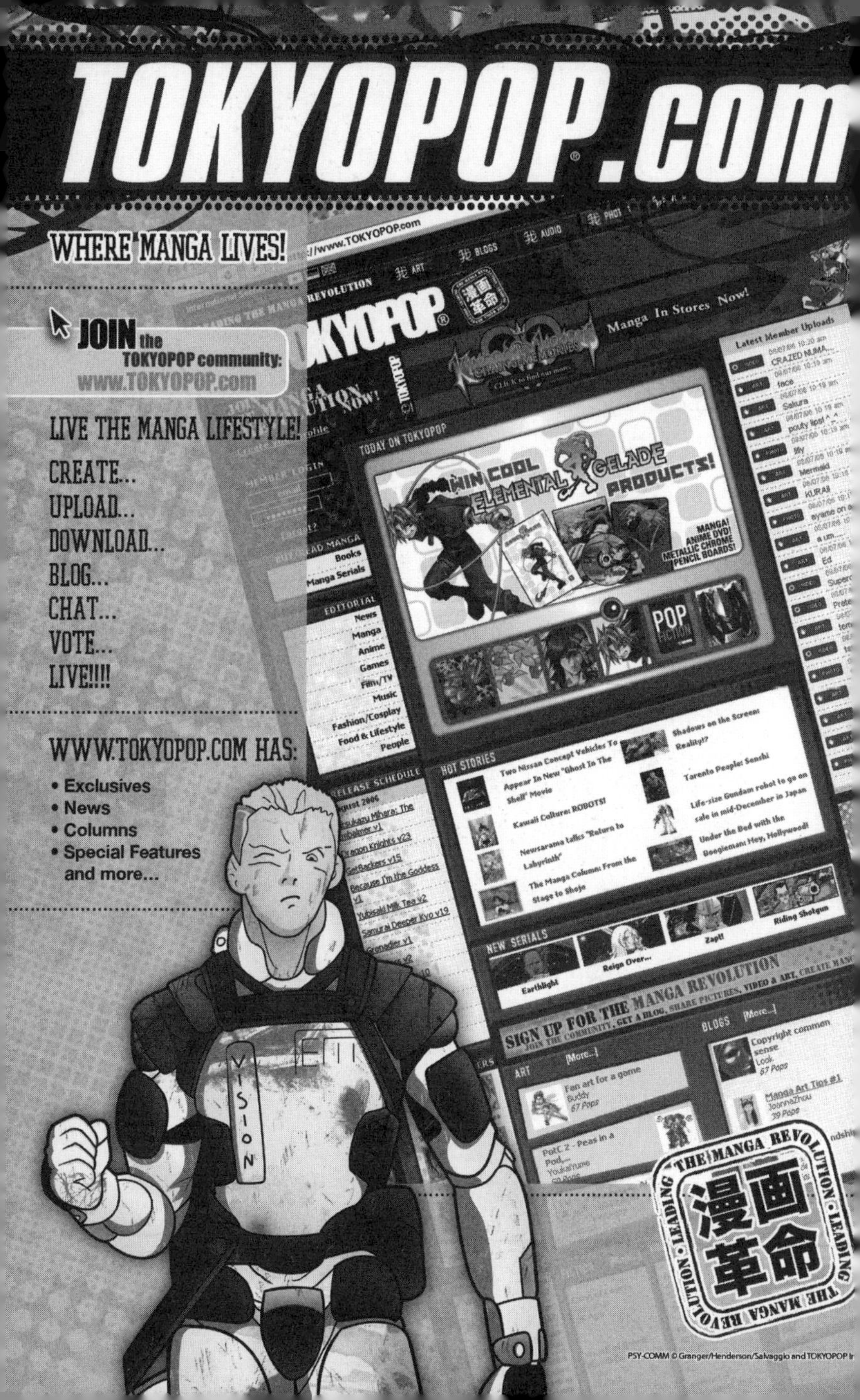
TOKYOPOP.com
WHERE MANGA LIVES!
JOIN the TOKYOPOP community: www.TOKYOPOP.com
LIVE THE MANGA LIFESTYLE!
CREATE...
UPLOAD...
DOWNLOAD...
BLOG...
CHAT...
VOTE...
LIVE!!!!
WWW.TOKYOPOP.COM HAS:
• Exclusives
• News
• Columns
• Special Features and more...
THE MANGA REVOLUTION • LEADING
漫画革命
PSY-COMM © Granger/Henderson/Salvaggio and TOKYOPOP Inc.

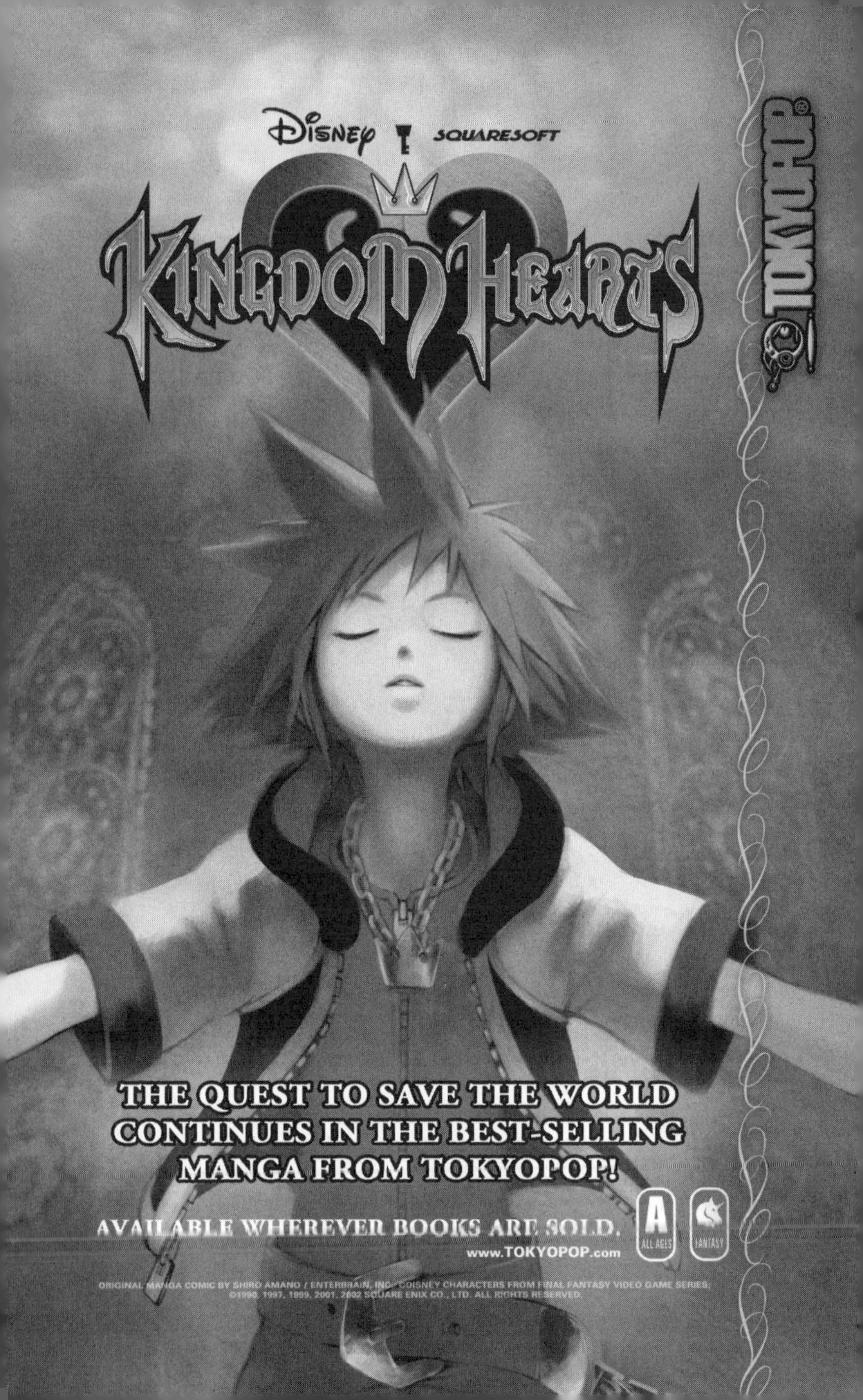

DISNEY SQUARESOFT
KINGDOM HEARTS
TOKYOPOP
THE QUEST TO SAVE THE WORLD CONTINUES IN THE BEST-SELLING MANGA FROM TOKYOPOP!
AVAILABLE WHEREVER BOOKS ARE SOLD.
www.TOKYOPOP.com
A ALL AGES
FANTASY
ORIGINAL MANGA COMIC BY SHIRO AMANO / ENTERBRAIN, INC. ©DISNEY CHARACTERS FROM FINAL FANTASY VIDEO GAME SERIES; ©1990, 1997, 1999, 2001, 2002 SQUARE ENIX CO., LTD. ALL RIGHTS RESERVED.

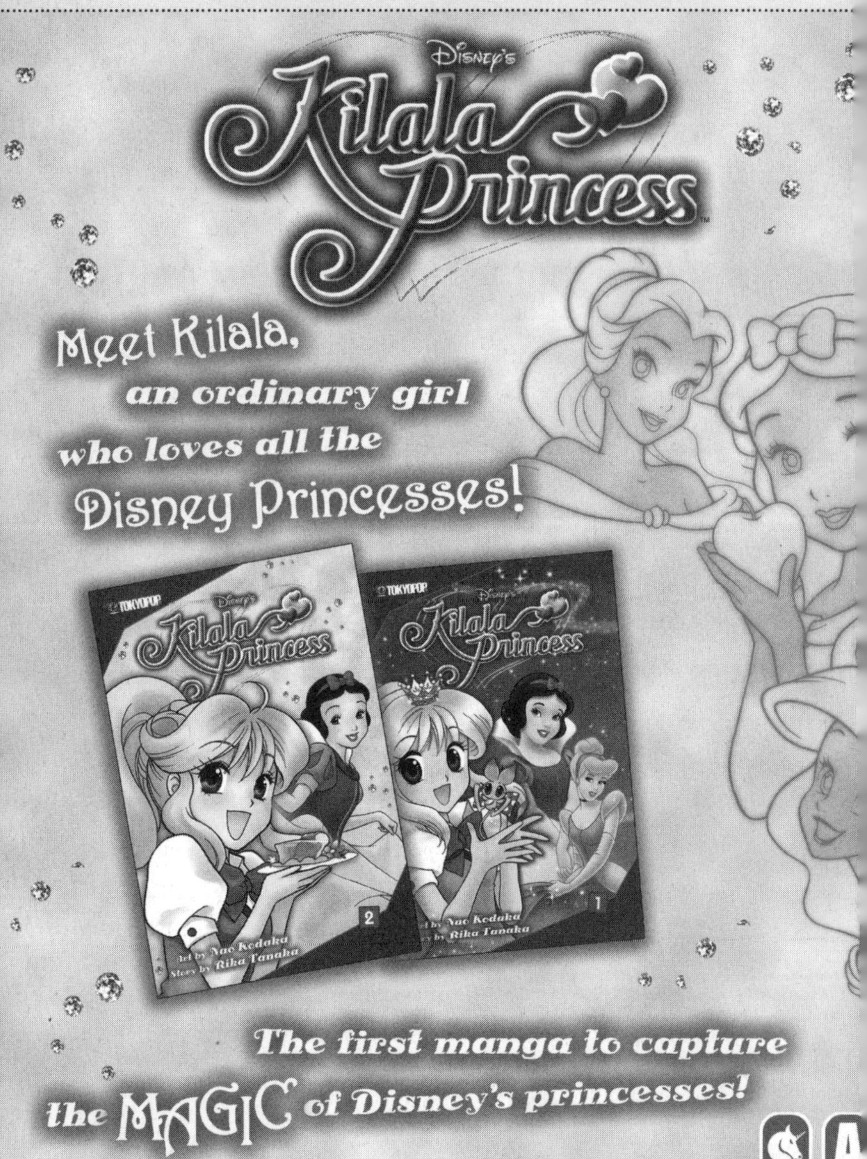
Disney's
Kilala Princess
Meet Kilala,
an ordinary girl
who loves all the
Disney Princesses!
TOKYOPOP
Disney's
Kilala Princess
2
Nao Kodaka
Story by Rika Tanaka
TOKYOPOP
Disney's
Kilala Princess
1
Nao Kodaka
Rika Tanaka
The first manga to capture
the MAGIC of Disney's princesses!
FANTASY

STOP!

This is the back of the book.
You wouldn't want to spoil a great ending!

This book is printed "manga-style," in the authentic Japanese right-to-left format. Since none of the artwork has been flipped or altered, readers get to experience the story just as the creator intended. You've been asking for it, so TOKYOPOP® delivered: authentic, hot-off-the-press, and far more fun!

DIRECTIONS

If this is your first time reading manga-style, here's a quick guide to help you understand how it works.

It's easy... just start in the top right panel and follow the numbers. Have fun, and look for more 100% authentic manga from TOKYOPOP®!